TO P. K. P.

Preface

STAGECRAFT AND SCENE DESIGN is primarily intended to aid the high-school, university, and community-theatre worker to establish satisfying standards of design and production and to help him develop sound and well-organized methods of work in the shops and on the stage. Although lecturers in the field of stagecraft and scene design will want to bring to the classroom additional materials gained from experience and special study, beginning designers and technicians will of course need at least a minimum knowledge of theory and practice if they are to be fully prepared to grow and develop in this field. To provide this basic knowledge is the purpose of this book.

The position of designer-technician is a highly challenging one. To be successful, such a person must ultimately have intensive first-hand experience with all the areas relating to the stage picture. Unlike the shop workers and the members of the various crews — who are in most cases aware only of their own individual responsibilities — the designer-technician must "see" the entire visual production from its conception to its presentation before an audience. To begin with, however, he cannot avoid learning the fundamentals, if he is later to capitalize fully on various opportunities to broaden his scope and develop his practical experience.

Moreover, the designer or technician who is somewhat skilled in one area often fails to recognize that his inadequacies in another may seriously affect his final efforts in production. Many technicians build admirably but paint crudely; others paint well but light badly. Some designers express themselves charmingly on paper, but cannot paint on a large scale. Still others paint scenery with considerable flair, but have little conception of the value of stage properties. The present text stresses the interrelation of all phases of scenic design, without which we can never expect completely pleasing and completely meaningful scenic effects.

Certain university and community-theatre workers disapprove of the term *non-professional* as applied to any phase of theatre work, feeling that all good theatre is *professional*. Others, more or less disparagingly, apply the term *amateur* to any theatre production which fails to use its working materials successfully. However, regardless of terminology, both professionals and non-professionals should attempt to prepare as perfectly coordinated productions as is possible within a given time and by means of available talent and money. Obviously, since professional builders and painters are highly paid and have had considerable practical experience, it is difficult to compare their results with that of beginning theatre students. Furthermore, a professional production involves the expenditure of many thousands of dollars; a non-professional designer is often fortunate to be able to spend a hundred dollars.

Scenery workers in the non-professional theatre have the opportunity to apply many of the professional practices that are in best repute. Although non-professional scenery work more often involves *re-building* than it does *building*, methods based on standard practice are none the less suitable. Professional painting techniques are similarly applicable to non-professional work even though the available painters are seldom truly skilled. Non-professional scenery need never be compared to professional work from the point of view of extravagance and cost. Needless to say, the renderings and drawings of the non-professional designer should be as nearly professional in quality and in conception as is possible, despite the limitations of the budget or the shops.

Few books are written without the generous assistance and warm encouragement of friends and colleagues. The author particularly wishes to express his indebtedness to the following: H. Darkes Albright, Robert B. Burrows, Lee Mitchell, Charles F. Hunter, and Edna L. Sterling. Because of their willingness to read manuscript and suggest improvements, the ideas within the book are more concisely related and the manuscript has been prepared without excessive delay.

The line drawings in the book are mainly the work of Raymond Barrett, Norman Buck, Homer Dietmeier, Alex Flett, Belle Gorman, William Rouse, and Charlyn Ryan.

H. P.

Contents

Figures

FIGURE

1

The Stage and Backstage Equipment

THE THEATRE is an institution which demands the time and the efforts of people from many different creative fields. The results of their work are usually presented to the public in buildings which have been specially designed so that audiences can satisfactorily view complete theatrical performances. Although first in importance are the script and the actors, theatrical performances usually display costumes, scenery, properties, and lighting as well. Each division of work is necessary but, above all, there can be no real theatre without an audience-player situation.

It is true that Shakespeare is occasionally offered in wooded glens with the onlookers seated here and there on the grass. Although Thornton Wilder's *Our Town* used no scenery, most people were delighted when they saw it produced on the stage. From time to time plays have been presented in churches, court houses, ballrooms, and public squares, and have drawn enthusiastic audiences. Actually, performances of this sort have been in the nature of novelties; a comfortable chair in a bona fide theatre building is still the ideal place from which to view a play.

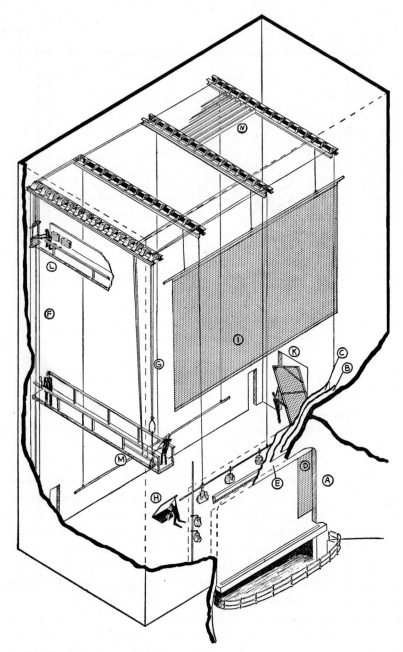

Fig. 1 *The stage house (for legend, see Fig. 2, opposite)*

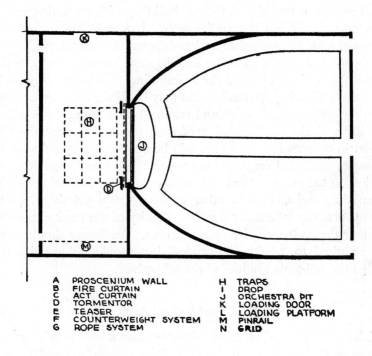

A	PROSCENIUM WALL	H	TRAPS
B	FIRE CURTAIN	I	DROP
C	ACT CURTAIN	J	ORCHESTRA PIT
D	TORMENTOR	K	LOADING DOOR
E	TEASER	L	LOADING PLATFORM
F	COUNTERWEIGHT SYSTEM	M	PINRAIL
G	ROPE SYSTEM	N	GRID

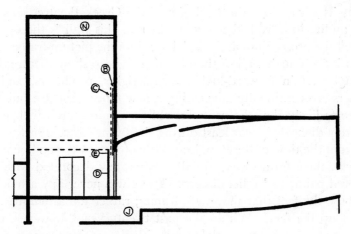

Fig. 2 *Stage and auditorium floor plans and cross section*

However, a traditional theatre building with an acting area is not enough. What the audience sees is a small part of what is necessary for the complete and satisfactory theatrical production. A theatre building is no better than its stage house (page 2) — that is, all the cubic feet behind the curtain line. No matter how architecturally pleasing the auditorium may be, if the stage house offers inadequate overhead space and cramped floor areas, there will be arbitrary limits to the staging of each production, and the time spent in overcoming handicaps will be out of all proportion to the energies expended on the visual aspects. Although working conditions in the theatre stand little better chance of becoming "ideal" than do those of certain other creative fields, primitive theatre plants actually take away from the dignity of the work and satisfy neither the craftsmen nor the audiences. Audiences should never be required to "make allowances" but should be permitted to judge the full-scale abilities of those involved.

The Proscenium Arch

The various locations within the stage house have precise names, many of which are centuries old. The proscenium wall, which takes its name from the *proskenion* of the Greek theatre, separates the auditorium from the stage house. In this wall is the opening called the proscenium arch, which outlines the picture-frame stage. This is the fourth wall of the present-day peep-show theatre; even though certain forward-looking playwrights, producers, and designers are continually advocating a new type of theatre building, it seems likely that the centuries-old proscenium arch will not be entirely discarded — at least during the twentieth century.

From the time of the Renaissance theatre until the end of World War I, these frames were usually elaborately decorated with gilt, colored paint, and relief designs. There was never any attempt to disguise the fact that they were frames; rather the attempt was to point up the fact. Within the past twenty years, however, there has been a tendency to do away with decorative frames and to make the division between audience and player less sharp. Frank Lloyd Wright's plans for a theatre at Hartford, Connecticut, actually show no proscenium arch at all, since the stage is to be lowered and raised and the scenery shifted in the basement.

Thirty feet is a desirable width for the proscenium arch, although forty feet is not uncommon on Broadway. Anything less than twenty feet suggests "experimental theatre," where emphasis on production is often slight and there is therefore less need for space. The height of the arch will, of course, depend upon the architecture of the auditorium. Fourteen- and sixteen-foot flats are in common use and thus the arch should be tall enough to accommodate units of this size. It is not difficult to cut down on the height of a tall proscenium by means of masking units, but certain stately and grandiose stage effects cannot be attempted when there is no height to the opening.

The Beam Spots and the Footlights

Although most of the important equipment and areas are backstage, some lighting units must necessarily be placed in front of the curtain line in order to light the downstage areas. Beam spots are usually the solution for this type of specific illumination. These spotlight instruments are mounted in the ceiling at a distance from the stage which will give them an angle-throw of roughly forty-five degrees to the downstage areas. A beam, structural or purely decorative, prevents the audience from seeing the spotlight instruments. It should be possible to adjust these lights from above the ceiling and behind the beam.

In older theatre buildings such as those found on Broadway, beam lighting is not possible. Therefore, in these theatres, lighting units are usually mounted on the front of the balcony or in the upper boxes. Light from the balcony front will, of course, be responsible for shadows on the back wall of the setting. None the less, this type of front lighting is adequate, and definitely more satisfactory for visibility purposes than units mounted above and behind the proscenium.

Footlights, in front of the curtain line, complete the lighting from the audience side, except for the occasional use of follow spots and effect machines from the projection booth in the balcony. Many lighting technicians disapprove of the use of footlights. There are older actors, however, who often demand this type of light, since they fancy that footlights are kind to their facial contours, and it is useful for special purposes, to be discussed later. Whatever the decision may be regarding the use of footlights for the acting areas, they will always be useful for lighting the act curtain as the house lights are being dimmed. However, they must be placed directly in front of the curtain line or they will tend to light the entire proscenium wall.

The Apron

Directly in front of the curtain line is the apron or forestage. The average professional theatre omits this feature and uses permanent built-in footlights at the curtain line. Portable aprons are used occasionally; such units can cover the orchestra pit and a few of the front seats if necessary. A specially constructed apron requires many people to set it up, and naturally there is considerable expense in connection with its original construction.

Many high school auditoriums have been built with large enough aprons so that lectures and recitals can be offered in front of the act curtain. While these aprons are useful at times, they will just as frequently become a problem to those who produce plays. The combination of a deep apron and an orchestra pit will place the audience farther away from the action than is desirable. Unless the apron is equipped with disappearing footlights it will not always be possible to light the stage adequately without placing portable footlights on the floor in front of the act curtain. Occasionally an apron is so deep that it requires the audience to sit literally on three sides of it, thus offering "theatre in the round" possibilities.

The Orchestra Pit

The main floor, commonly called the orchestra, and the orchestra pit both take their names from the *orchestra* of the Greek theatre. In English theatres the main floor is called the *pit*, a term originating in Elizabethan days. Regardless of what terminology is used or whether or not the theatre contains an apron, the orchestra pit should provide space for a grand piano and seating arrangements for an orchestra of no less than twenty musicians. As musicians play, their silhouettes should not be seen; therefore the floor of the orchestra pit must be somewhat below the audience level. Some of the newer theatres have been planned so that the musicians' chairs are placed on hydraulic elevators; the musicians can thus be raised to stage level or lowered out of sight. While such devices are undoubtedly most useful, the seating arrangements for the musicians are more important.

The orchestra pit must be wired to take care of orchestra stands, and it should be possible for the stage manager to blink these lights or to signal in some other fashion so that the orchestra conductor can be in contact with those who run the show. The musicians are in a world of their own, since they face the conductor rather than the stage. In order to conserve space, part of the orchestra pit is sometimes slightly underneath the front of the stage — not a pleasant location for those who must sit there during an entire evening.

The Fire Curtain, the Grand Drapery, the Act Curtain

City fire laws often require the use of an *asbestos fire curtain*. Usually, when such strict rules are in force, it is because of some tragic local fire of the past. The custom in New York City is for the fire curtain to be raised shortly before the show begins and for it to be lowered at the end of the last act. Chicago, however, requires that this curtain be lowered between the acts as well. Apparently the appearance of the curtain is to assure audiences that they are protected, although many patrons never see the curtain, since they arrive late and leave early. Ideally the asbestos curtain is of the drop variety; since it is a purely functional apparatus, it is often left plain and undecorated. In case of an onstage fire, the curtain is lowered and the audience protected from flames and smoke. If there is no fly space to install a drop fire curtain, a roll curtain may be necessary, despite the fact that such a unit is extremely awkward to install and to handle.

Directly upstage from the fire curtain is the *grand drapery*, an elaborate, tasseled, and fringed valance type of trimming for the top of the proscenium arch. Theatres designed in contemporary styles omit this decoration, but period-style auditoriums seem unfinished without it. Such a theatre as the Empire in New York

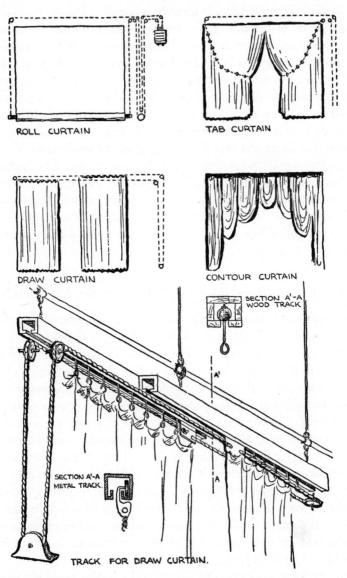

ROLL CURTAIN

TAB CURTAIN

DRAW CURTAIN

CONTOUR CURTAIN

SECTION A'-A WOOD TRACK

SECTION A'-A METAL TRACK.

TRACK FOR DRAW CURTAIN.

Fig. 3 *Roll curtain, tab curtain, draw curtain, contour curtain, and track*

City would seem undressed without a grand drapery, while the University of Wisconsin Union Theatre seems complete without one. Often the grand drapery is specially designed so as to cut down on the height of the proscenium arch and thus can aid in providing a more useful fly loft.

The *act curtain*, next in line, gives a clean-cut and sharp closing to a scene if it is a *drop curtain* or an *act drop*. When the stage has minimum fly space, a *draw curtain*, made up of two sections of curtain which part in the middle, is the second-best choice. A two-sectioned traveller or track (opposite), rigged with one-half-inch braided cotton rope, is necessary for this type of curtain. The most satisfactory travellers are of metal with metal rollers, but wooden tracks, using wooden balls, are also serviceable. Velour is probably the most suitable material for an act curtain, although certain of the newer theatres have used heavily textured self-patterned fabrics. The draw curtain must overlap at least eighteen inches and should just touch the floor so that light will not show beneath it.

Tab (tableau) *curtains* (page 8) and *contour curtains* (as at the Radio City Music Hall) are pleasing to look at but hardly suit a small theatre specializing in the three-act drama. Contour curtains are extremely difficult to rig and operate, but a draw curtain can easily be converted to a tab curtain for musical shows and ballet. For curtain calls, the Metropolitan Opera regularly uses a tab curtain with pleasing results.

The Teaser and the Tormentor

Directly upstage of the act curtain is the *teaser* (pages 2, 3), a horizontal frame, usually covered with black velour. Unless the production requires a specially designed *false proscenium*, the teaser serves as the usual downstage upper trim for the scenery. To insure complete masking, the teaser unit should be at least four feet wider than the proscenium arch. It should be possible to raise and lower this unit to accommodate settings of various heights. For example, an interior setting such as the lighthouse for *Thunder Rock* or the exterior for *All My Sons*, showing two floors of a house, both require considerable height. As a matter of fact, most stage settings have a more pleasing appearance when height is disclosed. Also, it is difficult for all the balcony patrons to see the back wall of a setting when the teaser is in too low a position.

The perpendicular masking frames placed Right and Left of the setting are called *tormentors* (pages 2, 3). These, too, are usually covered with black velour, and it should be possible to move them Off and On so as to display the exact width of stage that is desired. The units should be as tall as the proscenium height since, as already stated, there are occasions when great height is indicated.

The Light Batten, the Teaser Spots, and the Tormentor Spots

Part of the purpose of the teaser and the tormentors is to mask the lighting instruments which come next in line. The *light batten*, which holds the *teaser lights*, hangs directly behind the teaser, and the spotlights which are clamped to the pipe usually light the Up Left, Up Center, and Up Right areas. Since these lights should be easily accessible, often a bridge or catwalk is built above them; this walk allows workers to adjust and focus the lights without climbing ladders. Non-professional electricians often standardize the locations of these instruments on their light battens. Six instruments are considered to be the minimum for an average-sized stage.

Some theatres install so-called *tormentor lights* on pipes perpendicular to the stage and directly upstage of the tormentors. The lights are clamped one above the other, three or four for each side, and usually cannot be used if the setting is lashed directly to the tormentors. Sometimes the tormentors are attached to a tall pipe framework on casters which holds both the tormentor and the tormentor lights. Tormentor spots, like footlights, are favored by many older actors.

The Floor Space, the Fly Loft, and the Gridiron

In the past, architects have been loath to include adequate fly lofts in otherwise satisfactory theatre plans, since they have not known how to treat them from the point of view of exterior architecture. Architects have also been inclined to cut down on stage floor space because they do not know backstage problems. Recently a Western architect literally lived in a hospital for a year before beginning to draw up plans for a new hospital building. How fortunate it would be for the theatre if architects could follow through a number of actual theatrical productions before beginning their drawings.

Lack of backstage space is one of the most trying situations the technical workers have to face. If the proscenium arch is thirty feet wide, there should be no less than twenty feet on each side of the opening for storage space. While the settings will only occasionally demand a depth of over fifteen feet, the actual depth of the stage must be no less than thirty feet. If the effective height of the proscenium arch is fifteen feet, the ceiling of the stage house should be at least fifty feet from the floor in order to allow drops and other units to be flown completely out of sight. A fly loft which just misses being high enough is a greater architectural blunder than a low loft which frankly serves merely as a means for hanging stage draperies.

Six feet below the ceiling of the stage house is the open-work *grid* or *gridiron* (pages 2, 3) which supports the sheaves through which run the ropes of the rigging system. It is necessary to have the grid that distance below the ceiling in order to allow space above for workers to accomplish installation, adjustment, and repair work. Most lines hang at intervals of a foot or more, and when a permanent *counterweight system* (page 12) has been installed, the distances must remain constant. Where a combination rope and counterweight system is in use, the locations of some of the ropes can be changed occasionally by moving the sheaves.

The space below the gridiron is the *rigging loft, fly loft,* or *flies,* and it is in this space that flown scenery hangs.

The Pinrail and the Counterweight System

When the rope system for flying scenery is used, three lines, designated *Short, Center* or *Middle,* and *Long,* are required. These lines extend from the *pipe batten* or other unit which they are supporting, through the sheaves and *headblock,* to the *pinrail* and *belaying pins.* Sometimes an extremely wide stage will require four

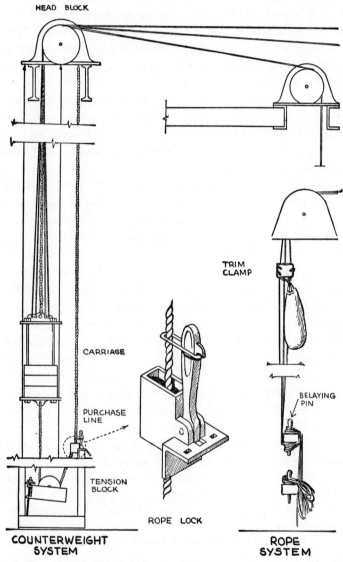

HEAD BLOCK

CARRIAGE

PURCHASE
LINE

TENSION
BLOCK

ROPE LOCK

COUNTERWEIGHT
SYSTEM

TRIM
CLAMP

BELAYING
PIN

ROPE
SYSTEM

Fig. 4 *Counterweight and rope systems*

lines instead of three. In that case the lines are numbered One, Two, Three, and Four, depending upon their distances from the pinrail. By means of *trim clamps*, it is possible to trim these lines relatively even and, if necessary, to hang sand bags or temporary counterweight arbors and weights.

Manila rope, three quarters of one inch in diameter, is commonly used for rope rigging. Braided rope is much better than twisted rope although the latter seems to be much more in evidence on the non-professional stage. Manila rope is necessary in any case where actual weight is suspended from it, and ropes must be checked frequently for signs of wear.

In addition to the pinrail, a *tie-off rail*, directly below, facilitates trimming, since lines can then be tied off as the object to be flown rests on the floor. The unit can then be flown and the ropes tied off at the pinrail proper. The operators stand on the *fly floor*, and the term *fly gallery* designates that entire area. Care must be observed to keep ropes from getting in a general mix-up on the fly floor, since serious accidents can be caused by flymen tripping and losing control of their lines.

Variations in the installations of counterweight systems are frequently found in up-to-date theatres. The *rope lock* and *locking rail* are often placed on the stage floor level and sometimes in a location which would correspond to that of an overhead fly gallery. Quite often theatres are rigged with a combination of counterweight and line systems, and this method naturally offers the maximum of flexibility.

Stage counterweighting is based on the principle that, since perfect balance is not always possible, the object flown must weigh a little more than the counterweights; thus the flown unit will always be under control at the rail and the weights will never come banging down. The counterweights come in units of ten, twenty, and thirty pounds and are placed in *arbors* or *carriages* which are guided by track-line steel bars or wires. All three lines from the pipe batten are connected to the top of the carriage, and a *purchase line* travels from the bottom of the carriage, through a *take-up block* on the floor, around through the head block to the top of the carriage. The rope lock holds the carriage in place and, if weighting is reasonably accurate, very little effort is required to raise and lower the heaviest of units.

The Scene Dock

A fly gallery placed at least eighteen feet above the stage floor will allow some sort of scenery dock or scenery storage space beneath it. If a counterweight system has been installed against a wall and the workers are to have access to it from the floor, the dock might better be placed on the opposite side. Guard rails can be placed in front of the lines, however, so that flats can be leaned temporarily on that side of the stage. The dock should not be considered as a place for permanent storage, but merely as storage space before set-up and during scene shifts. Space for permanent storage should be provided in the scene shop, so that the scene dock will always be free for scenery which is in current use.

The Sky Dome and the Cyclorama

In the 1920's there was a distinct inclination to stress the value of the *plaster dome* or *kuppel-horizont* as a means of representing the sky. While the dome takes light beautifully, relatively few interiors readily permit its use, since windows are so often on the side walls of settings. Furthermore, since no scenery can be leaned against a back wall that is of white plaster, valuable backstage space is tied up at all times. Certain continental theatres with tremendous backstage areas have demonstrated the effectiveness of the plaster dome; as a background for an exterior setting it is unsurpassed. However, such a theatre plant as the Mendelssohn Theatre at Ann Arbor, Michigan, since it has a minimum of backstage space, shows up the difficulties involved with such a built-in feature. It will be interesting to note how many theatres to be built within the next ten years will include sky domes.

A permanently installed *sky drop*, or a *cyclorama* (page 102) which can be flown easily, have few such disadvantages, yet will add much to the flexibility of the backstage area. At Hunter College, New York City, a pale blue velour cyclorama, stretched tightly and without seams, offers a convincing sky effect and is easily flown completely out of sight. Unfortunately, similarly shaped and rigged cycloramas with sufficient height and curve are standard equipment in very few non-professional theatres.

The Floor Areas

The location of the various backstage areas is functionally important. On the *working side* or *prompt side* are found the pinrail, the lighting controlboard, and the act-curtain pull; and the stage manager usually stays on this side. The *O.P.* side, known as the *opposite prompt* side, is the reverse side; and all the offstage space is known as the *wings*. In the stage directions of nineteenth-century plays, entrances are sometimes noted with such symbols as *L1* and *L2*. This means the first and second Left entrances upstage of the footlights.

A playing area of average size is usually divided into six parts: Down Left, Down Center, Down Right, Up Left, Up Center, and Up Right. Although a setting may sometimes be so shallow as to include only the downstage playing areas of the stage, most directors normally prefer more space.

The Stage Flooring

The stage floor must be of softwood so that scenery may be fastened satisfactorily to the floor, and no more than the extreme downstage area should be of hardwood. A *floor cloth* or ground cloth, covering somewhat more than the actual acting area, is usually desirable. Heavy brown canvas is the customary ground cloth material; it is either tacked to the floor with #10 carpet tacks or lashed to specially placed floor hooks. Actual carpeting is especially good for realistic interiors, and if the rug is to be a permanent feature, it is wise to place Ozite padding underneath it. These floor coverings will deaden sound and, in the case of barefoot dancers, serve as protection from splinters. Linoleum is very often used in musicals and certain revivals and, when waxed and polished, gives an extremely attractive finish to the floor. Eighteenth-century English plays should be as pictorially satisfying when staged with linoleum floor covering as plays from the Greek or the Renaissance. Whatever type of covering is used, there must be no hesitation about screwing stage pegs through the material when it is necessary to support various units.

The Traps

Most stage floors are trapped — that is, certain sections are removable to allow for entrances and exits from the floor. Some theatres have the entire acting area trapped, thus offering directors and designers out-of-the-ordinary opportunity for playing levels. A number of university theatres have the center portions of the stage on hydraulic elevators. While in most cases these elevators were installed to permit the removal of scenery to the basement, they are occasionally useful for trick staging. Many professional companies find it necessary to cut special traps since the permanent ones are not always the right size nor in the location that is right for a particular play.

The stages of medieval and Elizabethan theatres were usually trapped and scenes involving the Lower Regions and graves were thus possible. Audiences have always enjoyed such devices, and therefore the trap, together with smoke and flame effects, has often been used. When an opening in the floor is an absolute necessity for the development of a plot, it is sometimes possible to change the business slightly and to use whatever permanent traps are available. When the floor is not trapped or it is not possible to cut an opening into the floor, it may be possible to use some sort of substitute. A recent production of *The Skin of Our Teeth* made use of a temporary drop door, placed on the front edge of the apron; the actors got underneath the trap when the lights were dimmed. However, such a production as *Finian's Rainbow* would require a specially built trap and it is unlikely that any simplification of that device would prove satisfactory.

The Loading Facilities

Even though the scene shop is in the same building as the theatre proper, the backstage area must provide a *loading door* and a *loading platform* to allow for the delivery of supplementary supplies, properties, and, when necessary, scenery. The loading door and platform should be at stage level; moreover, when a truck is driven to the platform, the truck floor should be at the stage level. The weird loading arrangements encountered in theatres throughout the country cause many extra hours of labor for theatre workers. Scenery units are often heavy, yet the necessity for lifting units first up six feet and then down six feet is all too common.

Recently a school auditorium was built in the business section of a thriving community with the intention that it should house an occasional road show. When the plant was completed, it was discovered that all the backstage doors led to the high school corridors and that scenery could be brought in only through the main doors, a block away. Another relatively new building has a good loading platform but the roadway leading to it is so steep that few trucks can back into it when the weather is intemperate. Still another university theatre has a loading platform that is near the rear doors of several very permanent family residences. Late-at-night loading and unloading noises obviously displeased the neighbors; after a number of complaints were filed, the theatre had to revise its working schedule. It is certain that anyone who could visit theatre plants the country over would be able to compile a very interesting list of loading facilities.

The Lighting Controlboard

Although the lighting controlboard is usually placed backstage Right, a little above floor level, some authorities wish to place it in the orchestra pit or in the balcony. It is, of course, desirable that some of the lighting technicians see the stage during rehearsals. However, if the board is out front, the electricians will have to resist the temptation to make continual changes during certain performances, and thus call attention to light as light.

If the controlboard is placed in the balcony, the only means of communication with the stage is by telephone — and telephones have been known not to function. Although this means is satisfactory for productions in which it would be desirable for the lighting technicians to watch the stage, there are many times when it would be helpful for the stage manager to talk directly to those at the controlboard. There is little doubt that productions requiring ever-changing light such as *The Blue Bird* or Ibsen's *Brand* would definitely be smoother if the electricians were not working blindly. Theoretically the stage manager gives all light cues, but since he cannot see the stage, the sensitive qualities of the lighting may sometimes be lost.

The minimum stage facilities herein listed go to make up a plant which should permit smooth theatrical productions. If the backstage area is incomplete, concessions will have to be made in production, or at least the choice of plays will very definitely be limited. Certain plant reconstruction is possible and often necessary equipment can be added; but, generally speaking, an outmoded plant remains a trial — and a lesson for builders of new theatres.

PROJECTS AND EXERCISES

1. What are the height and width of the proscenium arch of your theatre? How is the arch treated decoratively? Does this treatment suit the architecture of the auditorium?

2. What lighting instruments are placed in front of the act curtain in the theatre in which you work? If beam spots are used, are they accessible? If your theatre is equipped with footlights, how frequently are they used?

3. How many auditoriums and theatres in your community have built-in aprons? Are they ever used during actual productions? Are they deep or shallow?

4. How many musicians can be seated in the orchestra pit of the largest of the local professional theatres? How much lower is the pit floor than the orchestra floor? List at least five musicals for which music could be provided in such an orchestra pit.

5. What are the regulations concerning fire curtains in the professional theatres of the community? In the state? Do the rules apply to the non-professional theatre as well?

6. What type of act curtain does your stage have and what were the obvious reasons for selecting a curtain of this type?

7. Examine the teasers and tormentors of three stages. How are they covered? What are their dimensions in relation to the proscenium-arch heights and widths?

8. Get permission to go backstage after the performance of some local non-professional production and note the number of teaser and tor-

mentor spots that are used. Try to discover at which floor area each is directed. If possible, examine similar lighting units at the close of some professional performance.

9. Using a scale rule, draw a floor plan of the stage on which you work. On the same page draw a plan which will show the recognized minimum essentials. Study the differences.

10. Which of the following productions could not be satisfactorily staged unless a fly loft were available: *She Stoops to Conquer, Oklahoma, The Corn Is Green, As You Like It, Harvey*? Give your reasons.

11. Does your stage have a fly loft? What distance is the gridiron from the stage floor? Can scenery always be flown out of sight? Are there any restrictions as to the weights of scenery to be flown?

12. What improvements would have to be made on the stage of the local college or civic theatre before it would have all the minimum essentials of dimension and equipment? Would such changes be practical?

13. If you had to choose between flying space and offstage space, which would you select? Why?

14. From the point of view of minimum essentials, examine a number of stage houses that are to be found nearby. Contrast with the stage on which you work.

15. On which side of the stage are the counterweight arbors or the pinrail of your theatre? How high is the fly gallery or the loading gallery from the floor? How many lines are provided?

16. Does your stage have a scenery dock? What height flats can be accommodated? Can it be used during performance?

17. As you attend various non-professional productions, note the sky effects represented. Is it obviously apparent whether the productions use sky domes, cycloramas, or sky drops?

18. Name three plays you have seen which have required traps. Could the productions have been staged satisfactorily without them? The road production of *The Madwoman of Chaillot* used a wall opening rather than a floor opening. Did this detract in any way?

19. List the various possible stage-floor coverings and suggest the type or types that might best suit the following productions: *A Doll's House, Dark of the Moon, Light up the Sky, Twelfth Night, Antigone, The Cherry Orchard*. Give your reasons.

20. From the point of view of the locations of the controlboards, examine the floor plans of as many college theatres as are available to you. What seems to be the most common location?

2

The Forms of Scenery

THE STAGE HOUSE and its equipment are quite likely to determine the forms of scenery that can be placed on the stage and shown to the best advantage. However, designers and technical workers need first to become completely familiar with the script before they attempt to make decisions as to the forms of scenery that are usable in a particular production. Scenic forms can be classified according to their shape with no reference to their actual design or style and, while a few of the classifications represent recent developments in stagecraft, a number of the forms can be traced back to Renaissance times. The mere knowledge of the forms is not important as such, but only as a basis for the clean-cut discussions which should precede the proper selections.

The Box Setting

During a recent Broadway season, fifty-four out of eighty-five productions required the use of realistic box settings. Even though it is not always necessary or possible to prepare such complete and detailed box settings as are seen on Broadway, this form of setting is obviously to be found in widest use in the non-professional theatre of today. In a sense, this is a definite advantage to many small groups with limited budgets since it will be possible for them to use standard equipment as the foundation for their work.

The distinguishing mark of the box setting is its completeness. The setting begins at one tormentor and ends at the other, and it has full height usually topped by a ceiling. Complete *backings* are used for the various entrance places and windows, and the audience is content that it is seeing everything it can and should see except the fourth wall. The box settings of the nineteenth century and the early twentieth century were usually painted with highlights and shadows from an arbitrary light source and seldom presented any actual third dimension. Such box settings were the final development of the sliding wing-and-backdrop mountings which originated in Renaissance days. In form and shape, late-nineteenth-century scenery was similar, none the less, to the present-day box setting and evidently audiences of that era got a similar satisfaction from viewing such scenery.

Fig. 5 *A box setting for Noel Coward's "Blithe Spirit."*   *Three-dimensional trim, a ceiling and carefully chosen set dressings are represented*

Three reasonably flat walls usually give better representation of an actual room than do many jogs, angles, and irregularities. Although it is true that walls may occasionally be broken up in accord with sound architectural reason, the mere introduction of the nook-and-cranny for its own sake is a bad and confusing practice. Thus the ingenuity of the designer will often be taxed as he tries to provide logical variety for his various box settings and as he attempts to give the solid and substantial qualities that are required with such scenery.

Whether the box setting is a three-wall or a two-wall interior, the downstage end on each side is lashed to the tormentor or to the *return*, a sort of second tormentor. When the return is used, it readily permits the use of light from the apertures between the tormentor and the return. If the return is black, it recedes and has no importance; while if it is given the same paint treatment as the setting, the room perhaps appears larger. Returns are frequently moved further onstage than the tormentors in order to decrease the width of a setting; if the returns on a small stage are placed further offstage than the tormentors, a setting will take on extra width.

Since the sight lines for balcony patrons demand rather higher walls than would normally be found in actual rooms, the stage interior often becomes partly a design problem focussing on what to do with the upper portion of the walls. Since these high walls are necessary, a fourteen- or sixteen-foot height is normal for the box setting on the stage of a large theatre. The combination of high walls and a wide stage will necessarily produce occasional box settings of an abnormal scale which, in the case of kitchens or attics, may be difficult for audiences to accept. In such cases, the settings are sometimes designed on a much smaller scale than the proscenium arch would suggest, and the unused space is masked off or treated to suggest the exterior of the building.

The Exterior Setting

The exterior setting is perhaps the most difficult form of scenery to present convincingly but, when successful, one of the most pleasing to look at. This type of setting usually requires the use of

Fig. 6 *A full exterior setting for "The Bartered Bride" including the use of a sky dome, profile steeples, and freestanding wall and house fronts*

a full stage and, because the first problem is one of masking, practically every scenic unit used has to be considered as a masking unit before its decorative potentialities are developed. Despite the desirability of spaciousness and authenticity in a realistic exterior, there will be no illusion if the patrons can see into the backstage areas.

Several important masking problems always exist. First of all, what to do about the sky? In the twenties and thirties there was no question regarding sky effects; a sky dome, a sky drop, or a cyclorama always took care of this problem. The addition of a ground row, a railing, a fence, or a wall usually completed that part of the stage picture and frankly hid the floor line of the sky piece. Today, we are inclined to give serious consideration to the painted backdrop inasmuch as a great deal more locale can thus be represented. This does not mean, however, that flat painted skies are not used in the present-day Broadway theatre. Mielziner's setting for *Summer and Smoke* made effective use of a large, plain sky piece, and both the exteriors for Samuel Leve's *Clutterbuck* scenery were enhanced by a brilliantly lighted sky piece.

How about horizontal masking? *Foliage borders* are the most

23

common type of scenery for this purpose, although occasionally some sort of architectural form is combined with the side masking to form a semi-exterior setting with emphasis on buildings and sky. If foliage borders are used, there will need to be a number of them unless the sky unit, whatever it is, is extremely high. Borders are usually hung progressively lower as they approach the upstage limits, and often light is kept off them in order to accentuate their silhouette qualities.

Although not all foliage on the stage is necessarily a masking device, there is always the question of whether foliage should be three dimensional or painted. Up until the twenties, naturalistically painted foliage was common; then for a time all greenery was artificial. Today, we like to mix both forms — a three-dimensional tree might stand near a painted backdrop or seem to branch out with foliage painted on a border above it. A foliage border might even be a combination of painted greenery with a few artificial leaves placed here and there where they would catch the light. However, regardless of whether or not the horizontal masking is leaves or architecture, it must never cramp nor overpower the stage picture unless, of course, the script suggests that it do so.

The fact that the complete exterior setting is a difficult form makes it a challenging project for the designer. However, the designer will often find that some one important practical item (a fountain, a statue, a well, a practical tree, a rock) will confuse and complicate his over-all design plans and seem to make the design less a creative challenge than a puzzle. None the less, no matter how attractive his sketch or water-color rendering may be, if, as a finished product, it does not mask, serve the action, or suggest the out-of-doors, it has not succeeded as a stage design for an exterior setting.

The Drop-and-Wing Setting

The recent renewed interest in the drop-and-wing setting has come as a delightfully refreshing change from the heavily built scenery of the twenties and thirties. Most present-day musical shows use drops and wings in some form or other, and the ballet

Fig. 7 *A drop-and-wing setting for Joseph Jefferson's "Rip Van Winkle" showing the use of foliage borders and painted house fronts*

presents this form of scenery today in much the same manner as it has always done. Although drops and wings first originated during the Renaissance, they have been in quite constant use ever since. From a practical standpoint, this form of scenery is probably less expensive than heavy, built pieces, although the skill required for painting is more specialized. It is therefore unlikely that many non-professional groups would attempt such a profusion of elaborate backdrops as were found in the Broadway productions of *Bloomer Girl* and *Up in Central Park*.

There are few limits to the interpretive possibilities of drops and wings, since anything imaginable can be painted on them. Their use is in no sense limited to exteriors, although the exterior no doubt offers the designer the greatest scope. Particularly effective as painted interiors are palace scenes and great halls which are so elaborate that their representation by means of building would be out of the question. For example, the backdrops for the Sadler's Wells production of *The Sleeping Beauty* presented architectural extravagance which could never have been represented on the stage by any other means than paint. The cathedral shell in *Brigadoon* would similarly have been almost impossible to build and

25

shift. Furthermore, from an interpretive point of view, the painted backdrops in these two productions were able to capture the mood better than any amount of building could have done.

Today, drop-and-wing settings do have a limited use which extends to musicals, opera, ballet, and revivals. While we do not usually present wings that slide in present-day productions, audiences often have the opportunity to watch drops go up and down and thus feel close to and a part of the total production. Unfortunately, a theatre without a fly loft cannot use this interesting scenery device which so simplifies the problems of scene shifting and helps the production to move rapidly and effortlessly. Technical workers will also always be impressed with the amount of free backstage area that this form of scenery guarantees.

The Unit Setting

During the twenties, unit scenery came very much into use and, while it then was a welcome relief from the previous elaborately painted scenery, its limitations were soon discovered. Early unit scenery was made up of more or less solid, three-dimensional units which were given interchangeable positions on the stage. Walls, columns, steps, ramps, arches, plugs, and trees were moved around the stage and the various new arrangements were supposed to suggest new locales. For example, in such a play as *Hamlet* a plugged arch might, on Stage Right, serve as the background for the king's throne and, later on, on Stage Left, unplugged, become one of the doorways leading off the hall. Trees, moved about to different areas of the stage, suggested different parts of a forest and might, when used in combination with arches and walls, help suggest roadways or gardens. There was also much use of complicated series of steps which were often given new arrangements as the play progressed. The steps which led up to the Queen's chamber in one scene could be combined with other steps to produce a palace terrace or some similar area.

Some designers thought they could end the scenic dilemmas of non-professional groups by designing a series of unit pieces to be used in innumerable combinations. It was soon discovered that there is always a limit to the number of arrangements possible, and that such stage picturization is too static to permit the inclusion of much atmosphere and locale. Whatever the merits of unit scenery as applied to Elizabethan plays and Greek plays, it seems obvious that the average contemporary drama demands a great deal more than such movable, utilitarian units can supply.

Certain variations from these early unit settings have been used recently and have proved more successful than the earlier type. A Broadway production of *The Tempest* had as its main scenic element a revolving unit which moved about from scene to scene to suggest various locations. Obey's *Noah* (page 28) is a play which is well suited to scenic representation by means of a movable unit that can be shown in different positions on the stage and thus both unify and simplify the production. It is in such productions, where a unit can be closely related to and be an active part of the stage picture, that unit scenery is most satisfactory. Indeed, it is possible that this type of unit scenery has never been fully developed and that soon some production will illustrate its use excitingly.

However, today we demand more from scenery than mere ingenuity. It may be disconcerting for an audience to be tempted to wonder where and how a unit is going to appear the third and fourth times. The less creative type of unit scenery obviously belongs to a specific period of development and progress in our theatre but cannot be considered as up-and-coming stagecraft today. Scenery must have meaning as well as form, and designers cannot be blamed for selecting forms which will not hamper their efforts toward interpretation.

The Skeleton Setting

Perhaps the most satisfactory type of relatively complete scenery which is in use today involves the use of one or more *skeletons* or frames designed to give a unifying effect to a particular production. A skeleton is a permanent frame; scene changes can be effected upstage of it frequently and quickly without halting any action that might be taking place downstage. While these frames are particularly well suited to such multi-set plays as those of Shakespeare and his contemporaries, they can often be used for present-

Fig. 8 *The unit setting. Two arrangements of a unit for Andre Obey's "Noah." The ark is on casters and is moved about from scene to scene*

Fig. 9 *Two skeleton arrangements for "Green Grow the Lilacs." Note the effects obtained by the changing of the side plugs, and the two additional center openings for the hay shed scene*

day plays that make unusual scenery demands. Such frames might also be planned for productions in which the time element in scene shifting is unimportant, but in which it would be desirable to create new and interesting stage pictures without changing the basic framework (see page 29).

Skeletons can be designed to accommodate both interiors and exteriors and, unlike many unit settings, they may express mood and locale, usually without the audience's being aware of any ingenuity that may be involved. If more than one frame is used, there will be increased opportunity for variety in playing areas. When a skeleton is used with stage draperies, a sort of false proscenium results, and this offers a definite downstage playing space for intimate scenes. Robert Edmond Jones' simple skeleton for *Lute Song* beautifully illustrates the pictorial opportunities of such type of scenery as do the elaborate frames for *Marco Millions* designed by Lee Simonson.

For some years students have had a tendency to use the terms *unit* and *skeleton* rather loosely. Theatre workers who really understand the chief differences between the two forms of scenery will hardly confuse the terms nor be likely to find a great deal of use for the former. Skeletons can be so versatile and chameleon-like that the designer is almost certain to consider the more static *units* as primarily useful for various formalized productions.

Minimum Scenery

Budgets and limited backstage areas frequently dictate the use of some sort of minimum scenery. While these forms of scenery adapt themselves best to musicals and non-realistic plays, sometimes they may be used for realistic plays — especially those which are episodic in form. Multi-set productions are often omitted from bills because they seem too difficult and expensive to stage. The number of settings in a play should not discourage the producers since there are these inexpensive methods of staging which, when carefully applied to a situation, often offer pleasing results. Scenery should never be evaluated by its measurements and weight. A great deal of scenery, unless it is absolutely right, can interfere with a production much more than minimum scenery, designed so that every square foot means something.

Fig. 10 *A cut-down setting for the laboratory in Maxwell Anderson's "The Star Wagon." The walls are cut down in direct relation to the architecture of the room*

THE CUT-DOWN SETTING

Cut-down scenery is a form of minimum scenery that usually contains units not normal in height, although the scenery is ordinarily complete as to floor plan, from tormentor to tormentor. Often the heights of the various walls are determined by certain architectural features of the room such as dadoes, windows, doors, and wainscoting. Horizontally placed flats, instead of perpendicular ones, can serve as walls, thus saving in materials and effort. The general effect often suggests solidity as far as the scenery goes, although there is, of course, no ceiling and the entire setting is usually placed in front of black stage draperies. Such scenery can be used in realistic plays as well as for plays in which style is of extreme importance.

The laboratory setting for Maxwell Anderson's *The Star Wagon* was planned in relation to the necessary cabinets, and the walls were cut down accordingly. When dealing with multi-set plays of this sort, it is necessary to think first of the most complete backgrounds

Fig. 11 *A selective setting for "Uncle Harry." The false proscenium stays throughout, the living room scene is set up permanently behind the black stage draperies, and the barroom (above) and the prison office are flown*

that might be possible and then to break these down to the final minimum wall essentials. Unfortunately, designers sometimes become beguiled with cut-down scenery as an idea with the result that the final products may become studies of angles and lines rather than suggestions of complete but simplified backgrounds.

There is no denying the fact that audiences will require longer to adjust to this type of minimum scenery than to full and complete box settings. However, once they understand what the scenery is trying to accomplish, it is probable that they might find such cut-down backgrounds interesting and stimulating. Surely theatre patrons must occasionally get as tired of the box setting as do designers.

The Selective Setting

Selective scenery, sometimes called *suggestive*, is often placed before black draperies, but here only one or two small wall sections are used. The height of this form of scenery is normal and the unit is architecturally complete at the top and sides. As in the case of cut-down scenery, the designer usually thinks first in terms of an entire room and then removes all that he considers non-essential.

32

Similar reasoning can be applied to the reduction of exteriors as well, although the use of sky effects makes it a more difficult problem.

Selective scenery is usually quite effective for realistic plays since one or two walls can often suggest an entire room. Thomas Job's *Uncle Harry* is an example of a solid and substantial play which lends itself nicely to this type of scenery. The realistic presentation of the play's three settings would be too difficult a task for many non-professional groups. Instead of a box setting, the selective tavern setting illustrated opposite shows all the details of one wall section and, aided by the set dressings, suggests completeness. The warden's office in the same play might be presented in similar manner by showing small wall sections containing barred windows, a chimney piece, and bookshelves.

Although selective backgrounds are considerably curtailed as to square feet, it is not necessary to omit important furniture from the stage picture. Furniture can be placed on the stage in any area where it can be used by the actors, and will not be a discordant note pictorially. The minimum walls will suggest the room, and the furnishings will complete it to the extent that is required. Certain tall pieces of furniture which are ordinarily placed against walls may be quite helpful in suggesting that the minimum walls make up a complete setting; if this is done, the various omissions will not be likely to disturb theatre patrons who are unused to this type of scenery.

THE FRAGMENTARY SETTING

Small irregularly shaped sections of a complete setting might best be classed as fragmentary. Such scenery is quite often painted rather than built; possibly it suits the non-realistic play better than the realistic. Fragmentary scenery may show a number of walls and will probably not be normal in height. Although the fragment may be sketchy, the designer gives considerable attention to the shape of the units so that the irregularities will help to define and point up the locale and mood. Basic architectural structure can often be emphasized in scenery of this type since, when a fragment of a wall is removed, the remaining section must necessarily reveal this construction.

Fig. 12 *A fragmentary painted setting for a cabin in "Dark of the Moon"*

Dark of the Moon is a good example of a play which might use this type of scenery to good advantage. The production requires many settings, and scene shifts must be fast and silent. Small settings are thus indicated and the very plot of the play suggests non-realistic fragments. Both the University of Iowa and the Broadway productions of the play took full advantage of this form of scenery with effective results.

In the professional field, George Jenkins has had satisfying results with fragmentary scenery. In such productions as *Strange Fruit* and *Lost in the Stars* he chose to set his fragments before painted backdrops instead of black velour, thus adding considerably to the visual appeal of these small units. There has been unlimited use of fragments in Broadway musicals for some years but, since producers of legitimate drama are inclined to shy away from episodic multi-set plays, fragmentary scenery has not had so great an opportunity for full development in the non-musical field.

THE PROFILE SETTING

Profile scenery, named after profile board (three-ply), attempts to represent a scene by means of one or two small irregularly

Fig. 13 *A profile setting for a hallway scene in the musical comedy "Anything Goes." All except the chairs is painted two-dimensionally*

shaped frames. These frames are usually covered with canvas and profile board and then painted in some non-realistic fashion, seldom with any attempt at literal three-dimensional form. Stage draperies or painted backdrops supply the background and may or may not remain stationary throughout the production. Since there is less scenery and so much attention is focussed on it, these frames must be all the more carefully composed. They can be shifted in an instant and, since they take up very little backstage space, innumerable profiles can be used in any one production, each frame reporting the very essence of a particular scene.

One or two small distinctive profile shapes can clearly indicate a definite location. For example, a painted steamship funnel and a short section of railing are sufficient to indicate a ship deck, or one carnival side-show tent-front is enough scenery to suggest a much larger group of such tents. The wall and painted doorway of the *Anything Goes* profile above leaves no doubt that the location is a hall or gallery. A stylized palm-tree silhouette plus some further identifying features such as significant furniture or a bit of native architecture might suggest Florida, Hawaii, or a more remote and less civilized tropical region.

Profile settings may not appeal to extravagant designers and producers or to audiences that are literal-minded. However, in musical shows, silhouettes are often shown which have such cameo-like elegance that it is difficult to believe that more scenery could accomplish as much. Directors might well consider this form of scenery for such episodic plays as *Beggar on Horseback*, *Alice in Wonderland*, or *The Insect Comedy*.

THE PROJECTED SETTING

While projected scenery has been seen occasionally in this country since World War I, it is chiefly a continental device; its uses are extremely limited and the results are likely to be fuzzy. The lens projector, similar to the "magic lantern," or the Linnebach lantern (page 327), with no lens, is necessary equipment for the presentation of this type of scenery. The lens projector, producing rather precise images, is usually hung above and in front of the screen or curtain, while the Linnebach lantern is often placed behind the screen; the Linnebach lantern uses slides which have very little detail and much emphasis on form and color. In either instance, slides must allow for distortion, since the projectors are not level with the screen. Interesting appearing and disappearing effects can be obtained by the use of two projectors and two dimmers.

The Federal Theatre used projections successfully for its various *Living Newspaper* productions, but the projected scenery for *Allegro*, a Broadway musical play, was generally considered unsatisfactory. The fact that this type of scenery is so infrequently used in the professional theatre surely indicates that it is questionable. Hazy, rather indistinct projected backgrounds will necessarily be unsuitable for a play which demands sharply conceived and sharply executed scenery.

The Simultaneous Setting

In the later years of medieval times it was not uncommon for an entire presentation to be set up in advance on one stage. Thus the players could move from area to area with no pause for the changing of properties and set pieces. Such a method of staging

Fig. 14 *A simultaneous setting for "She Loves Me Not." The central unit represents two rooms in a dormitory*

is frequently labelled "simultaneous" since all playing spaces are in evidence at one time. This system was, of course, preceded by, and was a natural development of, the medieval wagon stages which permitted scene shifts by means of wagons wheeled past the seating places.

In the present-day theatre, only an occasional play demands the use of several simultaneous playing areas. *She Loves Me Not*, a play dealing with certain incidents in a Princeton University dormitory, requires as many as three acting areas at one time. Although the illustration above shows four rooms, somewhat "minimum" in form, the original Broadway production (1933) used small complete box settings. Similarly, the simultaneous box setting for the Broadway production of *The Voice of the Turtle* was made up of three apartment rooms, including a kitchen with practical fixtures.

Even though the script does not demand it, if the proscenium opening is extremely wide, simultaneous staging might be useful in occasional episodic multi-set productions. The small incomplete acting areas could then be lighted when in use and the production thus become extremely fluid and alive. The simultaneous areas may represent both exteriors and interiors and, if most of the action

37

takes place within a definite location, the designer may choose to use this location as a unifying device.

Sometimes a number of these various forms of scenery are combined agreeably within one production, but usually the effect is better if a certain consistency is maintained. For example, it would be confusing to have Act I a box setting, Act II profile scenery, and Act III a drop-and-wing setting. A recent realistic Broadway production used box settings, profile scenery, and projections, and, although each setting was undeniably attractive, the final results seemed disconcerting. Certain other combinations might be more successful. A skeleton can be used satisfactorily with drops and wings and with profiles. Needless to say, the complete box setting and the complete exterior are always suitable within the same production as are fragmentary settings and profiles. Since full complete scenery is accepted quickly by everyone, while minimum scenery, as stated before, requires adjustment on the part of the audience, to introduce the patrons to one form and then shift to another may interfere with the true meanings of the stage pictures.

PROJECTS AND EXERCISES

1. Make note of the professional productions mentioned in Chapter 2. Try to find illustrations of the settings for these productions. *Theatre Arts* and *Life* are the most likely reference magazines. Study the pictures in relation to the discussions in the text.

2. What productions have you seen recently that used box settings? Drop-and-wing settings? Skeleton settings?

3. Examine the pictures in one of the bound yearly volumes of the original *Theatre Arts*. Attempt to classify the settings from the standpoint of form.

4. What forms of scenery seem best suited for the following plays: *Peer Gynt, The Critic, Nellie the Beautiful Cloak Model, The Late George Apley, Pirates of Penzance, Medea, Light up the Sky?* Give your reasons.

5. Have you seen any productions in which three or more forms of scenery have been used? Could you justify their use?

6. Consider a recent exterior setting that you have seen. Was the emphasis on architecture or foliage? Can you suggest any details

that might have been added but which actually were not necessary for the complete effect?

7. What recent professional productions have used drops and wings that were raised and lowered in full view of the audience? What did this accomplish?

8. List four realistic plays that might be staged with cut-down scenery and still retain the necessary authenticity.

9. Examine some well-known, elaborately fitted room in your community. Consider what you would do to represent it selectively on the stage in such a manner that it would be recognizable to those familiar with it.

10. Which type of background, stage draperies or painted backdrops would best suit fragmentary scenery for the following: *All God's Chillun Got Wings, Joan of Lorraine, Christopher Blake, The Cenci, Much Ado About Nothing*? Give reasons for your selections.

11. With which of the following musicals would profile scenery be most appropriate: *Of Thee I Sing, The Desert Song, Sweethearts, Three Penny Opera, Three to Make Ready, The Student Prince*? Why?

12. Which might be the most suitable for the following plays, a lens projector or a Linnebach lantern: *Peer Gynt, From Morn to Midnight, The Sunken Bell, Bury the Dead, Waiting for Lefty*? Give the reasons for your choice.

13. What contemporary plays require the use of several playing areas at the same time? What classic plays might be made more interesting by means of simultaneous staging?

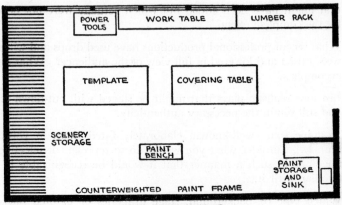

POWER TOOLS WORK TABLE LUMBER RACK

TEMPLATE COVERING TABLE

SCENERY STORAGE

PAINT BENCH

PAINT STORAGE AND SINK

COUNTERWEIGHTED PAINT FRAME

THE SCENE SHOP

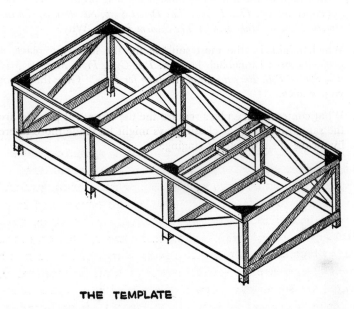

THE TEMPLATE

Fig. 15 *Scene shop floor plan and template*

40

3

The Construction of
Scenic Units

IN THE NON-PROFESSIONAL theatre, most of the workers who build
and paint stage scenery are usually relatively inexperienced beginners. As student carpenters and painters begin their shop
work, they will naturally be somewhat slow and perhaps not always
so accurate as is desirable. If, however, they study and practice
the basic principles of building, covering, and painting, there is
no reason why these workers should not turn out creditable-looking
scenery which can be set up and shifted with a minimum of effort.
Although stage-carpentry methods vary in different localities, most
practices are sound and bear a direct relation to the unique requirements of scenery as opposed to the heavier and more solid
building associated with the work of regular carpenters. Regardless of which building methods are used or how experienced the
workers, a special scene shop must be provided in which the work
can be laid out, built, covered, and painted.

41

The Scene Shop

The scene shop is second in importance to the stage and the stage house and is to be evaluated from the point of view of both space and equipment. Inadequate building and storage space can literally double the amount of work necessary for a production, and it is unfortunate, indeed, to find a shop which requires that scenic units must be moved about continually in order to find available working areas. At best, the preparation of stage scenery is a hurried and tiring job, and no detail of the shop arrangement and equipment should slow up the builders and painters or require them to do extra work. If building and painting are considered in relation to the progress of scenery through the shop, it is not likely that the working areas will be located illogically. When units move through the scene shop in assembly-line fashion, the efficiency of the shop arrangement has been proved.

Lumber storage is the first item to consider; such storage is best effected by means of lumber racks which are long enough to accommodate lengths up to sixteen feet. The various divisions of the rack should be arranged for specific sizes of lumber (i.e., $1'' \times 3''$, $1'' \times 2''$, $1'' \times 6''$, moldings, etc.), and bins should be provided for *corner blocks* and *keystones* as well as for scrap lengths. The lumber rack should be at floor level since all the stock must be within easy reach of the builders. Storing lumber near the ceiling may conserve floor space, but this method offers definite elements of danger. Finally, there must be an entrance door near the rack so that battens can be brought directly to the storage space without traversing the entire length of the shop.

No scene shop is complete without power tools. While there is a certain amount of danger in connection with the operating of such machinery, if its use is controlled to the extent that only the more experienced workers use the machinery, accidents should be at a minimum. The *table saw* is essential for ripping long lengths of lumber, although it is, of course, useful for crosscut work as well. The *band saw* is invaluable for use in cutting curved sweeps and certain irregular shapes which are not particularly intricate in design. These two essential machines are usually mounted on casters and must always have sufficient space around them so that,

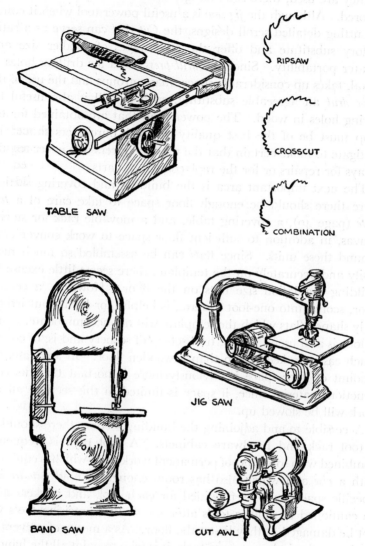

Fig. 16 *Power tools*

as they are used, there is no danger that the safety element will be ignored. Although the *jig saw* is a useful power tool when it comes to cutting detailed scroll designs, the *Cut Awl* can serve as a satisfactory substitute and offer the advantages of smaller size and greater portability. Since the *drill press*, used for drilling holes in metal, takes up considerable space, many groups find the use of the *Thor drill* an agreeable substitute: such a drill is also useful for boring holes in wood. The power tools that are obtained for the shop must be of the best quality and the purchasers should investigate to make certain that the manufacturers will never require delays for repairs or for the replacement of parts.

The next important area is the building and covering section. Here there should be enough floor space to take care of a *template* (page 40), a covering table, and a movable rack for storing canvas, in addition to sufficient floor space to work conveniently around these units. Since flats can be assembled so much more easily and accurately on the template, there seems little excuse for building regulation size flats on the floor. However, a cement floor, scored into one-foot squares, is helpful for laying out irregularly shaped flats which the template will not accommodate. Such a floor is also useful for the trial set-up of scenery and is, of course, much easier to keep clean than a wooden floor. In any case, the amount of floor space is obviously more important than its construction material since, if space is limited in this section, all the work will be slowed up.

Accessible to and adjoining the building section, there should be a tool rack and hardware cabinets. A tool rack is frequently combined with some sort of permanent work table which is equipped with a *vise* and which also has room enough to hold a *mitre box*. Specific space must be provided for each tool, and workers must be cautioned to replace tools after use so that precision tools will not be damaged as they lie on the floor. As a means of preventing the loss and misplacement of tools, it is wise to paint all the handles the same conspicuous color. The hardware cabinet must include separate bins for each item of regular and stage hardware; it is desirable that the name of the item and a sample of the hardware be placed at each opening in the cabinet to help workers to become familiar with the items and to aid in keeping the supplies in good order. Drawers are not so satisfactory as bins since quantities of hardware weigh a great deal and the drawers would often be rather unmanageable.

The paint section of the shop must include a large sink with hot and cold water; storage bins for whiting, wheat paste, dry color, and glue; and a variety of buckets. Also necessary is a work table on which is placed a double boiler and an electric heater with a pilot light — the latter to help guard against leaving the heat on when workers are not in the shop. The storage bins should be clearly labelled and each space provided with a scoop for removing painting materials as needed. If ample shelf space is provided for buckets and vegetable tins, these items will not be continually kicked about under the sink. As for the purchasing of supplies, many technicians feel that it is wise to buy by the barrel, and from these barrels to keep the bins full. However, scene-shop space is so important that unless there is a separate waterproof shed, it may be wiser to buy paint as needed since, as a rule, paint dealers do not offer wholesale prices to theatre groups.

The most useful equipment that has been devised to aid scenery painters is the *windlass-controlled paint frame*. This frame covers all or part of one of the shop walls and, when flats or drops are fastened to it, the frame can be raised and lowered, thus saving much extra labor. The height of the paint frame will usually be determined by the size of the drops that can be flown on the particular stage that the shop serves. In the absence of a paint frame, a *boomerang*, a step platform on rollers, will enable the workers to paint easily from various levels. A boomerang will, however, take up much valuable floor space and can therefore be used only in shops of considerable dimension.

The entire shop must be well lighted by powerful incandescent lamps, and there must be electrical outlets throughout the shop so that the power tools can be moved about when necessary. Too often insufficient light is responsible for building and painting errors, especially in a shop where there are many workers and out-of-the-way corners are used at all times. Needless to say, nervous and physical fatigue are increased greatly when workers cannot see their work clearly. Since most non-professional theatre workers do their building and painting at night, windows are not necessary for the purpose of supplying light but are required only if ventilation is provided by no other means.

A metalworking section would no doubt be a useful feature of a scene shop, but since the amount of metal work is usually so slight as compared to the wood work, it often seems advisable to omit this section and to depend on public metal shops for complicated metal work. A shop must be planned for predictable minimum essentials, all of which are justified by almost daily use. However, productions often demand some unusual item which may tax the space and equipment of a shop. Whether the problem is one of metal or wood — or both — is not so important as is the ability of the workers to adjust an unusual building problem to their particular plant facilities.

Even though it is sometimes necessary to use as a scene shop a building that was never built for such purposes, every effort should be made to modernize the area and to improve it so that scenery workers can employ their efforts in the construction and painting of scenery and not in overcoming the handicaps of the plant. Every effort should be made to keep the room warm and dry since hardware will rust and painting materials will become lumpy if much moisture is about. Paint will not dry quickly nor will glue set in a damp room, and time may be wasted as a result. Strictly from the point of view of morale, since technical workers spend so many hours in the scene shop, surely they are entitled to work in a clean, pleasant room where neither the elements nor the time of day can hinder their working efficiency.

The Construction Materials

TOOLS

Tools may be roughly divided into the following main headings: *measuring*, *gripping*, and *driving* (page 48), *cutting* (page 49), and *boring* (page 49). Certain tools will be used only occasionally and, unless a group has an extremely heavy production schedule involving much new building, it is wise to simplify the tool storage problem by limiting the tools to the really essential items. Since present-day costs are considerably out of line, no prices are suggested here.

Cheap tools are to be avoided, however, and emphasis should be on sturdiness, accuracy, and simplicity of adjustment.

Measuring Tools

6′ Folding (plastic or metal) rule for general shop measurements.

50′ Steel (or cloth) tape to be used when setting up scenery.

24″ × 18″ Steel square with white markings.

6″ Try square for marking cross grain on battens.

Trammel bar and points for drawing arcs.

18″ Carpenter's (spirit) level. Useful for both horizontal and vertical testing.

Cutting Tools

28″ Crosscut saw, 8 to 10 teeth to the inch.

28″ Ripsaw, 5 or 6 teeth to the inch.

Keyhole or compass saw. The keyhole size is smaller than the compass.

Coping (scroll) saw for cutting intricate shapes on three-ply.

Hack saw, using 10″ blades, for cutting metal.

Metal mitre box and 26″ backsaw.

10″ Drawknife for rough trimming.

Linoleum knife or jackknife for cutting canvas.

Block plane and smoothing plane.

Wood chisels. Sizes $\frac{1}{4}$″ through $1\frac{1}{2}$″.

14″ Rasp for rough filing.

Triangular file to sharpen bits.

Rat-tail file.

10″ Tin snips.

Gripping Tools

Vise attached to work table.

Slip-joint pliers.

14″ Pipe wrench. (Two are always necessary.)

Open-jaw wrench.

C Clamps and furniture clamps of assorted sizes.

Driving Tools

Claw hammer. (More generally useful than the rip hammer.)

Tack hammer. (Magnetic.)

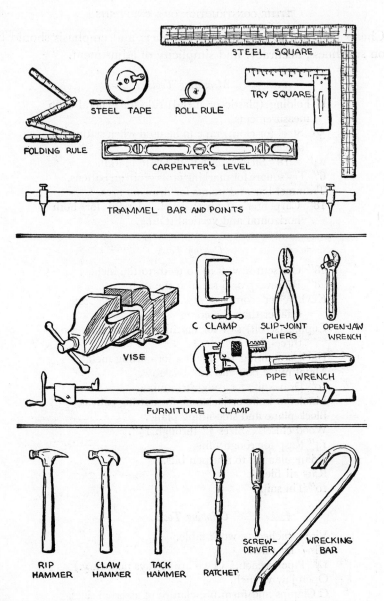

STEEL SQUARE

TRY SQUARE

STEEL TAPE   ROLL RULE

FOLDING RULE

CARPENTER'S LEVEL

TRAMMEL BAR AND POINTS

C CLAMP   SLIP-JOINT   OPEN-JAW
           PLIERS   WRENCH

VISE

PIPE WRENCH

FURNITURE CLAMP

RIP   CLAW   TACK   RATCHET   SCREW-   WRECKING
HAMMER   HAMMER   HAMMER   DRIVER   BAR

Fig. 17 *Measuring tools (above), gripping tools (middle), and driving tools (below)*

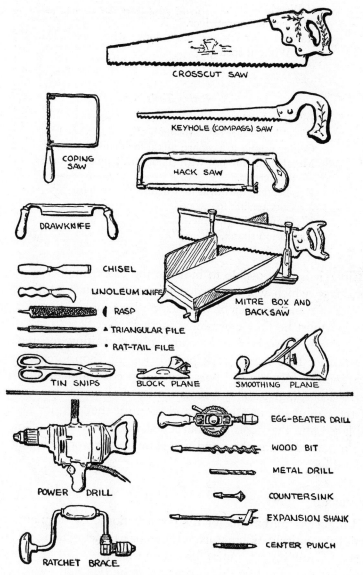

CROSSCUT SAW

KEYHOLE (COMPASS) SAW

COPING SAW

HACK SAW

DRAWKNIFE

CHISEL

LINOLEUM KNIFE

RASP

TRIANGULAR FILE

RAT-TAIL FILE

MITRE BOX AND BACKSAW

TIN SNIPS

BLOCK PLANE

SMOOTHING PLANE

EGG-BEATER DRILL

WOOD BIT

METAL DRILL

COUNTERSINK

EXPANSION SHANK

CENTER PUNCH

POWER DRILL

RATCHET BRACE

Fig. 18 *Cutting tools (above) and boring tools (below)*

49

2' Wrecking bar.
4" Regular screwdriver.
Ratchet screwdriver, 20" long when extended.
    Without spring.

Boring Tools

10" Ratchet brace.
Wood bits. Sizes $\frac{3}{16}$" through 1".
Center punch to prepare metal for drilling.
Metal drills for use with Thor drill, holes to take
    #9 screws.
Egg-beater hand drill and drills, $\frac{1}{8}$" through $\frac{3}{16}$".
$\frac{1}{2}$" Countersink for wood.
$\frac{1}{2}$" Countersink for metal.
Expansion shank, $1\frac{1}{4}$"–$2\frac{1}{2}$".

Since it is not possible to indicate the exact number of tools of each type which will be needed in the shop, such considerations as size of shop, number of workers, and amount of time for preparation must be the determining factors. Needless to say, time is wasted when workers must stand about waiting for tools. It should not take many work periods for the shop foreman to determine the number of items that are needed and to add to the stock accordingly. The foreman must also watch the condition of the equipment at all times and see to it that inferior items are replaced and that tools are sharpened when necessary. Dull tools are a hazard in the shop and will slow up the work schedule considerably.

LUMBER

Lumber requirements for the construction of scenery and properties are entirely different from those for cabinet making and other forms of building. Lumber for use on the stage must be light, easy to saw, non-splintery, well-seasoned, and without warp or an excessive number of knots. Northern white pine comes the nearest to fulfilling all these requirements and is, therefore, the most obvious choice. Scenery that is constructed of such lumber will hold its form indefinitely and will seldom add to the technical problems of those who must shift it.

Lumber is classified according to grade. There is theoretically a *Grade A* lumber; but, since this means *perfect*, it is seldom available these days and certainly is prohibitive in price. Therefore, the next grade, *Grade B or better*, is actually about the best grade on the market and is the choice of most professional builders. Since this quality is so expensive, *Grade C Select* is more often used by non-professional groups. *Grades D Select* and *Number 1 Common* can also occasionally serve where certain irregularities will not be detrimental to the building. Whichever grade is ordered, however, the purchaser should specify that the lumber is to be used for scenery construction, and often the dealer will be careful in his selections. It is unfair to go to the lumber yard and to select the best lengths, leaving inferior pieces for the next customers. A reliable lumber dealer is the scene technician's mainstay, and nothing must be done to provoke a strained relationship.

Although it is convenient to think of lumber by the running foot, the prices are all based on the 1000-board foot. Since dealers do not offer wholesale prices to schools and civic theatre groups, lumber will probably prove to be the most expensive single item on the budget. Prices will vary slightly in different sections of the country but, on the whole, lumber costs and grades have become somewhat standardized. In addition, the worker must be aware of the fact that if a piece of lumber is labelled as $1'' \times 3'' \times 12'$, this means that it is actually approximately $\frac{3}{4}''$ thick, $2\frac{3}{4}''$ wide, and a shade more than $12'$ long. When lumber is smoothed at the mills, this amount is lost in the planing and these variations in width and thickness will vary from order to order. Shop workers must thus measure each piece of lumber before using it and not assume any specific loss in the finishing.

While *white pine* is an ideal lumber for use in making flats, *yellow pine* and *fir* are not considered desirable for such use. These woods are heavy and splintery, contain pitch, and are difficult to saw. In an emergency, yellow pine (ponderosa) can be used for framing purposes but fir is never used for such building. It should be a shop rule that these woods be limited to temporary structures which will be dismantled after the run of a show. When extremely long lengths of lumber are desired, *redwood* might be considered although, since this lumber is not so strong as pine, care will have to be observed in the placement of the lengths.

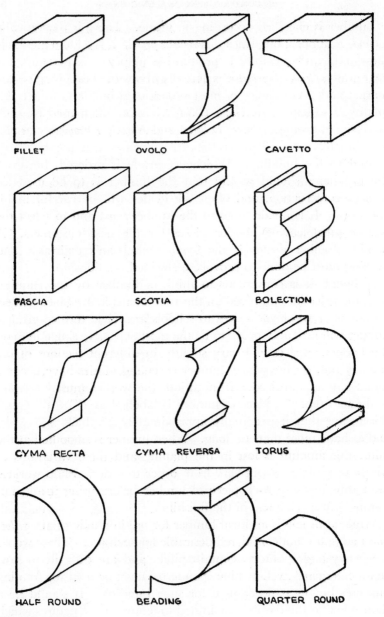

FILLET   OVOLO   CAVETTO

FASCIA   SCOTIA   BOLECTION

CYMA RECTA   CYMA REVERSA   TORUS

HALF ROUND   BEADING   QUARTER ROUND

Fig. 19 *Moldings*

52

Fir three-ply, $\frac{1}{4}''$ thick, is the most satisfactory material for corner blocks, keystones, and profile shapes of various sizes. Composition board is never a good substitute for three-ply, nor is Masonite, a brittle pressed wood product. However, many professional builders prefer to construct flats of $\frac{5}{4}''$ lumber; in such cases, $\frac{3}{8}''$ three-ply provides a much stronger joint. Three-ply comes in sheets 4 feet by 8 feet and is priced by the square foot.

MOLDINGS

The stock moldings available in the lumber yards today are all of designs based in part on those set up in the Greek architectural orders. Although each distinct architectural and design period is partly recognizable by its own moldings, actually these shapes are merely different arrangements of the original Greek curves. Unlimited opportunities for combining moldings are permitted the designer as he works out the construction plans for his interiors; picture moldings, chair rails, and cornices can often be represented by combinations of two or more moldings on different planes. It seems obvious that moldings will be necessary where there is any representation of three dimensions or suggestion of refined detail. Since accurate fitting is of prime importance, a good metal mitre box should be provided and all guess work discouraged.

NAILS, SCREWS, BOLTS, AND TACKS

Ordinary construction nails (page 54) are labelled as *finishing* or *common*, the former having a very small head and a thin shaft, and the latter, a large flat head and a sturdier shaft. Common nails are preferred for stage carpentry in which the construction is hidden from the audience; finishing nails are useful for moldings and for other trimming where it is desirable that the nail head be inconspicuous. Nails are also classified according to size — that is, a 6D (sixpenny) nail is $2''$ long and a 10D nail is $3''$ long. It is advisable to use screws instead of nails when there is sufficient wear and tear on a unit to cause certain sections eventually to become loose.

The *clout nail* is a small blue nail with a soft, flat point; if flats are constructed with these nails, the most suitable length will be $1\frac{1}{8}''$ if $\frac{1}{4}''$ three-ply corner blocks are used. This length will allow

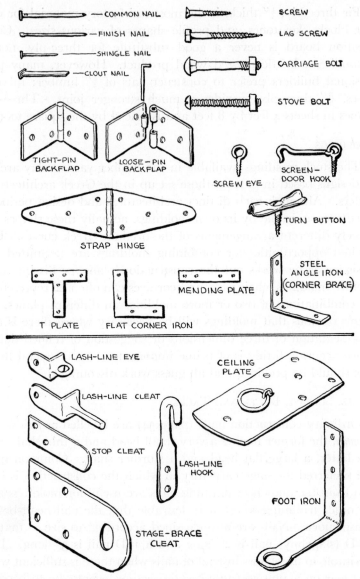

Fig. 20 *Regular hardware (above) and stage hardware (below)*

$\frac{1}{8}''$ to be clinched or bent-over on the opposite side. Much professionally built scenery is fastened together with clout nails and, since such scenery is seldom remodeled and rebuilt, this method is quite satisfactory. However, where scenery must continually be rebuilt, the clout nail is not so successful since it is impossible to disjoint the frames without ruining corner blocks that have been attached by this means.

Some professional builders prefer to use *resin-coated shingle nails* for flat construction. Three-ply of $\frac{3}{8}''$ thickness works better with this method, and the shingle nails must obviously be $1''$ long so that they will just miss going through the batten. A short time after the resin comes in contact with the wood it begins to stick, with the result that a firm and substantial joint is established. Use of these nails is recommended for permanently built flats since the corner blocks cannot be saved during rebuilding processes. As a matter of fact they work nicely wherever it is necessary to fasten any thin building material to a thicker piece of wood.

Where it is the practice to fasten $\frac{1}{4}''$ corner blocks to frames by means of *screws*, the #8 or #9 $\frac{7}{8}''$ size will prove to be the most useful, since this length screw will not protrude on the back side of the flat. Flat-head bright steel screws are generally considered the most useful, and the number of the screw states the size of the shank. The #9 $1\frac{1}{2}''$ screw is useful for fastening two $1''$ battens together or for construction work other than framing. There is considerable saving if screws can be purchased by the gross at wholesale prices instead of at regular hardware stores.

While *lag screws* are only occasionally used for actual building purposes, they are always essential when heavy stage hardware such as sheaves are installed. For example, lag screws are just as essential for the floor block of an act-curtain rigging as for the various loft blocks. Extremely heavy platforms and towers will be more solid and permanent if such screws are used to fasten the construction together. These screws vary in diameter from $\frac{1}{4}''$ to $\frac{1}{2}''$ and in length from $2''$ to $4''$; a wrench or a pair of pliers is necessary in order to get them firmly into the wood.

Carriage bolts and *stove bolts* are frequently necessary where there is danger that screws might pull out. For instance, it is never wise to install heavy casters with screws since, if the casters pull loose the entire unit will have to be turned over for repairs. Carriage bolts vary in diameter from $\frac{1}{4}''$ to $\frac{3}{8}''$ and are obtainable in lengths up to $10''$. Flat-head stove bolts are available with diameters of $\frac{3}{16}''$ or $\frac{1}{4}''$ and $2''$ or $3''$ in length. Since there is usually some pull and strain in connection with the use of bolts, appropriately sized washers must be used with all bolts. Far too few bolts are used by non-professional builders with the result that there are often annoying delays during the rehearsal period due to breakdowns. When these delays occur during performance, the results are, of course, critical.

There are two common uses for *carpet tacks* in connection with the covering of stage scenery. The #6 size, which is $\frac{1}{2}''$ long, is suitable for holding canvas to the frames so that the glue can be applied with ease. Since this fastening is a temporary measure, after the glue dries the tacks may be removed and used again and again. A larger tack, #10, is required when padding must be fastened to floors and steps. Tacks of this size are also useful for fastening rugs and carpeting to the floor but, once the tack has been driven full length into the wood, its point has become bent and it is usually not wise to try to use it a second time.

COVERING MATERIALS

One of the most widely used covering materials for flats is *duck canvas*. This material is available in natural or bleached color and, while it may be purchased in widths up to $120''$, the $72''$ width is wide enough for most covering purposes. It is usually more convenient and economical to purchase this canvas wholesale in bolts of fifty to sixty yards. The material is sturdy and should be used for all permanently built flats or for any covering that will receive unusual treatment on the stage; it is a nuisance to have to repair and patch flats during the run of a show.

Unbleached muslin is another choice as a covering material and is suggested for units which are of unusual shape, which will have temporary use, and which will not be subjected to severe treatment. Since muslin punches and tears so much more easily than does canvas, only the less flimsy grades of muslin should be used; four ounces should be the minimum weight per square yard. As in the case of canvas, money can be saved if the material is bought by the bolt. However, department stores can usually supply 72″ muslin when it seems advisable to buy the material in small quantities.

In the professional theatre there has been a recent vogue for covering flats with velour, gauze, and certain shiny and textured materials. Since this kind of covering is classified as *special* work, each covering problem must be studied and estimated as a specific case. The results of such work are often unusual although, of course, quite expensive. In the non-professional theatre, the workers will sometimes cover return, tormentor, and teaser frames with velour and, when this is done, the material is usually fastened to the rear of the frame by means of permanent tacks.

GLUES

Although *white flake glue* is considered by many to be the most desirable adhesive for use in the scene shop, *ground gelatin glue* is the kind that is most generally available in paint and hardware stores. Both glues may be used as a furniture glue, as a paint binder, as part of the mixture for fastening canvas to frames, and for papier-mâché. Glue must be covered with water, soaked for a time, and heated and dissolved over a double boiler before it is ready for use; great care must be observed that the boiler does not boil dry as the smell of burning glue is most unpleasant. Melted glue is about the consistency of molasses and, in this form, is only useful as non-waterproof furniture glue.

Casein glue, a skimmed milk product, can accomplish everything that gelatin glue can, although it is a bit more expensive. When it comes to covering flats, the worker can be assured that this type of glue will never stain the canvas and bleed through a paint job. The *Casco* brand is best suited for covering purposes and the easiest to mix; it is merely necessary to add water to the powder to form a paste. *Cascamite* and other brands are no doubt as strong and pure as *Casco*, but these other brands are not suitable for fastening canvas to wood. Only small amounts of glue should be mixed at a time as the paste is not so satisfactory the second day. This glue is waterproof.

Some sort of *flour or wheat paste* is required as a part of the flat-covering mixture and, although this flour paste is available in moist form, the powder form is the most economical. The following is a good recipe for a paste which will hold canvas to a frame and at the same time not stain the material:

> 1 part melted gelatin glue
> 1 part whiting
> 2 parts wheat paste

When mixing this paste, thin with water a little at a time until the mixture has the consistency of buttermilk. There is some likelihood of staining if mixtures are used that are not made fresh daily. *Swift's Glue Bond*, a liquid adhesive, may also be used for flat covering. This glue will not stain and it is not necessary to dilute it or mix it with other ingredients.

REGULAR AND SPECIAL STAGE HARDWARE (page 54)

In order to insure proper fitting and stability, special stage hardware should be placed on the various scenic units wherever possible. There are, however, a number of practical regular hardware pieces, useful on the stage, which may be purchased at hardware stores or from wholesale dealers. These items are to be used only when certain regular stage hardware does not serve better. Since all such hardware must be strong and durable, it is false economy to purchase lightweight, cheaper articles. Technical workers will find frequent use for the following items:

> *Tight-pin backflap:* square leaves; useful for doors, parallels, and books.
> *Loose-pin backflap:* square hinges with removable pins; for the temporary fastening of one unit to another. Wires are more easily removed than pins.
> *Strap hinge:* diamond-shaped; for heavy doors or swinging units; frequently used on the reverse side of the door thickness to clamp the door to the flat during a set-up.
> *Screw eye and screen-door hook:* a temporary means of fastening flats or heavier units.
> *Turn button:* useful for holding a canvas-covered door closed while it is being moved.
> *T plate:* might be used in place of the keystone for fastening extra stiles within the frame.
> *Flat corner iron:* a substitute for the keystone or corner block.
> *Mending plate:* used in pairs to lengthen battens. Also valuable as a means of preparing wide expanses for sweeps, unusual shapes, etc.
> *Steel corner brace* (angle iron): placed on the inner edges of a frame to insure extra strength.

All the various kinds of special stage hardware have been designed to take care of specific backstage needs. There should always be enough of this special hardware on hand so that workers are nevre tempted to use inefficient substitutes. Most of the items are extremely servicable and, while some of the pieces have limited and infrequent uses, many are regularly necessary for the proper construction and set-up of scenic units. Although stage hardware is sometimes available locally, many groups will have to order directly from such a manufacturer as J. R. Clancy of Syracuse, New York. Stage hardware is relatively expensive, but since it can be used again and again, the purchases should be considered as an investment in efficiency. Scene shops will need to have a plentiful stock of the following items:

Lash-line eye: holds the lash line at the top of the flat.

Lash-line cleat: staggered on flats to be lashed, except at the tie-off position where they can be placed opposite one another and used in place of the lash-line hook or the similarly shaped *tie-off cleat.*

Stop cleat: insures that flats butted together or lashed at an angle will remain in that position.

Lash-line hook: a substitute for the lash cleat; also useful where construction prevents the use of the lash cleat.

Brace cleat: fastened to back of flat. The stage brace is hooked to it.

Saddle iron: length determined by width of unit; used as a sill for a door or arch flat. May be cut from $\frac{1}{4}''$ thick and $\frac{3}{4}''$ wide strap iron.

Foot iron: solid or hinged; to fasten scenery or jacks to the floor. The hinged type will not foul when it is flown.

Ceiling plate: a steel plate ($7''$ by $2\frac{1}{2}''$) with a ring in the center. At one end are five holes and at the other a carriage bolt and wing nut. Serves to fasten the ceiling together and to provide a means for fastening the lines to it.

Other types of stage hardware, particularly identified with hanging, flying, and shifting rather than with construction, are noted and illustrated on page 150. Such items are indispensable since there is considerable danger involved with the use of scenery which is improperly braced or hung.

STAGE DRAPERY MATERIALS

The cost of a set of stage draperies is so great that there is often a tendency to select some inexpensive non-durable material such as *sateen* or some neutral-colored material like *monk's cloth*. Actually it is more economical in the long run to choose black *velour*, or maroon or deep blue, since these colors are rich and inconspicuous and the material heavy and durable. *Cotton rep* and *duvetyne* are also strong materials and have considerable body, but they will never hang quite so well as velour nor look so rich. If the draperies are to be professionally constructed, the labor cost will be equal to or more than that of the materials.

A 2″ upholsterer's *jute webbing* is required to strengthen and finish the top of the draperies, and cotton braided cord of $\frac{1}{8}″$ diameter (shade cord) is used for the *tie lines*. *Grommets*, a grommet set, and a grommet die are materials and tools needed for all drapery construction work. As for the bottom of the drapery, although velour draperies do not need a *link chain*, lightweight materials such as gauze or satin will not hang well without a chain. Painted canvas curtains will also require chains and should, of course, be finished at the top with the usual webbing and tie lines.

The Building Processes

JOINTS (page 62)

Since the joint is the foundation of all flat construction, it is advisable to understand the various methods of joining that can be used with satisfaction. Whatever the actual building preferences of the stage carpenter, he must always use practices which are economical of time and materials, and which employ sound construction principles. Although lightweight scenery is subjected continually to a great deal of strain, it must usually give the appearance of having strength and weight; it is the proper use of joints that will guarantee this strength.

The *butt joint* is the simplest and most commonly used joint and is the suggested method for flat construction in the non-professional theatre. It is true that this joint is perhaps not so strong as some of the others; nevertheless, building by this plan saves time, and supplies units which will withstand considerable strain. Of all the joining methods, the butt joint is the one which offers the least opportunity for error in cutting. If the shop worker is aware of the variation in widths of lumber, checks all his measurements, and marks his guide lines carefully by means of a try square, his finished product should be true. Furthermore, butt-jointed flats may be remodeled with practically no waste of lumber.

Since professionally built flats never have to be remodeled, they are usually put together with the *mortise and tenon joint.* Special machinery is required to prepare the lumber for this type of building, and the resulting units will undoubtedly be extremely strong and sturdy. In this case, the use of $\frac{5}{4}''$ lumber is preferable to that of $1''$ thickness since the thicker lumber will provide extra strength at the joint. Even though the non-professional builder does not have the time nor the machinery to construct flats by this method, he may occasionally find the mortise and tenon joint useful in the construction of various pieces of furniture. In the case of reversible flats, this method of fastening the frames together is often the only solution.

The *mitre joint* is advocated by a number of university groups and, while there is obviously nothing structurally wrong with this type of flat building, it is surely a longer process than the butt-joint method and undoubtedly presents certain salvage problems. Those who prefer this joint suggest that since each part of the flat will be cut to measurements equal to that of the finished product, there is little opportunity for error. It would seem, however, that the mitre joint can be very little, if any, stronger than the butt joint and, unless the builder were thoroughly experienced with the mitre box, there might be considerable opportunity for error in cutting the angles. Also, the mitred corners of the frame are inclined to chip as the units are shifted about over the stage floor. In any event, the use of the mitre joint is always necessary for the construction of picture frames, panelling, and certain chair backs and seats.

Tongue-and-groove lumber is specially milled so that flat pieces can fit together and support one another. Lumber of this type is useful for the construction of platform and wagon flooring, and parallel lids. Since such building is usually covered with padding

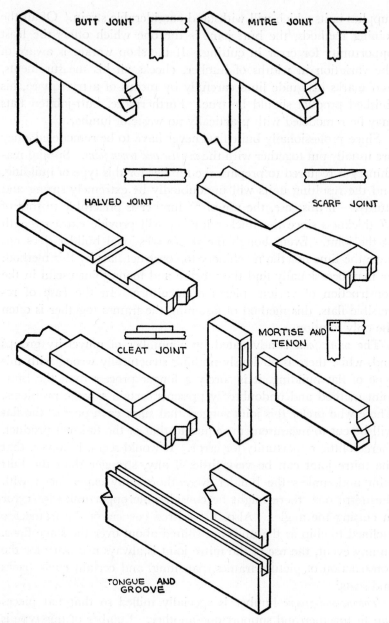

Fig. 21 *Joints*

and canvas, it is no disadvantage that tongue-and-groove lumber is often unfinished and contains knots. The fact that the pieces fit together will make only a minimum of underbracing necessary and thus help to keep the weight at a minimum.

Since battens are seldom available in lengths longer than sixteen feet, it becomes necessary, when large drops or ceilings are being assembled, to use some device to lengthen the battens, such as the *scarf splice*, the *halved joint*, or the *cleat joint*. The latter, sometimes called the over-lap splice or battened joint, is perhaps the strongest, and since a cleat of 1″ lumber tends to make an awkward joint, three-ply or metal plates are sometimes used. The other two joints are neat and serviceable where no great strain is involved.

FLATS (page 64)

Construction. The basic ideas involved in flat construction can be applied in part to many types of construction for the stage, since the flat itself illustrates, in one unit, many of the joining and fastening problems that are likely to arise. Accuracy is of prime importance, but such fine carpentry as is employed by the cabinet maker is not required since audiences are never close to the finished product. The builder who can construct a plain flat is not likely to have much difficulty with a *door flat*, a *ground row*, or even a *parallel*.

Let us take as an example the steps involved in building, out of 1″ × 3″, one flat 5′ wide by 12′ high. No professional units may be wider than 5′ 9″ since this is the limit that a freight-car door can accommodate. Despite this professional practice, there is no reason why a group should not build wider units if shop doors and loading doors are good-sized. There is actually more likely to be difficulty with the handling of unusually tall units than with those of extra width.

For the *stiles*, it is important to select lumber that is free from knots and not warped. Often a warped batten can be cut into pieces, however, and used for two or more *rails*. If the 1″ × 3″ is 2¾″ wide, the stiles will be 11′ 6½″ long and the top and bottom rails exactly 5′. The *toggle rail* will help to hold the frame in shape; it will be 4′ 6½″ long and placed in the center of the flat, parallel to the other rails. In the case of a very tall flat, more than one toggle may be required.

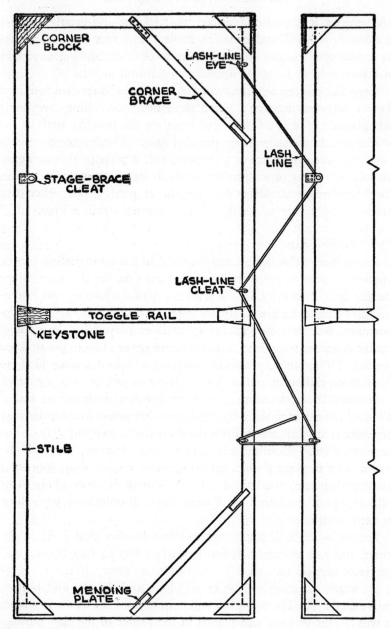

CORNER
BLOCK

LASH-LINE
EYE

CORNER
BRACE

LASH
LINE

STAGE-BRACE
CLEAT

LASH-LINE
CLEAT

TOGGLE RAIL

KEYSTONE

STILE

MENDING
PLATE

Fig. 22 *The flat*

Corner braces are placed at the top and bottom of the flat and must both be on the same side (rear view) if they are to accomplish their purpose, i.e., to keep the corners square. These braces should be made of 1″ × 2″ stock and will be, for this size flat, 3′ 6″ long, cut with 45-degree mitred ends. Narrower flats will require shorter corner braces, and extremely narrow flats, that is, *jogs*, will require none.

The flat must have four *corner blocks* of 9″ dimension for the matching sides, with the grain running across; and for the toggle rail two regular *keystones*, 6″ long by 3½″ at the wider and 2½″ at the narrower, with the grain running lengthwise. It is a nice touch to bevel the edges of the corner blocks and keystones, although, of course, this has nothing to do with the strength of the flat. Special parallelogram-shaped keystones, half keystones, or mending plates should be used to hold the corner braces to the frames since regular keystones are too wide for use on 1″ × 2″ stock.

If the shop is equipped with a *template,* the worker should next assemble all the wood on the table in the proper positions and check his measurements before fastening on the corner blocks and keystones. The position of the screws or nails is important, as their location in relation to the cracks has much to do with strengthening the joints. All corner blocks are placed ¼″ from the top and bottom and ¾″ in from the sides; the ¼″ placement will prevent the three-ply from catching on the floor as flats are shifted and at the same time will supply a maximum of support to the rails. Keystones are also placed ¾″ from the edge. This ¾″ measurement is a non-professional practice as flats will be used in different positions for different productions and might sometimes be butted together in such a manner that incorrectly placed corner blocks could interfere with proper fitting. A final caution is never to glue the corner block or keystones to the stiles if there is any likelihood that the flats must be salvaged.

If there is no template, assemble the lumber on the floor and, as the flat is being built, check the corners frequently with a steel square. Temporary shingle nails might be driven in part way to hold the pieces of three-ply in place. A final check can be made by measuring the diagonals with a piece of string. If the floor is cement, clout nails will clinch automatically; if the flat is built on a template, a *clinching iron*, either built-in or portable, will bend the nail points. The flat point of the clout nail should cross the grain of the frame lumber.

If workers use screws, holes should be drilled in the proper positions on the three-ply pieces, preferably from standard patterns — and slightly countersunk to prevent the screws from cutting the fingers of the scene shifters. The ratchet screwdriver will be an invaluable tool when it comes to putting the screws in place. Actually it takes about three times as long to fasten the parts of a flat together with screws as it does with clout nails. Only groups which have many workers can use this system to advantage, since time is always such an important element. There is, however, considerably less waste from the salvage of flats which have been fastened together with screws, since the corner blocks and keystones can be used many times.

Hardware and rope are often put on before the flat is covered, although there is no set rule for this procedure. The *lash-line eye* goes on the top right side, 18″ from the top, and the line is knotted and slipped through the eye and should clear the floor as it hangs; some technicians prefer to bore a hole in the corner block as a substitute for the lash-line eye. *Braided cotton rope* (sash cord) of $\frac{1}{4}$″ diameter will serve excellently for the 11′ 6″ of lash line that is required. The lower right *lash cleat, tie-off cleat,* or *lash hook* is 3′ 6″ from the floor, and the center right lash cleat is just above the toggle. A *brace cleat* on the left stile, 3′ 6″ from the top, does double duty as a brace cleat and a lash cleat. Occasionally it is necessary to vary this method of attaching hardware; however, in the main it is followed with little variation.

Additional lumber will have to be added to a flat frame if three-dimensional moldings representing a paneled room are a part of the front decoration. Usually two extra toggles and two vertical strips will be necessary for each panel, although sometimes the toggles alone will suffice. Also, when large pictures are to be hung, there must be vertical strips to take care of the hardware and the weight of the picture. The same principle follows in connection with the hanging of shelves and brackets. These extra pieces of wood can be removed when a flat is being remodeled so that there will be no unnecessary weight to the unit.

Covering. Before beginning the work of covering a flat, it is well to place the unit on a table or on wooden horses, smooth side up and corner blocks underneath, so that constant stooping may be avoided. Next, cut a piece of cloth about four inches wider and four inches longer than the flat. This material can be held in place on the frame by means of temporary tacks, one in each corner. Beginning in the middle of one of the long sides, place temporary tacks along the inner edge at intervals of about four inches. Two people may work on one side at the same time. After one side is tacked, follow the same procedure on the other side; and finally, make certain that the material is sagging ever so slightly and that the workers have not pulled on it. If muslin is used, the material should sag about $\frac{3}{4}''$ or what would be to the floor if the flat were not on horses.

If the above directions have been followed and the cloth has been accurately tacked, the ends of the cloth will practically take care of themselves as regards placement of material. The same temporary tacking method is used for the ends; whatever material is present is distributed evenly over the top and bottom rail. The four temporary tacks at the corners are then removed and the canvas is ready to be glued. For the gluing process, use Casco glue or the mixture of glue, paste, and whiting mentioned on page 58.

The free material is next folded back, exposing most of the stiles and the top and bottom rails. The glue mixture is applied generously to the main frame but never to the corner braces nor to the toggle rail, and the material is then folded back over the wood. Since the purpose of the glue is to hold the canvas to the frame, every effort should be made to see that the cloth sticks. The most satisfactory method is to rub the material vigorously and systematically with a damp cloth, making certain that no area is missed. Some people prefer to rub the cloth with a block of wood, but this method is not quite so thorough as the use of the damp cloth. As a final touch, four permanent tacks are put in the four outer corners.

There are two schools of thought as to the proper time to trim the surplus canvas from the flat — before the glue dries or after the glue dries. If the cloth is trimmed while the glue is wet, various spots which are not sticking properly can be noted and additional glue applied at the time. The wet glue, however, makes cutting more difficult and the knife has to be cleaned and sharpened fre-

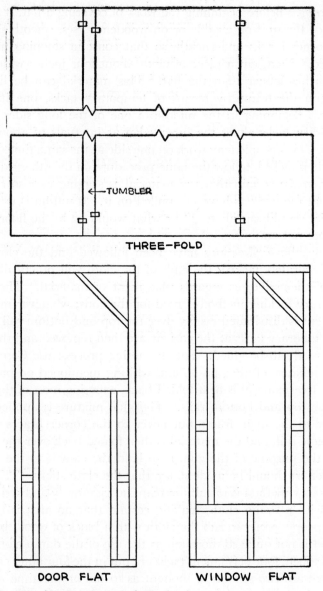

Fig. 23 *Three-fold, door flat, and window flat*

quently. If the material is trimmed after the glue dries, the poorly glued spots will have to be attended to a day later, and time may be lost before paint can be applied — a distinct disadvantage when one considers the usual tight working schedule.

Whichever system is used, the canvas is cut carefully $\frac{1}{8}''$ from the edge, and every effort is made to avoid a jagged cut. Most workers find that it is helpful to pull on the excess material with one hand while cutting with the other. Theoretically, the cutting pushes the edge of the material slightly into the wood, although it would seem that this is perhaps more true when the material is wet than when it is dry. After the glue dries, the temporary tacks are removed, since, if the tacks are put in permanently, dimples are likely to form around them and certain tacks will be conspicuous when the set is lighted. Never consider that the selvage can take the place of a trimmed edge; it will not shrink the same as the cloth itself nor will it stick as satisfactorily.

If the fire laws of a community require the use of flameproofed scenery, the shop workers should consult with the local fire department to get an approved flameproofing spray formula. The following solution satisfies some authorities:

1 lb. borax
1 lb. sal ammoniac
3 qts. water

Although flameproof canvas is available, such material will not remain flameproof since the chemicals eventually become inactive. Actually, if a flat is painted back and front it is fireproof.

Two-folds and Three-folds. After two flats are covered and trimmed, they may be *booked* together if necessary and the resulting unit will be known as a *book* or a *two-fold*. The advantage of the book is that it allows a large expanse of wall space with no cracks showing. While such units are heavy and somewhat difficult to shift, the shop workers should have little trouble with their construction and painting.

First, the two flats are placed on the floor, canvas side up, and made even at top and bottom. If the flats are 12' high, three tight-pin backflaps will be sufficient unless the stiles are warped. Four hinges are better for 14' and 16' flats. Place one hinge six inches from the top, another the same distance from the bottom, and a third in the center in such a manner that the hinges will fold together. Since the canvas is unpainted, it does no harm to step on the material while this work is being done. With a pencil, mark the hinges on the flats, remove them and, using a chisel, countersink a space of the exact thickness required by the hinge. Although the hinges on professionally built scenery are seldom countersunk, actually the units will look much trimmer and neater if this step is included.

The next step is to screw the hinges into place using #9 $\frac{7}{8}''$ flat-head screws. Finally, the crack and hinges are covered with a *dutchman* or stripper which is pasted and tacked into position, tacks being placed in the four corners of the dutchman and around the hinges. Wheat paste will serve as an adhesive although the best results are obtained with the mixture of melted glue, whiting, and wheat paste. It is important to make certain that the dutchman is no wider than the combined width of the two stiles underneath, and it must be wide enough to cover the entire hinge. If the dutchman stripping is rolled up, soaked in water, and wrung out before it is applied, it will be much easier to apply. Also, despite common belief, new material is easier to work with than painted material, and fits more tightly and evenly. A *wood wing* is assembled in exactly the same manner as a two-fold, the only difference being that one of the flats has an irregular tree-shaped form.

The construction of a three-fold is similar to the two-fold except for the addition of a *tumbler*, or a jigger, a length of $1'' \times 3''$ or $1'' \times 4''$, between two of the flats. This batten is joined to the flats by means of countersunk tight-pin backflaps, and the tumbler and two stiles are covered by a wide dutchman. If there is variation in the flat widths, the widest of the three flats should be placed in the middle and, when complete, all three flats will fold together making one, heavy, flat unit. In the case of both two-folds and three-folds, after the units are folded and unfolded a number of times, the creases may become rather noticeable; these creases are, however, much less objectionable than cracks would be.

Door Flats, Window Flats, Fireplace Flats, and Arches. The same building techniques are used in the construction of the door flat (page 68) as are used for the regular flat. In this case, however, the toggle rail becomes the top of the door and the legs are held together by a strip of strap iron the width of the flat, $\frac{1}{4}''$ thick and $\frac{3}{4}''$ wide, called the *saddle iron* or sill iron.   There is no great expense involved in having saddle irons cut and bored at a metal shop; nonetheless, it is often more convenient if this work can be done in the scene shop.   The preparation of the saddle iron is the chief metalworking job that is likely to confront the scenery worker; in order to do the work properly he will need to use the hack saw, the Thor power drill, a center punch, a metal countersink, and metal drills.

The legs of the door flat must be secure; therefore at least two $1\frac{1}{2}''$ screws must be placed through the countersunk holes in the iron and into each leg.   To accommodate this sill iron, the flat should probably be $\frac{1}{4}''$ shorter than one which has no sill; otherwise there may be an uneven line at the top of the setting.   Some builders like to think of the sides of the door opening as two short inner stiles.   Similarly, the short pieces which connect the inner stiles to the outer stiles might be called extra toggles.   Only one corner brace is necessary or possible on the door flat, and this piece is frequently omitted if other bracing above the door is required by the design of the particular setting.

Professionally built door flats are usually covered with a single piece of canvas; the door opening is cut out as one of the last steps. The non-professional worker, however, may wish to consider the use of three pieces of cloth: a top piece, and separate pieces for each leg.   Obviously the latter method is usually given consideration since there is a considerable saving of material.   If this method is used, it is wise to cover the legs first so that the material from the top section will overlap the legs, thus calling less attention to the joining of materials.   Exactly the same techniques of covering will apply here as apply to the covering of a regular flat although, of course, since the legs are not wide, it is not necessary to leave very much of the material slack.

A window flat (page 68) differs from a regular flat in that the toggle rail acts as the top of the window and a second toggle serves as the bottom.   Even though corner braces are used, it is sometimes necessary to place a vertical strip below the window to help support a heavy three-dimensional window unit which is placed

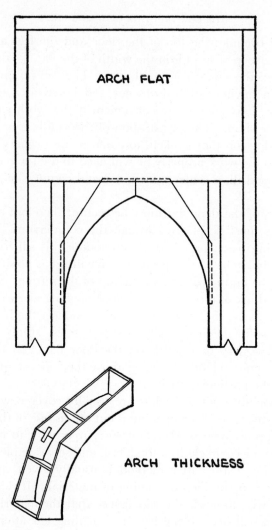

ARCH FLAT

ARCH THICKNESS

Fig. 24 *Arch flat and thickness*

in the opening. Additional strength is obtained from horizontal strips which connect the stiles of the window frame with the stiles of the flat. The worker has the choice of covering the flat with one piece of canvas or with four. If he chooses the second method, he will find it best to put on the bottom section first, then the two side pieces, and finally the top piece.

The fireplace flat can be likened to a door flat with a smaller,

72

lower opening. One corner brace is usually placed on this type of flat as well as a vertical strip in the center from the top rail to the top of the opening in the flat. Short strips separating the stiles of the legs are also usually necessary. While a saddle iron across the bottom is not absolutely necessary, the flat is much more convenient to handle if this feature is combined with it. Although the size of the opening in the fireplace flat may vary from setting to setting, a 3' wide by 2' 9" high space should serve most purposes and thus a certain standardization in building will be achieved.

The arch flat (page 72) is merely one with a larger opening than a door flat although it often has a curved top made from *sweeps*. These curved sweeps are set into the toggle and the inner stiles and are usually cut from 1" × 12" stock. In laying out the characteristic curves, it is usually best to place paper on the floor within the frame to serve as a pattern and, by means of string and pencil, to establish and mark the curves. The pattern can then be transferred to the 1" × 12" and the sweeps cut on the band saw. Occasionally, where a very large opening is desired, two flats will be booked together and half the arch will be in one flat and half in the other; a specially riveted saddle iron is required with such a unit.

When the arch opening is entirely within one flat, the *thickness* (page 72) is often merely strips of two-ply bent around the entire opening and securely fastened with screws. This method is not advised when storage space is at a minimum or when transportation problems are involved. The use of wallboard or Masonite is not to be recommended since it is so easy to damage the edges of these materials. In addition, it is very difficult to support such thickness materials in such a manner that the thickness curves will correspond exactly to that of the frame.

It should be clear that a booked arch, or an arch made from two flats and a header, must have *thicknesses which are removable* for transportation purposes. Such thickness pieces require considerable effort to build, but, if the workers are not rushed, this method is advisable even when the entire opening is within one flat. The thickness pieces are fastened to the frame by carriage bolts and it is usually wise to build the pieces in at least four parts: two perpendicular side pieces, and the curved part built as two units. This is

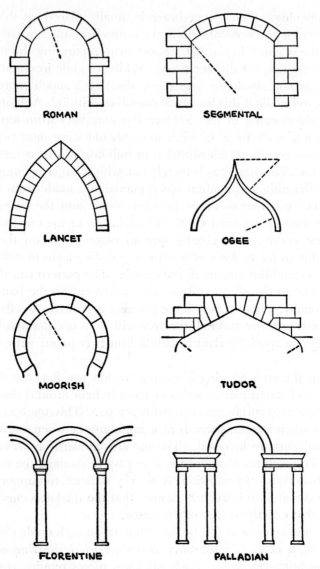

Fig. 25 *Types of arches*

precision carpentry and requires expert fitting, but the results are usually most satisfying from the standpoint of strength and maneuverability.

GROUND ROWS AND PROFILES

A ground row (page 76) is a long, low, horizontal unit of scenery the chief purpose of which is to conceal the bottom of a drop or cyclorama and at the same time to mask lighting units which are often placed upstage of it. While the ground row is usually irregular in shape, such scenery as a low wall or fence might be considered in this classification. If the unit is long, it must be hinged in the middle with countersunk hinges, and a dutchman should be placed over the crack. Instead of constructing ground rows of extreme lengths, it is frequently the practice to design two separate folding units which overlap in the middle, and thus are easier to shift and to stack. Often foot irons alone are capable of holding up the unit although, when the ground row is quite high, small hinged jacks are desirable.

Ideally a frame, roughly conforming to the general shape, is constructed first and the cut profile board fastened to it by means of $1''$ resin-coated shingle nails or $\frac{7}{8}''$ screws. No irregular section of three-ply should remain unsupported if it extends past the frame for more than $6''$. Finally the entire unit is covered with canvas as it is not possible to hide the grain of the plywood with paint. If wallboard is used in place of three-ply, the edges will be neither sturdy nor durable. Moreover, the wallboard will have to be covered with canvas also since, though it is without grain, it has such a different texture from that of cloth. Sometimes a ground row can be built using a regular narrow flat frame as the foundation. When this is done, irregularly shaped pieces of plywood are fastened along the front edge according to the demands of the design, and the entire unit is covered with canvas. This method of covering will hide the ridge which develops because of the addition of the three-ply.

While *profile* is the most generally used term for a large, vertical, irregularly shaped piece of scenery, the terms *silhouette* and *cutout* are often used. Occasionally the profile is of sufficient width and irregularity to make its construction problems similar to those of the ground row. Where there is height to the profile unit, it will be necessary to give particular attention to the placement of extra stiles and, unless the unit is so wide that it must be hinged, the

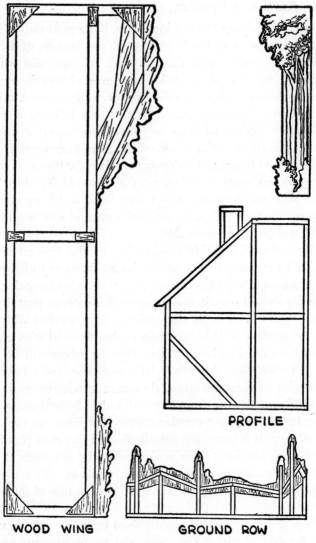

WOOD WING   GROUND ROW

PROFILE

Fig. 26   *Ground row, wood wing, and profile*

bottom rail should carry through. With so large a unit, it will often be wise, because of weight and expense, not to use plywood as a covering for the entire unit. If plywood is used only for the irregular edges, it should be fastened to the front of the frame and the entire unit covered with canvas in the same manner as is approved for the ground row. Since the unit is large and tall, jacks will always be necessary to hold it in a perpendicular position.

PARALLELS, LIDS, AND PLATFORMS

Just as the flat is the important scenic unit for defining walls and areas, the parallel and lid (page 78) are similarly important for supplying certain raised portions of the setting. A theatre group should eventually have enough parallels to take care of almost any problem dealing with height off the floor. Since these units are collapsible, little backstage space will be required for their storage during the run of a show; the units are light in weight, and therefore a minimum number of backstage workers will be required for handling the units.

The parallel is not a temporary unit; therefore it must be constructed accurately and with an eye to its future use. Basically a 3' by 6' unit is made up of five frames, two for the length and three for the width, constructed out of $1'' \times 3''$, and hinged together with $2''$ tight-pin backflaps in such a manner that the whole unit will fold flat when not in use (page 79). If the hinges are bolted rather than screwed on, the parallel will, as time goes on, seldom need to be repaired. The three frames can either be made all the same size or the two end ones can be wider than the center frame. Whichever system is used, it is important always to allow $\frac{1}{4}''$ at each end of the frame for the hinges.

Some technicians prefer to fasten the frames together with solid sheets of three-ply on three sides and to use corner blocks on both the fourth side and the center frame. Occasionally the mortise and tenon joint is used instead of the butt joint, or all the frames are held together with corner blocks. However, this last system will make it difficult to cover the frame so that it can be used without a *cover flat*, and the unit cannot fold together so flat as might be desirable unless all three-ply pieces are placed outside the frame. Regardless of the framing method used, it will be best to allow $1''$

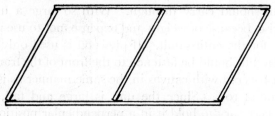

PLAN SHOWING HINGE PLACEMENT

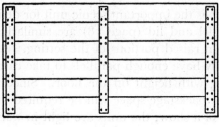

LID

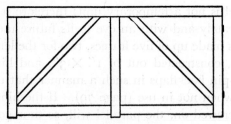

PARALLEL FRAMES

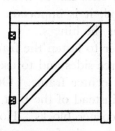

Fig. 27   *The parallel — plan, lid and elevations,*

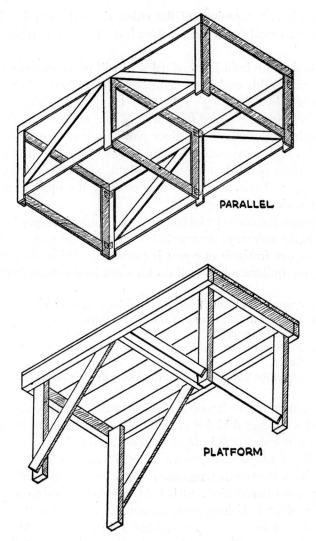

PARALLEL

PLATFORM

Fig. 28 *Parallel and platform*

79

legs which are extensions of the stiles, since the parallel is more likely to rest easily on a bumpy floor if the legs can straddle uneven areas.

Units that are built in standard sizes will prove more convenient to use than odds and ends of uneven dimensions. Lengths and widths of 3' by 6', 3' by 3', 4' by 8', 4' by 4', and heights of 1', 18", 2', and 2½' are considered standard. Three feet is about as high as these units are usually built, since parallels tend to wobble if there is much rough movement on them. Obviously, by using together a great many parallels of the same height, a considerable portion of the stage level can be raised, thus offering the opportunity for a greater variety of acting areas.

Although the correct placement of the hinges is a very important factor in the success of the parallel as a collapsible unit, the location of the center frame is of equal importance. When installing this frame, the builder might well do his work in the following order:

1. Screw or bolt the hinges to the sides of the center frame.
2. Hinge one side to one of the long frames.
3. Close the parallel.
4. Mark the relationship of the free hinges to the other long frame.
5. Open the frame and fasten the frame to the marked position.

If the center frame is not set in accurately in this manner, the parallel will never fold flat even though the individual frames may be perfectly constructed out of the best materials.

Although tongue-and-groove 1" × 6" lumber is most suitable for the lid of the parallel, regular 1" × 6" stock will do nicely. The flooring runs lengthwise and is held together by strips of 1" × 3" underbracing; it is important to make certain that these underbraces do not rest on the parallel frame in any way. Also it is desirable that two 1½" screws be placed through the underbraces on either side of each crack used in the flooring. Since the total widths of 1" × 6" used for the lid are not going to come out an even 3' or 4', it will be necessary to fill in with one or two narrower pieces. However, it will be well to avoid any widths less than 3"; a narrower width had better be placed on the edge rather than in the center. The lid is complete when it has been padded with Ozite and covered with canvas, the canvas being tacked to the under-neath side.

A *platform* should be a stronger and heavier unit than a parallel; therefore its framework and legs are usually made up of $2'' \times 4''$. Diagonal braces are required for the legs and there must be $2'' \times 4''$ bracing under the flooring at least every $2\frac{1}{2}$ feet. It is better to make a number of smaller platforms than an extremely large one which will be difficult to move and store. If the legs are fastened on with bolts and are easy to put on and to remove, there is little reason why the floor of the platform could not be used as the basis for a wagon. Although odd-shaped platforms are oc-casionally built and dismantled after a production, there is a definite value in attempting to standardize the measurements of platform units so that they can be used permanently.

STEPS AND STAIRS

In order that stairs may be useful with an accumulated stock of standardized parallels and will not always require special levels to be built each time they are used, it is wise to work toward a supply of 2-step, 3-step, and 4-step units which will be of standard size — that is, *risers* of $6''$ and *treads* of $12''$. While there might conceivably be some visual advantages to having the riser an inch higher or lower, it is actually difficult to mount or to descend steps gracefully when the treads are less than $12''$. However, when the script or the design requires steps which are definitely away from this norm (rickety steps with distorted risers or low, ramp-like steps), obviously these units will have to be specially built for the particular production and then taken apart after the last perform-ance.

Three *carriages* or stringers are usually considered adequate for units of three or four feet in width; two carriages will suffice for a unit two feet wide. These carriages can be cut from $1'' \times 12''$, and care will have to be taken in the cutting since the top and bot-tom riser and tread measurements will be different from the in-between ones. (*See* measurements on diagram, p. 82.) It might be well to make permanent paper patterns for carriages of different sizes and thus guarantee that all units will be of uniform size re-gardless of who builds them.

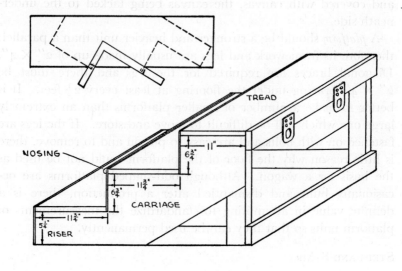

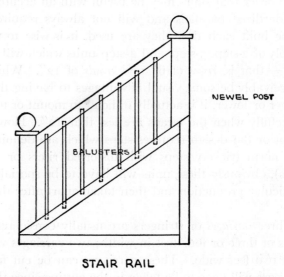

Fig. 29 *Step and stair rail*

After the carriages are cut, framing is added to hold them in the proper elevated position, and the treads and risers complete the unit. Sometimes only treads, risers, and carriages are used and the unit is hooked directly onto a platform or parallel. The treads are made of $1'' \times 12''$ and the risers of $\frac{1}{4}''$ three-ply ($1\frac{1}{2}''$ screws for the treads and $\frac{7}{8}''$ screws for the risers), and the stair unit is finally covered with padding and canvas. A nosing of $1'' \times 1''$ or half rounding is sometimes added to give the stairs a finished and more three-dimensional appearance.

Escape steps, not seen by the audience, can be made without risers; they may be either freestanding or of the hooked-on variety. If any height is represented, it is a good plan to provide simple railings so that the actors will not feel uneasy or nervous. In some formalistic arrangements, it may be possible to place cover flats in front of the skeleton escape steps in order to make them presentable for use on the set proper. Even though escape steps need not be decorative, they should be carefully and strongly constructed and considered as permanent standardized equipment.

The decorative woodwork which often accompanies the stairs in box settings is divided into numerous parts. The *balusters* or *spindles* are arranged in series; part of their purpose is to hold up the stair rail, the whole unit being called a *balustrade*. *Newel posts* are sometimes placed at the lower and upper ends of the balustrade and can help give stability to the unit. Decorative woodwork for stairs can be built as a separate unit like a cover flat and placed in front of the stairs; if the balusters must be seen as resting on the treads, the balusters and newel posts can be fastened directly onto the treads by means of very small steel corner braces. Since to-day it is difficult to buy new, turned balusters, it is a good idea to survey the various house-wrecking operations in the community and to lay in supplies of spindles for future use. As for stair rails, it is about as simple to construct them by means of built-up layers of three-ply and $1'' \times 3''$ as it is to remodel ready-made units. Newel posts, of course, are hollow and are not difficult to build out of $1'' \times 6''$; applied ornament can take care of the trimming.

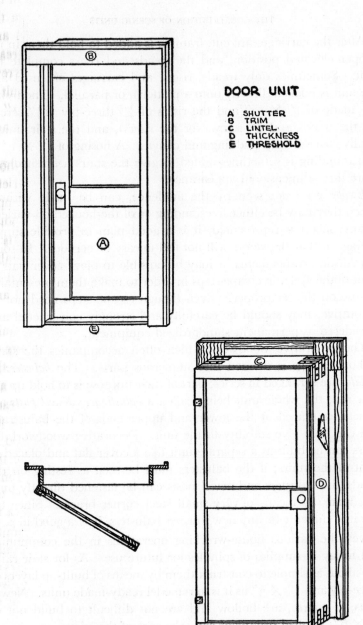

DOOR UNIT

A   SHUTTER
B   TRIM
C   LINTEL
D   THICKNESS
E   THRESHOLD

Fig. 30   *The door unit*

DOORS AND WINDOWS

As part of the average realistic box setting, it is desirable to have reasonably solid-appearing doors with three-dimensional trim. These doors must be built as lightly as possible so that their weight will not pull the unit out of line nor will the walls of the setting be shaken unnecessarily as the doors are closed. However, when a stage door is actually slammed, it is to be expected that the canvas walls will shake. Professionally built scenery that must take considerable punishment is often covered with three-ply; thus the door units can be heavy and the doors slammed at will.

A separate door unit has three main parts: the *trim* or *facing;* the *thickness* or *jamb*, made up of stiles, the *threshold*, and the *lintel;* and the *shutter*. Depending on the design of the door the trim may be either plain 1" × 6" or decorated with moldings, flutings, reedings, and decorative 1" × 1" regardless of whether or not the door swings off or on. The *doorstop* will help to prevent light leaks as well as to insure the proper contact between the shutter hardware and the thickness hardware. If the door swings off, it is usually hinged upstage so that its opening will help to mask the offstage space. Although most professionally made door units have a bevelled wooden threshold which makes allowance for the saddle iron of the flat which is underneath it, strap iron thresholds are sometimes used with success.

The chief problem involved with the fastening together of door frames is to select a method which will guarantee that the frame will always be firm and true. Neither the use of flat corner irons or mending plates on the rear of the trim nor the placement of angle irons at the corners of the thickness will accomplish this. However, if the trim is fastened together from the rear with large L-shaped pieces of three-ply and if strips of plywood carry along the edge, an extremely serviceable unit will result, and constant repairs will be unnecessary. Angle irons should still be placed at the corners of the thickness, but the strength of the frame will not be dependent upon this hardware.

Ordinarily the shutter should not be a regular milled door from the lumber yard but should be built (usually 3' by 7') like a flat frame with a 1" × 6" toggle and a 1" × 3" frame. If the door

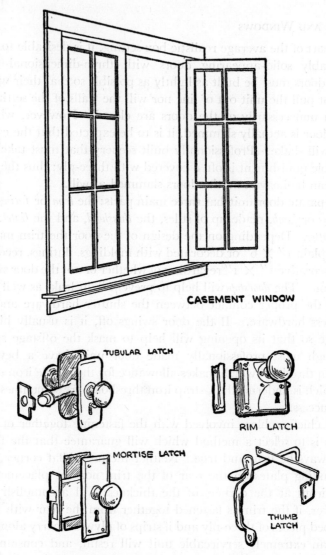

CASEMENT WINDOW

TUBULAR LATCH

RIM LATCH

MORTISE LATCH

THUMB LATCH

Fig. 31 *Casement window and door latches*

panel is to be plain, the frame can often be covered with canvas; otherwise three-ply will be necessary and molding panels or other decoration can then be fastened directly to it. If the door swings off, it is much easier to hang it from the rear of the thickness rather than inside the frame. If the shutter must swing on, it must be covered on both sides; thus, though the unit will be heavy, it will still be lighter than the average household door.

While regular household door hinges may be used to hang the shutter if it swings onstage, backflaps will work satisfactorily if the door swings offstage. Three hinges will usually be required, especially if the door is at all heavy or is slightly warped. A *tubular screen door latch* or a traditional *mortise latch* is good for a door which must swing onstage; the old-fashioned black-enameled *rim latch* is satisfactory for those which swing offstage. Rustic-appearing doors can often be fitted with the *thumb latch* which, although it is manufactured for garage doors and outer buildings, is mechanically the same as much Early American and Pennsylvania Dutch hardware.

During a scene shift, when it is necessary to move both a door unit and a door flat, it is often wise to move them separately. In such cases, strap hinges may be fastened to the offstage side of the thickness and serve as a quick method of fastening the door unit within the flat frame. If a door unit is to remain rather permanently within the flat frame, as in a one-set show, it is sometimes bolted there, and now and then doors and trim are actually built on as part of the flat.

The trim and jamb of the window unit are exactly the same as those of the door unit except for the differences in size. The top of the thickness is called the lintel but, instead of a threshold, a window has a sill; the sash takes the place of the shutter. Although windows vary considerably according to style and period, it is their actual use on the stage which will be of first concern to the builder. A *casement* window sash usually swings offstage like a door, and a *double-hung* window sash (page 88), if it is practical, raises and lowers. *French* windows are generally considered to be double doors, and their construction and fitting problems would thus be similar to those of the standard door.

The casement window sash (page 86) is a frame with oblong or diamond-shaped panes separated by sash bars which are usually

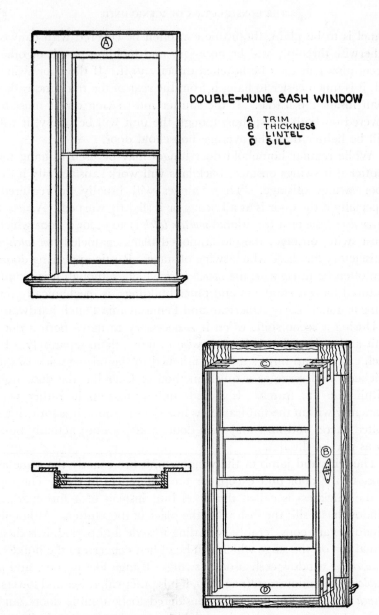

DOUBLE-HUNG SASH WINDOW

A TRIM
B THICKNESS
C LINTEL
D SILL

Fig. 32 *Double-hung sash window*

made of narrow widths of lumber or cloth tape. The frames should be held together with flat corner irons and mending plates instead of small strips of three-ply since the frames are often made of $1'' \times 2''$ stock. The frames can be hinged on with backflaps, but the fastening hardware should be of the correct household type. If the window must swing onstage, the problem becomes the same as that of a door which swings in similar fashion.

Since the top sash of the double-hung window does not usually have to be raised and lowered, it can be fastened permanently. However, if the lower sash is practical, it must slide up and down between strips of $1'' \times 1''$. A small spring can be placed at the height to which the window must be raised and, as soon as the window passes that point, the spring will prevent its being lowered until the spring is pushed back. If the window does not have to be raised, there is no reason why the entire window cannot be made as one solid unit. Since the frame rests on a rail of the flat frame, there is not much danger that the weight of the window will cause any trouble. Like the door, the window can be fastened into the frame by means of strap hinges or even built into the actual flat.

When glass curtains are hung at the window, it is seldom necessary to worry about any simulation of glass, especially if the curtain material is translucent. However, when the window panes are uncurtained, screening or black gauze is frequently used to suggest glass; black cheesecloth can also serve as an inexpensive substitute for gauze. Plastic materials of a translucent nature are often used to suggest the type of clouded glass that is found in the upper sections of some office doors.

CHIMNEY PIECES

Strictly speaking, the fireplace is only the actual area where the fire burns, and the decorative architectural treatment which surrounds this area is the chimney piece (page 90). The top of the chimney piece is called the *mantel*, and sometimes a mantel, together with the fireplace opening and the built-in brick or stone fronting, makes up the entire chimney treatment. The distinctive style of each architectural period is as much evident in the design of the chimney piece as it is in the appearance of the cornice or paneled walls; many chimney pieces are separate units of marble or wood which can be moved as easily as furniture.

made of narrow widths of linter or cloth tape. The frames should be held in position by corner joints and braced under the board of small sizes ...

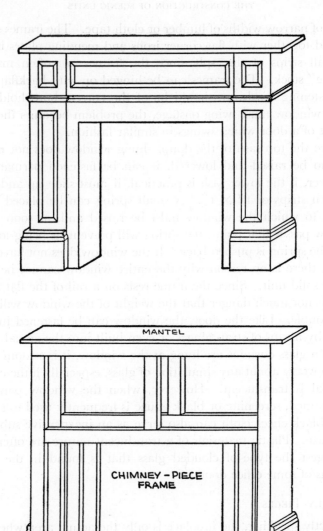

MANTEL

CHIMNEY – PIECE
FRAME

Fig. 33 *Chimney piece*

The front and back of the movable stage chimney piece may be built as two small flats with small strips of wood holding the frames apart and completing the framework. Unless the aim is to make a rather ugly and conspicuous unit, it is well to have the chimney piece protrude only slightly from the wall. Since the frames are so small, it will be wise to hold the parts together with small mending plates and angle irons instead of using corner blocks and keystones; if the unit is covered with three-ply on three sides, it will be possible to apply any type of molding or trimming. Movable chimney pieces are either bolted to the flat or clamped to the flat in a manner similar to the method used for door and window frames. If the chimney treatment consists mainly of a facing and a mantel, the facing should probably be painted directly onto the flat and the mantel bolted above it. With such an arrangement, a thickness piece will have to be applied to the top and upstage sides of the fireplace opening if the final effect is to be convincing. Finally, a low two-panel stone or brick backing completes the picture and allows sufficient depth to take care of andirons, legs, and special lighting equipment.

CORNICES

Most stage cornices (page 92) are separately built horizontal pieces which are bolted or screwed to the tops of the individual walls of the setting. At the same time that the cornice completes the room architecture, it thus helps to hold a series of wall flats in definite positions and to give a solidity to the setting. Stage cornices are necessarily deeper and more prominent than those found in actual rooms, because the high walls of the average stage setting demand them. Obviously a great deal of attention will have to be given to the design and construction of these units so that the result will be both pleasing to look at and accurate as to period.

Various stock moldings can be combined to give elaborate and heavy cornice effects and the use of the *cornice block* will tend to make the unit rather light in weight. There will seldom be any difficulty with the actual construction work although the accurate fitting of the corners which are not at a 45-degree angle will always be a problem. This fitting is ideally accomplished during the construction period and before the setting is painted. The floor plan

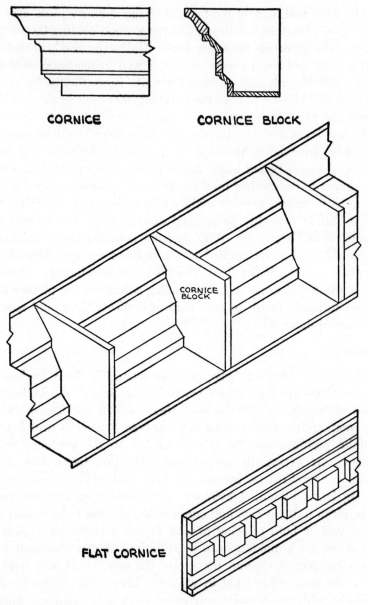

CORNICE   CORNICE BLOCK

CORNICE
BLOCK

FLAT CORNICE

Fig. 34 *Cornices*

of the setting is accurately chalked on the floor and the various cornice angles cut accordingly, section by section. If mistakes in construction have been made, it is much harder to make corrections after the setting is painted. Flat cornices are occasionally effective substitutes and, of course, are seldom difficult to fit. They give a three-dimensional effect but actually protrude little more from the wall than painted cornices. As for painted cornices, this method is frequently used in professional productions of the multi-set variety and for touring productions.

COLUMNS AND TREES

Realistic three-dimensional columns (page 94) for the stage must appear to be solid and substantial, but at the same time be light in weight and capable of firm attachment to the floor or to some sort of entablature. While it is usually not necessary to build the column with a complete circumference — the audience can see only the front — the *shaft* must often have a slight tapering or *entasis* if it is to appear graceful in line and correct as to period. Since the *capitals* offer the surest means of identification, it will be advisable to design and construct them with attention to form and detail. *Doric* capitals may be made of turned wood or layers of three-ply, but *Ionic* and *Corinthian* capitals are usually created with papier-mâché or carved from balsa wood.

The foundations of the stage column are a series of discs cut from $1'' \times 12''$, with $1'' \times 2''$ strips or lathe to connect the discs and hold the shaft together. The connecting strip framework is eventually covered with two-ply and canvas, and now and then such coverings as linoleum, oil cloth, textured material, or plastic are used. Flutings and reedings can be added in the form of half rounding, $1'' \times 1''$, or other strips of wood, depending on whether the desired effect is realism or stylization.

Cloth columns, suitable for some non-realistic plays, have a disc at the top (also occasionally at the bottom) and are hung from a pipe batten. The cloth is pleated around the disc or discs and the base sometimes anchored to the floor. Needless to say, these columns do not suggest much stability nor are they very durable. While well-made solid columns may be stored and used again and again, the cloth column must always be considered as a temporary unit of scenery.

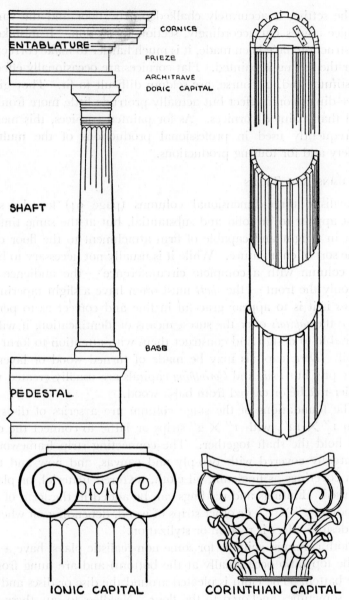

CORNICE

ENTABLATURE

FRIEZE

ARCHITRAVE

DORIC CAPITAL

SHAFT

BASE

PEDESTAL

IONIC CAPITAL

CORINTHIAN CAPITAL

Fig. 35 *The column*

94

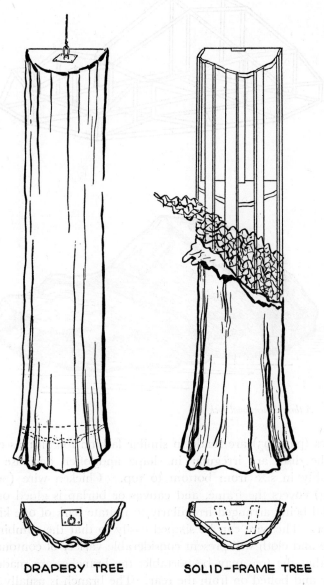

DRAPERY TREE　　　**SOLID-FRAME TREE**

Fig. 36 *Trees*

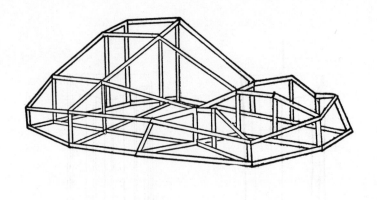

Fig. 37 *A three-dimensional rock*

Trees (page 95) are made in similar fashion to columns except that the discs are irregular in shape and often decrease quite noticeably in size from bottom to top. Chicken wire (poultry netting) covers the frame, and canvas or burlap is glued on, the material being arranged irregularly to imitate bark of one kind or another. The wire can be shaped easily so that the combination of wire and cloth will present considerable variety of contour. In order that the tree may be portable, the branches are made separately and bolted on from the rear. The branch is usually made from pieces of 1″ × 3″ fastened together in the appropriate shape and covered with wire and cloth. If it is necessary that the actors climb the tree, a ladder can be built into the offstage side of the tree and the entire unit given additional support from the fly gallery.

96

ROCKS

Rocks as represented on the stage may be either silhouetted or three dimensional — the choice depends on the style of the production. Silhouette rocks are merely profiles behind which levels and steps are sometimes placed. Practical rocks, however, must be carefully built with solid platform-like foundations which can be separated for moving and storage purposes. If the actors are to stand on the rocks, the best foundation covering material is Ozite or some similar rug padding; if the rocks must be three dimensional but not practical, chicken wire, fastened with staples and covered with canvas or burlap, will do nicely. While a great deal of the three-dimensional quality is achieved by paint, the shaping of the unit is very important, and designers and builders will do well to study actual rock formations from nature so that their work will be consistent and convincing. Such a play as *High Tor*, for example, demands that practically the entire stage be covered with rocks of a particular type and shape. Most of such building should be considered as temporary since most groups will not have storage space for such units after the run of the production.

CEILINGS

One or the other of the two types of stage ceiling, *book* and *roll* (page 98), is essential to trim and complete the box setting. A series of cloth borders as a substitute for the ceiling looks untidy and takes away whatever semblance of reality the room may have. Ceilings are considered as permanent equipment and, though the original outlay is considerable, the units will not have to be replaced often.

Of the two types, the roll ceiling is definitely the more practicable as far as transportation is concerned, since the stretchers can be removed and the unit rolled up like a drop. Either type should be constructed at least two feet wider than the proscenium and it may be two feet less wide upstage than it is downstage; twelve feet should be the minimum for the depth. The scarf splice will be useful in order to obtain long enough battens, or metal plates can be used to bolt two battens end to end.

The canvas covering for the roll ceiling, with seams running

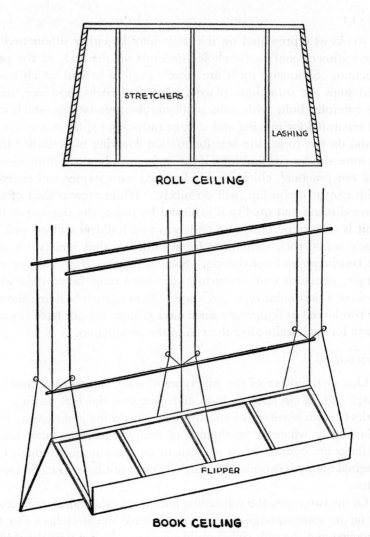

ROLL CEILING

STRETCHERS

LASHING

BOOK CEILING

FLIPPER

Fig. 38 *Ceilings*

lengthwise, is tacked and glued to the end battens, and when the unit is in its unrolled position, the four stretchers are bolted on by means of *ceiling plates* which also provide rings for attaching the ceiling to the pipe battens. The sides of the ceiling covering are hemmed and provided with grommets; after the sides of the ceiling are laced to the stretchers with sash cord, this masking piece is ready for painting. A neutral color is the most satisfactory since it will allow frequent use without repainting.

Two sets of lines will hold the ceiling above the setting and, when this unit is struck after a production, it can either be rolled up or hung like a drop on one set of lines. A flipper, covered with black velour and hinged to the front of the ceiling, effectively aids the masking, and it too should be constructed with removable stretchers so that the flipper will not interfere with the rolling process. There will be no difficulty about the hanging if the downstage pipe is fastened directly to the flipper instead of to the ceiling proper.

The book ceiling is actually two flats hinged together with countersunk backflaps so that it can be folded with the painted side in. At least nine ceiling plates or rings are permanently attached to its uncovered side but are used for hanging purposes only. Three sets of lines are required for the hanging of this unit and, when the ceiling is struck, only the center set of lines is in use. Since the book ceiling is so bulky and heavy to move, perhaps its use should be limited to theatres where such a unit can be hung permanently on certain specified lines.

STAGE DRAPERIES

Stage draperies (page 100) are extremely valuable for stages which are on a limited budget and must often use various forms of minimum scenery. Therefore, it is important for the drapery panels to be of such height and width that there will never be any problems attached to their use. Panels should be constructed in lengths suitable to the height of the proscenium and in widths which are not inconvenient to handle. Sixteen-foot lengths will be useful for most stages and an assortment of panel widths might include 12′, 18′, and 24′. Since the appearance of the draperies depends partly on the hang, no less than 50 per cent fullness (an 18′-wide panel to hang in a 12′-wide space) is desirable and as much as 100

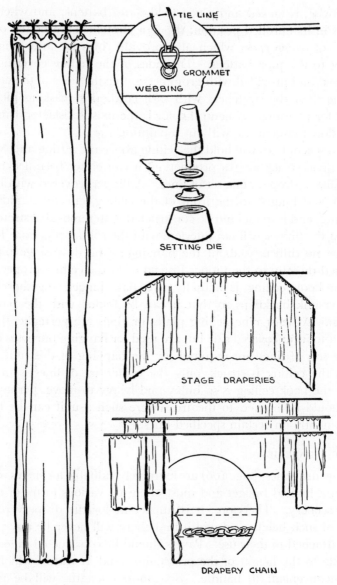

Fig. 39 *Stage draperies*

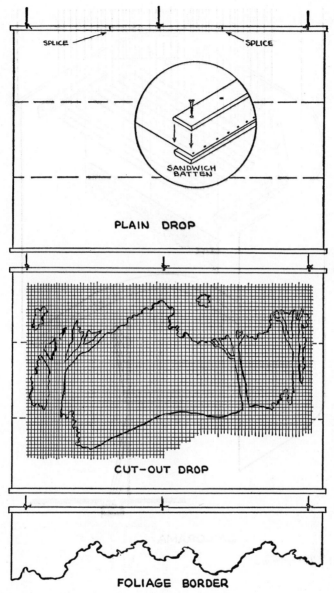

Fig. 40 *Drops and borders*

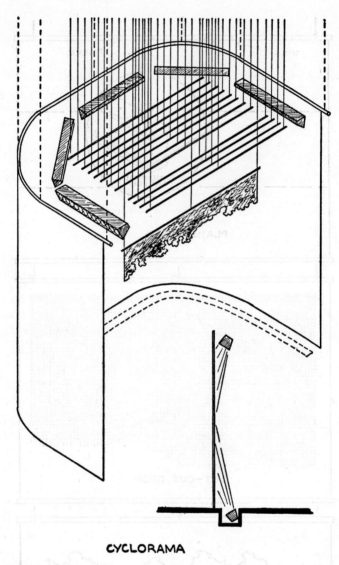

CYCLORAMA

Fig. 41 *The cyclorama*

per cent might be better. The panels must be cut so that the nap is the same for all sections, and the seams must go up and down with the selvage edge serving for the outer edges.

Each section of drapery is strengthened at the top with *jute webbing* and a 3″ hem. Grommets are placed every six inches along the top, and tie lines can be placed through two grommet holes at a time so that fullness can be tied in regularly. It is extremely unwise to arrange pleats in the tops of the panels and to sew these folds directly to the webbing. The bottom of the drapery must have a 4″ hem; and, while velour requires no weight at the bottom, a *link chain* should be included if the material is not heavy, so that the material will not move as people pass before and behind it.

Drops and Borders

The drop (page 101) is classified as an unframed scenic unit and, while the top and bottom are fastened to battens, the sides hang free. The canvas is always sewed with the seams running horizontally and it is tacked to two battens of 1″ × 3″ placed end to end. A length of 1″ × 3″ is then laid over the cloth and lumber so that it will straddle the crack. Extensions are finally placed on either end to make the entire double batten uniform in length and thickness. One-and-a-half-inch screws, placed on either side of the cracks and at intervals of eighteen inches, hold the battens together. The resultant double-thick batten is called either a *sandwich* batten or a *laminated* batten. This type of battening is placed at the top and bottom of every drop. The sky drop is put together in exactly the same fashion, while the *cutout drop* merely calls for the removal of cloth from certain areas and for the gluing on of netting from the rear to help hold the material in place.

Borders (page 101) are of two types: drapery borders, to match the stage draperies, and canvas borders, which are attached to sandwich battens and often cut into irregular shapes such as would be necessary for a foliage border. Drapery borders are tied directly to the pipe batten with tie lines and they thus hang like draperies; the batten on a canvas border is tied to a pipe batten in at least three places. Since one of the chief purposes of borders is to mask the fly gallery, it is necessary to use a number of them for each scenic arrangement.

CYCLORAMAS

Undoubtedly the cyclorama (page 102) is a most effective means for representing a large expanse of clear sky. If the cyclorama hangs without exaggerated wrinkles and is evenly lighted, it can be depended upon to give depth to the exterior setting. Curved C-shaped pipe battens, top and bottom, are necessary to hang the cyclorama properly; the unit must extend well past the proscenium width on either side in order to mask effectively. The top and bottom of the unit are finished with webbing and grommets, and tie lines secure the material to the pipe battens.

If the material has not been specially woven and seams are necessary, the stitching must run horizontally or the seams will be quite conspicuous. While painted cycloramas may not give so soft and deep an effect as can be obtained from dyed materials of less stiff texture, the paint will necessarily make any seams less noticeable and a smooth unwrinkled surface should result. None the less, when a sky-effect unit must be portable and capable of storage, there is no substitute for seamless dyed materials. Finally, students should guard against using the term *cyclorama* as synonymous with stage draperies which hang in folds on U-shaped pipe battens.

PROJECTS AND EXERCISES

1. If your scene shop has facilities for the storing of lumber, is the space readily accessible? What lengths of lumber may be stored?

2. During the construction phases of some particular production, note the frequency with which the various tools are used. If power tools were available, approximately how much time was saved?

3. If your shop includes a template, what width and length flats can be built on it conveniently? How many flats can be in construction at one time in your shop?

4. Draw up plans for an ideally arranged tool rack containing the minimum tools listed on pages 47 and 48.

5. What facilities does your scene shop offer for the painting of backdrops? What is the largest-sized drop that the shop will accommodate?

6. Select four pieces of 1″ × 3″ from the lumber rack. Make certain that no two were delivered from the lumber yards at the same time. Measure the width of each and note the variations. Do the same with pieces of 1″ × 2″ and 1″ × 4″.

7. Examine some professionally built scenery from the points of view of: kind of lumber, grade of lumber, thickness of lumber, and method of joining.

8. Visit the local lumber yard and note the various types of molding available. Make cross-sectional drawings of these moldings. Consider the various combination possibilities.

9. What recent professional productions have you seen that have used other materials than canvas for covering flats? What did this accomplish?

10. Mix small amounts of the various kinds of flat-covering adhesives. Test each type for strength and durability.

11. Examine a J. R. Clancy catalog and note the prices of the various commonly used pieces of stage hardware. From your local wholesale hardware dealer obtain the prices of the common forms of regular hardware. Make comparisons.

12. Visit several high school and college theatres to discover the types and colors of materials used for stage draperies.

13. Examine a chair and a table from the point of view of the various types of joints which are represented.

14. What height flats work to best advantage for box settings on the stage on which you work? Why?

15. According to the following dimensions, draw an "attic" window flat showing the placement of any bracing that is necessary: Flat, 5′ by 12′; Window, 2′ by 2′; Placement, 2′ from ceiling and 8′ from floor. Place the window equal distances from the sides.

16. At eighty-five cents a yard, what would it cost to cover a 4′ by 12′ flat and a 3′ by 12′ flat with 72″ material?

17. What productions have you recently seen in which it was obvious that various properties and scenery (not including flats and draperies) would have to be made fireproof?

18. How wide a wall can be formed conveniently by three-fold construction? Illustrate.

19. Draw an irregularly shaped profile and show what framework would be necessary to hold it in shape.

20. What professional productions have you recently seen that relied scenically on the elevation of a good portion of the stage? Which were probably used, parallels or platforms?

21. Have you seen any recent production in which step units were obviously not of standard dimension? What effect did this serve?

22. Note how the doors are hung in the next box setting that you see. Were the doors of the milled variety or probably covered with canvas?

23. How many practical windows have you noticed in stage settings? How important were they to the action of the play?

24. Discuss the various types of chimney pieces that you have observed in box settings. Why was each type chosen? Were the units built-in or portable?

25. Name four plays that would almost necessarily demand decorative cornice treatment for the upper portions of the setting.

26. *The Emperor Jones* is a play which depends considerably upon trees as scenery. What other plays have similar dependence on such scenic units? In each case would the trees need to be three dimensional or could silhouettes serve?

27. Although we commonly think of columns as particularly suited to Greek plays, what other plays or types of plays might find use for this kind of scenic unit?

28. The rocks in *Dark of the Moon* must be extremely practical. What other plays would demand similarly practical rocks? What plays might be produced before silhouette rocks?

29. If a ceiling must be struck during a show to accommodate an exterior setting, a book ceiling is often the easier to manage. Can you think of any cases where this might not be true?

30. For what types of productions can stage draperies be most effectively used? For what types of productions are they least effective?

31. If you saw such productions as *Bloomer Girl, Up in Central Park, Annie Get Your Gun,* or *Brigadoon,* were you aware of the number of drops in each? Since drops are so popular in today's musicals, be prepared to look for them when next you see a professional musical.

32. Contrast the effectiveness of two exteriors that you have seen, one of which used a cyclorama and the other, a painted backdrop.

4

Color and Paint

MANY PEOPLE are actually afraid of color and even hesitate to state their color preferences.   Other persons would like to leave color decisions up to experts, and then are suspicious of these very decisions.   While it is no doubt true that the color sense is more strongly pronounced in some persons than in others, with a little understanding of the subject, the color sense can be improved and this fear overcome — partially, at least.

In clothing and household decorations, drab neutral colors have probably been popular because their *inconspicuousness* theoretically tends to make the articles more lasting and serviceable.   In contrast to this, certain people enjoy *conspicuousness* and feel that an overabundance of color will call attention to themselves and their belongings.   As students develop and begin to understand the more subtle and less primitive color combinations, there will be a closer relationship between what they like, what they have learned, and what they select to use.

This is an age of formulas and slogans, many of which are repre-

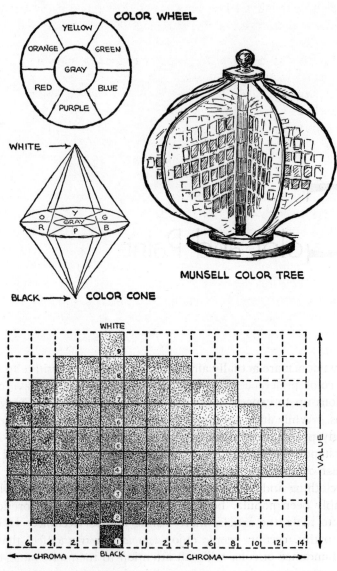

COLOR WHEEL

YELLOW
ORANGE   GREEN
GRAY
RED   BLUE
PURPLE

WHITE →

O   Y   G
GRAY
R   P   B

BLACK → COLOR CONE

MUNSELL COLOR TREE

WHITE

9
8
7
6
5
4
3
2
1

6 4 2 1   1 2 4 6 8 10 12 14
← CHROMA —— BLACK —— CHROMA →

VALUE

Fig. 42 *Color cone and Munsell color tree*

108

sented in magazine advertising. People expect to find rules to follow and expect that definite results will be guaranteed by the application of these rules. Manufacturers of decorative supplies, well aware of this tendency, attempt to furnish such information; as a result, much color information, as noted in advertisements, quickly becomes commercially dreary and uninteresting. An understanding of color involves much more than looking at Color #1 in Column #1 and learning that this color will not clash with #5 and #6 in Column #2.

The Color Wheel and the Color Cones

A ray of sunshine is made up of vibrations having a variety of wave lengths which affect the retina of the eye. When white light is refracted or broken down by means of a prism, the result is called the *spectrum*, a band of colored light containing red, orange, yellow, green, blue, purple, and, of course, many gradations between these colors. When the spectrum is bent into a circle, there is a rough representation of what is commonly known as the *color wheel*. Unfortunately, from this point on, there is confusion as to classification, and the explanatory charts advocated by various experts are likely to bewilder the beginning student because so few of the charts are alike. These actual spectrum colors cannot be used by painters and designers, but may serve only as a guide; certain chemical pigments, somewhat similar in color to the spectral gradations, make up the palette of the painter.

Many students are likely to consider the color wheel as the final word in color organization. Actually the problem is much more complicated, representing, instead of a wheel, two cones with bases together; the peak of the top cone represents *white*, the peak of the lower cone, *black*, and the center of the cones — from peak to peak — *gray*. The point of juncture of the two cones represents the color wheel and here are found the *color primaries*, *red*, *blue*, and *yellow*, and the *secondaries* (combinations of the primaries), *purple*, *green*, and *orange*. Primaries and secondaries combined are called *tertiaries*, but such colors are so complex that it is often difficult to classify them precisely by name. For example, a mixture of blue and purple would approximate such an indefinite color as *plum*. Color wheels can be established all the way up the cone to white, or down the cone to black. The colors will be lighter, of course, above the main color wheel and increasingly dark in the lower cone.

Colors opposite to one another on the wheel are called *complementaries.* Blue, for example, is the complement of orange — which is made up of yellow and red; red is the complement of green; purple, of yellow. Theoretically, gray can be produced by combining these colors in equal proportions but, because of the impurities in color pigment, exact results cannot always be predicted. Colors beside one another on the wheel are labeled *anolagous;* blue and green are side by side on the wheel, as are orange and red, and yellow and green.

Although the location of a color on the outer edge of the wheel indicates its *hue,* this location has no relation to the other color dimensions, *intensity* and *value.* The hue is the color itself and states that the color is blue, yellow, orange, etc. The intensity of the color is its strength and indicates its distance from the gray of the center of the wheel or cone. Color value is directly concerned with tint or shade or the light or dark quality which is usually obtained by the adding of black or white to the color. Obviously, a clear understanding of these three dimensions of color is necessary before the student can consider the use of subtle color relationships and apply them to his design problems.

Unfortunately, the names for these color characteristics are not standardized; therefore the student has the additional problem of becoming aware of the other terms used by a variety of authorities. Mathew Luckiesh, a leading color theorist and author of *Color and Colors,* prefers *saturation* to intensity, which he considers indefinite; when he speaks of neutralizing, he means de-saturation, or the adding of white to the color. Mr. Luckiesh thinks of pure blue as highly saturated or intense and considers sky blue as very low in saturation. He prefers the term *brightness* to value since value, to him, seems not to suggest brightness nor to imply shade. Mr. Luckiesh's terminology is similar to that of many physicists.

The Munsell color notation system, adopted by the American Standards Association, uses the term *chroma* instead of intensity and considers black as the color with the lowest value and white as having the highest. This system is made up of 398 colors and, by means of definite symbols and scales arranged around a color tree, similar in shape to the two color cones or color solid, an extremely accurate definition of color is possible. Although the Munsell color tree is so expensive an apparatus that most theatre groups will not find it possible to own one, there is a definite need for the exact color notation which its use permits (page 108).

Other systems of classification prefer *tonal value* in place of intensity, *brilliance* for value, *purity* for intensity, and *luminosity* for value. Still other systems prefer to consider tonal value and chroma as synonymous and use these terms in place of shade and tint. Some theorists even consider that there are four primaries instead of three — red, yellow, blue, and green. Since scenery painters use impure pigments, and since their problems are often so similar to those of the interior designer and the easel painter, rather than to those of the physicist, it seems wise for them to use the terminology approved by most art schools — hue, intensity, and value — and to work in terms of three primaries instead of four. Many designers have had their basic training in art schools; hence it will not be necessary to urge them to use these terms.

The Use of Color

When considering color terminology as related to paint mixing, the only safe procedure is to use the actual chemical names of the pigments. Trade colors, fabric colors, nature's colors, etc., are often misleading and can cause frequent misunderstandings. The student has only to ask himself the meanings of *Alice blue*, *Mediterranean blue*, or *azure blue* to realize just what he is up against when he strays from the chemical terminology. After the chemically named pigments are mixed, the painter may wish to compare his color with that of certain commercially prepared products; however, he will do well to ignore such color names as a basis for paint mixing.

As a matter of fact, the leading distemper or dry pigment colors are usually bought from firms which use the chemical names; manufacturer's color charts are as nearly standardized as is possible. Most of these colors are similar in color to oil paints of the same names and, since approximate primary colors are available, the painter should never be confused when it comes to stocking up with supplies. With the following paints on hand, the painter will be able to mix many of the colors he will need: *Medium Chrome Green, Ultramarine Blue, Vermilion, Burnt Sienna, Burnt Umber, Yellow Ochre, Light Chrome Yellow, Black,* and *White.* Other colors can be purchased in smaller quantities as needed, thus simplifying the paint storage problems.

Dry pigments and wet pigments (used for palette painting) are available in an extensive range of colors. Although many of these colors may be purchased in household paint stores, it is perhaps more satisfactory to deal with establishments which specialize specifically in scene paints. The following complete list is presented and the most useful colors are starred:

Dry Colors

*Danish Whiting — The most satisfactory whiting
*Light Chrome Yellow — Lemon in color
*Medium Chrome Yellow — A deep, gold yellow, similar to primary yellow
French Orange Mineral — Similar to the orange of the color wheel
*Turkey Red Lake — A brilliant scarlet
American Vermilion — A poor substitute for Turkey Red
Purple Lake — A deep purple
*French Yellow Ochre — A mustard color
*Raw Italian Sienna — Brownish yellow
English Dutch Pink — More intense than Yellow Ochre
*Raw Turkey Umber — A brown earth color
*Burnt Italian Sienna — A warm, reddish brown
*Burnt Turkey Umber — A deep, slightly reddish brown
*Ivory Drop Black — A satisfactory black
Swedish Black — Similar to Drop Black
Hercules Black — The blackest dry pigment
*Light Chrome Green — Similar to primary green
*Medium Chrome Green — Slightly darker than Light Chrome Green
Dark Chrome Green — A very dark green with considerable intensity
Italian Blue — A brilliant turquoise
Cobalt Blue — Lighter than primary blue
*American Ultramarine Blue — The nearest to primary blue
Prussian Blue — A dark blue
Celestial Blue — A deep gray-blue

Wet Colors

Turkey Red Lake — A brilliant scarlet
Solferino Lake — Magenta
Magenta Lake — A good substitute for primary red
Light Maroon — A deep, reddish purple
Dark Maroon — Has a brownish cast
Purple Lake — A deep purple
Yellow Lake — similar to Yellow Ochre, but deeper and more
   intense
Brown Lake — A deep brownish purple
Tapestry Black — A strong black
Emerald Green — A brilliant green
Malachite Green — A very deep green
Antwerp Blue — A deep subdued blue

There is no denying the fact that certain colors have definite psychological effects on individual persons. However, few people react in exactly the same manner to any one color since psychological reactions are entirely dependent on past experiences with colors. An individual may detest maroon as a color because he had to spend unhappy years in a house so painted; purple may displease him because an unpleasant relative chose to wear that color frequently. The psychology of color is so complicated a matter and so uncertain in its application to individual persons, that the designer will do well to consider psychology only in terms of the play and the characters in the play and to make few concessions to the usual varied and uncertain reactions of an audience. No designer can expect to satisfy every person in an audience by means of his choice of colors; if he makes up his mind to this fact early in his career, he will be realistically better adjusted to his work. Also, he must place his own color psychology in the background as he concentrates on the special requirements of a play.

Many people like to think that *white* usually has the correct psychological implication which is required to symbolize purity, or that *black* necessarily represents evil. However, although black is the accepted color for *cancan* hosiery and occasional scanty lingerie, it is also used for judges' robes and staid, correct limousines. *Red* might express great chic as well as shame and murder, and *green for envy* seems more like a trite saying than sound psychology or color symbolism. It is sometimes suggested that those with a fondness for *yellow* are in need of mental therapy, or that individuals who prefer *blue* are possessed of great repose and a calm mental state. Obviously, many normal people like yellow and it would not be difficult to find neurotic people who are satisfied by blue. It seems wise, therefore, to be cautious in the use of such color generalizations and, at the same time, to explore fully the psychological reactions of the characters within the play.

It is generally agreed that some colors are warm and others are cold; few will deny that yellow and red are usually warm, and there seems little doubt that certain greens and blues are cool. By way of illustration, during the course of a winter, a large employees' restaurant was repainted from yellow-green to blue-green. Immediately, all the employees complained so much of the inefficient heating apparatus, that it was necessary to restore the room to its original color. A warm, sunny climate is probably best served by cool colors and a gray, sunless region can use yellow, red, and orange to advantage. Such principles can often be applied to the design of stage settings, especially when a locale is closely related to the action of a play. For example, certain tropical regions are noted for the architectural use of specific colors as well as for an abundance of particularly colorful vegetation; thus the designer must combine principles with facts in order to obtain satisfying results.

It is also safe to state that some colors *approach* and others *recede*. Deep reds, deep brown, and purple come under the former classification and tints of green and blue are representative of the latter. An understanding of this basic principle is necessary when designing scenery or mixing paint colors since background colors cover so many square feet and must, therefore, approach or recede according to the nature of the play. A stage setting will decrease in size when approaching colors are used; at the same time contrasting colors will take on additional importance. Receding colors tend to be less conspicuous; thus their use is often limited to scenery which is relatively undefined and where detail is unimportant.

Some years ago it was a generally accepted fact that dark colors were suitable for tragedy and that lighter colors expressed comedy more suitably. In 1933, Donald Oenslager, by using deep blue-purple walls in the setting for *Forsaking All Others,* proved that comedy backgrounds need be neither neutral nor light in tone. The maroon walls of Mr. Oenslager's *Born Yesterday* scenery make certain that the results of his earlier experiment still hold. The professional production of Robinson Jeffers' version of *Medea* was played in a setting the chief feature of which was a dark gray edifice; certain other Greek tragedies have been staged before dark, cool, blue architecture. However, many exciting presentations of Greek drama have been presented with stark white columns as the chief background feature. It would seem wise then, for the designer to follow no slavish general rules as to choice of colors, but to be aware of general rules and to discard them knowingly and with reason when the play, together with his experience and understanding, suggests that he do so.

The use of color on the stage is always an engaging problem. While it is advisable to be aware of both general and specific color rules, the student must realize that, as in the case of general rules, the occasional purposeful breaking of a specific rule may bring a result which is completely satisfying. Specific color rules are used or discarded only after a careful study of the various color relationships has been completed. Since the beginning student usually needs to overcome his fear of color and to begin to rely on his own developing color sense, his ineptness as to color relationships will probably be overcome by a combination of "trial and error" and the study of specific rules. The following rather specific suggestions should prove helpful as a point of departure:

1. A color seems to have greater intensity when it covers a large area.
2. In most cases large areas should be kept relatively neutral.
3. Analogous colors may be used together in any proportion.
4. Complementaries should be used together in unequal proportions.
5. Color accents should be the complement of the main color.
6. Shades and tints of the same color may be used in any proportion.
7. A little bright red color outweighs much gray.
8. The values of nearby colors should be kept close together in order to bring out the hues of the colors.

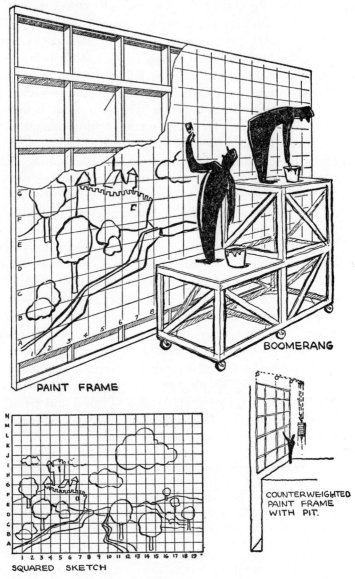

PAINT FRAME

BOOMERANG

COUNTERWEIGHTED
PAINT FRAME
WITH PIT.

SQUARED SKETCH

Fig. 43 *Painting a back drop on a paint frame*

116

9. A light color placed before a dark color will cause the latter to appear darker than it actually is.
10. A color should not be chosen merely because it is attractive in hue, intensity, or value. There should be definite reasons for the selection of each color.

The Painting Equipment

Anyone who has ever worked with a paint frame would be displeased, indeed, to give it up. This apparatus is perhaps the last word in the refinement of painting equipment; the installation of such a frame will pay for itself many times in the saving of labor and the accuracy of work which is possible by means of its use. A paint frame usually occupies a large portion of one of the long walls of the scene shop. When raised, the top of the frame touches the ceiling of the shop; when the frame is lowered, its top edge is a few feet above the floor level. Obviously the scene shop will have to be constructed so that there is space below the floor level to accommodate the frame when it is lowered. Since most paint frames are built with a protruding edge at the bottom, flats or other built scenic units can rest safely on and against the frame. In order for the frame to be used with safety it is counterweighted and checked by a windlass and winch so that the painters will have control over this heavy unit at all times.

A boomerang with two or three steps, and on rollers, will permit the painting of flats and drops from different levels. This is a much more satisfactory system than to have to work from ladders, as there is little danger of dropping pails of paint. However, many shops are too small to accommodate such a large and oddly shaped unit as the boomerang. The lack of a paint frame or a boomerang should not deter the workers since scenery can be painted flat on the floor or leaning against the wall; the results, despite the inconvenience, are perfectly satisfactory.

A paint shop should never be in need of utensils and brushes. A quantity of three-gallon pails should always be at hand and vegetable tins of the three-quart size are extremely useful for the mixing and storing of paint; a few five-gallon pails are also essential when it is necessary to mix large quantities of paint. As for stirring tools, the workers can either make their own paddles from three-ply or

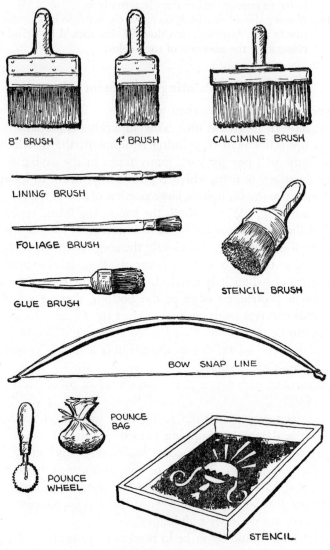

8" BRUSH   4" BRUSH   CALCIMINE BRUSH

LINING BRUSH

FOLIAGE BRUSH

STENCIL BRUSH

GLUE BRUSH

BOW SNAP LINE

POUNCE BAG

POUNCE WHEEL

STENCIL

Fig. 44 *Brushes, pounce bag and wheel, stencil, and bow snap line*

118

use the metal or wooden ones that are often given away for advertising purposes by various paint stores. Spatulas will also come in handy for scraping paint off the sides of buckets.

Paint must be stored in an orderly fashion, either in bins or in large cans placed on shelves. These bins or cans must be clearly labeled and the contents easily accessible so that a minimum of pigment will be spilled during the paint-mixing processes. Although pigment which is purchased in small bulk quantities is usually delivered in paper sacks, the practice of storing paint in such bags is not to be recommended since paper bags are impermanent and are easily torn as they are opened by painters in search of particular colors. Paint should be stored in a dry area, for otherwise it will cake and become lumpy; this is especially true of whiting.

The well-equipped scene shop will contain a sufficient quantity of paint brushes of various sizes so that all the painters can work when necessary. The most satisfactory brush for use in painting scenery has long, flexible, and stiff bristles. The eight-inch size with three rows of bristles is best for painting large areas; this size is frequently called a *calcimine brush* and is noted for its ability to hold a quantity of paint. Since these large brushes are very expensive, it is not likely that a shop can be provided with many of them. For filling in small, well-defined areas the *four-inch brush* is very useful. This size brush is not expensive and, therefore, should be stocked in quantity. Small *lining brushes* ($\frac{1}{4}''$, $\frac{1}{2}''$, and $1''$) and *foliage brushes* must also be provided, and such brushes should be of the best available quality because of the exact work they must accomplish. Although regulation stubby-bristled *stencil brushes* are desirable for stencil work, *two-inch brushes* can be used if the former are not available. If workers make it a rule always to use the correct type of brush for specific painting jobs, considerable time will often be saved. Never use a regulation paint brush in place of a special *glue brush!* Finally, it is wise to reserve the best brushes for water-color painting and to have a few inexpensive brushes at hand for the occasional oil painting that is required.

Great care should be observed in the washing of water-color brushes. The water should be warm but not hot, and all the paint must be removed from the bristles and *ferrule* (the metal strip which protects the top of the bristles). The brushes can be held under the water faucet in various positions and the bristles should be straight when the brush is put away to dry in a flat or hanging position. A mild soap does no harm to the bristles, but if the brush is washed *immediately* after using, soap is usually unnecessary. Alcohol is used to clean brushes that have had shellac in them; turpentine will remove oil paint from a brush.

The Painting Procedures

DRY PIGMENT

The mixing of paint is often likened to the first steps in following a cooking recipe; plenty of recipes are available, but the results are not always successful. It is true that certain proportions, when followed generally, will lead the paint mixer in the right direction. The final result, however, comes more often from an experience with the *feel* of the paint and from long-standing knowledge as to how various colors will react in liquid form and in combination with glue. The beginner must not expect perfect results in his first efforts, but should always attempt to analyze what is wrong with his paint so that each time he mixes ingredients he will be one step further along in experience.

First of all, the worker has the choice of melted glue direct from the double boiler or the use of *size water*. If he uses the latter, his proportion will be approximately one cup of melted white flake or ground gelatin glue to the gallon of water. This size water is stirred directly into the dry pigment; if the painter uses glue, water is first added to the color and the glue comes last. If ground gelatin glue is used, usually about half as much will be required as if the choice were the white flake variety. While it is no doubt more convenient to soak the glue overnight, this is not absolutely necessary as the glue can be dissolved and melted in less time than that. When soaking and heating the glue, always make certain that water completely covers the adhesive.

As the first step in paint mixing, it is a good idea to place the dry pigments in the pail — without water — since an approximation of color can be determined when the pigments are stirred together in dry form. It is not possible to state the definite amount of straight glue required per three gallons of paint although three cups is often suggested. The earth colors (ochre, the siennas, and the umbers) and whiting will require much more glue or size water than will the purer, richer colors.

Water or size water is added slowly; often it is necessary to use the hands to get the paint thoroughly mixed. Many painters like to use an electric or hand egg beater, after the pigment and water are fairly well mixed, thus making certain that all small lumps will be broken up. The final product should be similar to the consistency of good, rich milk. Running the solution through a sieve will insure a good mixture; if warm water or size water is used, the mixing process will be considerably easier. If it is necessary to use a batch of paint a second day, warming it up will help to get it in proper solution. The painter must always remember that whiting tends to settle in the bucket while certain other colors are likely to rise to the top; hence rather constant stirring is advisable while painting.

When the painter feels that the mixture is ready to use, he should test it first for color and second for the amount of glue. The usual procedure is to paint a small piece of wood and to dry it near heat without burning it. If the paint rubs off, more glue is needed; if it is shiny, there is too much glue and the paint will soon crack and break off. If size water has been used and the paint still needs more glue, straight melted glue must be added since additional water might make the paint too thin. Three gallons of scene paint will cover about five hundred square feet provided, of course, that the color to be covered is similar to that of the newly mixed paint. Be sure to mix more than enough paint as it is very difficult to match colors in case there is not enough paint to complete a job.

There follows a list of certain cautions and suggestions relating to the unusual results of pigment mixing as opposed to the theoretical discussions of pure color. Unless a painter has had a great deal of experience, he will be surprised at the results of some of the pigment combinations. While it would be impossible to list all the peculiarities of paint mixing, the following will serve as a guide to some of the more variable results:

1. Because of the impurity of the pigment, colors lose intensity when they are combined.

2. White changes the intensity and value of a color, but does not change the hue.
3. Black paint will neutralize a color as well as darken it.
4. Black will give yellow pigment a slight greenish cast.
5. In order to *key* all colors to one dominant color, add a little of the key color to each portion of paint.
6. Glue and size water will darken a color slightly.
7. A color can be grayed by adding a little of its complement.
8. The painter can usually predict the color which will be produced by combining pigments next to one another on the wheel.

The dry-pigment and melted-glue combination has a number of distinct disadvantages as well as advantages; therefore it seems wise to point these out and also to compare such paint mixtures with the *casein deep colors* such as Texolite. Dry pigment and glue are the traditional materials of the professional scene painter but, since the problems of the non-professional are considerably different, inexperienced workers will do well to consider all aspects of both paints before deciding which to use. If the following tabulations seem to present a one-sided picture, it is simply because the melted-glue and dry-pigment method, despite its common usage, presents many difficulties. At best, such paint is usually most successful when mixed by experts.

Advantages of Dry Pigment and Melted Glue

1. It is the cheapest method of painting scenery in the lighter colors.
2. The paint can be washed off the flats very easily.
3. There is no difficulty regarding the cleaning of buckets and brushes after the painting is finished.
4. This method offers an extremely wide range of unusual colors.

Disadvantages of Dry Pigment and Melted Glue

1. The glue pot is a nuisance and its odor is unpleasant.
2. Proportions of pigment and glue must be absolutely exact to insure a mixture which will be usable.
3. It is very difficult to get certain colors, such as red and black, to mix in solution.
4. The paint is difficult to apply without streaks.
5. The paint dries so much lighter than it appears in the

bucket that it is hard to predict the color as the paint is being mixed.

6. The mixed paint in the bucket lightens from day to day.
7. The paint dries satisfactorily only in warm dry rooms.
8. With this method it is difficult to cover dark colors with light colors; some colors (red, purple) will not cover at all.
9. Paint will deteriorate on the flats after a number of months.
10. Underneath coats will mix with the new paint as it is being applied.
11. Whiting has a tendency to drop to the bottom of the pail and certain colors will come to the top of the pail.
12. The paint deteriorates in the pails and the odor is offensive within a few days.
13. Usually only five or six coats can be applied.

Casein Paint

Casein paint comes in paste form and includes a sizing which is a skimmed milk product. The paint is placed on the market in cans of various sizes (pints, quarts, gallons) and it is only necessary to dilute it with half as much water to prepare it for use. One large Midwestern group buys white casein paint in large drums and uses this directly with dry pigment in place of glue and whiting. Undoubtedly there is considerable saving by buying in such quantity although such paint must usually be purchased from jobbers rather than from wholesale firms. If this kind of paint is always kept in airtight containers, it will last indefinitely and there will be no waste. The painters will do well to investigate all the casein paints which are on the market since new casein products are appearing from time to time.

Texolite, the best-known and most generally available product, comes in quite a wide variety of deep colors, most of which approximate the dry pigment colors. The Texolite deep colors are not to be confused with the tints — which are too light in value for use on the stage. However, these tints may be combined with deep colors and used in place of *Gardenia White*. The deep colors, like dry pigment, vary in price depending on the color. The following is the complete list of Texolite deep colors:

Light Yellow — Similar to Light Chrome Yellow
Medium Yellow — Similar to Medium Chrome Yellow

Burnt Sienna — Similar to the dry pigment
Raw Sienna — Similar to the dry pigment
Bright Red — Similar to Turkey Red
Red Orange — A bit darker than French Orange Mineral
Deep Blue — Similar to Ultramarine Blue
Deep Green — Similar to Light Chrome Green
Turquoise — Contains more blue than Medium Chrome Green
Burnt Umber — Similar to the dry pigment
Raw Umber — Similar to the dry pigment
Black — A shiny gray-black

Casein paint, like dry pigment and melted glue, offers both advantages and disadvantages. Although the following "advantage" list is the longer, those who object to the use of this kind of paint might point out that certain of the "disadvantages" are more important. An individual group will never know, however, which paint best suits its needs until each type of paint has been given a fair trial. There should never be any hesitation about using a product simply because it is not *traditional*.

Advantages of Casein Paint

1. Usually only one thin coat is required.
2. At least twenty coats of paint may be applied to a scenic unit.
3. The colors are pure, mix easily, and stay mixed.
4. It is almost impossible to leave brush marks.
5. When the paint sets, it is waterproof; thus it is ideal for outdoor theatres.
6. The paint dries only a shade or two lighter than it appears in the bucket.
7. The paint keeps in an open bucket for at least a week, even in a warm room.
8. There is no delay regarding mixing since a glue pot is unnecessary.
9. There is never any difficulty about one color covering another.
10. The color does not change from day to day.

Disadvantages of Casein Paint

1. The *Gardenia White* is a great deal more expensive than whiting.
2. The black color reflects light slightly.

3. The paint is somewhat difficult to remove from brushes and pails if there is any delay.
4. Casein paint cannot be washed off the flats easily.

DYES

Regular *analine* scenic dyes are usually available only in stores which specialize in scene paints. Analine dyes are also found on the market under trade names such as *Putnam* and *Diamond*, but most of the so-called tinting dyes (*Tintex*) will not be very useful. Since analine dyes are so concentrated, they are admirably suited for use in over-all dyeing and painting. When fabrics are to be dyed, the first step is to mix twelve ounces of dye into paste form and then to add about twelve teaspoons of salt to the three-gallon pail of water. In order for the dye to "set," the solution must be boiled. When the dye is to be used as paint, size water is necessary instead of salt and boiling water.

Dye serves much better than ordinary scene paint for painted draperies since the dye will not stiffen the fabric. However, extremely thin solutions of scene paint can occasionally be used in place of dye, especially such colors as red, purple, blue, and green. Because dye is translucent, it is well suited for painting stained-glass windows and translucent drops; interesting effects are obtained when scene paint and dye are combined in one unit. Such professional productions as *On the Town, Brigadoon,* and *Medea* offered drops which were strikingly painted with dye and scene paint.

Dyes are available in most of the colors that are found in dry pigment and can be combined to produce many interesting colors. All painting with dye must be done on new material and, if an area is painted too dark, it cannot be made lighter; areas painted light, however, can be darkened. It is sometimes effective to spray a unit with a dark dye and size water in order to break down the background color, although scene paint might be equally effective for such texturing. As a matter of fact, dyes have a very limited use, and the painter will never use dye when scene paint would be more satisfactory.

THE SIZE COAT

Professional scene painters usually give newly covered flats a size coat on the front and back, that is, a covering of size water and a little inexpensive pigment. This coat fills the pores of the canvas, shrinks the material, and helps prepare the units for later coats of special color. Non-professionals, to save time, frequently omit the size coat and apply the final coat directly to the new material. Such a practice does not always guarantee a successful paint-covering job although it does, of course, allow an extra coat of paint during the life of the scenic unit. The size coat is most easily applied with an eight-inch priming or calcimining brush and, while the appearance of this paint job is not important, the painter must be certain that he covers all the areas thoroughly.

THE PRIME COAT

Some professional painters apply a prime coat as the second coat of paint on a new flat. In non-professional scene shops, the prime coat sometimes takes the place of the size coat but, when this coat follows the size coat, a more successful result can be expected. When a number of older flats of different colors are to be used as the basis for a box setting, it is well to paint them all with some inexpensive neutral-colored prime coat before the final coat is laid on; this will insure a relatively even-colored final coat of paint. Prime coats are especially necessary when there are strong color contrasts between the various main flats which are to be used. The prime coat need not be so carefully applied as the final coat since it is mainly a preparatory coating of paint.

THE GROUND COAT

The final coat of paint, the ground coat, is usually applied before the texturing of the scenery is begun. Sometimes the ground coat is applied with a spray, but shop workers will be kept better employed and given greater experience when laying-in brushes are used. In most cases a smooth coating is desirable even though texturing will be applied over the ground coat; hence, brush strokes should be in various directions and without pattern. Sometimes a ground coat must be put on with indications of shading, from top to bottom. When such effects are desired, several colors may be required and the final result will seem somewhat in the nature of texturing. However, neither the solid color ground coat nor the multicolored ground coat is applied haphazardly; every brush stroke must accomplish something.

BACK PAINTING

The non-professional painter should give serious consideration to the idea of the general back painting of scenery. Since it cannot always be determined in advance exactly where lighting instruments will be placed — these units may spill light through the flats — there is much to be said for back painting an entire setting with some neutral, inexpensive color such as gray, white, or tan. Otherwise, it may be necessary to climb ladders and to paint the backs of flats after the scenery is set up on the stage. Ideally, back painting should be completed in the shop before the front painting is started, although no serious harm is done to the paint job if such painting is done later. While the front of the scenery is obviously more important than the rear, some technicians take particular pleasure in the neat and trim appearance which back painting gives to scenic units.

THE PAINT TEXTURES (page 128)

Very few paint jobs are complete until some sort of texturing is applied to the flats. Flat, painted scenery reflects light objectionably, looks completely unconvincing, and suggests little or nothing to an audience. On the other hand, textured scenery has a certain three-dimensional quality which is usually agreeable to view and which suggests solidity instead of canvas-covered frames. Even though the ground coat has been applied in a purposefully uneven manner, it is often necessary to texture such a surface to make it completely satisfying. Many non-professional painters think that if direct stage light is kept off the untextured flat, its appearance will not be objectionable. At best, however, such backgrounds will be meaningless and uninteresting.

Spattering. By far the most commonly used type of texturing is the spattering or flecking method. Spattering can, of course, be so heavily applied that the audience is aware of it; it can also be done lightly and thus serve purely as a method of breaking up a flat surface so that it will not reflect light noticeably. Painters can

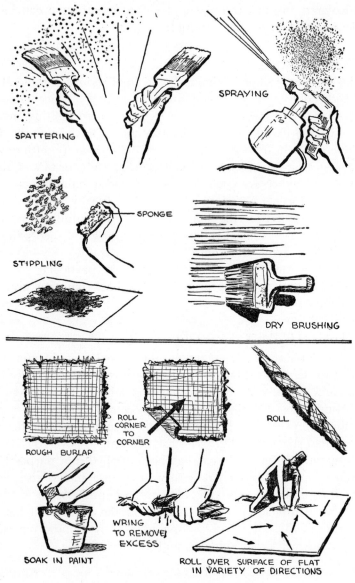

SPATTERING

SPRAYING

STIPPLING

SPONGE

DRY BRUSHING

ROUGH BURLAP

ROLL CORNER TO CORNER

ROLL

SOAK IN PAINT

WRING TO REMOVE EXCESS

ROLL OVER SURFACE OF FLAT IN VARIETY OF DIRECTIONS

Fig. 45 *Painting textures (above) and rolling techniques (below)*

develop great skill at flecking although the work is quite tiring and involves considerable strain of the arm muscles.

The process involves a near-dry, long-bristled brush and paint which has an extra amount of glue in it; if there is insufficient glue, the small dots will rub off and smear the surface. If the brush is held in a flat position with the thumb on the ferrule, it will be much easier to guide the directions of the spattering. The brush is dipped about one-half inch into the paint and then the spattering is tested on the floor or on some unused flat before any work is done on the newly painted scenery. A quick jerk of the arm, rather than a swing movement, will produce the best-sized dots of paint, although some painters prefer to tap the brush sharply against the side of the hand. No doubt there is much better control of paint for small areas by the use of this latter method. Whichever method is used, the direction of the flecking must be changed continually so that no pattern will be formed. Dots must be of assorted sizes but few should be larger than one-eighth inch in diameter; they must be distributed rather evenly. Scenery may be spattered either as it leans against the wall or as it lies flat on the floor; the latter position is perhaps less tiring for the painter, but it is easier to control flecking when scenery is off the floor.

The late Joseph Urban, distinguished designer for the Ziegfeld Follies and the Metropolitan Opera, advocated a system of spattering which is referred to as *pointillage*. This term applies to the flecking of several colors, often the pigment primaries, the idea being that scenery is more pleasing to look at when several colors are thus mixed rather than combined in the bucket and painted on the scenery as a solid color. Since the use of the pointillage system gives scenery a suggestion of richness and depth, this texturing principle is, of course, invaluable for use with many different kinds of scenery. Furthermore, colored light, similar to that of any one of the flecking colors, will cause the scenery to appear that particular color.

Spraying. The use of some sort of spraying device in place of flecking or spattering has a number of merits although the dots which result may be too small for some texturing purposes. Usually the spraying is the better method when the main purpose is to break down the glare of a flat surface rather than to suggest texture as such. Electrically powered sprays are preferable to hand sprays although the hand-operated spray such as is used by gardeners will serve when the aim is to simulate extremely rough cement or plaster. *DeVilbiss* and *Paasche* both make sprays with one-and-a-half horsepower compressor motors; these units take up considerable floor space and are abundantly noisy. Although these sprays normally give a very fine spray, it is possible to regulate the size of the dots to a limited extent. However, units of this type are rather temperamental and, when they clog and suddenly release paint, the results are most depressing. The metal jars which are available for these sprays are preferable to the easily broken glass jars which must be used with most motor-driven sprays. *Hudson* makes an A.C.-current motor-driven spray which has much in its favor since the small motor can be carried over the shoulder by means of a strap. This small, light spray must be kept in perfect running condition at all times; otherwise, continual heavy usage will cause the motor to break down.

Actually the most satisfactory spray texturing results are obtained from the use of the spray attachment which comes with most tank or cylinder vacuum cleaners. While it is true that this apparatus is rather cumbersome for a paint shop, there is no denying the efficiency and the ease of control which are characteristic of this type of spray. The size of the spray dots is usually regulated by the thumb, and the spray gun is very easy to fill and to clean. If the painters are satisfied with this method of spraying, it will pay them to purchase such a unit rather than to borrow continually from some household; obviously, the hose and cylinder will soon absorb scene-shop dirt and paint.

Stippling. When a texture is desired that is similar to that of very rough plaster or cement, brush or sponge stippling (page 128) should be the choice. There is always the danger of getting too much texturing on the flats at first; therefore it is well to apply paint to a small board with a brush and to touch the tip of the brush or sponge to the board rather than to the paint in the bucket before touching the actual scenery. Short-bristled stiff brushes as well as large genuine sponges which have a variety of hole sizes provide the best results; artificial sponges do not provide good texture. Texturing done in this manner will naturally be somewhat uneven in coverage, but this unevenness must be "studied" and must conform to the characteristics of natural cement or rough plaster. The sponging of several different colors will give greater depth to the uneven areas. For instance, brown and blue sponged over a tan ground coat will be much more interesting than merely to sponge with brown alone. When too much paint is sponged onto a certain area, the painter can sponge over this section lightly with the ground-coat color and thus disguise the error. Finally, it may be necessary to spray or spatter the entire setting after sponging has been completed in order to insure a more subtle effect.

Rolling. Sometimes a texture is required which must be so heavy and pronounced that it can be obtained in no other way except by the rolling method (page 128). For this purpose the painter takes a small square of burlap and rolls it up in triangular fashion. The roll is then dipped into paint, wrung out, and rolled over the flat in the various areas where roughness is desired. It might even be desirable to follow the rolling with sponging or spattering, thus softening the rolling texture somewhat. Rolling effects can also be accomplished by the use of a sponge although the results are perhaps not so easy to control. If the rolling, sponge or cloth, is done around the edges of a unit in a "criss-cross" manner feathering off toward the center, the results will be more pleasing than those which could be obtained by over-all coverage. Portions of the setting for the Evans-Anderson *Macbeth* production were given texture by the rolling method, and this heavy texturing suited that play admirably.

Blending. Occasionally a blended quality is necessary for a paint job, that is, the effect of several colors of the same value blended together with no apparent lines of demarcation. This type of painting, called either *scumbling* or *blending*, is often done on a damp ground coat, although satisfactory results can be obtained over a dry background color. Full brushes of paint are used and the painting is continued until they need recharging; occasional use of a dry brush will assist in the blending. Interesting rough stone effects are possible by this texturing method although, as with the other texturing methods, all the painting must be purposeful. Like most heavy texturing, usually the heaviest and darkest blending is concentrated at the top and sides of the scenic unit.

Dry Brushing. Dry brushing (page 128) involves the dipping of a brush lightly into paint and *dragging* it over the ground coat in an effort to represent graining or other defined texturing. As the brush is moved, it can waver slightly and thus suggest the irregularities of wood, and by dry brushing with several colors — yellow, blue, and red, for example — interesting varieties of wood can be suggested. This graining method is best suited to the indication of the rougher and less subtle wood effects; the more precise graining such as found in knotty pine, mahogany, etc., must be actually painted in naturalistic fashion after the painter has studied the characteristics of such woods. Dragging is also sometimes applied in crosshatch fashion to represent rough cement similar to that obtained by the rolling technique. Such dry brushing, like the graining effects, must be applied with both a free technique and a definite knowledge as to what each drag of the brush is to accomplish. Brush marks should be continuous and never jumpy; otherwise they will register as brush strokes rather than as specific texture.

Puddling. As the name implies, puddling is the running together of various small, colored puddles of paint. The painters shake the paint onto the scenery from heavily charged brushes and the results often suggest unusual depth and tone quality. This method is especially useful when a marble of varicolored pattern is desired and certain unusual plaster effects also can be simulated by the puddling method. Painting of this sort often needs to be toned down and softened, and sponging or spattering should take care of this satisfactorily. Although the results of puddling are bold and pronounced, this method requires as much or more skill and practice as any of the other texture systems, though it is perhaps used the least of any.

Appliqué. When actual three-dimensional texturing is needed, sawdust, ground cork, or papier-mâché can be glued directly to the scenic unit. If casein glue is used for this purpose, it is not likely that the applied dimension will loosen as the unit is painted; nor will the appliqué become soft, soak up moisture, or change its shape and dimension. Very convincing heavy stone work can be obtained by gluing irregularly shaped pieces of thick fibre board to a wall unit; such stone work is, of course, given additional texturing by means of sponging, spattering, or rolling. Paper representations of specific types of tree bark may be applied to the tree trunks of painted wood wings, thus suggesting a three-dimensional quality rather than the usual flat appearance. Since flats so treated are difficult to use again, it is well to work with units which must soon be recovered. The designer's ingenuity is the only limitation when it comes to the choice of materials for appliqué texturing.

Glazing. A glaze of size water, brushed or sprayed over a painted and textured flat, will give it a slightly glossy and mellow appearance. Scenic wallpaper is usually glazed after it is hung in houses; the same practice can be followed when representing such wall treatment on the stage. When sizing or thinned shellac is applied to scenery which has been painted to represent rough plaster, additional age and depth are suggested. Columns are particularly effective when glazed since their three-dimensional form then takes on a soft sheen which tends to recede, particularly in the upstage areas. Although some technicians feel that any glossy surface is undesirable on the stage, the occasional use of glazing actually comes as a welcome change from the constant use of large areas of non-glossy scene paint.

The Stencil. When painting wallpaper designs, a stencil (page 118) is invaluable as a means of securing uniform patterns. By means of chalk and a snap line, guide lines are snapped onto the units according to the size, shape, and placement of the stencil pattern. Lines may be snapped so as to provide spaces for *monogram, overlap,* or *diamond* patterns; great care must be observed so that these lines bear the proper relationships from flat to flat. In case a flat is not of a width or height that permits the snap lines to come out exactly even (for example, lines snapped every nine inches on a four-foot-wide flat will leave three extra inches), it is necessary to snap a perpendicular or horizontal line and to consider that line as if it were the edge of the flat. The stencil itself is cut either from special

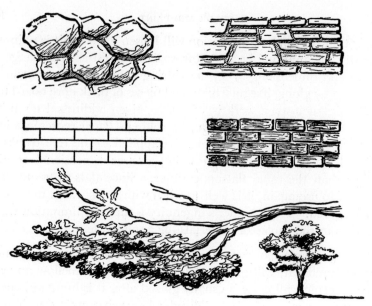

Fig. 46 *Bricks, stones, and leaves*

stencil paper or from thin cardboard which is coated, front and back, with shellac before it is used. Sometimes a wooden frame of $1'' \times 1''$ or $1'' \times 2''$ is built around the stencil, thus preventing the paper from curling or tearing as it is used. The pattern must be designed so that it will hold together after it is cut out; hence, certain parts of the design may have to be touched up by hand after the stenciling is completed. Where more than one color is required on the painted design, it is wise to provide separate stencils for each color. Although regular stencil brushes are desirable for this work, two-inch lining brushes will not be unsatisfactory.

Bricks. The most convincing realistic brick effects are obtained by first giving the unit a ground coat which represents the mortar color. After this paint has been applied, guide lines are snapped on regularly over the entire area to be bricked. If the bricks are to be reddish in color, at least three shades of this hue will be desirable; yellow or tan bricks would similarly require the use of a number of shades. Unless the painting is to represent very careful and precise bricklaying, the paint is placed within the outlines, leaving the snap lines exposed, and with not too great an attempt to make the outlines of the bricks clean-cut and sharp. As far as

134

possible, the colors should be moved about for the sake of variety and occasionally it will be necessary to paint regular arrangements of brick patterns. It is usually necessary to spatter or sponge the bricks, the amount of texturing depending, of course, upon the age of the bricks. In the case of non-realistic bricks, a brick color might be applied first as the ground coat and the gray mortar lines painted on with a lining brush. Obviously, there will be many slight variations to this latter method of brick painting since, unlike realistic bricks, which are relatively easy to classify, there are few limits to their non-realistic representation.

Stones. There are so many different types of stones and stone-laying methods that the painter should study and examine from life the type of work he is trying to represent. As in the case of brick painting, the workers have the choice of painting the mortar first or last. However, since painted stones are seldom a solid color, the ground coat is painted with several colors blended together before the colors dry; similar painting is applied to individual stones which have been sketched in. As a final touch, individual stones may be darkened on the lower edges and the entire unit sprayed or spattered to help cut down on the conspicuousness of the mortar.

Foliage. The representation of foliage is one of the most difficult problems that will face the scene painter. Very often silhouette foliage borders, wood wings, and ground rows are required, but there are many cases when detailed painting is necessary and leaves of a particular variety must be represented. The painter must remember that each leaf will be seen from a little different angle and that leaves have a characteristic manner of growing in groups. There must be a great deal of variation in color within a given area; therefore, so-called palette painting (wet or dry color and strong size water on a palette) or its equivalent will often be necessary. Black paint should be avoided when the painter is striving for realism, but non-realistic leaves are sometimes partially outlined in black in order to call attention to their specific shapes. When the results need not be completely realistic, the use of a foliage brush will simplify the application of paint daubs of various shades of green onto a more neutral green background.

THE BACKDROP

The backdrop offers more interesting painting opportunities than any other type of specially designed scenery. A designer's scale color-rendering or painter's elevation is, of course, the point of departure and, if beginning painters are observant and painstaking, there is no reason why they cannot complete such units satisfactorily. In transferring a design from a painter's elevation to a backdrop, the first step is to divide the elevation, or tracing of it, into one-foot squares, to scale (p. 116). Next, one-foot squares are snapped onto the canvas with a snap line. (The bow snap line can also be used where it is necessary to concentrate extra guide lines within a small area.) The painter is then ready to sketch with charcoal the main elements of the design, using the snapped chalk lines as guides; minute details are left to the final painting stages. Elaborate designs can be pricked into a cardboard pattern with a *pounce wheel*, and a *pounce bag* containing lamp black can be patted over the holes to transfer the pattern. In order to make certain that the unit will retain its shape, the edges of the canvas should always be tacked down, regardless of whether the drop is on a paint frame or on the floor. Areas are painted in order of their relative sizes; usually the upper portions are painted before the lower ones in order to avoid dripping paint on finished areas. Although professionally painted drops are seldom given over-all texturing, a light, gray spray will help to soften painting which has been accomplished by inexperienced painters.

SPECIAL PRACTICES AND PROCEDURES

There are many proved methods and practices in connection with scenery painting, and alert and ingenious painters will no doubt discover additional procedures as they work on particular productions. It is seldom that one painting job will be quite like another; hence the painter must have enough experience to know what methods to use as he interprets the designer's painting techniques. Since non-professional painters do not always have the opportunity to use fresh, new materials nor to work in ideally equipped shops, workers must be aware of the aids and methods which can be of use in helping to overcome handicaps. The following is a list of practices which painters may find useful at one time or another:

1. If oil spots, water marks, and areas of red or purple scene paint are given a coating of clear shellac, ordinary scene paint will cover them and prevent their bleeding through. This is not necessary, however, if the covering coat has a casein binder.

2. Scenery for out-of-door theatres, painted with dry pigment and melted glue, should be sprayed with a solution of one part formaldehyde and ten parts of water so that it will not be affected by rain.

3. A tablespoon of Lysol or carbolic acid added to the three-gallon pail of paint will prevent scene paint from decomposing so fast. Many people, however, will find the odor of the Lysol more offensive than that of the aged paint.

4. A solution of a handful of alum to a quart of water will toughen the paint on a flat and make it easier to cover the old paint with a new coat.

5. Backdrops will be less stiff if they have been painted with a solution containing one cup of glycerin to the gallon of paint.

6. Regular household oil paint is desirable for doors and other surfaces which are likely to become soiled with constant use.

7. Metallic powders, gold or aluminum, can be mixed in solution either with bronzing liquid or a glue solution which is twice as strong as size water.

8. If it is necessary to paint drops on the floor, painters will find it helpful to stand on a ladder from time to time in order to view the work.

9. Certain paints — such as red and black — will mix more readily with other paints if they are first stirred into paste form with a little alcohol.

PROJECTS AND EXERCISES

1. What are your color preferences and dislikes, and can you offer any reasons for your choices? Have you recently changed your opinion regarding some particular color? Why?

2. Note the latest department-store fabric colors exhibited in your

community. Attempt to analyze their color content in relation to the various dry pigments or casein paints.

3. What scenery have you recently seen which used colors which were predominantly "approaching"? Was this choice of colors justified?

4. What would you consider as suitable background colors for the following Shakespeare dramas: *Antony and Cleopatra*, *Twelfth Night*, *The Tempest*, *As You Like It*?

5. Select samples of several colored materials which might be used on the stage. How do you think various colored lights would affect the colors? Test the materials under colored lights to check your assumptions.

6. Make a diagram showing the storage facilities in your shop for paint, brushes, and cans. What improvements could you suggest?

7. How are drops painted in your scene shop? What size units can be accommodated? What is the greatest number of such units that your shop has turned out for any one production?

8. Is the paint in your shop mixed with size water or with melted glue? Why? What paint mixing mistakes have you noted recently and how do you account for them?

9. In a clean container, mix small amounts of any two colors in their dry form. In another container place the same amounts of color and add size water until the paint is in solution. Cover a small piece of wood with this paint and, when the paint dries, compare its color with that of the two mixed dry colors.

10. In order to check the effects of black on the various dry pigments, add a little black to small portions of each color of your palette. Add size water, paint small pieces of wood, and note the results as applied to change of color value.

11. Get casein color charts from the paint dealers in your community. Which brand has the widest color range? Which brand offers colors which are the nearest to the dry pigment colors?

12. Paint scraps of canvas with dyes to which various amounts of water have been added. After the materials dry, note the differences of translucency.

13. Paint ground coats on eight small canvas-covered frames. Apply one type of texturing to one half of each frame. Observe the results from a distance and under artificial light. As a further experiment, apply some spattering over the blending — and sponging over the puddling. What does this accomplish?

14. What methods of texturing have you observed in recent professional productions? Can you decide why these methods were selected?

15. Apply a coat of size-water glazing to the small flat frame which you textured by means of sponging. How does the glaze affect the ground coat? The sponging?

16. From a magazine, select some landscape advertisement which is of the approximate proportions of a backdrop. Place tracing paper over it and trace the main outlines of the landscape. Draw one-half-inch squares over the entire tracing. On a large piece of paper, enlarge the design to one-and-a-half-inch scale and note the problems involved.

17. Examine the bricks on at least three buildings. Note their sizes, their color variation, and their texture. Is any pattern suggested in the laying?

18. What types of foliage, silhouette or detailed, would best suit the following plays: *The Sea Gull, The Emperor Jones, Hansel and Gretel, On Borrowed Time?* Why?

19. Keep a list of any practices, procedures, or suggestions which you discover as you paint. Compare notes with the other students after each production.

The Support and
Shifting of Scenery

AFTER STAGE SCENERY has been constructed and painted, it must
be set up, fastened together, and moved to various positions on the
stage without waste of manpower. The designer must make plans
for these necessities in his original drawings. Thus the practicabil-
ity of the designs will be tested the moment the set-up begins. No
matter how attractive the flats, drops, or silhouettes may be, if
they can be neither supported nor shifted satisfactorily, the results
are wasteful of time and effort. Although professional scenery
must occasionally be discarded or rebuilt because it is cumbersome
and awkward to handle, non-professionals, usually working on
limited budgets, can seldom afford such extravagance. All mechanical problems must therefore be solved in advance on the
drawing board in order to insure economical, stable, and mobile
scenery.

Lashing

Because of the present-day tendency to use wide, unbroken
walls for box settings, the system of fastening one flat to another
by means of lash lines and special stage hardware is not used

so extensively as has been the case in the past. Flats which are booked together will prevent noticeable cracks and are therefore more desirable than units placed edge to edge and lashed together to represent a continuous wall; when flats are at an angle to one another, however, lashing is often desirable. While it is usually not difficult to lash flats which meet to form the corner of a room, flats which are butted together to form a wall surface which protrudes into the room can usually make good use of the *lash-line hook* for tying-off purposes. The lash line itself, #8 sash cord, must be pulled tightly and tied with a tie-off *slip knot* so that, if necessary, it will be possible to untie it quickly during scene shifts.

Skill in the lashing process comes only after considerable practice; an experienced stagehand can flip a rope on an eighteen-foot flat almost as easily as on a twelve-foot unit. It is best to hold the line near the bottom and to throw the rope as high as possible toward the top cleat, using a jerky movement. Although the line must be pulled back quickly just as it hooks around the top cleat, it does not require skill to get the line around the lower cleats. If the backstage workers bang the ropes against the back of the canvas, they may loosen the paint on some of the canvas and at the same time create considerable noise.

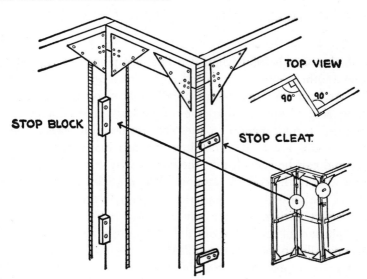

Fig. 47 *Stop block and stop cleat*

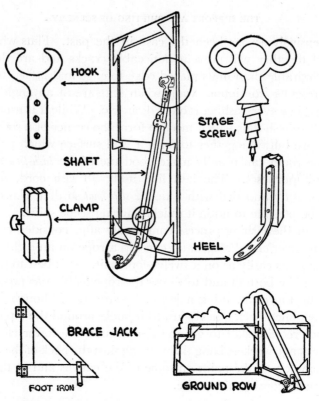

Fig. 48 *Stage brace and brace jack*

Stop cleats are helpful when two flats are placed at right angles to one another — forming a corner or joint *away* from the curtain line. At least three cleats are usually placed on the back of the upstage side of the flat that is more or less perpendicular to the footlights. (Small mending plates are also useful for this purpose.) If these cleats are used, each time the lash line is tightened, the stagehand can be certain that the corner is trim and that the flats are meeting in the correct position. When a joint is formed which is *toward* the footlights, at least three *stop blocks* are required to insure perfect fitting. These small $1'' \times 1''$ blocks are screwed three quarters of an inch from the edge of the flat which is more nearly parallel to the act curtain. When this type of corner is used, it may be necessary to use lash-line hooks altogether instead of lash cleats in order that the line may be pulled tightly without slipping off.

Even though a box setting is lashed on only two corners, this method of fastening justifies itself, particularly if the setting must be broken down quickly for fast scene shifts. If a setting need not be shifted during an evening and, furthermore, is going to be left standing for a number of days, the corners are sometimes screwed together, thus providing extra stability. Warped flats will not usually lash satisfactorily; hence, it may be mandatory to use screws when the setting is permanent — or screw eyes and wire hooks when quick scene changes are involved.

Bracing and Stiffening

Almost all types of scenic units must be braced from the rear so that they will stand erect and appear to be solid and substantial. Even so, scenery that is made up of lightweight frames, covered with canvas, will never withstand unlimited banging around without showing some movement. Although the technicians may know that the scenery is well-braced and in no danger of falling, it is certainly not reassuring to audiences to see a wall tremble flimsily. Sharp door slams are oftentimes extremely effective as stage business; thus, when it is obvious that scenery must take this kind of punishment, it may be advisable to cover some of the flats with profile board to help withstand the shock. The Broadway scenery for *Mr. Roberts* and *Command Decision* was almost entirely built of five-ply and therefore, since it was actually solid, the scenery could support weight and was in no danger from the robust activity of the players. While non-professional audiences can hardly expect this type of solidity, they should at least be spared the movement which is the result of careless incorrect bracing.

The two most common devices for use in bracing are the *stage brace* and the *brace jack;* the former is professionally constructed and the latter, shop constructed. The stage brace is made up of two hardwood *shafts*, and a cast-iron *hook, heel,* and adjusting *clamp.* These devices may be purchased in the short size which will allow an adjustment of from five to eight feet, or the more useful long size which will adjust from six to ten feet. While the shorter size is useful for low units and for giving extra support to stage doors, it is useless on flats of regulation height. Whichever size is used, the

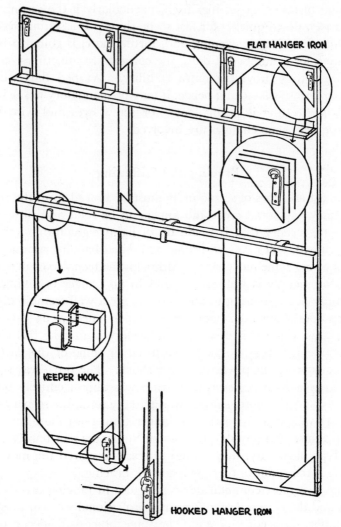

FLAT HANGER IRON

KEEPER HOOK

HOOKED HANGER IRON

Fig. 49 *Stiffening and hanging a stage wall*

backstage worker must make certain that, after the hook is placed in the hole of the stage brace cleat, the position of the brace is reversed and that it permits no play. After the stage peg is screwed through the hole of the heel, the clamp can be adjusted so that the scenery will be solidly braced. Since the brace is never permanently attached to the scenery but can be hooked on or unhooked quietly and quickly, the same braces may be used many times in a multiset show.

The right-angled brace jack is usually built of $1'' \times 3''$, using the general principles of flat construction. While the height of the jack will always be determined by the scenic unit that it is to support, its lower width (in order to conserve floor space) should seldom be over two feet. A *foot iron* is attached to the outer corner of the brace, thus permitting the unit to be anchored to the floor temporarily. If the jack is loose-pin-hinged to the flat, profile, or ground row, it can be folded against the scenery when it is not in use, thus conserving storage space. It will be well to consider brace jacks as more or less permanent equipment even though considerable lumber may be tied up by their construction. The jack will support a wall much more solidly than it can be held by a stage brace; hence the frequent use of jacks is recommended.

When it is necessary that several flats, booked or unbooked, give the impression of a wide wall expanse, the units must be stiffened and held together from the rear in order that the wall may be as straight as possible. For example, in order to hold three separate flats together, it will be necessary to screw lengths of $1'' \times 3''$ to the rear of the scenery. If the flats are at all warped, it is advisable to clamp them together from the rear before fastening on the battens. In the case of booked flats, two-fold or three-fold, which must be opened and stiffened, it will usually be satisfactory to loose-pin-hinge or bolt battens to the rear. When the scenery must be set up and struck frequently, there is much to be said for the use of bolts. *Keeper hooks* or S-hooks may be used at various positions along the top of an open book and in similar positions on the toggle rails as well; battens slipped into the protruding part of the hook will act as stiffeners. If the wall is trimmed by means of a built cornice and mopboard, these long members, bolted on, will act as upper and lower stiffeners; therefore, only the center stiffening battens will be necessary. Long wall expanses that are not stiffened by one means or another will tend to be flimsy and unconvincing and obviously can never be struck as a single unit during a scene change.

Running

By far the most common method of moving scenery is the running method, that is, the moving of scenery by hand without the aid of any contrivance or apparatus. While such moving of scenery is often difficult for beginners, the worker soon develops skill and is able to move tall and wide units easily. Years ago, when stage scenery was largely painted and consisted almost entirely of plain flats, lashed together, running was inevitable. Today, much of our scenery is assembled into units which are so heavy that special shifting devices must be used, with the result that the practice of running may be largely limited to the scene shop.

When running scenery, it is best to pull the units rather than to push them; unless the worker is left-handed, he will find it helpful to place his left hand at a height convenient for guiding and stabilizing purposes. The right hand, in a normal position, will lift the unit slightly and do most of the pulling. If the beginning backstage worker always places his hands in these positions, there will be little danger involved in the moving of scenic units, and there should be no waste of time and energy. Although an experienced stagehand can manipulate large, folded books with no difficulty, three-folds usually require two persons, one at each edge. Workers must at all times *look where they are going;* accidents caused by carelessness can injure bystanders as well as tear and break the scenery.

When a unit is to be raised from a flat-on-the-floor position, it is wise to have one person *foot* it, i.e., place his foot against the lower edge so that the second worker can *walk it up* without its slipping or sliding. After a two-fold or three-fold has had stiffening battens fastened to it, several persons will be required to walk it up — two or three others will probably be needed to foot it. Obviously, it will require several backstage workers to slide such a large unit to its correct position on the stage. The reverse of the above process, dropping the unit to the floor, is called *floating*. This method stirs

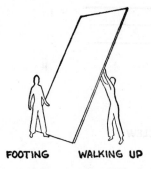

FOOTING   WALKING UP   FLOATING A FLAT

Fig. 50 *"Walking it up" and "floating"*

up a great deal of dust but, regardless of height, it can be attempted with any unit that is free from openings or built-on, three-dimensional trim.

The transportation of scenery from the shop to the stage, or from the stage to the storage room, can be responsible for considerable wear and tear. If the units are to be moved by truck, it will be necessary to consider the manner in which flats are lowered and carried. The simplest procedure is to float or lower a single flat to the floor and then to raise it on edge — the proper position for moving. Three-folds and books must be closed before they are lowered, not floated, to the floor and carried to the truck on edge. In order to avoid punching and scratching, it is advisable to stack flats with the painted sides together unless, of course, certain three-dimensional trim interferes. Flats are usually stored in a perpendicular position on the stage, in the shop, or in the storage quarters.

Flying

Technicians seldom find that backstage floor areas are commodious enough to take care of all the framed scenic units that are required for multi-set productions. No matter how carefully backstage space is apportioned, there will often be some units that are so large and bulky that it will be necessary to get them temporarily out of the way during some of the scene shifts. If the stage is equipped with a fly loft and sets of lines, no better method can be devised than to fly units which, because of their size, cannot be stored against the stage walls. Scenery can then be *let in* (lowered)

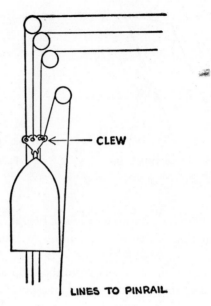

CLEW

LINES TO PINRAIL

Fig. 51 *The carpet hoist*

when needed; when the units are in the flies, valuable floor space
is made free.

Very often the entire back wall of a setting is got out of the way
by means of flying and, when the wall is lowered, the side walls are
run in and lashed to it.   Instead of flying only one wall, another
possibility is to hinge the side walls to the center wall, folding them
in and hooking them to the main wall before all three sections are
flown as one.   The three walls of a setting can also be flown in an
open position although this requires at least two sets of lines and
considerable teamwork on the part of those who pull the lines.
During the Katharine Cornell presentation of *That Lady*, one
small setting was flown, including the floor, although when the
production took to the road, the floor was dispensed with.

If the back wall is to be lifted as a unit, all the flats must be
fastened together by means of battens and the top of the unit fitted
with *flat hanger irons; hooked hanger irons* are necessary at the bottom
of the unit if great weight is involved.   Whenever it is necessary
to release the lowered lines to get them out of the way of a ceiling
or some other hanging unit, the lines at the pinrail must be equipped
with a special rigging device called a *carpet hoist*.   This rigging

allows the counterweight to be controlled at the pinrail by an extra line so that when the flown object is down and the counterweight up, the extra line can be tied off, holding the counterweight up until it is again time to connect the lines to the scenic unit. Sometimes a large, bulky object such as a motor car is got off the stage floor by flying it. Here, too, the carpet hoist will come in handy since, when the car is released from the ropes, the counterweighted lines must not get away from the stagehands. The original production of *The Star Wagon* handled the old-fashioned car in this manner; other Broadway productions have flown such objects as buggies, fountains, and mechanical contraptions, with little or no difficulty.

One of the most interesting possibilities in connection with the flying of scenery is the use of drops. Even in theatres where the fly loft does not permit that drops be raised in view of the audience, these units can be *tripped*, that is, caught up by the next set of lines in front. Revivals of such plays as *The Rivals*, or other eighteenth-century drama, are extremely effective when the drops can go up and down before the audience and thus change the scene in an instant. The use of *drop holders* is to be recommended as a quick and certain method of fastening the drop to the pipe batten; the drop holders are attached to short ropes or chains which are snapped or tied to rings on the pipe batten. Another possibility is to fasten *batten clamps* to the pipe batten and to clamp the lower end to the wood batten of the drop. When a drop must be fastened to the floor to prevent its moving as people pass behind it, the *floor stay* will prove a useful device (page 150).

While a ceiling is better known as a form of trimming than it is as an example of scenery, it makes definite demands on the flying system. The roll ceiling must be lowered to the floor before it is struck; therefore, it is a difficult unit to handle if there is a scene shift from an interior to an exterior. However, by the use of special rigging, a book ceiling may be manipulated by three consecutive sets of lines without lowering it below the height of the setting. The center of the ceiling is attached directly to the center pipe by the use of three short *snatch lines;* the outer edges of the ceiling are attached to the outer pipes with snatch lines which are twice as long. At each point where the center pipe is tied, two very short

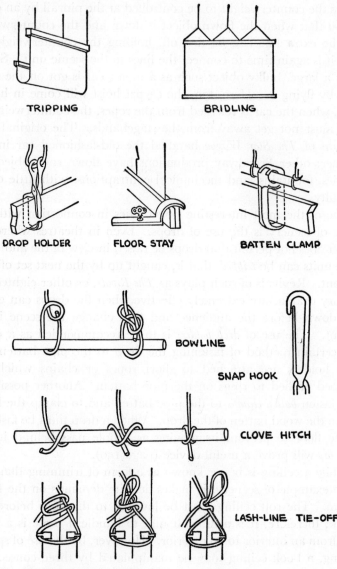

TRIPPING

BRIDLING

DROP HOLDER

FLOOR STAY

BATTEN CLAMP

BOWLINE

SNAP HOOK

CLOVE HITCH

LASH-LINE TIE-OFF

Fig. 52 *Tripping, the bridle, hanging hardware, and knots*

ropes with pulleys are tied on and the longer snatch lines, of course, go through these pulleys — six in all. Most of the weight is always on the center pipe. All manipulating must be done well above the set height; when the ceiling must be opened to a flat position, the outer pipes are raised and the entire unit lowered to rest on the top of the setting. When it is necessary to fold and strike the unit, these outer pipes are first lowered and then all three are raised.

When a set of lines does not hang in a position which will allow a bulky, flown unit to clear other nearby flown units, *breasting* may be the solution. This involves the temporary installation of one or two extra lines which can pull the unit slightly up or downstage so that it will be out of the way. Also it may be necessary to use *bridles*, loops of rope, at the top of extremely wide flown units in order to get the maximum of evenly distributed support from the lines.

The *knots* which are most commonly used on the stage are the *bowline* and the *clove hitch* since neither knot will slip and both are easy to untie. These knots are valuable both for tying ropes directly to wooden battens and for fastening units to pipe battens. One of the chief advantages of the bowline is that it may be tied in any position; the clove hitch is limited to use around a batten. In tying a bowline, two loops are involved, a large and a small. A small loop is first made by twisting the rope, the short end in front, at a point somewhat near the free end. Slack is allowed for the large loop before the free end is placed through the small loop, around the rope length, and back through the small loop. The clove hitch begins with carrying the short end of the rope around the pipe and crossing the long end before the second turn is made. After the second turn, the short end is placed between the second turning and the pipe. Thus, the short end and long end are parallel in direction and can be pulled tight. Since most stage lines should be equipped with *snap hooks*, except for the tying of heavy flown units, knots are used rather infrequently.

The chief disadvantage in the flying of scenery is the possibility of accident due to carelessness, miscalculation, and faulty equipment. Falling sandbags have been perhaps the worst offenders but now and then some larger unit falls. In theatres that are not equipped with pipe battens, it is usually the practice to use sand-

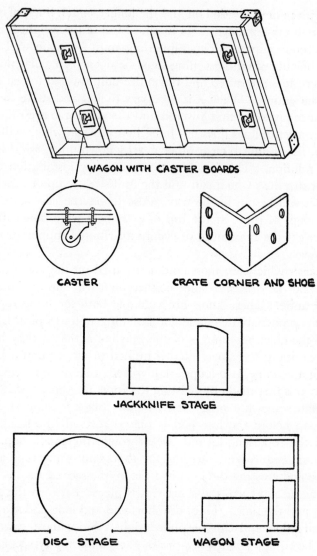

WAGON WITH CASTER BOARDS

CASTER

CRATE CORNER AND SHOE

JACKKNIFE STAGE

DISC STAGE

WAGON STAGE

Fig. 53 *The wagon, jackknife and disc stages*

bags to take care of free lines. It is never advisable to tie the lines directly to the ring which is attached to the sandbag; snap hooks save time and increase the safety element. There is particular danger in connection with the use of oversized sandbags such as are necessary for carpet hoists and the counterweighting of heavy units. Because of continual tension and friction, ropes must be checked frequently and replaced when they show signs of wear. Finally, although it is next to impossible to weigh all the units, there should never be any overloading of the grid. Technicians should not fly a heavy unit if it can be handled satisfactorily on the stage floor.

Rolling

In recent years there has been a definite trend toward the use of wagons as a quick scene-shifting device. Sometimes small wagons are moved in full view of the audience and at other times extremely large ones, of near-proscenium width, are moved while the curtain is down. Although some theatres are equipped with tracks and permanent wagons, most stage wagons are considered as special, extra equipment and can be pushed in any direction that is required. Wagons are not always silent, but they do permit the shifting of acting areas, complete with properties, in a matter of seconds.

Ideally, a theatre group should have in storage a number of small standard-sized wagons which can be fastened together to form large wagons when necessary; five by five feet or six by six feet are desirable sizes. Wagons can be attached to one another by the use of large mending plates screwed to the flooring and to the edges at the points of juncture. Tongue-and-groove lumber is especially good for the flooring, although regular $1'' \times 12''$ or $1'' \times 6''$ is usable. The use of $2'' \times 4''$ floor supports is mandatory if the equipment is to hold up for any length of time; $1'' \times 6''$ will do nicely for the outer edge of the wagon. If $1\frac{1}{2}''$ screws are used instead of nails, and a steel *chest and crate corner and shoe* is placed at each corner, the unit should be durable and solid.

Since the wagon must be moved silently and quickly by hand, the final success of the unit depends on the selection of ball-bearing, rubber-tired casters. Unless both the wheel and the swivel are packed in ball bearings, a heavily loaded wagon cannot be pushed easily in every direction. Six-inch casters are advisable so that the $1'' \times 6''$ edges can clear the floor by at least one-half inch. Four casters will be enough for a 6' by 6' wagon unless it is to carry extreme weight; regardless of the lumber, however, they must be placed so that they clear the supports in every position. Although a *caster board* is frequently recommended (an underneath plank to which pairs of casters are bolted), on small wagons, it is often sufficient to bolt the casters directly to the platform. In any event, if a caster comes loose, the only possibility is to remove the scenery and turn the unit over for repairs.

Although the chief difficulty involved with wagons has to do with the amount of offstage space that they require, ingenuity can often help determine how to use them. When the scene shop is separated from the stage by a large door, it is often possible to push a wagon into that area when it is not in use. If the proscenium opening is temporarily reduced in width and height by teaser and tormentors, technicians may "play checkers" with as many as four or five medium-sized wagons during one production. As a matter of fact, in present-day stagecraft, it is not at all uncommon for wagons to be closely associated with the players and their movements about the stage. Mielziner's use of three small wagons in *Dream Girl* always included actors as well as the simplified scenic units; these units were rolled on and off the stage, one at a time, to indicate new scenic locations. Even in *Inside U.S.A.*, Beatrice Lillie made quite a point of emphasizing amusingly her movements from the wagons to the stage floor.

However, if the wagon is not to be emphasized scenically, it is common to build up the front of the stage, just above the curtain line, to a height equal to that of the wagons. This built-up section is bevelled toward the audience and, when a wagon is butted against it, the patrons have the illusion that they are seeing the regular stage floor. This method is particularly popular when *jackknife* stages are used for quick scene changes. The jackknife wagon is anchored at one side of the proscenium and pivots at the fastening point so that it can swing offstage or on. This type of wagon is usually rectangular or semicircular in shape and its width is about that of the proscenium. The jackknife is an extremely adaptable device in that it can be used in combination with many other systems; for example, the use of two jackknife stages with flown scenery will allow for three different settings.

Very few theatres are equipped with permanent *revolving stages* or discs since such installations are so costly; therefore, when professional productions require such a device, most of the stage must be built up to a new level. If a revolving stage is to be placed dead center, this unit must be constructed like a round wagon with the edge exposed. It must be anchored at the center by means of a heavy flange and pipe, and be amply supported with heavy rubber-tired casters. Beginning with a bevelled edge at the curtain line, the stage floor is then built up around the disc, leaving just enough space for it to turn easily. Since such equipment is heavy, cumbersome, and very awkward to store, its non-professional use is infrequent. None the less, many Broadway productions have made excellent use of these temporarily installed discs. *I Remember Mama* used three of them and *Lady in the Dark* was able to shift from reality to the dream world by the use of four such devices; also, the ship's deck of *Mr. Roberts* gave way to the cabin scenes by the use of a revolving stage. Because of the labor involved, professional companies on tour often have to allow an extra day for setting up if their scene shifting is dependent on the revolving stage.

Breakaway Scenery

Occasionally a play demands the use of scenery which must separate in full view of the audience and disclose certain units placed further upstage. This is quite an interesting device for an audience to observe since the patrons enjoy the feeling of being "let in" on complicated scene shifts. The use of breakaway scenery is particularly effective when the exterior of a house rolls or is flown away and the rooms within are revealed, or when small wagons are pushed onto the stage and fitted together to complete a large spectacular unit. While relatively few plays are written with such scenery as a necessary part of the production, often designers and directors can find opportunities to use such scenery — thus adding to the scenic interest.

Sometimes the moving scenery is placed on two wagons or outriggers and moved on cue, one wagon to the Right and the other to the Left. An interesting effect might be obtained by using a third wagon in the center and having it move forward after the side wagons have left the center of the stage. In order to insure that the wagons will move to specified positions, grooves, made of strips of $1'' \times 1''$, may be helpful to guide the casters. Interesting breakaway effects can also be obtained by the use of jackknife stages; two jackknives, the combined widths of which are equal to that of the proscenium, can be anchored at either side of the arch and, on cue, swing away to disclose scenery that is already in place and to make way for units that are to be let in. Precision building is definitely necessary for scenery of this type since, when two units are together on the stage, they must seem as one.

Breakaway effects are often successful when simple sliding walls or frames are moved from in front of previously set scenery. Grooves of $1'' \times 1''$ can be fastened to the stage floor and the walls held erect by means of jacks that are equipped with casters and held perpendicular to the flat by means of hinged pieces of $1'' \times 3''$. Although low units will move especially smoothly in these improvised tracks, such a system has been used successfully with flats as high as sixteen feet. Sliding walls might be necessary for *Androcles and the Lion* if the setting made use of a square central unit equipped with a central pivot. In moving the unit around to show the rear side, it would be necessary to slide the connecting walls away and return them to their original positions after the central unit was turned; if this movement could occur in full stage light, the audience would be able to see the Emperor start through the doors and come out on the other side. The Radio City Center Theatre's production of *The Great Waltz* relied on revolving stages for spectacular breakaway effects which also included wagons and flown units. Today, Radio City Music Hall is perhaps best known for the similar stage effects which it frequently offers to its patrons.

The Tip Jack

When it is necessary to move an entire wall along the floor during a scene shift, and the shifting must be fast and the placement accurate, it is often wise to use tip (tilt) jacks for this purpose. If a

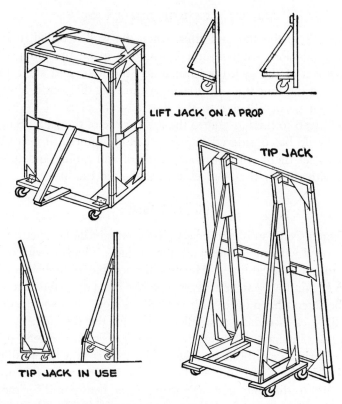

LIFT JACK ON A PROP

TIP JACK

TIP JACK IN USE

Fig. 54 *The tip jack and lift jack*

setting is made up of three walls, it may be possible to place two or three tip jacks on each wall so that the entire unit can be moved by two crew members. The downstage edges of the walls can then be lashed to the returns and the corners of the room lashed together. The chief problem in connection with the use of these units has to do with the amount of backstage space that is required for storing extremely large walls. Even though there is not sufficient space available to roll an entire wall, it may be possible to use the tip jack for smaller wall sections. Furthermore, the use of this device is particularly effective for heavy walls, complete with architectural trim, chimney pieces, and elaborate wall decorations.

The tip jack is built like a brace jack except for the slightly less than forty-five-degree angle at the base and the casters that are placed on the lower edge of the rail. The slanting stile is loose-pin-hinged to the flat and thus, when the wall is rolled, it is in a slanting position; when a unit is standing in an upright position, the bottom of the jack does not touch the floor and stage braces must hold the unit up. To make certain that the jack is always in a position perpendicular to the flat, a short piece of $1'' \times 3''$ is often hinged to the flat and to the lower edge of the jack. Since tip jacks should be considered as permanent equipment, it is advisable to construct them out of a good grade of white pine and to equip them with rubber-tired swivel casters of good quality.

The Lift Jack

When a scenic unit is so heavy that it cannot be fastened to a flat and moved with the entire wall, the lift jack, a lever device, can be used to good advantage. Heavy chimney pieces, cabinets, bookcases, or window seats, either as separate units or fastened to walls, can be lifted and moved with very little effort with such a device. The lift jack is usually a smaller unit than the tilt jack; it, too, is triangular in shape although it includes one caster instead of two. The contrivance is built so that the lumber is in a flat position in relation to the lifted unit — the short arm hinged to the upright piece and to the long arm. To prepare the heavy unit for moving, the only effort required is to push down on the long arm of the lever and to lock it, thus raising the built piece and allowing it to rest entirely on the casters. After the scenery or property is in the desired position on the stage, the arm is released and the heavy piece will be lowered to the floor, the casters no longer in use. Many units will require the use of at least two lift jacks — one on each end — and they must, of course, be manipulated in unison. Regardless of the number of jacks that are used, the object will always be in a perpendicular position and never tilted, as in the case of units which are moved by the tip jack.

Backstage Organization

Whatever types of scene-shifting devices are selected, every effort must be made to use these devices in ways that will conserve manpower and time. Even though ten minutes is allowed between acts for a scene shift, the work must be so organized and planned that each worker will have specific assignments in relation to the work as a whole. While audiences will usually accept emergencies gracefully, they do not like to be held up because inefficient stage-hands are unfamiliar with their duties and seem unable to realize the relationship that their work must necessarily have to the entire production. It is true that, while an occasional extravaganza makes demands with which a stage force actually cannot cope (Orson Welles's *Around the World*), most scene shifting can be re-hearsed sufficiently so that it will not delay the action of the play.

In order to avoid confusion, it is wise to appoint one or two definite "lead" workers or crew "heads" through whom all scene-shifting matters are cleared. Technicians can advise with crew heads in planning the over-all work, but definite authority must be in the hands of the chief technician. Also, it is a good idea to ex-plain the reasoning involved in connection with the various phases of the scene shifts — work that is intelligently accomplished stands a better chance to be accurate and consistent. Non-professional backstage workers sometimes feel that their work involves too much sitting about and waiting. When this is the case, the technical director must make them understand that, despite certain periods of inactivity, the crews are needed desperately at other times; the show could not be presented without them. Since the *set-up* and *strike* always seem remote during the run of a show, the crew work for a one-set production may be a bit harder to justify than the crew activities for a multi-set show.

Rehearsals will normally be classified as either *technical* or *dress* and, combined, should not be fewer than five. Unless a show is particularly complicated scenically, two technical rehearsals should be sufficient; special scene-shifting practice can always be held, if necessary, when the actors are not present. The final dress rehearsal should be as nearly like an actual performance as possible, with no stopping unless absolutely necessary. Obviously, then, these rehearsals are for the purpose of refining and sharpen-ing the details of the production but should not have to include work which would normally have been completed in the shops and the practice rooms. Crew members should spend this period of time in learning their various duties and in becoming proficient in the coordination of their work with that of their co-workers.

It is usually a good idea to use special mimeographed forms for the listing of the backstage duties so that no worker will ever be in doubt as to what is expected of him. First of all, an over-all list is prepared which analyzes the scene shifts or the set-up and strike into a number of definite *moves*. After it is decided how many crew members are necessary for a certain phase of the shifting, lists of individual duties are prepared. These lists need not be complicated in nature but must be complete, even to the use of stage braces and pegs. Unless the workers perform exactly the same duties at each rehearsal, there will be little opportunity to check the completion of the shift or to work out the necessary routine which will result in a saving of time and effort.

If the scene shift involves changing from an interior to an exterior setting, the first problem will be to raise the ceiling. When the unit is a book ceiling, at least four people will be required — two for the center and one each for the upstage and downstage lines. As soon as the ceiling clears the setting, the stage crew begins its work, removing first the backings and then the main walls. While the ceiling is being raised and the backings are removed, the property crew can place in the center of the stage objects which might be damaged by the moving of the flats. Actually, the question of which walls to remove first cannot be determined until certain main *traffic lanes* are established and *furniture storage areas* are selected. Great care must be observed not to *bury* anything that will be needed during the performance.

While one person can handle a light flat, it is usually advisable to assign two persons to a flat which is in any sense unwieldy. The current practice of fastening door trim, window trim, and shutters directly to the flat adds considerable weight, as do various decorations that are often attached to the walls and not struck during the shifts. When it comes to the moving of large wall areas made up of several flats battened together, the efforts of from three to six people will usually be required even though the use of tip jacks is involved. The moving of these heavy units requires a sort of team work since serious damage might result to the scenery if even one worker is careless.

After the stage is completely clear of scenery and properties, the crew "stands by" in readiness to manipulate or disconnect the ceiling — depending upon how it is rigged. If the stage is equipped with a roll ceiling, four people will be required to untie or unhook it from its downstage lines and to fly it from the upstage lines; if there is no fly loft, the roll ceiling can be stood against the back wall. Again, the members of the stage crew must work in unison in order to prevent possible damage to the ceiling and to make certain that there is no loss of time. Haste and speed are never profitable when they are at the expense of accuracy.

In setting up a simple exterior, four crew members should be able to take care of the work without any difficulty unless the shift must be extremely fast. Pairs of workers can set up such units as wood wings and house fronts after which the foliage borders and backdrop can be let in. Two people might be assigned to each side of the stage and, later on, all members might assist in *letting in* the units from the fly loft. All locations should be carefully *spiked* (painted or chalked on the floor) in order to avoid any form of guess work. Like most scene shifts, setting up the exterior requires that each person complete his work in the correct order in relation to the work of the others. For example, the shifting will be slowed up considerably if the foliage borders are let in before the wood wings and architecture are in place. Backstage workers who understand the reasoning involved in connection with their work are not likely to upset a scene-shifting routine.

Ordinarily, actors will not be on the stage while scenery is being shifted. But occasionally, during an especially fast shift, actors must be nearby. In such instances, actors must be given special instructions as to where to stand so that they will not be in any danger. The backstage areas can become very crowded when actors, electricians, property crews, and scenery crews are all at work. Indeed, it is not uncommon for one crew to stand aside until another crew has completed a certain part of its work. Furthermore, during a performance, the stage crew is often under a nervous tension and must, therefore, give special attention to cooperation and attitude. While temperament, anger, and unreasonable demands can ruin the morale of a stage crew, tremendous difficulties can be overcome if everyone is considerate and helpful. Backstage work may not always be fun, but it surely should *never* be drudgery.

PROJECTS AND EXERCISES

1. Examine a photograph of a stage setting from the point of view of the lashing problems. Make a rough floor plan of the setting and indicate where you think lashing was required.

2. Practice lashing in the scene shop or on the stage; use flats of various heights. After you have become somewhat skilled, prepare a list of suggestions for beginners.

3. How many stage braces would probably be needed to support an unbroken stage wall eighteen feet long? Why?

4. As you visit backstage after some professional or non-professional performance, note the uses of the brace jack. When you find the jack in use, try to find out the reasons for its selection.

5. Draw to scale a simple floor plan involving at least two long un-jogged walls. How many stiffening battens would you need and how long should each one be?

6. In the scene shop or on the stage, practice running small flats, one person to a flat. Increase the size of the flats up to $5'9'' \times 14'$. With the assistance of another student, run a folded book; a folded three-fold.

7. Float a regular flat on the stage floor; then float a window or a door flat. Be certain that there are no tools on the floor as you drop the flat. What are the results of floating the window flat?

8. Discuss the relative merits of running and flying for such a play as *The Streets of New York* or *Nellie, the Beautiful Cloak Model*. Would wagons be suitable for such productions?

9. Make a list of plays which would require the flying of some heavy three-dimensional unit. Could these plays be done on your stage? Why?

10. Which of the two types of ceiling would be the more satisfactory for use when producing the following: *The Late George Apley, Berkeley Square, The Three Sisters, The Innocents, The Alchemist, Thunder Rock*? Which of the above plays could be presented without ceilings? Give reasons for all selections.

11. Is there ever an occasion to use breasting or bridles on your stage? Explain in detail.

12. Examine the sandbags on your stage. How are they constructed and in what condition are they? Could you suggest any improvements to make them safer?

13. Using a theoretical set of six 6' by 6' wagons and four 3' by 6' wagons, show by means of a simple floor plan how you would arrange them to take care of a small box setting. How could they be used to hold two house units for an exterior setting?

14. Make a list of plays which might be presented in a style similar to that of *Dream Girl*. If this method could be used, how large would the wagons have to be?

15. What productions have you seen that have used revolving stages? How did the use of this device help the movement as a whole? What was the audience reaction?

16. The Broadway production of *Rat Race* used a large upper-floor section of a rooming house, enclosed by a gauze frame painted to resemble the exterior of the house. From time to time, the frame was raised to allow full visibility of the room. List a few plays that might use a variation of this method. Consider the use of at least one secondary playing area.

17. How many stagehands would be required to move a wall twenty-five feet wide by fourteen feet tall if the unit were placed on tip jacks?

18. Which of the following units might best be moved by the use of lift jacks: wardrobe, puppet theatre, automobile, window seat, counter, bookcase, and sofa?

19. Develop a simple all-inclusive chart which will show the backstage duties of a stage crew during the set-up of a one-set show.

20. For how many dress rehearsals does your group provide? What general rules of deportment are followed and how much time is usually allowed?

21. Describe in detail and in the correct order the necessary duties involved in shifting from an exterior to an interior.

22. Select a two-set play such as *The Madwoman of Chaillot* or *Life with Mother*. Draw simple floor plans which will indicate the number of solid walls involved. Attempt to estimate the number of crew members that would be required for satisfactory shifting.

6

The Styles of Scene Design

No MATTER how accurately the student may be able to classify scenery according to form, or how exact may be his knowledge of the various parts of the scenic unit, if he has no appreciation of the styles of scene design, he must always work somewhat blindly and without true understanding as to the real purpose of his finished product. Although the student is likely to be considerably perplexed when he first begins to use style terminology, he should not consider that he is dealing with the mysterious nor the esoteric. Fortunately, since most of the style terms have been borrowed from literature and painting, the beginner necessarily has some background in this connection. Despite the fact that these terms are often bandied about in hit-or-miss fashion, theatre students must make every effort to avoid such vague usage; the chances are that when a theatrical production offers an unfortunate mixture of various styles, at least some of the blame can be traced to the original production conference where inexact terms were used.

One of the chief reasons for confusion is the fact that seldom is one style found in its pure form; combinations of two or more styles are the rule rather than the exception. Unlike an easel painting, scenery must present a condensed and precise background effect which will interpret but not intrude. Since scenery is, at all times, subservient to the play itself and to the actors, it can never demand the focus-of-attention that applies to easel paintings, nor can it become so close to an audience as the style of a long novel is to a reader. However, even painting and writing styles are combined to the extent that a finished product is sometimes difficult to label. Students who have attempted to classify literary styles and have been confronted with various combinations should feel no special confusion when similar combinations are noted in connection with stage scenery.

Naturalism

Pure, naturalistic scenery is seldom found in present-day theatre; it is only in occasional films that such stressing of excessive detail can be noted. The naturalistic style, as applied to the stage picture, implies that every possible effort has been made to load the setting with all the objects and three-dimensional or painted detail

Fig. 55 *A room containing naturalistic detail which might be suitable for a production of a play such as "A Doll's House"*

that it can stand up to. Most of such decorations, obviously, would serve very little real purpose since they might bewilder rather than define and interpret. The cluttered stage room shown on page 165 would be distracting to an audience which was watching such a play as *Ghosts* or *A Doll's House;* although the room is authentic as to period, it neither explains the play nor is selective in its use of detail. A stage setting is so much larger than an actual room that a naturalistically treated stage kitchen, for example, might contain sufficient supplies and equipment to feed a family of twenty and, at the same time, suggest a display room.

David Belasco headed the naturalistic school in this country, and many interesting stories are related concerning his insistence upon minute detail. He once bought an entire cheap boarding-house room — complete with wallpaper, architectural trim, and furnishings — for his production of *The Easiest Way*. Actually, when the room was placed on the stage it did not prove to be sufficiently theatrical, but the naturalistic intent was there none the less. On another occasion Belasco had the aroma of coffee forced out through the ventilating system at the same time that the actors were drinking coffee on the stage. A Belasco cabinet was likely to contain a carload of ornaments, and his tables were often littered with objects, very few of which were necessary or useful. Whatever Belasco used, however, had to be the real thing and no near-right substitute would serve; a Belasco kitchen often showed real food cooking on the stove and a real icebox complete with ice. When such naturalistic touches are used today, audiences seem to be impressed, but it is unlikely that they would appreciate a great profusion of such details within one production.

Interesting analogies can be drawn using novelists and painters as a means of comparison. Theodore Dreiser and Thomas Hardy, for example, are well known for the detail in which they have set down every thought, speech, and movement of their characters. Since many of these thoughts and speeches are often extremely uninteresting, the more streamlined observations of such writers as John O'Hara or J. D. Salinger seem better suited to the times. So-called "calendar art" painting may show every detail, sometimes to the point of being almost photographic, but it does not take an art critic to inform most people of the shortcomings of such work. These naturalistic methods are in no better repute today than is stage scenery of the same sort; even though we find examples of this style mixed with today's realism, a little of it goes a long way, indeed.

The naturalistic backgrounds found in motion pictures are sometimes legitimate and often successful, especially when they focus on meaning instead of detail — when they tend a bit toward realism. Everyone knows of the tremendous amount of money that is available for film productions and of the great number of people who are employed to prepare the backgrounds. An historical film can offer exact duplications of buildings from other centuries and the results will usually seem authentic. The recent trend toward filming on actual "location" is a further example of the type of naturalism which is especially suited to the films. Because of these elaborate film productions, the "typical moviegoer" is not usually impressed by the realistic scenery that he sees on the stage and he is quick to suggest that the scenery seems incomplete and unconvincing.

Movie naturalism can sometimes be carried to ridiculous extremes, however. Some years ago, a certain film had, as its finale, a technicolor view of the hero and heroine beneath apple trees in full bloom. To heighten this effect, apple blossom scent was forced through the ventilating system. The results were somewhat surprising in that the patrons usually looked to the floor to see if someone had dropped part of her shopping. When naturalism is handled intelligently, however, it has a rightful place in the films since it requires little or no imagination on the part of the audience; film audiences, for the most part, want to see clearly rather than to worry about illusion or aesthetic distance.

Realism

Since the present-day theatre seems to be mainly concerned with realism, it is only natural that the realistic scenic style should predominate on Broadway. Although realism in the theatre has its roots in naturalism, realism stresses the element of selectivity and we get not a photographer's view but a clean-cut, sharpened version with the unnecessary details removed. Realism does not

Fig. 56 *A realistic background for George M. Cohan's "Pigeons and People" — a bachelor's apartment in one of the contemporary styles*

imply austerity nor severity but rather suggests a tight, well-knit quality which reinforces the stage picture but does not intrude in any manner. As opposed to naturalism, realism deals with needed essentials, whether decorative or atmospheric. While realistic scenery must never look bare, the selectivity that has been employed may be forthright rather than sly and evasive. Although the contemporary feeling of the *Pigeons and People* setting above necessarily dictates limited furnishings and décor, the room is intended to show a realistic bachelor-apartment as conceived by an interior designer. Theatre patrons should understand what such a realistic design is attempting to accomplish; furthermore, they must set aside all comparisons with the films.

Three dimensions are normally associated with realism although, whenever paint can serve as a satisfactory substitute for building, technical problems will be simplified. Skillfully painted door panels surrounded by three-dimensional trim may, if properly lighted, present quite a realistic effect. Similarly, a painted cornice, at least on the center wall, will decrease the over-all weight of the scenery and, even though the audience realizes that the cornice is painted, the results can be considered as realistic. Realism is a matter of intent and results rather than of methods and comparisons; illusion need never be sacrificed at the expense of simplification.

Naturalistic touches can often be found within realistic settings; although usually these inclusions serve specific purposes, occasionally they seem a bit incongruous and unnecessary. The dirt floor of *Tobacco Road*, for example, presented a marked contrast to the painted scenery. While the use of antique documents and letters in *The Barretts of Wimpole Street* was not distracting, it surely would seem to be an unnecessary touch of naturalism. As a matter of fact, the current professional practice of using antique furniture for period plays smacks of naturalism in addition to creating almost constant repairing problems. Even though *The Voice of the Turtle* kitchen was trimmed and dressed as selectively as possible, the running water and electric icebox would have been especially interesting to Belasco audiences. Some naturalistic touches, then, may attract attention which may be out of proportion to their real value as an aid to the pictorial effectiveness of the realistic setting.

Realistic scenery has been very successfully used on Broadway in such productions as *John Loves Mary*, *O Mistress Mine*, *State of the Union*, *The Fatal Weakness*, and *Light up the Sky*. While no one of the above plays required a great amount of subtle interpretation, in each production set dressings were kept to a minimum and the basic settings were not overloaded with detail. On the other hand, such realistic plays as *Angel Street*, *The Innocents*, *Another Part of the Forest*, *The Little Foxes*, and *Come Back, Little Sheba* demanded and received unusual selective scenic treatment, each individual item and motif helping to interpret the script.

Occasionally, realism is simplified to the extent that it approaches symbolism. In other words, one scenic unit or property unit is recognizable as a part of, or representative of, an entire location: a stack of wooden crates could symbolize a loading wharf, or a row of steamer chairs, a ship's deck. Such simplified realism almost always implies the use of special lighting which will focus attention on a small portion of the stage. Experimental, simplified realism is often intelligently conceived and sometimes ingenious, but it is seldom exciting; furthermore, if the results are not sharp and positive, it may even confuse an audience. Regardless of its use, however, students must realize that symbolism is not limited to its association with realism but is likely to crop up in connection with many of the other scenic styles.

Impressionism

Pure impressionism seldom appears in the theatre today although it is often found combined with the other styles. In painting circles, impressionism is commonly understood to be the painter's idealistic (or romantic?) impression of what he sees or what he thinks he sees; mood, therefore, plays an important part. Since the impressionist *interprets* what he sees, there is considerable likelihood that some emotion is represented and that the emotion will carry over to the onlooker. Theatrical impressionism interprets and de-explains the details of realism and while there is often considerable selectivity, the characteristic subtlety and indirect method of painting is of primary interest to the designer.

The Katherine Hepburn production of *As You Like It* made bountiful use of handsomely painted backdrops and wood wings which were obviously emotionally idealistic impressions of the forest — complete with non-detailed painting; the illustration shown below is a similarly impressionistic view of a forest. Mielziner's use of scrim in *A Streetcar Named Desire* was impressionistically realistic in intent and his sparse use of detail was noteworthy; the

Fig. 57   *Impressionistic drop-and-wing scenery with a forest locale*

location was recognizable, yet the transparent walls and sketchy trim were atmospheric rather than literal. This production made interesting use of precise area lighting as well, a lighting method which is often associated with impressionism on the stage. Mr. Mielziner's somewhat representative scenery for *Winterset* was also impressionistic in feeling since we were here presented with impressions of recognizable places — not with actual locations.

If a play is episodic in form and definitely concerned with mood and atmosphere — but at the same time offers characters, situations, and locale which are somewhat recognizable — the chances are that impressionism, combined with some other style, will be a possibility. Obviously, *Dear Ruth* is not in this category, nor are *Claudia, Command Decision,* nor *The Heiress.* However, such plays as *Family Portrait, I Remember Mama,* or *The Glass Menagerie* offer excellent opportunities. Very few plays call for and demand impressionistic scenic treatment; designers with a feeling and liking for this style will have to be on guard in order not to include such touches when they are neither needed nor desirable.

Expressionism

Many theatre students are inclined to consider the expressionistic style as merely distortion — not realizing that scenery of this style must show the mentality, the emotions, and the point of view of the characters within a play. While expressionism often involves distortion, exaggeration is as likely to be from the point of view of color as of line. Like impressionism, expressionism turns to realism for its framework; the source of any distortion must be immediately recognizable. Since the distortion of such scenery may express either an intellectual or an emotional upheaval, the designer must make certain that every change of proportion and shape is motivated by the lines of the play and is never arbitrarily a pictorial problem. The distorted lines in the setting for the expressionistically stylized production of *The Inspector General* shown on page 172 were indicative of the fantastic situation presented by the plot. The Meyerhold production of the same play made use of innumerable oversized skeleton doors for similar expressionistic reasons.

Expressionism is ideally suited for plays containing dream se-

Fig. 58 *An expressionistic minimum setting, on a wagon, for an interpretative production of "The Inspector General"*

quences and representations of the subconscious: the *Beggar on Horseback* has amusingly horrible dreams as to what it would be like to marry into a certain rich family; the *Lady in the Dark* brings back her past from her psychoanalyst's couch; the *Dream Girl* imagines herself as having all sorts of strange experiences. While expressionism often presents such frivolous versions of the workings of the mind, this style is perhaps most successful when it is called upon to point out the hidden meanings of a more serious tragic play. The backgrounds for the Broadway production of *Crime and Punishment* (with Gielgud) were slanted and distorted to an extent that its insanity was made clear from the start. A great many of the satirical scenic effects in the original production of *The Adding Machine* were obtained mainly by an expressionistic use of scale and line. The workings of *Christopher Blake's* subconscious were similarly illustrated by means of exaggerated proportion and color.

Although, at first glance, many plays seem appropriate for expressionistic treatment, the designer must be extremely careful not to read more into a script than the dialogue or the director calls for. A realistic play, for example, which deals with the mentally unbalanced, would probably be better off without specific expressionistic support from the scenery. In such a play as *Outward Bound*, a distorted ship would be wrong since the audience, for a time, thinks the characters are on a regular passenger ship. In the revival of a melodrama an amusing distortion of line might be handled in a stylistic manner as to period and locale; if the backgrounds attempt to penetrate to any hidden meanings, the scenery is probably on the wrong bent.

Expressionistic painting and scene design, then, are extremely adaptable and purely creative methods rather than highly mannered simplifications of reality — and, like impressionism, are often found in combination with other styles. The expressionistic stylization such as was presented in *The Cabinet of Dr. Caligari* is an important design landmark in the history of the films. The same combination of styles is also often suitable for topical musical comedies and revues although, in such cases, the emphasis is frequently on the style. Surrealism, often classified as a weird form of expressionism, relies almost completely on the subconscious; in its pure form, involving such items as strange torsos and great expanses of sand, it has been offered to ballet audiences a time or two.

Expressionistic symbolism, of course, is usually an extremely simplified distortion with concentration on one central scenic unit. While the settings for *Johnny Johnson*, for example, employed some use of symbolism, the effect was mainly of stylized expressionism. Such expressionistic combinations are actually more interesting than the style would be on its own since pure expressionism could be so startling that it might detract from the production as a whole.

Stylization

Many theatre patrons are inclined to apply the term "stylized" to any type of scenery that is not realistic. While it is true that stylization is quite often combined with the various non-realistic styles, it is necessary to have a more exact understanding of its meaning. In the main, stylization is a method of exaggeration which emphasizes a conventionalized style of decoration in some individualistic manner. In order to provide suitable themes for stylistic emphasis, the designer uses such interpretive means as a period, a decorative motif, an era, a style of painting, or a method of staging. Whatever theme he chooses will necessarily be treated somewhat abstractly and with objective application.

Fig. 59 *A light-spirited, funereal stylization for Noel Coward's "Family Album"*

The first noted example of stylization on the American stage was the work of Robert Edmond Jones (1915) for *The Man Who Married a Dumb Wife*. Since this design is generally considered to be our first example of genuine, complete scene design, the beginnings of stylization in the American theatre can be dated accordingly. Since that time, stylization has become increasingly popular, especially for productions which are in the lighter vein. Lee Simonson's *Amphytrion 38* scenery presented stylization of Greek architecture and decorative motifs — a suitable solution for so stylish a play. Other examples of stylization include: Lemuel Ayers's sketchy, indicative designs for *The Pirate*, the same designer's Grant Wood-inspired *Oklahoma* scenery, Howard Bay's Currier and Ives *Up in Central Park* backdrops, and Jo Mielziner's version of the flora and fauna of the *South Pacific*. While the above-mentioned productions represent more than one style of scenery, in each case the conventionalized decoration is perhaps the most important feature of the scenery.

The use of such decorative motifs as shells, flowers, and ribbons might be an important feature in the stylization of a frivolous production set in the Louis XV period. Such decorations, enlarged and given unusual color treatment, would clearly point out the style and thus definitely indicate the essence of the production;

similar use of different motifs would be effective for *The Rivals* or for any other eighteenth-cent⟨ury⟩ Oversized, distorted Chinese motifs should ⟨…⟩ ylized, slightly expressionistic production of ⟨…⟩ s were the more traditional Jones's stylization ⟨…⟩

Exaggerated use of the primitive color combinations and bizarre decorative motifs of Southern Europe would be especially striking for such musicals as *The Chocolate Soldier* or *The Bartered Bride* since the scenery for those non-real productions should hardly be expected to probe very deeply into the minds of the characters. Noel Coward's *Family Album*, a play ⟨…⟩ 174), could be set with black and white striped ⟨…⟩ amusing funereal aspect. Tomato-red uphols⟨…⟩ ure would add a stylized note from the point ⟨…⟩ particularly if the costumes were all in black a⟨…⟩

Many directors and designers are o⟨…⟩ nion that stylization is especially well suited to plays for children. This is likely to be true if the play is so sophisticated that it appeals both to adults and young people (*The Blue Bird, Alice in Wonderland, Peter Pan*, etc.). However, this style would seem too artificial for the general run of children's theatre where the subtlety of the scenic effects is often secondary to the story. There are also those who hold that stylization is not successful for serious plays. Even though present-day serious drama is perhaps best handled by the use of realism, stylized décor — cold, formal, and austere in feeling — is suitable for many Greek tragedies. Also, such Shakespearean tragedies as *Othello, Julius Caesar, Romeo and Juliet*, and *Anthony and Cleopatra* have been given similar stylistic scenic treatment on Broadway within recent years.

Stylization is so difficult to place within definite confines that many designers conclude that, combined with other styles, there are few limits to its usage. No sooner does one state that stylization does not belong within a particular production than a Broadway showing proves otherwise. It seems safe to state, however, that certain designers (Jones, Simonson, Chaney, etc.) have a special feeling for this style of scenery and can usually be depended upon to turn out extremely decorative exaggerations.

Formalism

Pure formalism is seldom found in the professional theatre of today; however, this style is frequently combined with other styles to provide backgrounds for presentational productions. Formalism is particularly concerned with such scenic units as arches, columns, steps, platforms, screens, and draperies, and with the playing areas that these units can provide. Since formalistic designs make little attempt to locate a play or to set the mood and atmosphere, the use of color often becomes a costume problem. The scenic effect, then, is one of neutral plasticity, with nothing on the stage which will detract from the actors or help the audience to analyze the play. Although the setting for *Antigone* below, for example, may attempt to suggest the exalted aspects of the play by means of line and mass, the background serves mainly as a formalistic framework for the play.

Nowadays, Shakespeare is occasionally presented on stages which are reasonably accurate replicas of those of late-sixteenth-century English theatres. In such cases, the producer's aims are

Fig. 60 *A setting for Sophocles' "Antigone" providing a formalistic background emphasizing primitive Greek architecture*

probably formalistic, but it is questionable as to whether or not the backgrounds completely recede as they did in Shakespeare's times. If certain architectural liberties have been taken with the design of these backgrounds, the scenic effect may be one of stylized formalism — with emphasis on the decorative, pictorial qualities. In like manner, special reproductions of Greek and Roman stages, or Oriental stages, can never guarantee that a production will be purely formalistic; audiences may well be attracted by the novelty of the production.

Formalism, in its various combinations, is no special possession of the experimental theatre; Broadway has been particularly successful with such scenery — especially in multi-set productions where continuous action is the chief technical problem. The Anderson-Evans production of *Macbeth* used a stylized formalization which permitted a number of different acting areas. From the point of view of design, the revolving rock unit in Margaret Webster's production of *The Tempest* was an interesting combination of formalism and stylization, at the same time offering considerable variety. Mielziner's formal background for *Anne of the Thousand Days* took on impressionistic qualities as well, mainly because of the lighting. The New York production of *Lute Song* was so very decorative that many in the audience were probably unaware of the formalistic nature of the main framework. The Galantière version of *Antigone*, as staged by Katherine Cornell, made generous use of stage draperies, the stark dignity of which was completely in accord with the script. Robert Edmond Jones's exquisite sculptured column-arches for *Lucrece* were almost pure formalism, despite the fact that a number of important changes of large properties took place before them.

It is difficult to conceive of the realistic use of formalism unless, perhaps, a play happens to be set before some edifice with classic proportions; in that case the realistic elements of the background would take on considerable importance and hardly permit the scenery to be unobtrusive. Some authorities, however, are certain that they see a sort of formalism in arena staging, despite the fact that realistic plays are most often presented in such theatres, and scenic effects are sometimes attempted. In the traditional theatre, when formalization is used with realistic intent, the realism usually takes precedence and the formalistic nature of the design is more or less disguised.

⌈Symbolism, on the other hand, combines readily with formalism and, conceivably, each might contribute an equal tonal quality to the production. As a matter of fact, symbolism is often an integral part of formalized stylization since, however non-representative the décor may be, it is rarely meaningless. In combination with the use of space staging and concentrated beams of light, certain conventionally accepted objects might even be considered as symbolistic formalizations which could stand for complete locations, i.e., a lamp post for a street, a blackboard for a school room, or an easel and canvas frame for a painter's studio. Such simplification is, of course, best suited for multi-set productions where considerable variety is required during the playing time.⌋

Theatricalism

As the name implies, theatricalism is theatre in its pure sense, with little scenic attempt at realism or subtle interpretations of the motives of the characters. Since backdrops and wings are frequently associated with this style, paint, rather than building, is the logical means of expression. During the nineteenth century and earlier, theatrical scenery was often so seriously and elaborately painted, complete with three dimensions and shadows, that there seems little doubt that naturalism was the intent. Today, however, theatricalism takes on a different slant in that painting is seldom literal; instead, the effort is to point up the style of the painting and to make clear that the artificiality is more important than even a suggestion of realism. The backdrop for *The Rivals* shows the important wall decorations of the room plus a number of pieces of furniture painted directly onto the backdrop. Even though this type of painting may be skillful and the lighting advantageous, it is not likely that an audience would confuse such a painted backdrop with a three-dimensional room.

Present-day Broadway theatricalism is usually quite broad and often combined with stylization or impressionism. The stylized theatricalism of the *Oklahoma, Bloomer Girl,* and *Up in Central Park* backdrops is somewhat representative of today's trend in musical

Fig. 61 *Highly mannered theatrically painted frames and backdrop for "The Rivals"*

comedy backgrounds. This combination has also been used pleasingly for such Shakespearean comedies as *A Winter's Tale, The Merry Wives of Windsor, Twelfth Night, As You Like It,* and *The Taming of the Shrew.* Professional designers have also caught the flavor of some of the witty plays of the Restoration (*Love for Love, The Country Wife*) and the eighteenth-century English satiric plays (*The Rivals, The School for Scandal, The Critic*).

During the first quarter of the twentieth century, vaudeville theatres were usually equipped with painted backdrops representing various locations — streets, parks, beaches, hotel lobbies, and the like. The drops were painted with great detail and the attempt was not to suggest painting styles but rather to represent pictorially exact places by means of paint — like huge, colored photomurals. At one time, vaudeville backdrops were taken seriously, but later there was a tendency to bang them about; often, comedians would try to open painted doors, drink from painted fountains, sit on painted chairs, or pick painted flowers. Theatrical painting is seldom emphasized in such fashion today; elaborate and decorative backdrops are usually recognized and accepted for what they are. However, Broadway's use of realistically painted backdrops as window backings should not be confused with theatricalism **as a style.**

179

Examples of this style of design are sometimes found in other forms of scenery besides drops and wings; profiles or silhouettes also can be painted theatrically. Although the uninteresting, painted box settings of the early twentieth century need not be imitated today, still — if a revival of a play of that period should be attempted — highly stylized, theatrically painted box settings would add considerable comment to the production. Since the success of fragmentary settings usually depends upon the use of paint, theatricalized versions of these scenic forms should be of special interest to the designer. Whatever form of theatrical scenery is used, and regardless of whether the painting technique is laborious or relatively free, today's audiences will usually accept paint for what it is.

Constructivism

Constructivism was first observed in the Russian theatre directly after World War I, under the sponsorship of Meyerhold. While this type of scenery has a number of aims and purposes, the chief reason for its development probably had to do with the scarcity of materials. Pure constructivist scenery depended largely upon rough, uncovered frames, scaffolding, ramps, and steps, completely non-decorative in design. Like formalism, this style, in its early days, attempted to provide a great variety of playing areas and levels, meaningless but functional. Some of the Russian constructivist designs were so weird that they must have detracted from the production far more than would have been the case with decorative units.

Meyerhold's so-called bio-mechanical productions often stressed the importance of engineering, mechanical devices, and machinery — pictorially and otherwise. His actors had to be extremely versatile as he frequently required them to apply trapeze and tumbling techniques. However, not all Russian constructivism was carried to such extremes; sometimes this style was agreeably combined with formalism or stylization. The constructivist formalism of the setting for the Moscow Art Musical Studio production of *Lysistrata*, for example, had considerable style despite its sketchy framework. Antonin Heythum's well-known house frame

Fig. 62 *Skeleton frames for a constructivist version of "The Skin of Our Teeth"*

for *Desire Under the Elms* would probably shock a New Englander; nevertheless, it provides a bit more than the minimum scenic essentials for the play. Another example, Alexandra Exter's design for *The Merchant of Venice*, uses constructivist units but decorates the units so that they take on a slight suggestion of locale.

On Broadway, the structural honesty of Mielziner's *Death of a Salesman* gables and Aline Bernstein's frames for *The Dybbuk* have generally been admired; such structural designs have their roots in architecture rather than in engineering, and help to interpret the play rather than to suggest the smart-aleck whims of a producer. Mielziner's attractive, polished frames for *Two on an Island*, placed against a drapery background rather than a bare stage, were at the same time functional and indicative. Such a play as O'Neill's *Dynamo* naturally suggests a sort of mechanically constructivistic décor; Lee Simonson's settings for the New York production were in this spirit. The use of a bare stage, ladders, planks, and rehearsal furniture for *Our Town* can be classified as constructivism although the original production of that play illustrated certain other styles as well.

Combinations of constructivism and other styles should be especially appropriate for multi-set plays which stress ideas rather than characterizations. Distorted constructivistic touches might

181

also be possible for expressionistic plays like *The Adding Machine*, *R.U.R.*, and *From Morn to Midnight*. Such settings might easily be as attractive as certain constructivistically stylized designs which, of course, are pleasing mainly because of the stylization. It is conceivable that contemporary plays like *Dream Girl*, *The Time of Your Life*, or *The Skin of Our Teeth* (p. 181) might be staged by means of modified constructivistic indications. Since the Wilder play is purposefully confusing as to time and place, and the house is merely a framework as a contrast to the out-of-doors, the use of stylized constructivism should be suitable. Generally speaking, however, this style has a very limited use, either in its pure form or in combination with the other styles, and any attempt to force it on an unlikely play can lead only to confusion.

The designer's use of the scenic styles must necessarily depend upon the script itself and the method of production that has been selected by means of conferences; special preferences and tastes must be subordinated to the finished product. Designers may unconsciously be influenced by certain scenic trends of the times, but these trends must never be followed arbitrarily. For example, although during the past decade, paint — in all its glory — has pleased many audiences, there are occasional productions which are not helped by paint. If a designer has a particular fondness for the use of stylized, painted, decorative motifs or realistically painted landscapes, he must be on guard not to use these styles in productions where they do not suit. Similarly, a designer who favors impressionistic forms must realize that his own impressions are less important than the requirements of the play.

A knowledge and understanding of the scenic styles is necessary so that all those concerned with a production will speak the same language at the conferences. If realism means naturalism to the director, stark selectivity to the designer, and impressionism to the costumer, the final results can be most confusing. Since such confusion sometimes exists on Broadway, it is not surprising to find it in the non-professional theatre as well. Although occasionally a unified production results despite misuse of terminology, if the designer and the director are vague as they work together, they will be even more vague as they work separately. Even if the styles of acting within a production vary considerably, at least the pictorial elements — scenery, costumes, and lighting — should be in agreement since they are more tangible and easier to control.

Whatever styles are selected, the process is one of indirection; the designer should begin with a clear mind so that style can be the outcome rather than the point of departure. In many cases, plays suggest one style so clearly that there can be little question as to choice. Other plays, however, seem to offer so many design opportunities that, before a solution is reached, it will be necessary to evaluate and combine, discard and re-apply, most of the scenic styles. While the final results may not please everyone, at least the choice will be clean-cut and sound, and the production will tie together pictorially.

PROJECTS AND EXERCISES

1. Watch a film, contemporary or period in setting, from the point of view of naturalistic detail. Make a list of the items and decorations that serve no useful purpose.

2. Examine one of the recent Burns Mantle collections to note which plays on the "ten best" list include the use of realism. Try to find pictures of the settings for these productions. What decorative details might have been added to each setting to give a cluttered and junky appearance?

3. Which of the following plays might be treated with impressionistic scenic indications in combination with some of the other styles: *First Lady*, *The Blind* (Maeterlinck), *The Women*, *The Skin of Our Teeth*, *Shadow and Substance*, *On Borrowed Time*, *Anna Christie*, *Elizabeth the Queen*?

4. List ten comedies in which some expressionistic combination of scenic styles might be used in certain scenes. Make a similar list of six serious plays. Be able to explain in detail why you think these combinations are suitable.

5. Examine pictures of at least ten recent musicals, noting the stylistic tendencies. Try to find pictures of musical comedies of the first twenty years of the century. Do you find any evidences of stylization?

6. What would be your train of thought as you decide upon such elements as scale, proportion, and decorative motifs for formalized

stylizations of such plays as *The Imaginary Invalid* or *Ralph Roister Doister?*

7. Draw simple floor plans for formalistic productions of Greek, Elizabethan, and Oriental plays. What similarities do all three floor plans have in common? What opportunities might there be for the use of symbolism?

8. Of the following professional productions, which offered examples of broad theatrical painting? Which of the plays used realistically painted backdrops and backings? Which were completely three dimensional? *The Iceman Cometh, The Innocent Voyage, Jacobowsky and the Colonel, A Bell for Adano, Home of the Brave, Blithe Spirit, Daughters of Atreus, St. Helena, Victoria Regina, The Great God Brown.*

9. Post-World-War-I Russian constructivism enthusiasts seemed to feel at home with Shakespeare or such contemporary American dramatists as O'Neill. What would you think of this style for Molière, Maxwell Anderson, Noel Coward, or George Kelly?

10. By the use of a simple floor plan, show how you could stage a complicated melodrama in constructivistic fashion. Suppose that the play involved the following technical difficulties: a tenement fire, a drowning, a noise race, and a cops-and-robbers chase.

7

Scene Design Procedures

THE VARIOUS DISCUSSIONS involved in the planning and preparing of scenic drawings and designs usually concern the entire staff of a non-professional theatre at one time or another. The very first meeting or conference, however, may involve only the director and the scene designer and will, in all probability, cover chiefly the general requirements of the play, the style of the production, the openings in the settings, and the minimum properties which will be required. Obviously, at this point the director and the scene designer must know the play well and each should contribute ideas; if either the director or the designer takes an "I want this, and I want that" attitude, the meeting is not a conference. Although it is not possible to begin these discussions without pre-conceived ideas concerning a production, it certainly should not be impossible to discard some of the ideas when better ones are suggested.

Since the more technical aspects of the production cannot be settled until specific floor plans have been selected, there is no

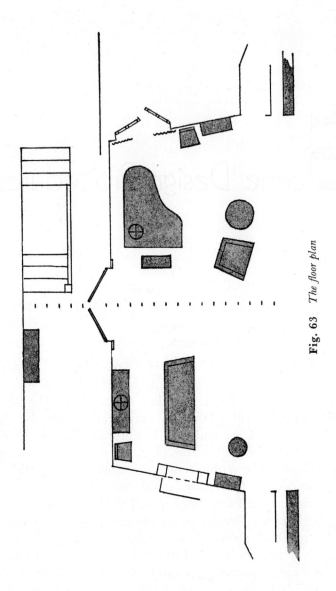

Fig. 63 *The floor plan*

186

reason why the lighting expert or the technical director should sit in on this first meeting; similarly, unless special emphasis is to be placed on costuming, the costume designer will not be needed until a later meeting. A close working relationship is desirable at this point and the presence of extra staff members may serve to confuse the issues at this stage. Unfortunately, as the actual work on a production gets into full tilt, the designer and the director become so busy that they will have little opportunity to continue working together; hence, if they do not start with perfect understanding and agreement, the final results may be questionable.

The Plan

After the important angles of the production have been discussed, the next step is for the designer to prepare a *floor plan* (ground plan) drawn to scale; this plan must show the arrangement of all the important features of the setting as they would appear as one looks down to the floor from the fly loft. Certain directors are well equipped to think in terms of floor plans while others will have difficulty understanding these space and plane relationships. In most cases, however, the openings in the setting and the placement of the furniture are suggested by the director — the scene designer later develops these basic requirements into plans and finished designs. The first floor plans are necessarily roughly drawn, possibly on graph paper, and a number of them will no doubt be discarded before the finished scale drawing is completed.

So that there will be no misunderstanding as to the placement of the setting on the stage, it is advisable to draw the floor plan within a scale drawing of the actual plan of the stage. This floor plan of the stage should include indications of the placement of rigging, wall protrusions, the lighting controlboard, floor pockets, traps, stairs, loading doors, and various cupboards. In order to help conserve the designer's time, it is well to have a supply of these printed stage plans on hand so that he can concentrate immediately on the actual floor plan of the stage setting.

If the floor plan is to be accurate, the designer must be supplied with suitable drafting equipment. There follows a minimum list which students should find useful although most designers would consider this list as a point of departure:

An 18″ × 26″ drawing board
A 26″ T square with plastic edges
An architect's scale rule, flat or triangular
An 8″ 45-degree plastic triangle
A 10″ 30-60-degree plastic triangle
2H and HB pencils
A compass and divider
A sandpaper pad
An eraser
Drawing paper, 18″ × 24″
Thumbtacks or Scotch drafting tape

This equipment should be of good quality although it is not necessary for the individual pieces to be of the de luxe variety. The designer will usually find it to his advantage to work on a large well-lighted table where he can have all his equipment easily at hand.

Most students have no difficulty developing skill in the use of simple drafting equipment. Since the finished drawing must be precise, sharp, and clean-cut, inexperienced designers must often give almost as much attention to the use of the drawing tools as to the plan itself. The following list of specific cautions should assist the designer to prepare drawings that are accurate and satisfying as to appearance:

1. Always use the same edge of the drawing board, and the upper edge of the T square.
2. All perpendicular lines must be drawn with the triangle placed against the T square.
3. Use the scale rule for measurements only and never for drawing lines.
4. Draw lines forward but never backward.
5. Never use the same thumbtack holes twice or use strips of Scotch tape the second time.
6. Keep pencil carefully sharpened at all times.

These rules apply to any kind of drawing-board work, regardless of whether it is a floor plan, an elevation, or a working drawing for the builders. Furthermore, if the scale rule is not used correctly, there are likely to be many construction difficulties.

The actual floor plan of a box setting usually begins with the returns, showing their relationship to the tormentor and to the setting proper. While some designers prefer to draw the wall lines as thicker than a pencil line, sufficient accuracy can be assured with the thinner lines. If the doors and windows have three-dimensional thickness, this should be indicated on the floor plan; other trim (paneling, mopboards, cornices) need not be drawn. All backings, whether of the standing or hanging variety, must be shown. Stage draperies, ground rows, and set pieces must be similarly drawn.

The floor plan must also show the important pieces of furniture in their correct relationship to the walls and the openings of the setting. Exact furniture sizes cannot always be shown on the plan but it is better that a maximum-sized piece be indicated so that, later on, there will be no difficulty regarding crowded playing areas. Many floor plans will need to show several furniture groupings, one of which is of primary importance; the floor space that furniture requires will have a great deal to do with its importance on the stage. As a matter of fact, many directors start with a furniture plan and consider the walls as second in importance. Although the placement of furniture within the room is largely the responsibility of the director, the designer can often be of assistance in pointing out blocking problems that show up on the floor plan. All concerned, however, should realize that ideal sight lines are for a limited number of seat locations only. Unless the stage is bare, someone in the audience will always find something to ob-struct his view at least part of the time.

Since many stage settings make generous use of steps and levels, the designer must be prepared to illustrate such arrangements when they are called for on the floor plan. The usual practice is to connect the opposite corners of the raised unit with straight lines and to draw a circle around the dimension which states the height of the level from the floor. Steps are represented by drawing only the tread and circling the dimension which will tell the amount each tread is elevated from the floor. Because of the fact that floor space is involved, offstage *escape steps* must be drawn in addition to the more elaborate units which are in full view of the audience.

The problem of sight lines is one of considerable concern both to the director and to the designer. While the sight lines of the setting are mainly the responsibility of the designer, it is, of course, up to the director to center important action in areas that can be readily seen. The usual testing method is to draw imaginary lines from the extreme seats of the house across both sides of the proscenium to the various openings and locations on the setting. These lines will indicate clearly which onstage and offstage areas can be seen by all the audience. A cross-sectional view of an exterior setting is also often important in order to make certain that the horizontal masking is satisfactory.

Very often the floor plan will point out inconsistencies in the arrangement of the openings of a box setting. It is always well to think of the entire house in relation to a specific room — i.e., kitchen and living room, hallway and main doorway, etc. Although some playwrights are often a bit vague as to such matters, there is no reason why the director and the designer should not attempt to make a room arrangement plausible. In like manner, peculiar furniture relationships will show up quickly on a floor plan. Completely life-like arrangements are scarcely ever possible on the stage, but often such effects may be suggested without sacrificing any important playing space.

Most designers prefer not to litter up a floor plan with dimensional markings, for such markings are likely to be more confusing than helpful. All dimensional lines should be outside the playing area and should end with arrows which show the extent of the measurements. In addition, there will be much less opportunity for error if such a dimension as seven feet is written as 7′ 0″. The depth and width of the setting are essential as well as an indication of the amount of rake to the side walls. It is not always necessary to draw dimensional lines for windows, chimney pieces, and the like, since there is seldom much variation in such measurements. A simple uncluttered floor plan will present a clean-cut view of the playing space and, later on, be of value to the crew members who must set up the finished product on the stage.

The Sketch

At the second meeting of the designer and the director, the scale floor plan is presented and, if the first conference was a success, only very minor changes should be required; perhaps it may be necessary to rake a wall an extra foot, to widen a door, or to move a piece of furniture. Since there is nothing mysterious about a floor plan, all space relationships should be settled at this meeting so that, when the painted sketch is shown at the next meeting, the chief concerns will be such problems as color, style, mood, and atmosphere. It is assumed, of course, that each design is practical and that, where quick scene shifting is required, no unforeseen difficulties will arise.

Most experienced designers draw a number of rough thumbnail sketches in conjunction with their floor-plan work. These simple black and white drawings are for the designer's use only, and their main purpose is to prove that the floor plan will work. Since thumbnail sketch indications are often very slight, such drawings might confuse a director rather than help him visualize the appearance of the setting. If the designer's ideas are to be presented clearly and effectively, it is necessary, then, for him to prepare a scale sketch, carefully drawn and painted — and nicely mounted. The late Christian Bérard may have drawn his sketch for *The Madwoman of Chaillot* on a paper napkin, but most designers will find that their sketches must usually be displayed to better advantage. Indeed, a certain type of salesmanship may be involved before all final decisions are made.

PERSPECTIVE

There are a number of perspective systems which are in common use and each method has certain specific advantages. The method that has been selected for presentation on these pages is as simple as any other, and at the same time is not dependent upon the use of a drawing board. The drawing paper needs to be only slightly larger than the finished product, since the floor plan, on a separate sheet of paper, can be referred to whenever necessary; if $\frac{1}{2}''$ scale is used for the floor plan, the same scale is desirable for the sketch. The sketch may be drawn directly onto a $12''$-by-$16''$ water-color sketch block and thus be ready for painting in a minimum of time. A scale rule and a large 45-degree triangle will prove of considerable assistance in laying out the general proportions but the T square should not be necessary. The mechanics of perspective are necessary only to set up the general shape and openings and to locate the furniture; smaller detail and decorative work are

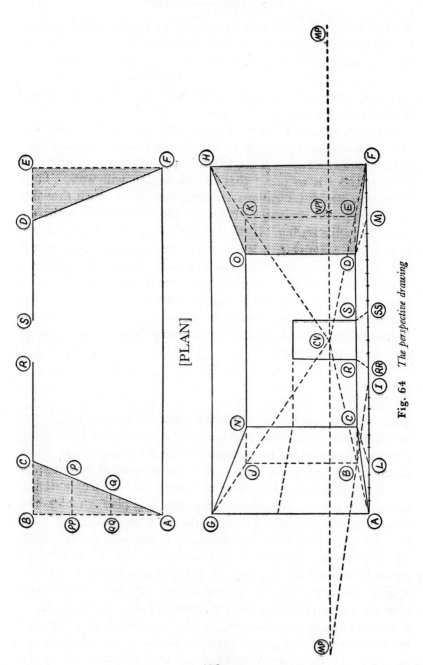

[PLAN]

Fig. 64 *The perspective drawing*

192

usually a freehand proposition. Although the sketch is not primarily an architectural exercise, the beginner must know what to expect of perspective before he can accomplish very representative freehand drawing.

The first step in preparation for the perspective sketch is to enclose the floor plan in the smallest rectangle which will take care of its over-all dimensions. The floor plan ACDF (opposite) is enclosed by ABEF; AB and EF indicate the full depth of the setting and AF, the width of the proscenium. This rectangle is to become the foundation for a rectangular one-point perspective box which will inclose the setting proper.

Next, the designer draws a rectangle on his drawing paper which will be the width of the setting, AF (*ground line*), and the height of the flats, AG or FH. This is the *fourth wall* of the setting, or the *picture plane*, through which the spectators will view the scenery. At this point, it will be helpful to divide AG, FH, and AF into one-foot divisions before going further with the sketch, since some of these marks will be referred to frequently.

The question of the *eye-level line* (horizon line) must next be settled. Some designers prefer a high eye-level line so that they seem to be looking down on the setting; others feel that the eye level should be at the floor. The average theatre patron sees at least a bit of the floor; therefore it is probably best to compromise with the two extremes and to consider the eye level as three feet above the floor. At points three feet above A and F, lightly draw a connecting horizontal line and extend it on either side of AG and FH to the *measuring points* (MP). (It is desirable that these points be located about twenty feet — to scale — on each side of the drawing. Temporary pieces of paper can be placed at either side of the sketch block and the measuring points located thereon.) The exact center of the eye-level line will be called the *center of vision* (CV) and lines are next drawn connecting CV with A, G, H, and F. Since these are construction lines, they must be drawn lightly or drawn as dotted lines.

The designer is now ready to draw in perspective the temporary construction lines for the rectangular box which encloses the three-walled box setting. If AB on the plan is ten feet, the student counts to the right ten feet from A and may call this location I. One end of the drawing square is placed on I and the other on the left MP and a light line is drawn; where this line crosses the A–CV line, the student makes a dot which corresponds to B on the floor plan. A line drawn to the right from B, parallel to AF, will intersect CV–F at a point which will be the same as E of the floor plan. Perpendiculars are next erected from B to the line CV–G and from E to CV–H, and the points of intersection, J and K, are connected. The rectangular box in perspective is now complete and the student is then ready to draw the stage setting which fits inside it. The front wall of the box is AGHF, the side walls are ABJG and FEKH, and the back wall is BEKJ. When a box setting is rectangular in shape and has no rake, no further perspective steps are required.

The floor plan on page 192 indicates, however, that the setting has a four-foot rake on each side, that is, BC and DE are four feet each. The next step, the location of C and D in the perspective, is accomplished by referring to the line AF. Measure four feet to the right from A and four feet to the left from F and label these points L and M. Place one end of the square on L and the other on CV. The point where the connecting line crosses line BE will locate C; on the other side, a line from M to CV will cross BE at D. Connect A with C and F with D to form the side floor lines in perspective. The erection of perpendiculars from C to the JK line and from D to the JK line will determine the points N and O which, when connected, will supply the ceiling line of the back wall. The stage-setting perspective can now be seen as follows: Stage Right wall — ACNG, Stage Left wall — FDOH, Floor plan — ACDF. Obviously, too much ceiling shows at this point, but this can be trimmed down after the sketch is complete.

The placement of openings in the setting is of next concern and this will involve perpendicular measurements as well as floor dimensions. Let us assume there is a door on the Stage Right wall and a door on the Center wall. On the floor plan (Fig. 64), PQ will indicate the width of the side door and RS, the width of the Center door. To locate the side door in perspective, draw light lines to line AB on the floor plan, parallel to AF. The points at which P and Q cross AB will be called PP and QQ. Assuming that the distance from PP to A is seven feet on the plan and the distance from PP to QQ three feet, refer next to the perspective (Fig. 65) and count seven feet to the right of A to locate PPP. Place the square from PPP to the left MP and, where the square crosses AB, make a mark which will be the same as PP on the plan. Next, draw a parallel (to AF) from PP on the sketch to the point where it intersects AC. In order to locate Q on the sketch, the same steps are followed in exactly the same order.

To get the height of the side door, the designer must first locate the vanishing point for the Stage Right wall of the setting; this point (VP 1) is obtained by extending GN and AC until they cross somewhere on the horizon line. If the door is seven feet high, measure up seven feet from A on the AG line. Place one end of the square on this point, and the other on the new vanishing point (VP I). Where the square crosses the perpendiculars erected from P and Q, the top of the door will be indicated in perspective. Had the door been on the Stage Left wall, similar drawing would be necessary in reverse.

If the other door is dead center, first locate the exact center of AF on the sketch (Fig. 64). For a door four feet in width, measure two feet to each side of this mark (RR and SS) and then place one end of the square at RR and the other at CV. Where this crosses CD, make a mark and erect a perpendicular; apply the same procedure in the case of SS. The height of the door is determined by a height located on AG; the vanishing point for the Stage Right wall will take the height to line CN after which it becomes parallel to AF and determines the top of the door.

By checking with the floor plan, furniture can be located in perspective on the floor of the sketch, using the MP points and the CV (Fig. 65). Indicate furniture heights within the setting by drawing a line from the corner of the perspective furniture plan down to the ground line, using CV as a guide. Where the line crosses the ground line, erect a perpendicular the height of the furniture and, using the CV, return the line to where it crosses a perpendicular line from the corner of the furniture. The beginner will find it helpful to draw a box-shaped solid which will enclose an entire piece of furniture and to remove what is not needed as he sketches the characteristic shape; the eye-level line will be useful to tell the designer the amount of the top of a piece of furniture that will be visible. Furniture that is parallel to the side walls of

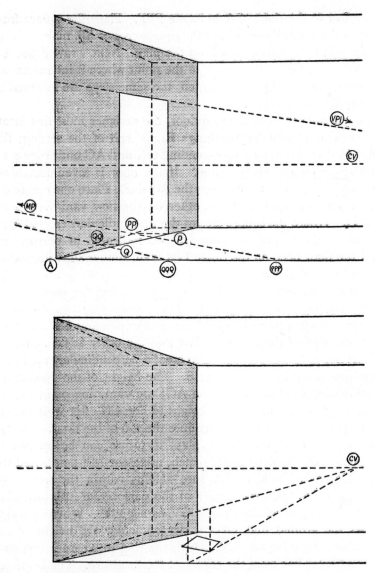

Fig. 65 *The perspective drawing — Enlargements of side door and furniture areas (for items not included here see Fig. 64, p. 192)*

the setting is the easiest to draw since it will use the same vanishing points as the side walls.

Since many exterior settings have side masking pieces which are similar to the side walls of a box setting (the sky drop will not be unlike the center wall), the above method of perspective is useful for almost all types of scenery sketching. There will be plenty of opportunity for the application of drawing techniques and color relationships *after* the main framework has been set up. From this point on, all trimming, pictures, draperies, furniture, and wood-work can be sketched in, using these fundamental perspective directions. However, if the student attempts the sketch without the framework, the results may be out of scale, badly proportioned, and misleading. A sketch which is drawn to scale offers excellent opportunity for the study of most of the elements which make up the static stage picture; furthermore, such furniture blocking as has not been discovered in the plan will usually be apparent in the sketch.

WATER-COLOR RENDERING

The use of water color for the painted rendering requires considerable skill and, until the student has practiced painting actual landscapes, furniture, and various small objects, his scenic sketches are likely to appear flat and uninteresting. A thorough understanding of shade and shadow is necessary before the student can paint well; this knowledge must be gained from the continual observation of the effect of light on the three dimensions he sees in life. Although many designers object to the use of *rough* paper, on the grounds that it serves as a crutch, scene designers will, none the less, find this paper useful since it helps to supply texture to the water-color rendering. In addition, it is much easier to apply paint to paper that has a slight *tooth.*

Certain designers insist that only the most expensive Windsor and Newton's water colors are useful because these colors are extremely permanent and pure. Obviously, the use of such inexpensive paints as are supplied in the average grammar school paint box may limit the designer. However, he will do well to try various qualities of paints until he finds a reasonably priced grade that he can handle easily. For example, Schmincke's

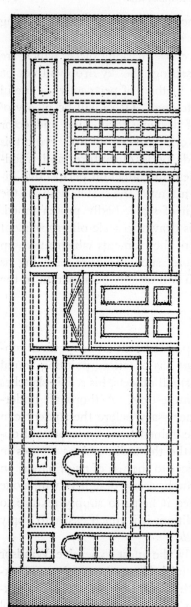

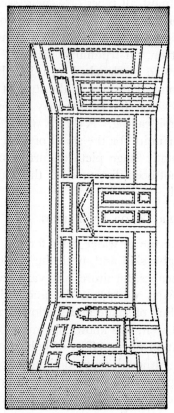

Fig. 66 *The front elevations — the model*

Horadam colors are preferred by many since it is almost impossible to apply an uneven wash with these paints. Whatever paints are used, the best painting results are usually obtained when a number seven (or larger) sable brush is used.

The student should study the various water-color painting techniques that are representative of the finest commercial and non-commercial work of the present day; eventually he should attempt to develop a characteristic technique of his own. Some designers prefer to take great pains with the pencil work for their renderings and to apply the paint with great speed; other designers spend very little time with the drawing work, preferring to concentrate on the painting. Scenic representations should not be rendered in a tedious, pinched manner but should have a free quality. This freedom, however, must not get out of hand so that the completed water-color rendering will be vague. It should be possible to *indicate* by means of paint so that an object will be recognizable without being overdetailed.

Occasionally it may be necessary to include groupings of human figures within the rendering; when such is the case, detailed forms are unnecessary since interest will usually center around the height and color of the figures. Furthermore, if all the light sources are clearly indicated on the rendering, the painting can suggest lighting effects which might be desirable. Regardless of what is included on the rendering, however, the student should never forget that the primary purpose of the scenic sketch is to give an impression of the scenery as it will appear on the stage. While the sketch is not an end in itself, occasionally these renderings have special merit as examples of water-color work.

The Model

After the sketch is finished, the designer and director meet again and, if the setting is a relatively simple one, the director will probably not require further proof as to its space relationships. In that event, the costume designer and the lighting technician are called in and the conference turns to their particular problems. If, however, the director cannot as yet visualize the backgrounds, he may ask for a model of the setting; most directors will be particularly anxious to see a model of a setting which involves a great many steps and levels.

Since the purpose of the model is to supplement the sketch, it should not be necessary to include in it every little detail. Wall decorations can easily be painted directly on the model. Miniature scale furniture is not usually included, especially if very detailed. If the floor plan on which the model rests provides the furniture placement in plan, the director will be able to test the playing areas satisfactorily. However, without the furniture, color relationships can not always be checked; hence, the sketch will probably be of more use for this purpose than is the model.

Most models are made to a scale of $\frac{1}{2}'' = 1'$, using a cardboard such as Bristol Board or Illustration Board. The various walls can either be cut separately and fastened together with drafting tape or the entire setting can be drawn in one continuous piece and the wall divisions scored with a *mat knife*. So-called "airplane glue" will be especially useful for models which require the actual representation of thickness and other three-dimensional building. As for the walls, the drawing and painting need not be done meticulously, but all scale relationships should be clear; the designer's particular drawing and painting techniques are just as appropriate on the model as in the sketch. Since many designers draw and paint rough front elevations of the various walls before making perspective sketches, it should not take long to translate the same material into model form. (In many cases the various walls of the model will even be satisfactory as painter's elevations.) A simple black proscenium arch usually accompanies the model; all backing pieces are included as well.

The model may even serve as a substitute for the sketch. The technician can then show the building plans (working drawings) on the rear of the model; thus the model can be of use to the shop workers as well as to the director. Lighting technicians will also find the model of considerable value since the floor plan does not emphasize perpendicular relationships. In addition, the model may be of interest to the costume designer although the colored sketch will present a better over-all picture of the colors which are to be used.

The Elevations

When director and designer have agreed on the plans, models, and sketches, it is still necessary to prepare elevations and working drawings before construction of the setting can begin. Usually the technical director drafts the working drawings and the designer is responsible for the detailed front and side elevations and the painter's elevations. The front elevations are always two-dimensional views showing length and width but no thickness or perspective. As the technician makes the working drawings he will have an opportunity to discover and analyze all the important building problems. However, since the purpose of the elevations and working drawings is not to demonstrate mere drafting ability, the views which are shown are only those which will be of real guidance to the builders and painters.

Scale drawings of the front elevations of each wall are always necessary so that the technician will be aware of all trimming and can make provision for it from the rear of the flats. The designer must also indicate such detail as cross-sectional views of moldings, newel posts, papier-mâché work, balusters, etc. if front elevations

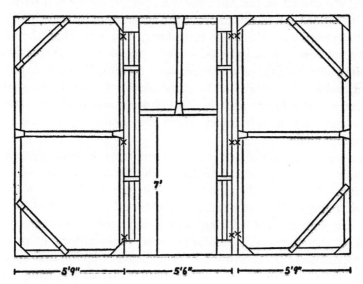

Fig. 67 *Working drawings*

do not make them clear. Such items as baseboards, chair rails, cornices, pilasters, and applied molding are shown, but drawing detail is not repeated where it is identical. Although the designer is not required to draw such construction as tumblers, hinges, and stage hardware on the front elevations, he has usually designed his scenery in such a way that the technician will have no difficulty to break up the wall for construction and transportation purposes. Furthermore, the front elevation usually contains over-all dimensional marking as well as the dimensions of doors, windows, panels, cornices, etc.; these dimensions will be of value to the technician as he prepares his working drawings although side elevations or sectional views may also be required of some units. Where there is considerable use of molding or intricate overhang trimming, such drawings are really more properly a part of the technician's working drawings.

The designer is responsible for front and side elevations of all specially built furniture that is to be used for a production. Although the individual pieces of furniture, in drawing form, may appear satisfactory, it is important to check their relationship to the setting as well. Since all furniture that touches the wall is usually included in the front elevation, the designer can often use the elevations as a means to prove the accuracy of his scale, balance, and proportion. He must remember, however, that the front elevation cannot always be depended upon since the proportion of a piece of furniture, or a pilaster or a cornice, depends upon the relationship of all three of its dimensions. Cylindrically shaped objects such as lamps and shades, columns, and urns are particularly confusing in this respect since they appear much the same from any angle.

The painter's elevations are also front-view scale drawings and include all the colors and textures which are to be used on the setting. Because of the amount of white in so-called "show card" paint, many designers feel that such paint offers a better likeness to the dry pigment and whiting combination than do water colors, and is therefore more satisfactory for the painter's elevations. These painted elevations must, of course, give attention to draperies, wall pictures, murals, and other similar decorative trim. The designer is also responsible for scale wallpaper patterns and for

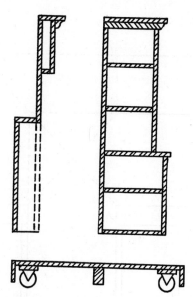

Fig. 68 *Cross-sectional drawings*

suggestions and samples as to color mixture. As for backdrops, the colored sketches must be divided into one-foot squares so that the design can be transferred to the backdrop as it hangs on the paint frame. Painter's elevations, unlike the colored sketch, do not attempt to show the effects of stage lighting; they are an exact representation of what is expected from the finished product as it leaves the shop.

The Working Drawings

In most cases the designer's floor plan will be sufficiently accurate for use by the technician. By reference to this floor plan and to the detailed designer's elevations, the technician can prepare working drawings which will show the various sections of the setting which must be built, transported, and handled on the stage. The rear view of each of these units must be drawn complete with stiles, toggles, corner blocks, keystones, hardware, and lash lines; and all over-all dimensions should be clearly indicated. It is advisable to draw all the flats of an entire wall, side-by-side, so that stiffening devices and hinging can be illustrated; in addition, the drawings should indicate which sections of the setting (doors,

203

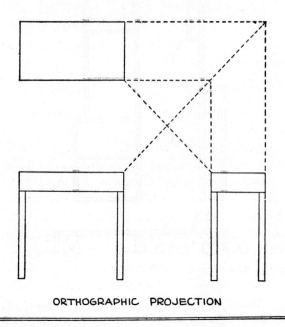

ORTHOGRAPHIC PROJECTION

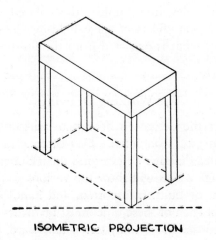

ISOMETRIC PROJECTION

Fig. 69 *Orthographic and isometric projections*

windows, chimney pieces, etc.) do not require canvas. Although many draftsmen insist that working drawings should be almost self-explanatory, simple written instructions often accompany the working drawings.

CROSS-SECTIONAL DRAWINGS

If a scenic unit is so complicated that it cannot be illustrated satisfactorily by means of a plan and a rear or side elevation, cross-sectional drawings may be required. A cross-sectional view suggests that the three-dimensional unit has been cut in two; the cut parts are cross-hatched and the parts which are farther away are represented by thin lines (p. 203). Such three-dimensional building as chimney pieces and cornices, which include moldings and special hollow construction, are often much easier to build when cross-sectional drawings are available. Cross-sectional drawings, particularly those which involve moldings or unusual joining methods, are often shown in a larger scale than that used for rear elevations. While drawings of such units as rocks and platforms may not require a larger scale, in most instances cross-sectional views will be desirable.

ORTHOGRAPHIC PROJECTIONS

The *orthographic* projection is sometimes useful for demonstrating the relationship of an object to its side elevation and plan since most three-dimensional objects (bookcases, cabinets, chimney pieces, steps, etc.) require at least three views before their dimensions are apparent. The orthographic projection has been devised as a two-dimensional method of presenting three dimensions. The usual procedure is to place the views at equidistant right angles to one another so that lines from the front elevation can be projected up to indicate the width of the plan, and lines projected from the top and bottom of the front elevation will indicate the height of the side elevation. Obviously, these projections can show only the exact height, length, width, and thickness of a unit, without the use of perspective; therefore, extremely complicated building methods may have to be presented in some other manner. The orthographic projection is primarily a method for recording the precise shape, the important dimensions, and the elevation detail of a scenic unit or a piece of furniture.

ISOMETRIC PROJECTIONS

Because of the distorted view that it offers, *isometric* drawings are only occasionally used to illustrate complete stage settings. However, such drawings often provide a simple, graphic, three-dimensional method of illustrating the form and construction of furniture, architectural trim, step and platform arrangements, and complicated joining arrangements. The isometric drawing or projection often starts with a plan which is placed on the paper by means of a 30–60-degree triangle in such a way that right angles are obtuse. The slant may be any number of degrees, however, depending upon the purpose of the drawing. Perpendiculars, the exact height of the object, are extended from the corners of the plan and the details drawn in, using the exact measurements of the object. When illustrating joints and architectural trim, the draftsman need not use a plan; jagged lines will suggest that the woodwork continues some distance further than there is space for the drawing to indicate. Despite the fact that the parallel lines of the isometric drawing can be measured accurately, no diagonal lines will present accurate measurements. This is scarcely a handicap, however, as most important lines have to do with height and width.

Some General Principles of Scene Design

Many beginning designers expect to find specific rules to aid them in their various scene design problems; fortunately, no such rules are available. Theoretically, design for the theatre is an individual matter and it is unlikely that any two designers would be in exact agreement regarding a particular production. These differences of opinion have served to keep present-day scene design more or less out of the rut and to place a premium on straightforward, honest, non-eccentric scenic solutions. While it is true that definite scenic trends can be noted during a particular decade and that experimental playwrighting is often quite largely responsible for these trends, no two designers are likely to interpret these trends identically. Indeed, stage scenery would not be held to its present form were it not for the fact that most plays are inclined to follow the "well-made-play" formula. Most experienced designers seem eager to break away from the traditional and would thus never welcome a set of specific rules to guide them.

However, the beginning designer will do well to keep certain general principles in mind as he works on a production and to apply these principles intelligently rather than blindly. The designer must always consider that a stage setting is a place rather than a picture such as might be conceived by an easel painter. While a painting usually has one main point of interest, a stage setting may have several — although they may not be of equal importance. Both the stage setting and the painting must be attractive regardless of subject matter; a country landscape would seem to offer more possibilities for stage picturization than a junk yard, but the latter need never lack beauty as illustrated by scale, proportion, balance, line, and mass.

Perhaps the most difficult problem that will confront the beginning designer is the question of scale and proportion (page 208). A stage setting is a much larger and intensified representation of a location than its counterpart in life, and therefore size relationships are especially important. Not only must an object or a section of the stage setting be in itself proportionately well-formed but it must be equally pleasing in relation to everything else on the stage. A well-scaled piece of furniture will accomplish nothing in a setting which is formed of badly proportioned door and window openings and includes splotchy undersized wall trimmings. Similarly, the relationship of nearby pieces of furniture is of importance — an overscaled chair, for example, will take on a different effect if placed near a delicate table or chair. Obviously, the original sketch is the best means for checking scale and proportion, and the problem is primarily the concern of the designer rather than the director.

Although the *balance* (page 209) of a stage setting is influenced by color as well as by line and mass, it is the latter that must be considered first in the scenic sketch. Symmetrical balance presents identical items on either side of center while optical balance achieves a pleasing approximation of symmetry with a variety of line and mass. Symmetrical balance perhaps suggests more formality than does the optical form although, of course, the question of formality involves much more than mere balance; a Greek temple is both formal and symmetrical but many symmetrically designed

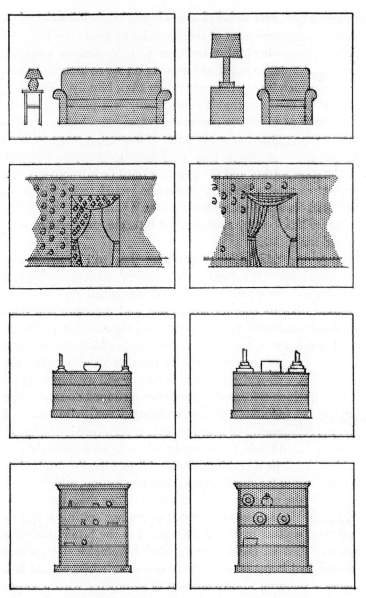

Fig. 70 *Extreme examples of good and bad scale and proportion*

Fig. 71 *Examples of various forms of balance*

Fig. 72 *Line and contour*

rooms are basically informal. In most instances, however, when an informal effect is desired on the stage, optical balance will be desirable. A window and a secretary on the Stage Right wall should balance a large draped archway on Stage Left, or a house exterior on one side of the stage might balance a solid-looking wall on the other side. After all the relationships of line and mass are settled, the question of color must be considered. Since bright colors weigh more than neutral ones, considerable experimentation may be required so that a line and mass balance will not be disturbed by the introduction of color.

A scene design for a one-set play must have sufficient variety of line, contour, and mass to make sure that an audience will not tire of looking at it during an entire evening. While such variety must not be an end in itself nor must it attract attention to the extent that it competes with the actor, there must be enough variation in form to avoid monotony. Even when the script calls for a relatively simple setting, there can be a variety in the contour of the larger wall masses and in the shape of the openings of the setting. In like manner, a scenic design made up of an unusual amount of detail must use such detail in a variety of ways in order to hold the interest of an audience. Openings into the setting may very well represent diversified heights and decorative treatments but, unless extreme formality is desired, these features must be balanced and interestingly arranged. Although certain areas will necessarily receive more emphasis than others regardless of the methods used for achieving pictorial variety, the final results should present a scenic unit. For a multi-set show, this minute attention to variety is of a different nature since the constant shifting from scene to scene can offer the necessary diversity; at the same time, the repetition of the design style assists in unifying the production.

Most designers agree that a scenic sketch must interpret rather than present a literal background although there is often disagreement as to how far this interpretation can and should be carried for various plays. Can a rather tragic play take place in a smartly designed New York apartment or must the room suggest at first glance the overtones of the play? Must an amusing realistic play of Midwest farm life be presented in a setting which says *comedy* the minute the curtain rises? Can the stage design of a room in a well-known hotel tell an audience what to expect as the play unfolds? What about the appearance of a pleasant little country inn, taken over by gunmen, with murder as the plot of the play? Similar questions will continually arise and it will be up to the director and the designer to make their decisions with the entire production in mind. Here, as in the case of other scenic principles, the suggestions can only be general; it should not be difficult to suggest cheer and warmth when they are needed nor should cold gloom prove troublesome. When a play particularly demands that a stage setting be completely in contrast to the material of the play itself, the designer is interpreting the play no less by providing an environment that seems more like a background. However, the scenic sketch must represent a *designed* room or exterior rather than a decorated location, and its relationship to the play must be apparent at least soon after the play begins to progress.

In order for the scene designs to contribute to the production, they must often suggest *mood and atmosphere* as well as locale. Although many of the slick contemporary comedies demand very little from the scenery except locale, more serious plays actually need the reinforcement that atmospheric scenery can supply. Unfortunately, beginning designers often fail to take advantage of opportunities for such scenic interest, and also occasionally weigh a production down with unnecessarily perceptive designs. A sensitive and ingenious designer, of course, takes advantage of every opportunity for scenic interest but may have to be curbed slightly if his sketches stress elements which are not of primary importance. It is conceivable that, even in a serious play, scenery that is loaded with mood and atmosphere might rest rather heavily on a highly emotional play which has not the substance to support such designs. In such an instance, the designer may have followed some principle or other instead of studying the demands of the play. Whatever the reason, the designer need never go far astray if the script is his guide and he and the director are in perfect agreement.

PROJECTS AND EXERCISES

1. Select some play which requires a box setting and, following the author's directions, draw a $\frac{1}{2}''$ scale floor plan which will include openings, backings, and furniture. Give special consideration to sight lines, blocking, and important playing areas.

2. Following the perspective instructions given on pages 192–193, lay out, in pencil, the perspective framework for your floor plan. After the walls and openings are located, sketch in the furniture and the wall trimmings.

3. Paint your sketch with water colors, attempting to represent as much third dimension and lighting as is possible. Cast shadows on the floor wherever this will assist in giving depth to your sketch.

4. Draw and paint a model of your setting with the idea in mind that the individual walls of the model can serve as painter's elevations as well. If possible, use "show card" paint and include no shadow or shade. Compare the results with the painted sketch.

5. Select the most interesting wall of your setting and draw a detailed front elevation of it which will include all the decorative and trimming features. Do not repeat identical design elements.

6. Draw rear elevations of all the scenic units which make up the wall which you selected for question 5. List the units which would benefit by the inclusion of cross-sectional drawings. Draw a cross-sectional view of any one of these units.

7. By means of an orthographic projection, show the form of some item from your setting such as a chimney piece or a bookcase.

8. Use an isometric drawing to illustrate the cornice or a step arrangement which is to be found in your sketch.

9. Check the effectiveness of your scenic sketch from the following points of view: scale, proportion, balance, line, and mass. What does your sketch show of locale, mood, and atmosphere? What unity devices have you used in connection with your design? Is there enough variety of contour to interest an audience?

10. Examine some reproductions of professional scene designs from the point of view of painting technique, accuracy of indication, three-dimensional quality, and representation of lighting effects. Are any of the painting techniques of special interest to you? Why? Note the painting techniques represented in a current issue of *House and Garden* and apply the above tests.

8

Stage Properties

STRICTLY SPEAKING, any item included in the stage picture, not labelled as scenery, is considered to be a property of one kind or another. However, the distinction between scenery and properties is sometimes difficult to define since the budget or the availability of workers within the two fields often determines the classification. Actually, such properties as furniture, draperies, paintings, and objets d'art make much more of an impression upon an audience than do painted flats. The designer thus has the special responsibility of controlling the emphasis of these design elements so that properties will take on no more individual identity than is necessary. Needless to say, if the choice of properties demonstrates that the designer is insensitive to the period styles, an emphasis of the wrong sort may result. Since all the furnishings of a stage setting must usually appear to belong there rather than arbitrarily to have been placed there, such questions as quality, type, color, and scale must also be considered in relation to every single item in the room. In most cases an approximation of the desirable

214

properties should appear on the scenic sketch so that there is no danger that scenery and furnishings will become unrelated.

Scene design involves a great deal more than the sketching of authentic decorative backgrounds. A knowledge of period furnitrue and architecture is often necessary before a variety of completely integrated designs can be conceived. Furthermore, few stage interiors have any particular intent until they are complete with the properties which are suitable to the play and to an over-all scenic conception. There is always the danger, however, that a beginning designer may concentrate on this phase of the work to the extent that his sketches may seem to represent interior design rather than scene design.

The Classification of Properties

Visual, decorative stage properties can be divided into three main divisions: *set* properties, *trim* properties, and *hand* properties. These divisions often overlap and any final classification must be determined by the use to which they are put on the stage. The actual subdivisions of properties are not important in themselves but merely serve as a means for helping students and crew members to organize their work to better advantage. If the production requires the use of a period sofa, it must be built, borrowed, or rented as well as shifted by the property crew; what happens to it within the setting during performance is the director's responsibility. Special *visual effects* and *manual sound effects* are also sometimes considered as properties. These will be treated in detail on later pages.

Set properties, frequently called scene props, include all furniture and rugs which are placed on the floor of the setting as well as the decorative objects (lamps, vases, candelabra, etc.) which may rest on the various pieces of furniture. Set properties for an exterior setting might be represented by grass matting, garden furniture, a bit of statuary, or a unit of three-dimensional shrubbery. These properties, then, are the larger, more impressive pieces which help to accentuate the scale and composition of the setting and which contribute most appropriately to the flavor of the background as conceived by the designer. It is conceivable that, in the absence of scenery, a play might be presented using only decorative, well-scaled set properties.

Although film studios are likely to apply the term *set dressings* to all room decorations, stage workers usually consider trim properties and set properties within a more specific classification. *Trim properties* are related to the walls of a stage interior or to certain decorative refinements of a large exterior unit. Such items as draperies, pictures, hanging shelves, sconces, and wall clocks often serve as essential trimming for a period room. Trim properties for an exterior setting might be represented by three-dimensional features like hand-made leaves, blossoms, fruit for a tree, or glass curtains and blinds which can be seen as the audience looks through a window into a building.

Despite the fact that *hand properties*, sometimes called action props, are primarily utensils for the actors, they must at the same time belong visually to the stage picture. A tray of silver and china for a tea-serving scene is a hand property and must suggest the taste and financial status of those who belong in the room. If jewelry is merely worn by an actress, it is a costume problem, but a bracelet or necklace that is handled by the actors becomes a hand property. Food, liquor, cigarettes, and magazines are additional examples of hand properties which find frequent use on the stage. Such properties are placed in specific positions onstage for various scenes, or are picked up by the actors from offstage property tables. Occasionally a hand property may be a trim property as well: i.e., the paintings in *Kind Lady* or *The Late Christopher Bean*.

The Types of Furniture

Before the student can use furniture on the stage with any degree of proficiency, he must first become familiar with the various general types of period and non-period furniture. Although most furniture dealers use much the same basic terminology, establishments which offer antiques or high quality reproductions prefer to use precise foreign terms whenever possible. Furniture types are recognizable by silhouette and bulk rather than by detail. Though the same types may be found in many different periods, certain types are associated with specific periods; for example, the *chaise longue,* a long chair, is best represented by the Louis XV and XVI periods, regardless of the fact that many present-day versions of the chaise longue are on the market.

Similarly, the *highboy* and *lowboy* (page 252) were developed in William and Mary times although, today, most people are more familiar with reproductions of the eighteenth-century American adaptations of these pieces. The lowboy, with a mirror hung above it, serves nicely as a dressing table; knee space is provided by the high opening in the apron and the use of an X stretcher to connect the four legs. The highboy is a chest of drawers with a lowboy as its foundation. The top of the chest is trimmed with either a plain cornice molding or a broken-hood cornice. Since knee space is not necessary, four front legs often complete the design.

While there are characteristic sofa styles for most of the decorative periods, two very popular non-period sofas are in more frequent use today than are the general run of period pieces. The trim, tailored lines of the *Lawson* sofa and the knife-edge silhouette of the *Tuxedo* sofa are in much better proportion than a great deal of the overstuffed furniture that has been manufactured within the past twenty-five years. Lawson *love seats* (two sections) and *club chairs* (one section) are equally well proportioned although the Tuxedo shape does not look so well in chair form. There are some middle-class stage interiors which demand an ugly, mushroomlike, overstuffed *davenport,* a piece of furniture which is often more easily procured than the Lawson, the Tuxedo, or sofas offering the best in contemporary design.

While many present-day upholstered chairs are ungainly and ugly, there are a few more or less standard pieces besides the Lawson which have considerable merit. The popular *barrel* chair suggests a vague eighteenth-century elegance; the chair is recognized by its back, similar in shape to that of half a barrel. Sometimes the chair-back upholstery is tufted, but a fluted effect is much more common. The *wing-back* chair, another pleasing model, is definitely reminiscent of certain eighteenth-century French and English chairs. The tall back, complete with side pieces, also suggests the trim simplicity of eighteenth-century American furniture. Although there is much tawdry French furniture on the market,

LAWSON SOFA

LAWSON CLUB CHAIR

DAVENPORT

TUXEDO SOFA

BARREL CHAIR

Fig. 73 *Types of furniture*

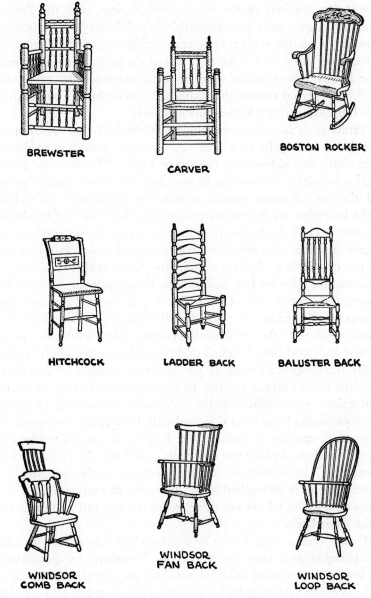

BREWSTER

CARVER

BOSTON ROCKER

HITCHCOCK

LADDER BACK

BALUSTER BACK

**WINDSOR
COMB BACK**

**WINDSOR
FAN BACK**

**WINDSOR
LOOP BACK**

Fig. 74 *Types of furniture — Chairs*

219

present-day versions of the *bergère*, closed arm, and the *fauteuil* (page 243), open arm, are often entirely satisfactory. The bergère is usually available with a loose seat cushion and, when provided with a large stool, can serve as a sort of chaise longue. Although these French pieces are suitable for use in stage settings representing French period rooms, the chairs are also useful in combination with English furniture for less formal effects.

Certain early New England chairs, although they are not always classified as belonging to a limiting decorative period, nevertheless have distinctive silhouettes (see page 219). The *Brewster* chair, Pilgrim in origin, is noted for its wooden seat, heavy, turned posts, and the use of many turned spindles or balusters. This chair might be called an American provincial version of the Jacobean. The *Carver* chair is similar in silhouette to the Brewster chair although it has a characteristic rush seat and makes considerably less use of spindles. Another chair, the *Boston* rocker, is noted for its decorative spindles but, in this case, the spindles are usually not turned; the wooden seat of the rocker is often curved upwards and the top rail of the back is painted with detailed designs. The chief characteristic of the nineteenth-century *Hitchcock* chair is its painted fruit and flower stencil designs, although the chair back is faintly reminiscent of some of the Sheraton designs. Since there is considerable current interest in these painted chairs, many reproductions are available today. Although occasional Chippendale style chairs have been designed with horizontal slat backs, the seventeenth-century American and English provincial versions of the tall *ladder-back* chair are especially noted for this characteristic silhouette. The *baluster-* or *banister-back* chair, another seventeenth-century piece, is recognizable by the series of perpendicular balusters or spindles which are attached to the top rail and cross rail of the chair back.

Windsor chairs, first made by early-eighteenth-century English wheelwrights and later developed by American cabinetmakers, are known for a variety of silhouettes (see page 219). While many of the original Windsors had fiddle-shaped back splats and cabriole legs similar to Queen Anne chairs, the simplified American splayed-leg versions often used only spindles to define the *comb, fan,* and *loop* backs. Windsor chairs are available in light farm woods or in mahogany, and are sometimes painted. For present-day use, a padded seat will add to their comfort and introduce a touch of color. These chairs are particularly suitable for informal country houses and do not combine readily with the more decorative Georgian pieces.

In recent years there have been many reproductions of the Queen Anne and Chippendale *piecrust* table; the simpler American versions of this table have been reproduced even more frequently. The piecrust table, with its molded and scalloped edge, often appears in the *tilt-top* form, complete with *squirrel cage*. When the tilted table stands in a corner or against the wall, it takes on a special decorative quality; since the table is light, it is easy to set up and to move about the room. Piecrust tables are equipped with a three-legged pedestal base which is sometimes highly carved and complete with claw and ball or pad feet. The *dumbwaiter*, a tiered table, also usually has a piecrust edge although the table is, of course, not collapsible. Another pedestal table, the *drum* table, is known for its deep apron containing a series of drawers. Since these pedestal tables (see page 222) are in excellent taste, they are suitable for use in rooms where refinement is to be stressed rather than ostentatiousness.

Butterfly and *gate-leg* tables (also shown on page 222), in contrast to the piecrust pedestal models, are less sophisticated since they are of Jacobean and early-eighteenth-century American origin. The butterfly model is equipped with drop leaves which are supported by butterfly-shaped brackets; when the leaves are raised, the table is either oval or circular in shape. This type of table is often small enough to place beside a chair or sofa to complete an informal furniture group. On the other hand, the gate-leg table is much larger and more substantial, though equally informal. Its drop leaves are supported by swinging legs which are hinged to the center framework. Because of its size, this table is shown to the best advantage when it is placed against a wall or behind a sofa. Another drop-leaf piece, the eighteenth-century *Pembroke* table, often on casters, has leaves which are supported by brackets. In contrast to the butterfly table, the Pembroke table displays considerable refinement of scale and detail.

Although in actual rooms, desks and writing tables (see page

DUMBWAITER

DRUM TABLE

PIECRUST TABLE

BUTTERFLY TABLE

GATE-LEG TABLE

PEMBROKE TABLE

KNEEHOLE DESK

KIDNEY TABLE

SECRETARY

CARLTON TABLE

BLOCK-FRONT CHEST

Fig. 75 *Types of furniture*

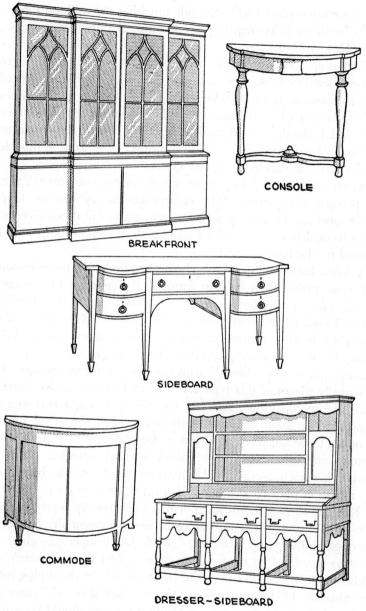

CONSOLE

BREAKFRONT

SIDEBOARD

COMMODE

DRESSER-SIDEBOARD

Fig. 76   *Types of furniture*

223

222) are often placed with one side touching the wall, on the stage such furniture is frequently placed completely free from the wall. The *kidney* table or desk, because of its concave front and over-all kidney shape, looks especially well in such a position. The regular flat-top *kneehole* desk, however, with drawers on either side of a center opening, must have decorative paneling on all four sides if it is to be placed away from the wall. The most attractive part of any desk is the drawer side; this is especially true of the eighteenth-century American *block-front* slant-top desk. The front of this piece of furniture is divided into one concave and two convex carved sections and a drop lid opens to reveal various compartments and to provide work space. The eighteenth-century English *Carlton* table must also be seen from the front to get its full decorative value since it consists of a table with a series of drawers and compartments placed on the back of the top.

When a large wall space must be broken up by the use of movable furniture rather than built-in features, the *secretary* (page 222) or the *breakfront* may offer possibilities. Both these pieces of furniture are tall and, when the shelves are filled with books or objets d'art, can provide an extremely decorative note to a wall area. While many breakfronts are equipped with a drop leaf which serves as a writing space, the cabinet features are of more importance. Occasionally pieces of this type are extremely elaborate and ornate, but the majority are suitable for dignified eighteenth-century rooms. The *dresser-sideboard*, sometimes called the *Welsh* dresser, is also a large tall piece of furniture, but, because of its unsophisticated form, its use is mostly limited to rural cottages. Since the shelves are open, a considerable amount of color can be introduced by means of plates and other bric-a-brac (see page 223).

Regular dining rooms are not often completely represented on the stage although portions of such rooms occasionally are shown through archways. The *sideboard* (buffet), developed in eighteenth-century England, is an example of a typical dining room piece. However, certain other pieces, used frequently in the dining room, are also suitable for other rooms; the *side chair* is as satisfactory at a desk as it is at the dining room table; a *commode* should be equally decorative against a dining room or living room wall space. The many different varieties of *consoles*, when used with mirrors, can often lend dignity to a hall, living room, or dining room. Although some one-legged and two-legged consoles are often slight and must be supported at the wall, a freestanding four-legged console is usually quite substantial. Some of these pieces are illustrated on page 223.

The Parts of Furniture

Most pieces of furniture have recognizable parts which are essential to the construction and without which the units would not hold together. Chairs, tables, and chests of drawers all offer essentially the same basic framework regardless of the fact that the decorative treatment and scale of the pieces vary as to period. Designers must be aware of these parts and their relation to the finished product since no furniture design can be successful unless it is first structurally sound.

The main parts of the *chair back* (page 226), for example, include the *top rail*, the *cross rail* (at the bottom), and the *back posts* which are a continuation of the back legs. Sometimes the top rail is so broken up by the design of the chair back that it is difficult to prescribe; none the less, there is always a structural member which serves this purpose. If the chair back is to be upholstered, the basic parts will remain the same even though padding or stuffing will be required as a foundation for the covering material. The terminology is essentially the same for the average chair *seat frame*. The *side rails* connect the back posts to the front legs and an *apron* or skirt holds the two front legs together. (A provincial chair like the Windsor has no apron or side rail; the seat is usually a solid piece of wood.) An armchair will require *arm stumps* to connect the arm and the side rail, regardless of whether the chair is of the open-arm or closed-arm variety. When a wooden arm is fully exposed, as in certain Victorian and French upholstered pieces, the *arm pad* often adds a decorative touch. Many chairs will require *stretchers* to give extra rigidity to the legs. The most common types of stretchers include H stretchers, which consist of side and cross stretchers; diagonal X stretchers; and box stretchers, which continue around from leg to leg.

Tables, like chairs, are equipped with aprons and side rails.

PARTS OF A CHAIR

A   TOP RAIL
B   CROSS RAIL
C   BACK POSTS
D   SIDE RAIL
E   APRON
F   ARM STUMP
G   ARM PAD
H   STRETCHERS

PARTS OF A TABLE

A   APRON
B   SIDE RAIL
C   STRETCHERS

PARTS OF A CHEST

A   BACK PANEL
B   SIDE PANEL
C   FRONT POST
D   BRACKET FEET

Fig. 77   *The parts of furniture*

226

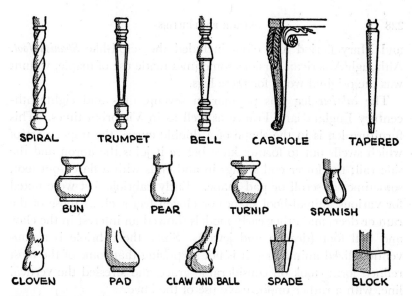

Fig. 78 *Furniture legs*

Stretchers are also frequently employed on tables although, in the case of writing tables, such supports offer considerable interference. The use of an elaborate stretcher on a console table can be an extremely decorative feature since these tables are usually designed primarily for the sake of appearance. On the other hand, stretchers will be of little value on a chest of drawers since the frame rests so near the floor. However, the chest contains back and side panels in addition to *front posts* and *back legs*.

The *spiral* or *twisted-rope* leg was often employed on furniture legs of the early seventeenth century in Flanders, England, and France — although it was originally introduced through Spain. Occasionally the twisted turning included only part of the leg but in most cases the design was continuous and complete with a *bun foot*. (Variations of the bun foot were provided by the oval shaped *pear foot* or the *turnip-shaped foot*.) Spiral-turned legs are more often seen on tables and highboys than on chairs.

During the last half of the seventeenth century there was considerable use of the *trumpet* leg and the *bell* or *inverted-cup* leg. The former has the silhouette of a square or round trumpet turned upward with the bun foot at the bottom. The graceful bell leg, connected by flat stretchers, is especially characteristic of the William

227

and Mary period and often included the scroll-like *Spanish foot.*
Although American versions sometimes made use of maple, walnut
was the original wood for these legs.

The *cabriole* leg was popular in seventeenth- and eighteenth-
century England and France as well as in Victorian times. This
furniture leg is in the shape of a double curve, the upper part of
which swells out to form a knee before it joins the apron and the
side rail; the lower end swings in and ends with a flared-out foot,
sometimes of scroll or pad shape. Early cabriole feet were noted
for various animal-hoof shapes or cloven feet such as those of the
ram or deer, and other early models showed an interest in the claw
and ball foot (dragon and jewel). Since the cabriole is a conventionalized animal leg, it is not surprising that some of the most
refined forms took on considerable grace and stressed the vertical
line, with a rather unobtrusive use of the knee.

The *tapered* legs of the late-eighteenth-century French and English periods are perhaps the most graceful of all. Round and
square legs were equally popular, and fluting, reeding, and brass
sheathing at the bottom were often a means of decoration. While
some tapered legs had no feet as such, many of these legs were finished with *spade* feet, tapered like the shaft of the leg and unen-
cumbered by stretchers. Carving and inlay work were a frequent
form of decoration although such treatment was often limited to
the more conspicuous front legs. Variations of the tapered shafts
were used by Duncan Phyfe in the form of legs suggesting reverse
curves and finished with brass animal feet, dog or lion, and small
casters. Slender, straight furniture legs that are not tapered
sometimes end with a square, boxlike *block* foot. Chinese Chippendale legs are usually finished in this manner.

The Decorative Motifs

Regardless of whether ornamentation is carved, painted, or inlaid, the chief purpose of decorative motifs is for the surface enrichment of architecture, furniture, and objets d'art. Since certain
decorative motifs are characteristic of particular periods, the
student will find it necessary to become familiar with the most frequently used decorative forms and to understand how they con-

TREFOIL QUATREFOIL GREEK FRET SWASTIKA DIAMOND POINT HEXAGON

EAGLE AMORINI

GRIFFIN ATLANTES SPHINX CARYATID

SHELL DOLPHIN

ANTHEMION ACANTHUS

URN CORNUCOPIA SWAG TREE OF LIFE

VASE GUILLOCHE DIAPER

EGG AND DART

RINCEAU ARABESQUE LINEN FOLD

Fig. 79 *Decorative motifs*

229

tribute to visual effect in combination with other ornament. The line and form of good period furniture is usually enhanced by means of surface ornamentation. Although the best period furniture is not loaded with ornament, scene designers must frequently design rooms and furniture which are loaded with detailed forms. In such cases, special skill will be required since an excessive use of decorative motifs can be distracting.

Most decorative motifs, regardless of their historic origins, can be classified specifically as to their form and inspiration. *Abstract* forms (page 229) often have definite geometric sources; the *trefoil* and *quatrefoil* forms are completely contrived, as are the *Greek Fret* and *swastika*. Jacobean decorative motifs, for example, illustrate such abstract forms as diamond points, hexagons, double rectangles, and similar angular forms. *Conventionalized naturalistic* forms, however, have more varied sources. Many such motifs are based on *human* and *animal* forms like the eagle, the griffin, and the dolphin. *Amorini* (cherubs), *caryatids* (female figures), and *atlantes* (male figures) are equally representative of this form of conventionalization. *Plants* are another inspiration for conventionalized motifs with such forms as the *acanthus* leaf, the *anthemion* (honeysuckle), the palm leaf, the tree of life, the wheat ear, the olive branch, and the fleur-de-lis as appropriate examples. The *rock and shell* motif is still another naturalistic conventionalization. *Classic objects* make up a third decorative motif form by the use of such objects as vases, urns, musical instruments, ribbons, bows, swags, festoons, Prince of Wales' feathers, cornucopias, and fasces.

The manner in which decorative motifs are used is of considerable importance inasmuch as the placement of a form often determines its proportion and scale. If motifs are repeated, side-by-side or alternately, this use of form represents a *border* (or band) *pattern*. The *egg and dart* ornament is an example of a border pattern by alternation; the *guilloche* represents a continuous geometric pattern. The *rinceau* is another continuous border pattern although in this case the inspiration is from nature and the design has considerable width. Decorative border patterns are often used to enrich table aprons and the architectural cornices of classically inspired rooms. Decorative motifs which are used in an allover, regularly repeated manner, make up what is called a *diaper pattern;*

wallpaper and textile designers find this pattern of particular value. Finally, if the forms are especially shaped to fit an area of specific size, the result is the *panel pattern*. The classic *arabesque*, intertwining flowers and leaves, is designed to fit a specific panel as are most seventeenth-century *linen-fold* designs. Carved, geometrically designed panels were frequently a part of the decoration for Jacobean cabinets and wainscot chair backs.

Period Furniture and Decoration

A knowledge of period furniture is often essential before a designer can formulate, express, and carry out his scenic ideas. Period design must not, of course, be used as an end in itself, but only as a legitimate means to the end — an interpretive design. An over-all knowledge of the period styles is invaluable in helping the designer to select and relate the proper furniture and decorative forms. Furthermore, since most period design is based on a *way of living*, in order to get the *feel* of a period, the designer will usually find it necessary to consider furniture as it relates to the modes and manners of the times. It must be remembered, however, that there is no clean-cut division between one period and another; as a result, transitional furniture is sometimes difficult to classify.

THE EGYPTIAN STYLES

The history of ancient Egypt from the days when the Upper and Lower kingdoms were combined, until the time of Alexander the Great, roughly includes the years from 3200 B.C. to 332 B.C. Since Egypt was an isolated country during these several thousand years, the Egyptian styles remained fairly constant, with the refinement of existing forms as the chief decorative development. Temple walls and columns were often elaborately carved with animals, human figures, and inscriptions, arranged to tell stories. Because perspective was unknown, the representations show a sort of half side and half front view of the human figure. These figures were brightly painted, red and yellow being the popular colors. Decorative motifs consist of open-winged vultures, sphinxes, swans, spiral designs, lotus blossoms and buds, acanthus leaves, beetles,

VULTURE

LOTUS BORDER

LOTUS BUD

SPIRAL DESIGN

TABLE

STOOL

ARMCHAIR

COUCH AND HEADREST

STOOL

Fig. 80 *The Egyptian style*

and snakes. The popular running border designs involve the wave pattern, lotus and papyrus plants, and various flower shapes.

By present-day standards, Egyptian furniture must have been very uncomfortable, yet many of the pieces are well proportioned and make excellent use of ornamentation. Stools, chairs, tables, stands, and couches (page 232) are the most prominent types of Egyptian furniture. Some of the stools have rush seats and others are of the folding variety with X-shaped bases and leather seats. Chairs frequently made use of carved animal legs, particularly those of dogs, bulls, and lions. Tables were solid and substantial and were also equipped with decorative animal legs or heavy columns and stretchers. The characteristic yoke-shaped headrest was a necessary addition to beds and couches, regardless of their shape or style. Cedar, sycamore, and olive woods were most commonly used and the pieces were often painted or varnished; many of the most elaborate pieces were inlaid with such decorative materials as ivory, ebony, mother-of-pearl, precious metals, and semiprecious jewels. Chair seats and couches were sometimes given a sort of padded treatment, but loose cushions, covered with silk or linen, were more often used.

In the design of the smaller decorative objects, Egyptian artisans were no less skilled. Most of the small statues, vases, jewelry, and boxes that have been found in recent excavations illustrate exquisite scale and demonstrate the skill and honesty of the craftsmen. It is not difficult to understand why Egyptian motifs, contours, and forms have been the source of considerable inspiration in the succeeding ages.

The Greek Styles

Although Greek civilization may be said to extend back to 3000 B.C., it was not until the so-called Golden Age in the fifth century B.C. that artistic development came to full flower. While it is true that the Egyptian and Mycenaean civilizations had some influence on early Greek architecture and decoration, the Golden Age was a period in its own right and its designs have never been equalled since. Although Greek decorative motifs were somewhat limited as to number, there was considerable variety as to the manner in which they were interpreted and combined. Abstract

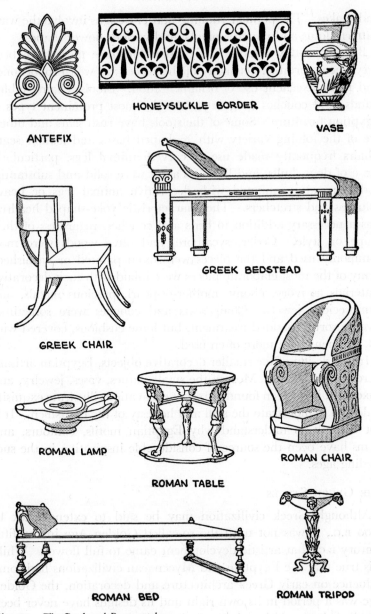

ANTEFIX

HONEYSUCKLE BORDER

VASE

GREEK CHAIR

GREEK BEDSTEAD

ROMAN LAMP

ROMAN TABLE

ROMAN CHAIR

ROMAN BED

ROMAN TRIPOD

Fig. 81 *The Greek and Roman styles*

designs such as the Greek key and the guilloche were often represented as well as conventionalized plant designs of the palm leaf, the acanthus leaf, the honeysuckle, and the lotus flower. The Greeks also used decorative animal forms of horses, lions, sphinxes, and griffins.

One of the most distinctive characteristics of the Greek chair, the *klismos* (opposite), is the curved top rail of the back. These chairs were either equipped with dog or lion legs or else the entire leg was plain and curved so as to be in agreeable relationship to the curved back. Bed and couch silhouettes, adapted from Egyptian designs, are usually rather high off the floor. Tables are low, however, and are mostly of the four-legged variety. Although there was much use of olive and yew wood for furniture construction, occasional pieces were made from bronze and marble. The pieces were often painted or carved, and inlay work was not infrequent. Upholstery, as such, was not characteristic, but cushions were sometimes used with chairs and couches.

From the study of Greek pottery, we learn many of the specific details of the décor of the period. The best examples of pottery were decorated with pictorial Greek designs as well as pure ornamental enrichment. Drinking cups, pitchers, and bowls — complete with accurate representations of furniture, musical instruments, and costumes — give the student an opportunity to study the customs of the day. Most of the smaller Greek decorative pieces were exquisitely designed, illustrating the best principles of scale and proportion.

THE ROMAN STYLES

The finest examples of Roman design appeared between 100 B.C. and 300 A.D.; however, since the works were primarily Greek in inspiration, they cannot be labelled as truly creative. The Romans used most of the Greek decorative motifs and, in addition, found considerable use for ox-head, ram's-head, scroll, serpent, cherub, and fish-scale forms and certain grotesque, imaginary figures. The use of such forms as the arabesque, the garland, and the festoon for household décor suggests a playful, light-spirited attitude.

The Romans made frequent use of the three-legged table and

the pedestal table (page 234). Table legs were often carved to represent animal legs, and table tops were usually round or rectangular in shape. Chair shapes included the folding stool, the settee, and both high- and low-backed chairs; curved backs continued to be characteristic. Since the Romans dined in a sort of reclining position, the couch, with its pillow rest, was an especially important piece of furniture. Tripods and pedestals were particularly popular in these times and were often surmounted by lamps. Furniture materials included bronze, marble, and native woods and the use of carving, inlay work, metal appliqué, painting, and varnishing served as decorative methods. Decorative fabrics were pretty much limited to silks and tapestries but there was considerable use of metal threads in the weaving.

Aside from urns, pitchers, bowls, and various other utensils, the chief small decorative objects were lamps and candelabra. Bronze and silver were the chief materials used for this purpose and the serpent and the ram's head were represented freely as structural decorative aids. At one time or another, most of the motifs and border patterns were used to enhance and enrich small decorative objects. Greek utensils, however, are usually considered to be better scaled and to offer a more judicious use of ornament.

THE MIDDLE AGES

The Middle Ages included a period of roughly a thousand years, from the fourth to the fifteenth centuries. Most of the finest architecture and decoration of that era was religious in nature, with exalted forms in direct contrast to the miserable state of the common people. The various decorative characteristics of the Middle Ages were somewhat regional, however, and the final *Gothic* development was influenced by a number of specific historical events.

The *Byzantine* styles, developed in Constantinople after the fourth century, were a mixture of Roman, Persian, and Arabian forms. Decorative motifs were used profusely and usually had religious significance. The motifs were mainly stiff and sharp abstract forms; conventionalizations of animal and leaf forms were applied by means of carving and inlay. Mosaic murals of ecclesiastical subject matter were particularly effective, and the use of deep blue, red, and purple, combined with gold, gave exceedingly rich effects. While the craftsmen of the period were not much concerned with domestic furnishings, their brass and enamel work often showed great skill. After the Crusades, and before the fall of Constantinople in 1453, the Byzantine forms were introduced into Europe. To this day, the influences of the Byzantine civilization can be noted in the Russian and Greek styles.

The *Romanesque* period extends roughly from the ninth through the twelfth centuries and its beginnings are especially associated with the French king Charlemagne. The English Normans also developed a similar style and these French and English versions of the Romanesque eventually led to the Gothic style. Decorative motifs made use of geometric patterns such as the checkerboard and chevron shapes, and crude, awkward representations of the acanthus leaf and domestic animals were not infrequent. Windows were made of varicolored glass and offered mosaic patterns held together by strips of lead. The bareness of domestic interiors was sometimes relieved by means of tapestries and wall paintings.

The *Gothic* period, extending approximately from the twelfth through the sixteenth centuries, continued to illustrate the place of religion within the lives of the people of the Middle Ages. Undoubtedly the Crusades were largely responsible for the shift from the somewhat severe Romanesque forms to the elaborate and rich Gothic forms. Gothic decoration made use of a number of geometric and conventionalized forms that had not been used previously to any great extent. Oak foliage, acorns, stars, ivy plants, linen fold, coat-of-arms representations, and heraldic emblems were all popular. Although the pointed arch characterizes the entire Gothic silhouette, it is the elaborate stained-glass windows of the period that are most noteworthy.

In early Gothic days, furniture consisted largely of oak storage chests which could be moved easily. After the fifteenth century, however, the cabinet, the cupboard (credence), the bench, and the chair began to appear. High-back chairs were often constructed so that the seats provided chest arrangements. Planks on trestles served as dining tables, and canopies and curtains enclosed elaborately carved bed frames. Since furniture forms and carved decorations were borrowed from the architecture of the period,

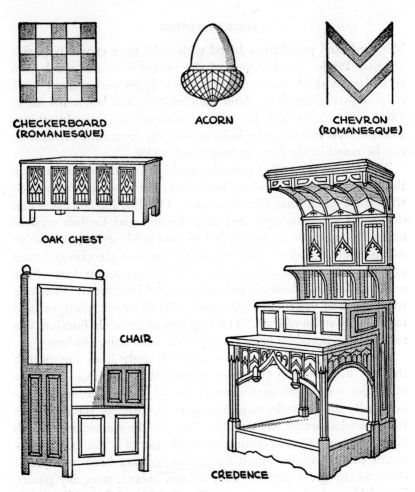

**CHECKERBOARD
(ROMANESQUE)**

ACORN

**CHEVRON
(ROMANESQUE)**

OAK CHEST

CHAIR

CREDENCE

Fig. 82 *The Romanesque and Gothic styles*

the pieces were usually ecclesiastic in feeling and their construction included such logical building principles as the use of the mortise and tenon joint. Early oak furniture was left in its natural state but, in later years, paint was applied. Silks, linens, and tapestries were among the fabrics, and color emphasis favored rich, deep greens, reds, and blues. The Gothic period was especially noted for the development of armor, silver utensils, and various types of enamelware. Wrought-iron hinges and elaborately designed locks contributed to the decorations of most of the Gothic chests and credences.

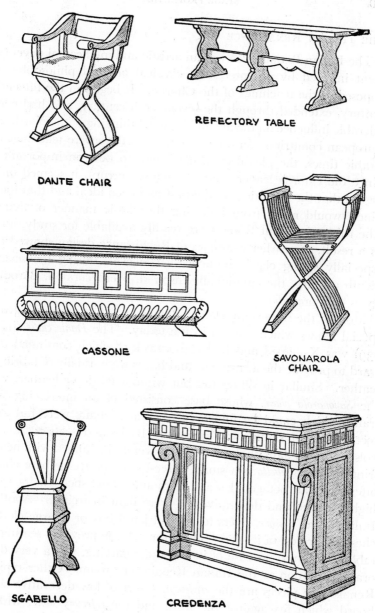

DANTE CHAIR

REFECTORY TABLE

CASSONE

SAVONAROLA CHAIR

SGABELLO

CREDENZA

Fig. 83 *The Italian Renaissance style*

239

THE ITALIAN RENAISSANCE

The Italian Renaissance was an artistic and intellectual development inspired by an interest in classical art and philosophy as opposed to the teachings of the Church. It began in the fifteenth century, extended through the seventeenth century, and had considerable influence on the art and political thinking of the Northern European countries. In direct contrast to the severe teachings of Gothic times, the pleasures of life began to take on importance. Since the Church leaders had become so corrupt, it seemed only logical that the conditions of the past had been ideal and that happiness would result from imitating the classic manner of living. The ruins of ancient Rome were readily available for study, and, as a result, the earlier examples of Renaissance design showed an especially strong classic influence. However, during the seventeenth century, the emotionally inspired, overdecorated, Baroque styles took precedence.

Most of the important Italian Renaissance furniture was given special names which are still in use today. The *Dante chair* (page 239) was X-shaped and had elaborate legs which continued upward to provide the arms; seats and backs were usually of fabric or leather. Similar in silhouette, but without fabric or leather, was the *Savonarola chair*, whose base consisted of an interlacing slat frame which could be folded. Other arm chairs were tall and rectangular in shape, and often the backs and seats were upholstered with damask, brocade, or velvet and trimmed with heavy fringe. The *sgabello* is a small, three-legged or trestle-base chair, often with an octagonal seat. Although some such chairs were highly carved and decorative, all were light in weight. Another Italian term, *cassone*, refers to a small jewel box or a large clothes chest, regardless of its size. The large cassone provided seating or table space and, because of its elaborate carving, was a very decorative addition to the Italian Renaissance room. Other typical Renaissance pieces are the *credenza*, a sort of low decorative sideboard which fits against the wall, and the *refectory table*, with a plank top and columns or trestles connected by stretchers. Walnut was the chief wood, and the classic motifs and patterns were carved or inlaid with ivory, semiprecious stones, or contrasting woods. A plastic cast ornament known as *gesso* was applied to early Renaissance pieces, and the use of gilt helped to bring out the detail of the gesso.

Small decorative objects in Renaissance times were abundant, and included household items as well as those which were purely decorative. Framed relief panels of religious subject matter, majolicaware decorated in scenic style, and bronze statuettes illustrate the variety of design which was represented. Bronze was also used for lanterns, candlesticks, andirons, and door hardware. The delicate Venetian glass of the period is well known, as are the mirrored glass pieces. So great was Renaissance man's interest in beauty that there was scarcely a staple item of daily living that was not pleasingly designed.

THE FRENCH STYLES

The French Renaissance. During the late fifteenth century the Gothic styles in France were definitely on the wane, mainly because they failed to offer the luxury and comfort which seemed desirable for a conquering nation. From the time of Francis I, in the early sixteenth century, until the beginning of the Baroque period (Louis XIV) during the last half of the seventeenth century, the Italian Renaissance had a great influence over French design. Francis I invited many painters, sculptors, architects, and craftsmen to work at his court. The influence of these men, together with the effects of certain minor Spanish and Flemish artistic trends, eventually completely routed the final traces of the Gothic.

Benches, stools, and the four-legged *caquetoire* (page 242), a narrow-backed chair (often without arms), were the main pieces of sitting furniture. Tables were of various shapes and bases were elaborately carved. The *tall cabinet* or two-layer cupboard, resting on bun feet, was perhaps one of the most characteristic pieces of the period and its elaborate inlay work of tortoise shell and bronze illustrated the detailed furniture decoration of the times. Decorative motifs were mostly of Italian inspiration although, during the reign of Francis I, the salamander was important. While oak and walnut were the popular furniture woods, at the start of the seventeenth century ebony became popular. Fabrics included velvet, damask, and tapestries; heavy fringes served as trimming.

CAQUETOIRE

HENRI II CABINET

SALAMANDER

CONSOLE

CHAIR

CABINET

Fig. 84 *The French Renaissance style (above) and Louis XIV period (below)*

FAUTEUIL

SHELL

PAGODA

BOMBÉ COMMODE

BERGÈRE

MANDARIN

CHAISE LONGUE

Fig. 85 *The Louis XV period*

The Louis XIV Period. It was not until the reign of Louis XIV that French décor took on definite national characteristics. Although the fabulous decorations at Versailles involved the work of the leading Italian and French artists of the day, the rich Baroque designs were not mere imitations of the Italian. During the reign of Louis XIV, 1643–1715, interior design emphasized an expansive formality which placed furniture as second in importance to the room architecture. Decorative motifs involved the use of geometric and conventionalized forms; among the latter were included masks, sun and sun-ray forms, flowers and leaves, animals, weapons, musical instruments, and certain Chinese forms.

The King's cabinetmaker, Boulle, was responsible for most of the extravagantly decorated seventeenth-century French pieces; tortoise shell and silver marquetry, known as *Boulle work* (or *buhlwork*), and the use of applied bronze decoration, *ormolu work*, were his special contributions. Since furniture was placed flat against the wall, rectangular lines controlled the shapes of most of the pieces. Typical early Louis XIV legs were square and tapered and often included a carved block top decoration; heavy scroll-shaped chair legs were featured later in the period. Although the high-back armchair and the freestanding table were equipped with stretchers, the tall, heavy, massive, decorative cabinets rested so near the floor as not to require this bracing. The *console* table (page 242), a development of the period, often included a marble top and carved legs, painted white and gilded (*boiserie*). The chaise longue, another development of the period, was later to become a distinctive Louis XV piece. A luxurious stately touch was provided by bed canopies, trimmed with fringe and hung from the ceiling.

The Louis XV Period. Louis XV became king in 1723, eight years after the death of Louis XIV. These intervening years make up the transitional period which is called *Régence* or French Regency, during which time straight lines gave way to the free curves of the Louis XV taste. Such Chinese motifs as the pagoda and the mandarin supplemented the rocks and shells, scrolls, ribbons, and pastoral forms of this rococo period; none of these motifs, however, was ever used symmetrically. Interior architecture was elaborate; and curved marble chimney pieces, fireplace equipment,

URN

BOWKNOT

ROSETTE
WITHIN BLOCK

FESTOON

SOFA

GALLERY-TOP
TABLE

ARMCHAIR

WRITING TABLE

Fig. 86 *The Louis XVI period*

245

and large mirrored overmantels were often impressively featured in many of the rooms.

Despite the ornate wall treatments of the period, for the first time French furniture became important in its own right. The cabriole leg, combined with the free curves of the furniture frame, gave the appearance of delicacy and grace. Side chairs were often provided with cane seats and backs which were made more comfortable by the use of loose cushions. During these years the *chaise longue*, the *fauteuil*, and the *bergère* (page 243) were developed into comfortable, attractive furniture units. The important wall furniture included *chests* and *commodes* with *bombé* (swell) fronts and elaborately carved *console* tables which were attached to the walls in architecturally sound locations. Many table tops were of marble although marquetry decoration was equally favored. The popular furniture woods were oak, mahogany, and the various fruit woods, all of which were sometimes lacquered or painted in pastel colors. The brass ormolu mount was an important furniture trimming and similar bronze work was a decorative feature of many smaller objects such as candelabra, clocks, Sèvres porcelain urns, barometers, etc. Fabrics were represented by satin, moiré, damask, brocade, needlepoint, and toile-de-Jouy, a hand-blocked cotton material with repeated pictorial designs.

The Louis XVI Period. About ten years before Louis XVI began his ill-fated reign (1774–1789), straight lines began to take precedence over the free curves that had been used so consistently during the previous fifty years. The nobility were tired of the extravagant Louis XV forms and, since money was scarce, they were aware of public disapproval; hence, simplicity and restraint came into vogue. The Pompeiian and Herculaneum excavations were responsible for a renewed interest in the classical forms. Many of the Greek decorative motifs were represented as well as such forms as urns, lyres, swans, bound arrows, festoons, swags, flower wreaths, and the bowknot (see page 245). The Petit Trianon at Versailles, although built during the reign of Louis XV, is generally considered to represent the best Louis XVI architecture and décor that is on display today.

Furniture legs were straight and tapered, often fluted, and usually

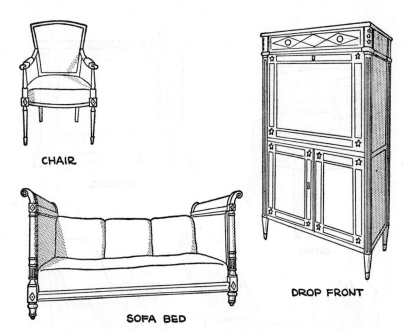

CHAIR

SOFA BED

DROP FRONT

Fig. 87 *The Directoire style*

decorated at the top with a carved rosette block. Brass galleries were frequently placed around table and commode tops, and brass moldings added a decorative trim to furniture panels. Sofas, love seats, writing tables, powder tables, bergères, and fauteuils were offered in natural mahogany or painted finishes. Painted designs were occasionally substituted for carving in an effort to simplify construction. Pastel colors continued to be popular and silk materials and toiles were preferred for draperies and upholstery work.

The First Empire. The transitional *Directoire* decorative period began with the French Revolution in 1789 and lasted approximately until the coronation of Napoleon in 1804. Although there was little in the way of Directoire architecture, the furniture of this period had a few definite characteristics. The delicate classic lines of the Louis XVI period continued to be popular but new military decorative motifs were introduced. Such forms as Liberty Caps, diamond shapes, drums, stars, spears, and arrows were used because of their subject matter, but any motif that was reminiscent of the French kings was held in disfavor. During these years, na-

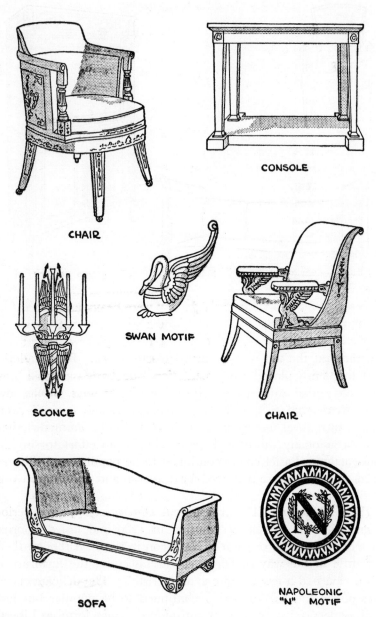

CHAIR

CONSOLE

SWAN MOTIF

SCONCE

CHAIR

SOFA

NAPOLEONIC "N" MOTIF

Fig. 88 *The Empire style*

248

tive woods were used instead of mahogany, and simple carving continued to be a decorative feature.

During the First Empire (1804–1814), Napoleon, through the appointment of David as the official art director, made every effort to establish a style which was typical of the spirit of the Empire and suitable for the new aristocracy. The chateau at Malmaison is the outstanding example of Empire décor and architecture, although certain rooms at Fontainebleau and Versailles were redecorated in the Empire manner. Decorative motifs were of both Egyptian and classic origin and included such forms as obelisks, sphinxes, winged vultures, eagles, swans, lotus flowers, palm leaves, acanthus leaves, bees, and cornucopias. Fabrics were either plain, striped, or block-patterned, and rich deep greens, reds, purples, and yellows were the most representative colors.

Much Empire furniture seems badly scaled in comparison to that of the Louis XVI period. However, many of the pieces were decoratively pleasing even though they were heavy and overgrand in design. Since large areas of the furniture were left plain and often veneered, the grain of the mahogany and fruit woods took on added importance. Ormolu mounts and stamped brass designs were the chief method of ornamentation, but chairs and table arms and legs were sometimes carved. Chair backs were curved and legs either flared or finished with carved dog's paws. The Récamier sofa, higher at one end than at the other, was one of the Empire versions of the chaise longue. The period was especially noted for its use of heavy mirror-back cabinets and consoles, round tables with pedestal bases, and low sleigh- or boat-type beds. The Empire influence was felt strongly in early-eighteenth-century England (Regency), Germany (Biedermeier), and America (Federal).

THE ENGLISH STYLES

The Tudor-Elizabethan Period. Throughout Queen Elizabeth's reign during the last half of the sixteenth century, there were strong evidences of the Italian Renaissance influence. Elizabethan furniture was mostly of oak and consisted largely of substantial chests, chairs, stools, tables, sideboard-dressers, wardrobes, and beds. Although the pieces are structurally Gothic, the decoration

JACOBEAN
STRAPWORK

MELON BULB LEG

ELIZABETHAN BED

ELIZABETHAN TABLE

JACOBEAN STOOL

JACOBEAN CHAIR

ELIZABETHAN CUPBOARD

Fig. 89   *The Elizabethan and Jacobean styles*

was usually Renaissance in feeling. The use of the *melon bulb leg*, with its acanthus leaf and gadroon carving, is the most distinctive decorative characteristic of the period. These bulbous legs, connected by stretchers, usually supported the long, heavy tables; guilloche carving was often a feature of the table apron. Chairs have wooden seats and wainscot backs and their turned legs were also connected by stretchers. The massive four-poster beds of the period were equipped with wooden canopies and side draperies, and ornamented with strap work, carved figures, melon bulb shapes, and scrolls.

The Jacobean Period. While some authorities prefer to classify the years from 1603 to 1689 as the Stuart or Jacobean period, the following divisions present more accurate distinctions: *Jacobean*, 1603–1649; *Cromwellian*, 1649–1660; *Restoration*, 1660–1689. The Puritan influence was strong in Jacobean times and ornament was limited mainly to such forms as the hexagon and the double rectangle. Chairs were used more frequently during Jacobean times than had been the case in the preceding years, and simple, turned legs and stretchers supported the chairs. The wooden chair backs were usually carved in geometric patterns and often trimmed with scroll arrangements at the top. *Spiral* or *twisted-rope* turning (page 227) appeared on some of the chairs and tables although many tables were designed with bulbous legs of a simplified form. The *drop-leaf* table was Jacobean in origin and such pieces appeared in various sizes and shapes. Late in the period, upholstery was introduced for chair backs and seats, and heavy fringes were occasionally used as trimming.

During the Civil War in England, the chief trend to be noted was the further simplification of furniture detail.

The Restoration Period. With the return of Charles II from Flanders, however, the Baroque styles made a definite impression upon the décor of the next fifteen years, and the work of Inigo Jones and Sir Christopher Wren helped to emphasize the crudities of the sixteenth and early seventeenth centuries. Restoration furniture (sometimes called *Carolean*), in contrast to the severe designs of Puritan times, took on ornate qualities. The *Flemish scroll* (page 252) became popular, especially for chair legs and stretchers, and

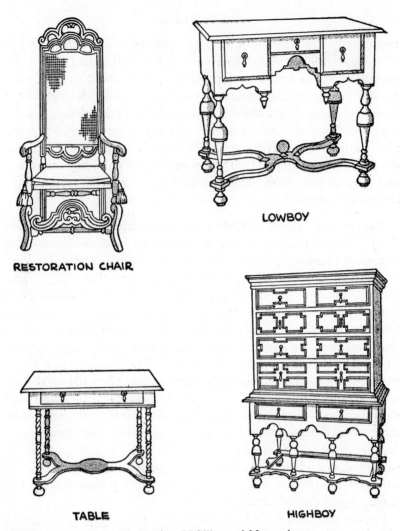

RESTORATION CHAIR

LOWBOY

TABLE

HIGHBOY

Fig. 90 *The Restoration (top left) and William and Mary styles*

spiral-turned chair and table legs appeared occasionally. Chair
seats and backs were often caned, with bright colored seat cushions
adding to the comfort of the chairs. The *baluster-* (banister-) *back*
chair often used a scrolled Spanish foot, and a carved headpiece
decorated the top of the chair back above the balusters. Such
relatively new furniture types as day beds, wing chairs, round
tables, and sofas were popular during these years. Furniture was

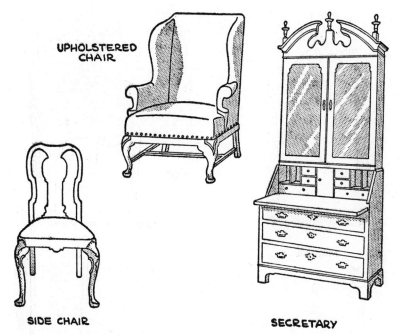

UPHOLSTERED CHAIR

SIDE CHAIR   SECRETARY

Fig. 91 *The Queen Anne period*

largely constructed of oak and walnut and there was occasional veneer work. Such decorative objects as crystal chandeliers, sconces, mirrors, fire screens, clocks, and silver vases were often prominently displayed in Restoration rooms.

The William and Mary Period. Because of the Holland background of King William and Queen Mary, the William and Mary period (1689–1702) was essentially Dutch in feeling. The decorative excesses of the Restoration were shelved and clean-cut lines and a more delicate scale prevailed. Elaborate *seaweed* marquetry patterns soon became more popular than carving, and large areas of highly polished walnut veneer work gave special emphasis to wood grain; lacquer work, involving the use of oriental motifs, was also in high style. Chair and table legs were straight and often designed with bell or inverted-cup shapes and carved Spanish feet. Spiral and trumpet legs were also represented, with flat stretchers giving support to the legs. Of the new pieces of furniture, the *lowboy* and the *highboy* were perhaps the most characteristic, although William and Mary sofas, love seats, and upholstered arm-

MIRROR

CHINESE LATTICEWORK

LADDER SLATS

GOTHIC
CHAIR BACK

SOFA

INTERLACED
RIBBON

Fig. 92 *The Chippendale styles*

chairs were not without distinction. The deep colored drapery and upholstery fabrics included velvet, crewelwork, needlepoint, damask, brocade, and tapestry.

The Queen Anne Period. Although Queen Anne's reign extended only from 1702 to 1714, the characteristic furniture silhouettes of this period were adapted and redesigned during early Georgian days up to, and including, the time of Chippendale. The Baroque forms of the period were Dutch in inspiration rather than French; the predominately straight lines of the preceding period gave way to the cabriole leg, the curved seat frame, and the pierced or plain *fiddle-backed* chair back. Chair stretchers were discarded later in the period and the claw and ball foot soon became popular. The grace and elegance of the Queen Anne chair extended to the other furniture as well; piecrust tables and other small tables came into popularity due to the new tea-drinking habit, and the glass doors of the cupboards and cabinets allowed for the display of colorful china. Lowboys and mirrors continued to serve as dressing tables, and highboys were often designed with elaborate broken pediment tops. Upholstered sofa and love seat backs were similar in silhouette to the wooden chair backs, including the characteristic carved detail. Decorative motifs were mostly limited to shells, acanthus leaves, and various oriental designs, although marquetry and carving were considered of less importance than the highly grained walnut surfaces. For window draperies and upholstery work, there was continued use of velvet, damask, needlepoint, and tapestry.

The Chippendale Styles. Although *Early Georgian* (George I) furniture was similar in silhouette to the Queen Anne styles, it was much more elaborately carved and decorated. Thomas Chippendale's early designs were of this type and were brought officially to the attention of the public in 1754 with the publication of his book, *The Gentleman and Cabinet-Maker's Director.* Chippendale is best known as an adapter; he had the ability to combine the best details of the popular styles and to carry on a very successful business. During this time, mahogany came into its own and has since been the most popular of woods.

The Chippendale chair back is perhaps the most easily recognizable feature of his work. *Fiddle-shaped splats,* carved *Gothic tracery, interlaced ribbon* carving, *Chinese latticework,* and *ladder slats* were all adapted from Queen Anne, Gothic, Louis XV, and Chinese designs. Chippendale cabriole legs were often of the claw and ball variety and usually included acanthus leaf carving at the knee. Straight legs, however, were likely to be found on the pieces showing the Chinese influence. Stretchers were omitted on chairs designed with cabriole legs although they were usually provided on straight-legged chairs. The aprons or skirts of the Chinese-inspired pieces were often carved with fretwork, or, if the legs were carved to represent bound lengths of bamboo, similar carving was likely to be found on the apron. (See page 254.)

Chippendale's Chinese designs were particularly well displayed in his elaborate mirror frames, overmantel designs, candle stands, brass hardware, and sconces. Commodes and serving tables were frequently decorated with Chinese motifs, and occasional highboys and secretaries were also carved in the Chinese manner. As a matter of fact, some Chippendale furniture included Chinese, Gothic, and classic motifs all used together. The upholstered camel-back sofa, the wing chair, and the open-arm upholstered chair were featured by Chippendale. The legs on such pieces were either cabriole or straight; upholstery materials were usually damask or brocade. Chair-back sofas and love seats, done in the styles of the popular chair models, were a pleasing substitute for the upholstered pieces. Most of the beds of the period were equipped with tall posts, and elaborate canopies were sometimes included.

The Hepplewhite Styles. George Hepplewhite's career as a designer and cabinetmaker extended from about 1760 to 1786. Although much of his work is noted for its delicate carving and inlay work, Hepplewhite was responsible for the introduction of painted furniture decoration. His use of wheat ears, corn flowers, paterae, ribbons, sunbursts, swags of flowers, urns, and other similar classic decorative motifs was especially characteristic. The fact that the Prince of Wales was one of his clients was probably responsible for Hepplewhite's frequent use of the Prince-of-Wales plumes as a decorative motif. Satinwood veneer became popular during the

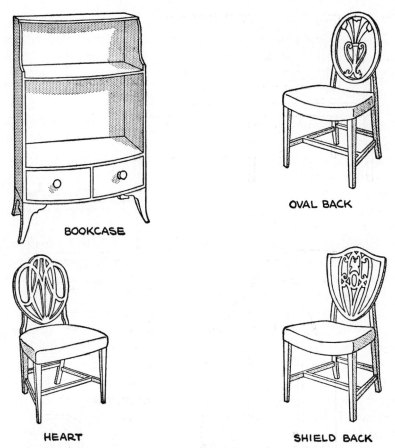

BOOKCASE

OVAL BACK

HEART

SHIELD BACK

Fig. 93 *The Hepplewhite style*

latter part of the century largely because its use was stressed by Hepplewhite.

Chair backs (above) made use of curved lines to produce oval, hoop, shield, and heart silhouettes; decorative carved splats were a distinctive part of the chair-back design. Chair legs were usually straight, tapering to form a spade foot. Reeded or fluted legs were typical although inlay designs were not uncommon. Because of the slender proportions of the chairs, stretchers were necessary to insure proper strength. The chair apron was seldom decorated, although — when pull-over upholstery was used in place of the slip seat — studding frequently completed the upholstery work. Hepplewhite furniture designs also included such pieces as side-

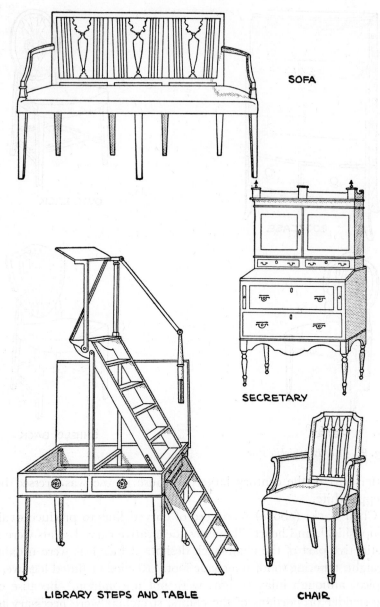

SOFA

SECRETARY

LIBRARY STEPS AND TABLE

CHAIR

Fig. 94　*The Sheraton style*

258

boards, dining tables, china cabinets, chests, commodes, consoles, card tables, drop-leaf tables, flat-top kneehole desks, and secretaries. These pieces were often decorated with inlaid or painted designs, particularly on such areas as the apron and the drawer and door panels.

The Sheraton Style. Thomas Sheraton's career as a furniture designer may be said to have begun in 1791 with the publishing of his book, *The Cabinet-Maker and Upholsterer's Drawing Book.* Sheraton's designs were influenced by the Louis XVI styles as well as by the classic forms of ancient Greece and Rome. However, his designs in the Directoire and First Empire manner, in his later years, were not considered as pleasing. Sheraton's use of straight lines and segmental curves was particularly characteristic, and the simplicity and restraint of his designs were ideally combined with sound construction principles.

Sheraton legs were likely to be of the taper-turned variety with reeded or fluted shafts and turned feet which were sometimes covered by brass sheathing. Chair backs made use of rectangular lines; ornamental splats were held in place by horizontal top and bottom rails. Chairs were decorated with restrained carving and inlay work. Sheraton secretaries and cabinets were of excellent scale and proportion and were often given interesting pediment treatment. Many Sheraton pieces were most ingenious in design, specializing in such devices as disappearing drawers, secret compartments and locks, remarkably equipped dressing tables, tambour panels, or steps which folded to disappear within a table. Sheraton sofas, often upholstered in striped silk, were designed with a silhouette similar to that of the side chair. Other Sheraton pieces included sewing tables, chests, sideboards, dining tables, and drop-leaf tables.

The Adam Style. The Brothers Adam were architects as well as furniture designers and their work was inspired by their first-hand contact with the classic styles and with the work of Palladio. The most important of their designing was completed between 1762 and 1792 when Robert and James Adam were architects to George III. For the first time, entire rooms were designed so that interior architecture and decorative detail were closely related.

Adam furniture (page 260) is best represented by the large pieces

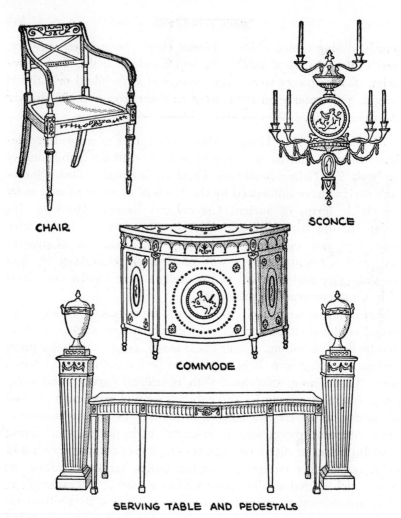

CHAIR

SCONCE

COMMODE

SERVING TABLE AND PEDESTALS

Fig. 95   *The Adam styles*

of wall furniture which were specially designed for particular rooms. Sideboards were originally made up of two pedestals and urn-shaped knife boxes placed on either end of side tables; the combination of these three units developed into our present-day sideboard.   Furniture was decorated with carved or painted classical motifs such as lyres, urns, swags, ribbon bows, honeysuckle forms, bell-shaped flower pendants, paterae, wheat husks, and such running patterns as the Greek fret and the egg and dart.   Adam chair

SOFA

CHAIR

TABLE

Fig. 96 *The English Regency style*

backs were either rectangular, shield, wheel, or oval in shape and chair legs were tapered and usually decorated with carved, inlaid, or painted pendant designs. Since the Adam brothers were not cabinetmakers, it was necessary for them to work with such men as Hepplewhite; hence it is often difficult to label a piece of furniture as definitely "Adam" or "Hepplewhite."

The Regency Style. Before George IV came to the throne in 1820, he served as Regent for a period of about ten years, thus naming the English Regency style. This style was inspired by the architecture and decoration of ancient Greece and Rome. Since many Regency designers had mainly an archeological interest in the styles of antiquity, their work was not particularly creative. Decorative motifs were often developed as applied brass ornament and included such classical forms as the honeysuckle, the cornucopia, and the Greek fret. Although furniture was not specially designed for comfort, the curved Greek klismos chair back was often pleasingly used. Large pieces of wall furniture such as bookcases or sideboards often depended on architectural principles for their decorative interest. Architectural interest was also obtained by the use of marble busts and statues placed in niches and on pedestals. The end of the period, however, saw many poorly scaled and overdecorated pieces.

The Victorian Styles. During the long reign of Queen Victoria, 1837–1901, English designers tried almost every imaginable type of revival with generally unfortunate results. The furniture inspired by Louis XV was perhaps the most successful, but there was no dearth of Gothic- and Turkish-styled furniture. Since novelty was the chief aim, little attention was given to scale and proportion or meaningful use of ornamental motifs. The rosewood and black-walnut Louis XV versions (opposite) were either carved with flower, leaf, and fruit forms or inlaid with florid mother-of-pearl designs. Chair seats were rather low and backs were usually oval in shape. The Gothic and Turkish furniture was especially noted for its dreary gingerbread and unfortunate scale. Victorian colors were bold with special emphasis on red, purple, blue, and green. The typical elaborate floral fabrics and wallpapers, when combined with the overdetailed furniture, gave a consistently *busy* effect. Neither the serious Gothic adaptations of Sir Charles Eastlake nor the *Arts and Crafts* designs of William Morris were able to guide late-nineteenth-century design trends into aesthetically pleasing channels.

MISCELLANEOUS STYLES

The Spanish Renaissance. The Moors first invaded Southern Spain during the eighth century A.D. and, for the next five hundred years, had a definite influence on the artistic development of that country. Moorish tile work made plentiful use of such decorative motifs as triangles, crescents, stars, and crosses. In addition to Moorish decorative tile work, jugs, dishes, pitchers, and vases were used for decorative purposes; these utensils were extremely bright in color and were also decorated with geometric motifs. Tooled leather, another important Moorish contribution, was often used

SOFA

TABLE

CHAIR

TABLE

Fig. 97 *The Victorian styles*

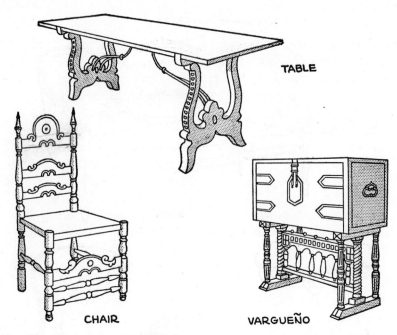

TABLE

CHAIR

VARGUEÑO

Fig. 98   *The Spanish Renaissance style*

for covering walls and furniture.   Furniture largely consisted of a profusion of cushions and low tables.

After the expulsion of the Moors, during the sixteenth century Gothic and Italian Renaissance designs were introduced and combined with Moorish decorative forms.   The strong, rectangular walnut and oak furniture (above), noted for its strength, was either painted or inlaid with bone, silver, or tortoise shell.   Slanted, heavily turned table legs were often braced by means of curved wrought-iron supports.   In rural areas, extravagantly carved or painted ladder-back chairs were popular, with elaborate shell designs on the top slats and on the stretchers.   The Spanish foot, based on the Flemish scroll, was sometimes featured on chairs, settees, and small tables.   The box-shaped *vargueño* desk was of special importance, however, since it was an original form.   This desk was given interesting decorative treatment, complete with drawers, partitions, and impressive hardware.   Heavy cupboards with carved or grilled doors offered many opportunities for decorative treatment.   Tooled leather was an important covering and upholstering material, complete with decorative nail heads in rosette and star shapes. Other covering materials were velvet, velour, brocade, damask, and tapestries, with colors tending toward bright reds, blues, and warm yellows and oranges.

The Oriental Styles. Previous to the seventeenth century, Chinese furniture — except for ceremonial pieces — was extremely scarce. During the Ch'ing-Manchu dynasty (1644-1851), furniture, pottery, and rugs were produced which, as has already been pointed out, had considerable effect upon European design trends of the seventeenth and eighteenth centuries. Chinese furniture was extremely practical since all the pieces were designed in relation to the specific problems of daily living. The construction was remarkable and the woods were either beautifully polished or heavily lacquered.

The Chinese *wardrobe* is an ingenious affair, often built in two separate layers and designed to be used with as many as four sections forming one large unit. Cabinets for the display of vases and statues often made use of zigzag shelves combined with sections set off by doors. One of the most interesting sitting pieces is the *K'ang* or couch on which K'ang tables were placed between two people; such tables are sometimes used today as coffee tables. Writing tables and tall side tables were also important types as were extremely low tables, sometimes with scroll feet, which were used to display elaborate coffers or chests, decorated with carved brass hardware.

Chinese decorative flower motifs were numerous and lavish, particularly when applied to vases and rugs; such flowers as peonies were represented singly and in groups. Dragons, horses, lions, and cranes were also popular as were butterflies and landscapes. Carved fretwork and cloud heads often helped to accentuate chair and table aprons. Blue on white or white on blue was an extremely popular color combination for the pottery of the Ming dynasty (1368–1644) although polychrome combinations later became popular.

Japanese designs, on the other hand, have had a greater all-round influence on the contemporary styles, from the time of William Morris until the present, than have any of the other ori-

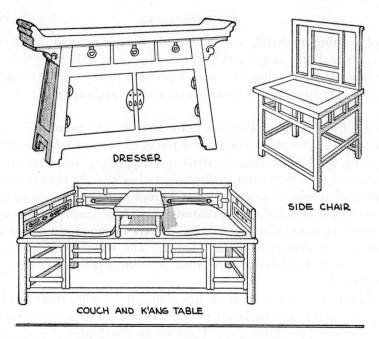

DRESSER

SIDE CHAIR

COUCH AND K'ANG TABLE

Fig. 99 *The Oriental styles: Chinese (above) and Japanese (below)*

ental forms. The spaciousness and lightness of the traditional Japanese room (opposite), with its plain walls of varying textures, and recessed areas, offers the essence of functional design. There has never been much freestanding Japanese furniture, however, since built-in chests, cupboards with sliding doors, sleeping mats, and low tables have largely taken care of the furniture needs of the people. Such furniture as was used was usually given a handsome lacquer finish which included specks of gold floated in the lacquer. Floors often contained a box-like opening in which charcoal was burned. Although most of the elaborate Japanese silks were designed for wearing apparel, occasionally materials made generous use of such motifs as Mt. Fuji, cherry blossoms, elaborately dressed women, and landscapes of pine trees.

The American Styles. The American versions of most of the eighteenth-century English styles were an important feature of the artistic development of this country. There has been a tendency, however, to consider the American styles in rather a general fashion without much attention as to dates. The term *Early American*, for example, is often loosely applied to all American decorative designs, and sometimes late-eighteenth-century pieces are called *Colonial*. Such confusion of terminology is particularly bewildering when a designer is attempting to discuss furniture with a director.

So-called *Early American* design is correctly associated with the seventeenth century. Most of it is based on the tastes of the Jacobean and William and Mary periods, although usually offering less detail. Native woods were used for the simpler pieces, and cabinetmakers considered sturdiness as more important than refinement of design. On the other hand, the eighteenth-century American *Georgian* styles, imitative of the English designs of the same century, were more sophisticated and more detailed, and usually made interesting use of wood and grain. Since most American furniture of these centuries is based on the English styles, it is well to label the pieces as such; thus we have American Jacobean, American Chippendale, and American Sheraton. Some authorities apply the term *Colonial* to the Early American and Georgian periods.

The early-nineteenth-century American styles, sometimes called *Federal*, show both French and English influence. The designs of Duncan Phyfe were a part of this period and, of course, have special distinctions of their own. The Federal period made generous use of such motifs as the pineapple, the American Eagle, cornucopiae, heavy scrolls, and various classic decorations. Although considerable use was made of such woods as mahogany and rosewood, the decorative chairs of Lambert Hitchcock were of lighter woods stained or painted in imitation of darker woods.

Many Victorian manufacturers in America, like those in England, were overly preoccupied with the Gothic styles. Ornateness took on more importance than did taste, and interiors were often a conglomeration of clashing colors and extraordinary ornamentation. Those Victorian pieces which were based on Louis XV lines were not necessarily offensive; however, Romanesque and Moorish carved motifs, frequently combined with Gothic or Renaissance decoration, necessarily produced weird, meaningless detail.

The Duncan Phyfe Style. Although Duncan Phyfe's designs were based largely on Sheraton, Hepplewhite, Directoire, and Empire styles, his work was sufficiently distinctive as to be recognizable. The best of his New York designs were completed between 1790 and 1830 during the so-called Federal period. The most successful of the Duncan Phyfe designs are known for their pleasing proportions, clean-cut lines, and conservative use of ornament. Duncan Phyfe was particularly fond of pedestal-base and lyre-base tables. He also made considerable use of reeding for legs, chair arms, and table edges. As decorative motifs, he preferred simplified acanthus leaves, water leaves, oak leaves, acorns, laurel leaves, eagle's claws, dog's feet, ribbons, and lyres. Chair and table legs were often completed with brass mounts. The use of carving, simple inlay work, ornamental hardware, and veneer helped to give a richness to many of the pieces.

Chairs, sofas, and tables are the most characteristic of the Duncan Phyfe pieces of furniture. One of his most often reproduced side chairs is noted for its curved, reeded legs and lyre back (see opposite). Phyfe tables included card, dining, sewing, and console pieces. Dining tables sometimes had as many as three pedestals, and library

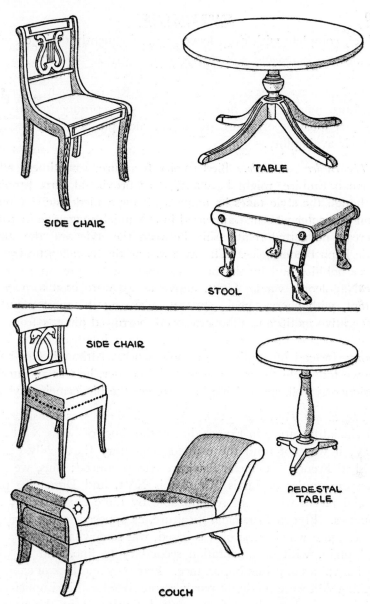

SIDE CHAIR

TABLE

STOOL

SIDE CHAIR

PEDESTAL
TABLE

COUCH

Fig. 100 *The Duncan Phyfe style (above) and Biedermeier style (below)*

269

tables, complete with drop leaves, were frequently designed with lyre bases. Sofas and love seats were usually designed with carved wooden rails at the top of the back. Love seats sometimes had curved arms and legs similar to those of a Roman couch. Today's furniture market is so flooded with Phyfe reproductions that a designer must be on guard not to use such pieces simply because of their availability.

The Biedermeier Style. Biedermeier furniture, sometimes called German Empire, might be classified as provincial First Empire. Although the style takes its name from Papa Biedermeier, a cartoon character who first appeared in a Munich magazine in 1815, there is no actual relationship between the style and the stuffy little Papa Biedermeier. The style was originally taken up by the lesser nobility and by the business people who were profiting by the Napoleonic wars. Light, native woods were used to a great extent, with cherry, pear, and apple among the most popular. Decorative motifs and silhouettes were borrowed directly from the Empire period but decoration was mainly painted, or inlaid with ebony, instead of applied as ormolu work. Although Goethe is known today chiefly as a poet and philosopher, he was an interior designer as well, specializing in the use of the Biedermeier style.

The French Provincial Styles. Although there was considerable provincial furniture in France during the times of Louis XIII and XIV, it was not until the eighteenth century that really distinguished French Provincial furniture was produced; thus, we find many examples of Louis XV, Louis XVI, and Directoire provincial pieces which are recognizable by those characteristic silhouettes. French Provincial furniture, as opposed to the Parisian pieces upon which most of it is based, was somewhat conservative and plain, with ornamentation secondary to line, and its utilitarian values of prime importance. Economy and lack of cabinetmaking skill were no doubt partly responsible for this simplicity.

The typical furniture forms varied somewhat in the various provinces but the *armoire* (as a substitute for the closet), the canopied bed, the rush-seated ladder-back chair, the settee, the commode, and the buffet were generally in use in the provinces. Chairs that were not upholstered sometimes made use of loose cushion seats.

Toile-de-Jouy was popular for upholstery and draperies and was sometimes used to cover entire wall areas. Woods were almost invariably oak, cherry, walnut, and elm and carving was extremely simple. Pewter and copper utensils and wrought-iron chimney piece fixtures were used appropriately with these charming furnishings. Since there has lately been a specific commercial interest in French Provincial furniture, such pieces are likely to be readily available to the designer.

The Contemporary Styles. Although the *Arts and Crafts* work of William Morris was among the first to attempt pure design as opposed to traditional ornamentation, it was not until around 1900 that *Art Nouveau* really attracted the attention of the general public. Like Morris, Van de Velde, the original exponent of Art Nouveau, used nature as a source for his design motifs. Beetles, dragonflies, waterlilies, tomatoes, poppies, daffodils, and crocuses were used with a vengeance, and a profusion of vines and branches often connected these various motifs. While Art Nouveau designers insisted that their work was functional as well as new and nontraditional, actually they thought mainly in terms of decoration. The weird, twisted, badly proportioned furniture often made use of unusual materials such as stained glass and metals. In America these influences were shown in the peacock vases and iridescent glassware of Louis Tiffany and in the products of the Roycroft Shops. Germany took to this trend to the extent of permitting Van de Velde to found the Bauhaus at Weimar in 1902. Later on the Bauhaus, under the influence of such designers as Gropius and Moholy-Nagy, developed a more satisfying set of decorative principles.

In 1925 the Paris Exposition displayed considerable furniture which today is often labelled *Art Moderne.* The furniture was known for its peculiar shapes, lush upholstery, and pure novelty. The term *modernistic* is also frequently applied to those unpleasant pieces. Stepped-up bookcases, zigzag decorative motifs, frosted-glass wall brackets, horizontally striped draperies, pretentious and meaningless streamlining, circular unframed mirrors, and the use of weird woods were particularly characteristic. Most of the French Line ships in the late twenties and thirties were treated in this

ART NOUVEAU MOTIF

ART NOUVEAU

ART MODERNE

EAMES

MIES VAN DER ROHE

BREUER

SAARINEN

HARDOY

Fig. 101   *The contemporary styles*

manner, and Radio City Music Hall is not without its Art Moderne influences.

In considering present-day non-traditional furniture, many designers prefer to use the term *contemporary* instead of *modern* since furniture manufacturers often refer to reproductions as modern in contrast to antiques. Contemporary design is and always will be in a constant state of development. The best contemporary design stresses functionalism, restraint, and the use of quality materials. Much contemporary furniture is beautiful because of its simplicity and honesty, and lack of ornamentation. The most highly regarded contemporary furniture makes excellent use of space, and its form is determined by the use to which it is to be put. Even though some designs are slightly reminiscent of traditional forms, the prevalence of light colored woods always guarantees a contemporary feeling.

Obviously, certain styles of contemporary design are associated with particular present-day designers (see page 272). Marcel Breuer in Germany, for example, was largely responsible for the cantilevered S-shaped chromium tube chairs. Ludwig Mies van der Rohe, from the same country, insisting that form follows function, used strips of metal in place of chromium tubing to produce similar silhouettes. In all probability such furniture was first developed as a result of a subconscious worship of machinery; the expression "Dentist's Office Modern" has frequently been applied to the more commercial versions of these pieces. From Sweden the designs of Bruno Mathsson and the use of curved laminations by Alvar Aalto from Finland are examples of an interest in craft as opposed to the machine. In America, Frank Lloyd Wright has shown a similar interest in craft although his actual room furnishings are often of the built-in variety. Charles Eames's rhythmic chairs with their molded plywood seats and backs are held by many to have particular present-day significance.

Such a designer as Eero Saarinen, known for his big sculptured chairs, feels that the furniture of today, in order to be in tune with mid-twentieth-century living standards, can well afford to make use of such materials as foam rubber, plastic, and other experimental materials. The antitraditional writings of Robsjohn-Gibbings are well known as are his slender graceful designs for The

Widdicomb Company, usually executed in light woods. The work of George Nelson and Edward Wormley makes similar use of light woods and graceful lines. The more extreme sculptural-biological work of Noguchi attempts to suggest living tissue in motion; Noguchi designs cannot be taken lightly since they are always sincere if not intelligible to the average person. An interesting Italian chair, the *Hardoy*, has become famous because of its crossed legs and suspended seat.

Many of the present-day contemporary designs will no doubt be considered out-of-date in a few years. Too many of the designs are so experimental that their only accomplishment is that they resemble none of the traditional forms. The very best of the designs are so expensive that they are out of the reach of the average buyer; the markets, however, are flooded with bad contemporary pieces to which the term *modern* is loosely applied. When the scene designer is called upon to use the contemporary styles, he must give special consideration to the particular era or quality of the work required. A contemporary stage room which must express "avant garde" highbrow qualities must obviously suggest also the soundest theories of present-day contemporary design.

Decorative Metalwork

Decorative hardware for use on the furniture in stage period rooms need not be neglected because it is not readily available. As a matter of fact, most commercial or special-order period hardware is too expensive for groups that are on limited budgets since the hardware might then cost more than the built pieces upon which it is to be placed. However, designers will find it helpful to refer occasionally to various hardware catalogs for suggestions as to the silhouettes of certain decorative hardware pieces. Needless to say, if the designer-technician ignores this feature of the stage picture and lacks ingenuity as to the preparation of substitutes, his work will often seem incomplete and may occasionally appear to be incongruous.

Many types of hinges, drawer knobs, keyhole plates, and drawer handles can be simulated by means of three-ply, papier-mâché, and paint. Salvaged handles and knobs from wrecked furniture

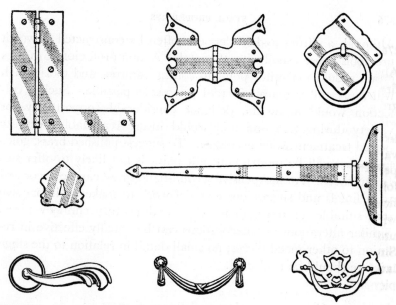

Fig. 102 *Decorative metalwork*

are often useful after being given special decorative treatment. Although carved balsa wood does not have sufficient strength for general use, if thin muslin is glued over the carved portion, the wood may be sufficiently durable provided it need not be handled violently. Sometimes the part of the fixture that must be handled can be practical, with three-dimensional painting suggesting additional form and decoration.

The student will note in the illustrations above that there is a specific relationship between hardware forms and the spirit of a period as illustrated by its popular decorative motifs. The Louis XV scroll and the Louis XVI swag, for example, were commonly used for drawer handles. Regency and Empire ring pulls made considerable use of the lion's head, and Adam urns often appeared on keyhole plates and drawer knobs. Many Chinese Chippendale pieces abound with elaborate hardware of oriental design. In contrast to the above styles, cock's head and butterfly hinges are suited to the less elegant early-English and Colonial furniture.

Andirons, fenders, grates, fire tools, and firebacks are usually necessary if a chimney piece is to seem convincing on the stage.

275

Although andirons and fenders can often be constructed of wood, fire tools must usually be of metal. A non-professional theatre group should make it a point to collect andirons and tools which will represent as many different periods as possible. Such a collection would allow the designer considerable opportunity for variety during a season and would insure reasonably accurate period treatment when necessary. To suggest polished brass, gold-foil paper will be most useful; gilt paint is not likely to offer sufficient sheen. An inexpensive second-hand grate can be decorated with finials and suggestions of relief work to make an impressive unit suitable for use with an eighteenth-century chimney piece. Similar alterations and decorations can be equally effective in relation to other metal pieces; no small detail in relation to the stage picture should be neglected.

Renting and Borrowing

Groups that have neither the time nor the facilities for the building of furniture and special properties must either rent or borrow such items. Unfortunately, the amount of effort expended in locating furniture, obtaining permission for the renting or borrowing, and transporting the pieces to and from the stage, often exceeds the time which might be required for simple remodeling and building jobs. Furthermore, borrowing and renting is not usually so satisfactory as building since it is so often necessary to settle for articles that are not quite right. Unless elaborate period pieces of furniture are to be built, the designer will do well to locate such pieces before including them as part of his original water-color rendering.

The larger communities are often well supplied with used furniture stores which have a variety of interesting furniture and bric-a-brac for sale. Such establishments will sometimes rent furniture for a fee ranging from five to ten per cent of the value of the items. The difficulty involved here has to do with the possible sale of the merchandise; articles that are selected a month in advance may not be available by dress rehearsal and performance time. Used furniture is seldom a trial to backstage workers, as small scratches can be touched up and soiled spots cleaned without changing the market value of the pieces. Used furniture looks particularly well on the stage since it is less likely to give the impression of being straight from the sales floor.

As for borrowing, persistent designers will find a great variety of furniture available at little or no cost. However, there is always considerable worry regarding the care of the articles and, if damage to borrowed furniture becomes habitual, ill feeling will soon develop between a theatre group and the community. Damage to properties seems to come mainly during the transit from the house or shop to the stage; therefore, extra consideration must be given to moving methods. In case any breakage occurs, the group should not haggle with the owners but should immediately pay what is asked. Designers are perhaps justified in feeling a certain loss of dignity when they literally must go from house to house looking for furniture. Socially the problem also presents difficulties; hostesses may fear, and rightly, that a designer will necessarily catalog the contents of their rooms for possible future use. None the less, since a non-professional theatre contributes to a community, the community should not be above contributing to the theatre. While program credits are usually not desired by those who loan, complimentary tickets are usually appreciated as are "thank you" notes. All items must be *returned promptly*.

Furniture Building, Remodeling, Refinishing, and Upholstering

Specific productions occasionally demand specially shaped and scaled furniture which can be neither borrowed nor rented. When this is the case, the designer must design the units in such a manner that they can be built in the shop. Since large wall units such as bookcases, cabinets, and cupboards need not always be practical, the builders may often construct large frameworks, held together by mending plates and flat corner irons, and cover portions of the frames with wallboard, three-ply, or even canvas. Moldings and hardware and various applied ornamentation can be fastened to the unit if three dimensions must be featured. Occasionally, large units must have one small section that is practical — a drawer must pull out or a book must be taken from a shelf. In such cases, it will be possible to insert a box-like structure into the proper position leaving the balance of the unit purely decorative. In the case of book shelves, actual binding backs can be attached to the shelf divisions to create a three-dimensional effect. Half-round battens are sometimes used as a substitute, as are vari-sized cardboard tubes. A large open shelf unit might well be backed with canvas, thus cutting down considerably on its weight. The use of casters is advisable if large furniture units must be shifted during performance.

The first consideration in connection with specially built tables is their stability and bracing. While tables of a certain style or period may be visibly braced, others must have freestanding, rather delicate legs. An Elizabethan table must be as solid as a rock and visible stretchers may be utilized for bracing purposes. Eighteenth-century English tables, however, are usually braced under the apron. In order to obtain a variety of levels and attitudes, directors frequently have the actors sit, stand, or lean on tables; thus the table must be prepared for any eventuality. Carved or turned table legs had better be made from white pine since other woods are so difficult to work with. Detail need not be so exact as would be required for household cabinetmaking, but scale and proportion must be correct. Paint can help to bring out carved detail, and the final over-all finishing coat should suggest the specific qualities of the wood. If the table is to be realistic, the use of shellac, varnish, or some glossy finish will give it an interesting contrast to the flat paint of the walls.

Side chairs present much the same bracing problems as do tables; visible supports are typical of some periods but not correct in others. The use of furniture glue, screws, and angle irons is necessary if the chair is to be solid and the stiles of the chair back must always be a continuation of the rear legs. Since cabriole legs and fluted legs of various styles are available at furniture-manufacturing firms, it will probably be better to purchase these rather than to attempt to carve them. Architectural supply houses have interesting displays of molded three-dimensional ornaments which, while not inexpensive, will prove invaluable for various knee and top-rail chair decorations.

Upholstered chair and sofa frames, except for size and scale, are, of course, similar in construction to those of the side chair. Since upholstered furniture for the stage need not be comfortable in the household furniture sense, it is often wise to build hollow arms and backs which, when covered, will appear to be cushioned; strips of lathe, layers of three-ply, or wallboard are ideal for this purpose. In this connection it is particularly important that the framework be strong since, once the unit is covered, it is difficult to reinforce the frame.

If a theatre group possesses an ample supply of various types and periods of furniture together with odds and ends of turnings, relief designs, and hardware, it will be possible to do considerable remodeling and thus change the contour and color of furniture. Non-professional theatre organizations should let it be known that they will always accept every donation of this sort. The designer must also become a frequent shopper at such stores as those run by the Good Will, the Junior League, and the Salvation Army. He must buy goods that seem to have remodeling possibilities even though the pieces may not be needed at the moment. Auctions and sales are also important contributory sources. Theatres that have been renting or borrowing for years will obviously have nothing in their storerooms; such a situation is likely to limit the pictorial effects which they can obtain inexpensively.

Too often shop workers hesitate to cut up, simplify, enlarge, or paint and refinish some reasonably good period piece which they own. On the contrary, furniture should be considered only as related to particular productions since exquisite lines and patina will have no particular value in storage. Many mongrel pieces of furniture of excellent wood and finish need only slight remodeling to make them appropriate for use with furniture of a particular period; others will require refinishing after drastic alterations have taken place. Sometimes a basic framework can be completely disguised to produce a realistic or stylized piece of real distinction. Whatever method is used should guarantee that the furniture will be exactly right in feeling, scale, and color for a particular room.

When furniture is remodeled, in its completed state it is likely to represent woods of various colors and finishes; for that reason, it is almost always necessary to refinish the pieces. Since the removal of varnish and paint is a laborious process, it will be wise to

Fig. 103 *Upholstering and slip-covering*

consider some substitute for this process. The simplest method is to give the furniture a coat of Texolite paint of a color somewhat similar to that of the desired finish. This coat can be grained in the manner of a particular wood and the entire piece then coated with shellac or a varnish stain of the appropriate color. The finished product must then be rubbed with steel wool so that the gloss disappears and a dull polish applied as the last step. Such a method is particularly successful when an imitation of fumed oak is desired.

If furniture is to have a painted finish rather than to show the grain of the wood, it is best to use oil paint or Texolite; scene paint, unless it is heavily loaded with glue, is likely to rub off onto the costumes. Furthermore, scene paint offers little contrast to the walls of the setting. Texolite has the advantage of being relatively easy to remove at a later time, but it will never offer the gloss that can be expected from an enamel. Often rustic furniture can be painted to suggest unfinished wood since, in such a case, a glossy finish would not be desirable.

The chief requirements for stage upholstery are that the work be neat and trim in appearance and that the material be firmly attached. Upholstered pieces for the stage should not be equipped with springs since it is not desirable to have actors seated in such positions that it will be difficult for them to arise gracefully. Cushions can be filled with padding or scraps of cloth, and padding or layers of burlap should be satisfactory for the arm and back foundations.

Unless old upholstery is in very bad condition, it need not always be removed before new material is put on. A borrowed or rented upholstered piece, of course, must be covered by the use of stitching instead of tacking so as not to cause damage to the foundation material. Regardless of the condition of the original piece, the material must be cut to fit the various sections of the furniture such as the arms (inside and outside), back (inside and outside), and seat (top, bottom, and thickness). Expert upholsterers pin the material directly to the chair and trim the excess, allowing a couple of extra inches for joining and six or more inches for tucking in at the seat and back. To avoid waste, beginners will probably do well to make paper patterns. When printed material has a pattern which must be matched, an extra yard of material should be ordered.

If the material is to be tacked to the frame, and the upholstered piece is of the style which requires the use of a welt edge (cord, covered with material), the arm covering must be either sewed in advance by sewing machine or sewed in position on the frame using a strong thread and a curved needle. If gimp (ornamental braid) is to be used where the cloth joins, blind-tacking may be necessary. Blind-tacking involves tacking the back side first and then folding over the material to the finished side. This type of tacking will be especially useful for most open arm chairs. Unless a welt edge is required, the material may be tacked underneath the chair rail using #4 tacks.

A removable slip cover requires basically the same patterns as an upholstered piece although more yardage will be necessary. A slip cover, complete with welt edges or piping, is sewed together completely except for one seam which is zipped or snapped together after the cover is adjusted. The following yardage table for *plain fabrics* should prove useful to those who must order the materials:

	Upholstery	Slip Cover
Club chair	6	7
Love seat	8	11
Sofa	11	14½

When patterns must be considered, extra material must be provided. Chintz, cretonne, linen, satin, and rep are excellent slip-cover materials since they are light in weight, of sufficient body, and easy to sew. Slip covers must fit perfectly or they will not add distinction to a room. One or two pieces of furniture are frequently slip covered with the same material as the draperies.

Window Curtains and Draperies

Curtain and drapery fabrics for the stage need not be of the best quality but neither should they be so cheap as to appear sleazy. Since materials must often be dipped or dyed, heavily sized materials will necessarily become limp after such treatment. Although materials should be bought wholesale, by the bolt, whenever possible, occasionally department store sales or sellouts will offer unusually low prices. Most materials must be toned down or textured in some manner; therefore it is not wise to borrow curtains or draperies. In addition, stage windows are so much higher than house windows that borrowing is not practical.

Glass curtains which are also called sash curtains, fit next to the window frame. If the roller type of window shade is used, the glass curtains will be placed in front of this shade; windows equipped with Venetian blinds usually dispense with glass curtains, especially in public buildings. The most frequently used glass-curtain materials are marquisette, organdy, scrim, gauze, lace, and silk, rayon, or cotton net. Curtains of this type are usually finished at the top by means of shirring or a French heading, and hang to the sill or, in a formal room, to the floor. Glass curtains have a softening effect upon a room and are particularly desirable in rooms with an eighteenth- or nineteenth-century feeling.

Draw curtains are sometimes placed over the glass curtains, especially when there are no window shades. Since such curtains cut off the view and keep out direct light, they must be of some material such as shantung, pongee, rep, or taffeta. Draw curtains

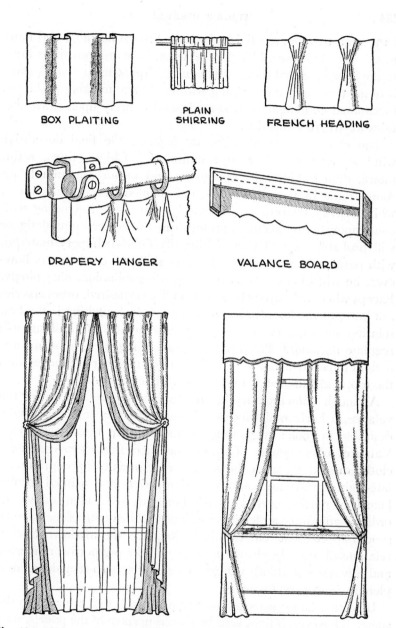

BOX PLAITING

PLAIN SHIRRING

FRENCH HEADING

DRAPERY HANGER

VALANCE BOARD

Fig. 104 *Glass curtains, overdraperies, pinch plaiting, and special hardware*

hang on a traveler, are finished with a French heading, and hang
to the sill. However, like glass curtains, they are sometimes hung
to the floor in formal rooms. The use of draw curtains on the stage
is of great assistance in helping with backstage masking problems.
Occasional contemporary rooms depend entirely upon draw curtains for window covering.

The choice of materials for *overdraperies*, the final decorative
window treatment, is almost unlimited. Chintz, linen, satin,
moiré, damask, brocade, brocatelle, and velour are suitable for
rooms done in the eighteenth- and nineteenth-century manner,
while heavily textured plain materials are more interesting with
contemporary architecture and furniture. The beginning designer
will probably do well to avoid heavily figured drapery materials
with patterned walls. As he develops skill and competence, however, he will discover how to use such combinations charmingly.
Except where an extremely informal effect is desired, overdraperies
are hung to the floor. *French heading* or pinch plaiting is the best
solution for drapery panels since this method of finishing will
regulate the folds. Pinch plaits consist of regular groups of three
folds at intervals of four to six inches, sewed together five inches from
the top, and stiffened at the back with buckram.

Although contemporary rooms do not require the use of the
valance, a horizontal window trimming, such a device is usually
desirable in rooms suggesting the more recent traditional styles.
Valances often consist of shaped wooden frames covered with
cloth; draped valances, however, are especially appropriate for
late-eighteenth-century and Victorian rooms, and painted cornice
boards or mirror-covered valance boxes are often used today. In
order to guarantee a pleasing relationship, the depth of the valance
should approximate one eighth the height of the window. Such a
relationship must be clearly indicated on the perspective rendering
and elevations so that it will never be necessary to remodel a completed window treatment.

It is often unnecessary to line drapery panels that are used on the
stage. However, if light is to be placed upstage of the panels, they
must sometimes be interlined with a black material. Sateen is the
customary lining for household draperies but muslin will be satisfactory for stage use. Panels will hang much better if the selvage

is cut at regular intervals and the sides of the panels hemmed by hand. Machine-made draperies and curtains are likely to be stiff and angular. Sewing for the stage need not pass as close inspection as work done for a house, but the work should, none the less, be strong. Triple thickness hand-sewn hems are desirable on all draperies, four inches wide at the top and two inches wide at the bottom.

Unless the panels are sufficiently wide and full, they will give the impression of a pair of shoelaces. For example, if a window is four feet wide, neither panel should be less than four feet wide. Since the drapery patterns in the panel must match, it is always well to order an extra yard; if the design is small, a half-yard will suffice. Panels are weighted at the bottom with chain or dressmaker's weights. Tiebacks are suitable for both formal and informal draperies and are usually placed one third the distance from the top or the bottom of the panels. A considerable variety of tiebacks are possible (flat belts, cords, metal ornaments, etc.); the choice will depend upon the period involved and the character of the room.

Draperies on the stage should ordinarily not be hung with lightweight household hardware. Sometimes it is advisable to tack the panels directly to a batten or wooden valance which in turn is hooked to the wall by means of *picture-frame hooks and sockets* (p. 291). If the window treatment demands the use of poles and rings, *drapery-pole hooks and sockets* (p. 283) will be invaluable. Draw curtains may be hung with household tracks but this apparatus should be fastened to a batten which is hooked to the wall so that it can be removed easily.

Many types of traditionally designed draperies require the use of trimming of some sort before they appear complete. Trimming includes such possibilities as accordion-plaited bands, ribbons, ruffles, gimps, or fringes. Fringes are broadly classified as cut, uncut, ball, tassel, or molded, and are available in silk, cotton, wool, or rayon. Cut and uncut fringes include the moss, chenille, and bouclé varieties while ball fringes depend on cotton, silk, woolen, crystal, or wooden balls for their decorative effects. Molded fringes, often specially designed and handmade, frequently consist of unusual crystal or wooden pendants combined with loops

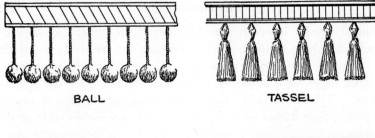

BALL   TASSEL

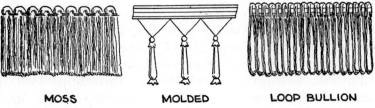

MOSS   MOLDED   LOOP BULLION

Fig. 105 *Fringes*

of heavy silk thread and tassels. Late-nineteenth-century rooms made particular use of elaborate trimmings on runners and cushions as well as for draperies. Trimmings should usually be of the same material as the decorative units that are to be trimmed. Draperies in rooms that stress contemporary design seldom require the use of trimming of any kind.

The Arrangement and Selection of Furniture and Decorative Objects

Although most stage furniture cannot be placed in positions which would be considered as normal in an actual room, yet, unless the script demands unusual placement, effort must be made to suggest arrangements which bear some sort of relationship to room architecture. If the designer first considers the entire room, with its four walls, and later removes the fourth wall, he will be working in the right direction. Heavy, tall pieces such as secretaries, breakfronts, and cabinets are ordinarily placed against a large wall expanse. However, if sofas are flat against a wall, they will not be easily accessible to the actors. Chairs and tables are of most value when they are freestanding and permit actors to play around them.

Most stage interiors are planned with emphasis on two or three

286

Displeasing   Pleasing

Fig. 106   *Furniture and picture arrangements*

furniture groups, one of which is of primary importance. A group might consist of a table and two chairs or a downstage sofa, parallel to the act curtain, with a long table or desk upstage of it. If a room contains a chimney piece, it would seem logical that furniture placement should not ignore this architectural feature; nearby armchairs should surely not be backed against the chimney piece. Sometimes directors and designers, in striving for originality, contrive furniture groupings that offer playing variety but look stiff and unconvincing. Stage interiors in the professional theatre are sometimes so large and contain so many groups of furniture that the various groups appear to be almost as isolated as those in a hotel lobby. In contrast, small non-professional stage settings are occasionally so filled with furniture that it is difficult for the actors to walk about. Unless a cluttered effect is required, designers and directors will do well to concentrate on bare essentials and to fill in wall spaces with pieces which are necessary for dressing the setting.

If a grand piano is correctly placed within a stage setting, it can add character and refinement to a formal or semiformal room and at the same time give the feeling of belonging. Ordinarily, a grand piano is placed with its straight side against a wall and with some relationship to outdoor and indoor lighting; an awkwardly placed piano will suggest that it is a showpiece and seldom used. Although a limited amount of piano-top decoration is permissible, real musicians do not load their pianos with shawls, photographs, vases, and lamps. Tall, upright pianos should never be used on the stage except where called for in the script; an upright piano for *Fumed Oak* is exactly right. While the present-day version of the spinet piano is not an unattractive instrument, it can hardly substitute for a spinet of the sort needed for *Ladies in Retirement.* In such a case, perhaps it might be better to use a remodeled spinet desk and offstage music. Miniature uprights look rather well in stage game or rumpus rooms and in small apartments, without suggesting the dreariness of tall upright pianos.

Traditionally styled present-day rooms should offer informal furniture arrangements which *illustrate* the tastes and habits of those who live in them. Informality can be emphasized by using an occasional skirted piece as a relief from the stiff exposed furniture legs. In contrast, the furniture in an authentic period room must be arranged in a manner appropriate to the life of the times; "leg" problems will be of little concern in this connection. Arrangements of contemporary furniture, complete with numerous built-in pieces, should probably point up a *manner of living* rather than illustrate it graphically. Certain liberties must necessarily be allowed when the contemporary styles are used on the stage since it is not usually desirable that stage furniture line the walls nor that the center stage areas remain free of furniture.

Wall *pictures* and *paintings* must be planned for in the designer's original renderings, and not hung in hit-or-miss fashion after the setting stands on the stage. Size relationships between pictures and furniture must be studied on paper so that the best use can be made of wall spaces. Since stage walls are so much taller and wider than those found in actual rooms, it may be necessary to increase the scale and number of such wall decorations in rooms which must not appear barren. A few large, well-spaced paintings will usually suggest a more formal effect than a profusion of smaller pictures, hung in groups.

As a rule, an up-and-down picture is more pleasing above a chimney piece or a heavy piece of furniture than is a horizontal picture. However, horizontal pictures may be used in groups to build an over-all perpendicular effect. Pictures on the stage must be hung somewhat higher than in a house — the eye-level line becoming the minimum low placement rather than the high extremity. Ordinarily the eye should not jump up and down as it follows various pictures or picture groups around the room; nor should pictures be placed above or higher than the openings to a setting unless a particularly quaint or grotesque effect is desired.

The designer must study the picture-hanging and framing methods of the twentieth century and of various earlier times. In the twenties, cords and tassels frequently called attention to the hanging method. Pre-World-War-I pictures were often hung with visible wires hooked onto low picture moldings. Eighteenth-century paintings and etchings were always hung with invisible supports as are present-day framed pictures. Oil paintings are never matted and are often heavily framed and lighted with individual lighting fixtures. Etchings and water colors, however, are matted and often framed inconspicuously. In most cases, oils and water colors are not combined within a particular wall grouping although, if the designer has a particular flair, such arrangements might prove interesting for stage rooms occupied by certain Noel Coward characters. Dramatic picture arrangements similar to those often featured in the interior design work of William Pahlmann should prove especially effective for highly styled stage rooms.

It is usually advisable to prepare pictures in the shop since exact sizes, subject matter, media, matting, and framing are difficult to track down in the stores. A piece of three-ply of the exact size can serve as the foundation. After the mat paper and picture, or the picture alone, are fastened to the three-ply, molding can be applied around the edge. The whole picture is then ready to spray and, since it is without glass, it can be toned until it is relatively inconspicuous. If crew members are not prepared to paint suitable pictures, magazine pictures are often usable. Color reproductions of famous paintings are available but the cost is usually prohibitive. Beware of using recognizable reproductions of paintings from famous museums when the stage room would obviously be hung with originals; the *Kind Lady* setting that includes the Mona Lisa or a popular Picasso will be completely out of focus, no matter how attractive it may otherwise be.

Special stage hardware for hanging pictures is more satisfactory than picture wire since the hardware guarantees that the picture will not jostle around. The picture-frame hook is fastened to the back of the picture and the socket is attached to the flat; heavy pictures may require hardware at both top and bottom. Borrowed pictures cannot be hung in this manner as the attaching of the hardware might damage the frames. (See page 291.)

The small decorative objects used with a stage room must be chosen as carefully as the larger items and must represent the same attention to scale and proportion. Contemporary design favors a few large items rather than a collection of smaller objets d'art which are considered suitable for traditional rooms. Arrangement by pairs will always suggest greater formality than groups which appear less studied, although informal arrangements may be just as carefully planned. Overloading with bric-a-brac is, of course,

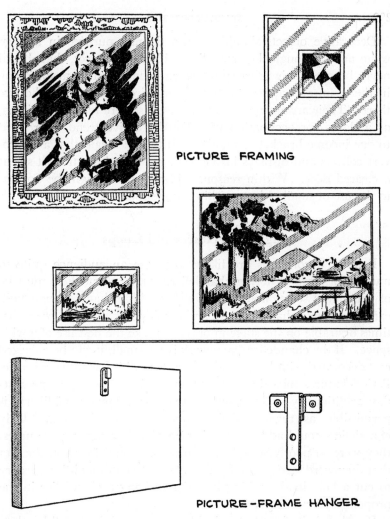

PICTURE FRAMING

PICTURE-FRAME HANGER

Fig. 107 *Picture framing*

representative of the worst Victorian years and of the Gay Nineties. Bric-a-brac is not difficult to locate in second-hand stores — nor should the cost be prohibitive. In recent years, the various utility stores have offered assortments of crude china figurines, many of which can be painted, toned, and substituted for valuable eighteenth-century pieces. It is not wise to borrow expensive objets d'art for use on the stage.

Decorative objects should serve a definite purpose in a stage room and, although they sometimes fill empty spaces, that should never become their primary purpose. They must seem to belong in the room and appear to have been selected by those who live there. Their arrangement may suggest a sincere manner of living, or a slavish preoccupation with the decorative trends as related to one income bracket or another. It has been said that an introvert collects and displays his belongings while the extrovert sits at a cleared desk. Within reason, this suggestion might be applied to the use of small objects within a stage room.

Lighting Fixtures and Lamps

Few set decorations are likely to please an audience quite so much as a large glittering chandelier. Stage chandeliers must be of very large scale; household fixtures seldom have enough bulk except for use in hallways and arches. Two chandeliers are sometimes desirable on the stage in order to make the best use of a wide space. If the chandelier framework is too small, it can be enlarged and decorated with beads and pendants until it has sufficient scale. Period fixtures must be truly representative although in present-day traditionally styled rooms, a reasonable amount of liberty is permissible as regards their silhouette and trimming. Ugly chandeliers could add an amusing note to the stage picture unless they were so poorly scaled that emphasis would focus on the fact that they were inadequate for the space. Oftentimes it is necessary to cut a hole in the ceiling in order to hang a chandelier in the proper position.

If a chandelier is not practicable, sconces or wired wall brackets may be used. These also must be overscaled if the stage picture is to be pleasing. If sconces are placed about the room consistently, they can serve as light sources. These fixtures may be plain or decorative, according to period, and are normally arranged so as to be related to such architectural features of the room as the chimney piece, panels, archways, etc. Less orthodox arrangements are often used for purposes of humor or to illustrate poor taste. An amusing touch might involve the attachment of a floor lamp cord to a wall bracket, directly over it. Candle shades or shields have been used off and on during the past fifty years, but are not usually suitable for traditional rooms.

The use of table lamps for the stage interior is usually limited to those areas where a lamp would not block the action of the play. Tables, desks, and chests that are placed against a wall make the best use of lamps for decorative and light-source purposes. Lamps must bear a scale relationship to the furniture upon which they are placed. Thanks to Dorothy Draper and her influence upon the scale of lamps in particular, it is not difficult to find inexpensive lamps which can be refinished and toned to suit a distinctive room. Unfortunately for the market, but fortunately for the designer, many ridiculously small lamps are still available for use by designers who assemble stage rooms which must display picayune trimmings. Although either translucent or opaque shades are useful on the stage, the former perhaps present a softer warmer quality to a stage room.

The floor lamps and bridge lamps of the twenties and thirties have been almost entirely replaced by table lamps except by the contemporary designers. A floor lamp, topped by an ornate, fringed silk shade, is almost a trademark of bad taste, especially when such a lamp is placed beside an upright piano. Bridge lamps with plaited or beaded parchment shades represent the days when homecraft novelty work was a national pastime. Many contemporary floor lamps, however, are highly representative of the work of important contemporary designers and are a far cry from their early originals.

Foods and Beverages

Among the more difficult hand properties are food and beverages, since here the actors' preferences are likely to be of as much concern as are the requirements of the scene. Stage food must be palatable and not unpleasant to look at although it need not always be expensive nor exactly what the lines of the play suggest. Most actors accept substitutions for such items as filet steaks, caviar, and lobster; however, substitutions must not be made which will involve allergy problems or strong individual dislikes.

It sometimes seems that authors must take special pleasure from requiring the use of food and drink on the stage. A long list of breakfasts, lunches, and buffet suppers could be tabulated from the productions of any recent Broadway season. Perhaps when an author temporarily runs out of dialogue, he uses coffee, tea, or cocktail conversation to fill in. At any rate, the problem must be met frequently both at rehearsals and during performance, and food must usually not be stringy, gummy, highly seasoned, nor served in unclean dishes. As a general rule it will be wise to avoid such foods as crackers, stew meat, cold mashed potatoes, peanut butter, caramels, and celery. On the other hand, ground beef, cold cuts, fresh bread and cake, hardboiled eggs, bananas, and rice are easy to eat and, with a little ingenuity on the part of the property crew, these foods can suggest many different foods. If food is served in a steam dish, dry ice will help to give the suggestion that the food is warm even though the ice will make the food cold to the taste.

As for beverages, cold tea, cold coffee, and cider will be the most useful substitutes since, when they are diluted, they give the appearance of such liquors as whiskey, sherry, or vermouth. The combination of grape juice with a little lemon is pleasant to the taste and at the same time looks like port wine. Imitations of the various pink wines can be concocted from diluted grape juice or plain water and vegetable coloring. Pale ginger ale can be served as a substitute for champagne if it is poured into a champagne bottle of the proper shape and brand. If the champagne cork must be removed onstage, it can be whittled down before it is inserted into the bottle, and the actors can turn the bottle slowly in the approved manner in order to remove the cork — an offstage "pop" will add a realistic touch. Because of the head which develops as beer is poured, it is difficult to substitute for this beverage. As for milk, although professional property men frequently prepare milk for the stage by adding a bit of condensed milk to water, obviously real milk will be more pleasing to most actors.

Miscellaneous Properties

Most stage productions require a considerable variety of properties, eccentric or otherwise. A comprehensive list of the average properties that might be needed during a season would hardly be possible since such plays as *You Can't Take It With You* and *Angel in the Pawnshop* would upset any normal list of properties. However, certain items keep reappearing on property lists and are therefore worth consideration at this point.

1. *Newspapers.* Wherever possible, the correct papers should be obtained. Since audiences are quick to detect errors of this sort, it is well to glue the proper heading at the top of the sheet even if an actual, complete paper is not available.

2. *Luggage.* Unless the script specifies otherwise, luggage should show some signs of wear. It should also usually be weighted so that actors do not have to pantomime the weight.

3. *Cigars and cigarettes.* The actors' preferences should be followed as far as possible although, of course, with reasonable regard to expense. Date and locale must be considered in selecting the shape and size of the cigars and cigarettes. Cheap tobacco should be avoided as far as possible. Pall Mall and Tareyton cigarettes should be satisfactory for such plays as *The Sea Gull* or *The Three Sisters.*

4. *Matches.* Since book matches were not in general use before 1930, small boxes of matches or kitchen matches must be used if the play is set at an earlier date.

5. *Guns.* Even though blank cartridges are always used for stage guns, the gun should never be pointed directly at another actor. After guns have been fired they must be cleaned with gun-cleaning compound, cleaning fluid, or soap and water before re-oiling. Unless this is done the re-oiling will not prevent corrosion. Many gun experts feel that blank cartridges foul a firearm much more than do ball cartridges.

6. *Swords, knives, and daggers.* If these sharp instruments are borrowed, Scotch tape can be placed across the edge for safety purposes. If the articles belong to the producing group, it will be advisable to grind the edges and the points.

7. *Ash trays.* If a little water is placed in the tray, ash trays will not smoke. Unless comic business requires a tippy ash tray, large substantial pieces are the most useful.

8. *Razors.* Most groups will find it desirable to purchase a straight-edged razor and to grind its edge. It is not otherwise safe to use such a razor on the stage.

9. *Packages.* All stage packages should be wrapped in a manner suitable to the contents and the occasion. A laundry package should not resemble a gift package, or vice versa. If a slip knot is used for the cord or ribbon, the package can be untied in a hurry.

Artificial Flowers and Foliage

The use of artificial flowers for interiors and exteriors can accomplish a great deal toward dressing a stage setting. Whether growing or in vases, flowers help to indicate season, locale, and the personal preferences of the characters. Greenhouse flowers are not useful on the stage since the lights will fade the natural colors. Such flowers are also an extravagance since they must be replaced frequently during the run of a show; artificial flowers, if properly cared for, should last over a period of years. When the flowers are handled by the actors, the slight sound of the rustling of paper may disturb some literal-minded patrons. However, this is really not a serious criticism since very few decorative properties are actually real and everyone knows it.

Some productions may require as many as six different large flower arrangements during the performance. If artificial flowers of high quality are purchased outright for such use, the cost might easily exceed a hundred dollars. Therefore, such utility stores as Woolworth's and Kresge's should be watched closely over a period of weeks — stock often changes quickly. Some florists' supply jobbers have splendid artificial flowers made in accurate copy of actual plants and blooms. Many of these are made of cloth and sheet rubber and do not rustle. They cost as much or more, of course, than the flowers they represent. Quantities of expensive and inexpensive flowers of various kinds and colors should be purchased as available and stored in long florist boxes *between* layers of tissue paper. Although these purchases will involve considerable money, yet, because it is a long-range plan, the purchases should not be considered as an extravagance. If the colors of these flowers are too bright, they can be touched up carefully with scene paint or Texolite. Homemade artificial flowers, unless a real expert is available, are seldom satisfactory.

Artificial leaves are relatively simple to construct and are much more suitable than real leaves which soon wither and lose whatever color they may originally have had. Actual tree branches are often stripped of leaves, covered with strips of canvas, and dressed with artificial foliage. This method usually guarantees impressive results although the process is somewhat tedious. Property people

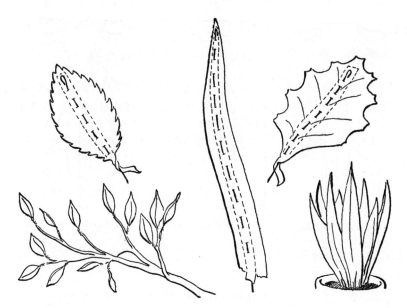

Fig. 108 *Foliage*

must study the characteristic shape of the leaves in question and make patterns of leaves of a variety of sizes. The green cloth-paper used by book binders, shiny on one side, is ideal for making leaves, but if this is too costly, stiff green paper such as is used in grammar school art classes will be reasonably satisfactory. (Plexiglass, with cord or wire, can also be painted on both sides and used for leaves although this is not an inexpensive material.) After the green art paper is shellacked on one side, it is ready to be cut into leaf shapes of various sizes. If necessary, leaves can be touched up with red and orange paint to suggest autumn.

Lengths of ordinary black stovepipe wire, eight to ten inches, are next punched in and out so that the wire will not loosen. A small strip of green shellacked paper can be glued over the wire on the dark side of the paper; the other end of the wire is then free to twist around the tree branches. Students will note that leaves grow in groups and that leaves of various sizes appear within a group. A similar use of leaves is just as satisfactory for vines as it is for tree branches.

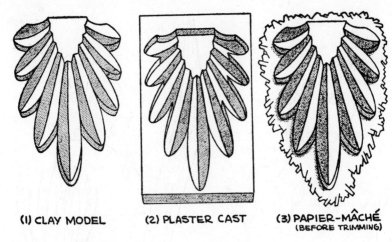

(1) CLAY MODEL   (2) PLASTER CAST   (3) PAPIER-MÂCHÉ
                                                   (BEFORE TRIMMING)

Fig. 109   *Papier-mâché work*

Papier-Mâché Work

It is frequently necessary to prepare a number of lightweight three-dimensional forms that are exactly alike. Such forms as capitals, carved ornament, and urns may be made of papier-mâché and attached to scenic units to suggest solidity and to reinforce the detail of the stage picture. The first step is to model the desired form out of molding clay. The clay form is coated with vaseline or oil before it is covered with the plaster of paris which is to serve as the papier-mâché mold. After the plaster hardens, the clay is removed and the inside of the mold rubbed with graphite powder or a soap solution. Layers of thin paper are placed in the mold, layer by layer, and held together by the use of mucilage, thin glue, or a combination of wheat paste, glue, and whiting. Thicker paper and sizing may be necessary if the details of the mold are broad rather than minute and detailed. After the glue has hardened, the masklike form of the original clay model is gently removed. This mask must be given special support before it is used as part of the scenery. If the mold is to be of considerable size, it may be best to approximate its shape in wire or scraps of lumber, thus requiring the use of less clay.

There is practically no limit to the objects that can be formed in this manner. Shelves of bottles, vases, bowls, and jars are often too heavy for use on the stage; if these items are of papier-mâché, their weight will be negligible. Life masks can be made by providing the subject with nose straws through which to breathe during the process. Extra decoration can be applied to furniture and pottery by means of a paste made up of paper and size water. This mixture is not difficult to mold into the desired shapes and designs. All papier-mâché work can be painted with any type of paint. *Celastic,* a new colloid treated material, may be substituted for certain kinds of papier-mâché work. Although this product permits extremely fast and accurate work and guarantees durable results, the cost is somewhat greater than that of papier-mâché.

Property Plots

Unless stage properties are carefully listed and their whereabouts taken into account at all times, there is likely to be considerable confusion during performance. Experienced professional property men are able to perform their duties with the aid of informal placement lists and shifting notes. Beginning backstage workers, however, must organize their work in graphic fashion on paper so that their lack of experience will in no way prevent a smooth technical production.

A complete over-all listing of set and hand properties is desirable as a point of departure. Properties should be itemized under such main headings as furniture, rugs, pictures, vases, china and silver, food, etc. with indications as to scenes involved. Such a list cannot be obtained from the back of a Samuel French edition of the play, but must be worked out with the director and the designer. This complete list is, of course, subject to slight changes, mostly additions, during the rehearsal period. After the list is complete, it will be up to the designer and the technical workers to decide which items must be built, which borrowed, which rented, and which purchased.

If a property is to be *constructed or remodeled*, it is desirable to make *drawings* which will illustrate what is to be expected of the finished product. Drawings for property construction or remodeling, orthographic or isometric, must indicate dimensions, together with lists of supplies which will be necessary in order to complete the work. Bolts, studding, gimp, relief designs, paint, stain, etc. may all be required to prepare a single chair for stage use. Advance planning of this sort guarantees orderly, accurate shop work which will budget working time to the best advantage.

It is usually advisable to keep account of the *production expenses* involved with the property work of the various productions. Such expenses may be classified under two main headings — *permanent* and *current*. The permanent list will include all materials and objects such as furniture, artificial flowers, dolls, silver, dishes, and vases that were purchased for a particular show; the current list should include such items as cigarettes, food, and liquids which must be replaced frequently during the rehearsal and performance period. Both lists should make use of such headings as *name of item, use, store*, and *price*. Property shop expenses have a way of increasing in leaps and bounds until they sometimes equal or exceed the cost of the scenery. Occasionally it is well to estimate in advance the costs of the various work divisions from the point of view of their relative importance to the final pictorial effect. In case a show is repeated, production expense listings will prove invaluable in preparing the budget.

Special *lists of borrowed and rented properties* are usually necessary in order to make certain that all items are returned to the proper persons. These lists should contain the following information:

Property	Delivery		Source	Approximate Value	Returned	
	By	Date			By	Date

It may also be a good idea to have the merchant or householder initial the printed form. This may serve as a protection to all concerned. Occasionally people forget that some small item has been returned; when such cases arise, misunderstanding and ill feeling are likely to result. A group that is lax in returning properties may discredit the reliability of all the theatre groups within a community.

While property-crew members may have no specific duties related to dressing a one-set show for the first time, their *duties during performance* are of a precise nature. In a multi-set show, wall properties are often semipermanently attached to the walls; therefore, property shifts are primarily concerned with furniture placement.

Before specific duties in either a one-set or a multi-set show can be carried out satisfactorily, crew members must know exactly where and when each property is to go on and off the stage setting. In addition to ground plans showing furniture relationships, it is necessary to draw up a plan for the top of each piece of furniture that has a horizontal surface. These plans should show the exact arrangements of such items as lamps, ash trays, books, and vases — scene by scene. Similar plans should be drawn for each offstage property table.

The *specific duties* of the various crew members must be listed in some organized fashion so that the work can be checked easily and accurately. Duties will normally include setting the stage before performance starts, the placement of small hand properties before performance and between scenes, striking small objects between scenes, and striking furniture and bulky wall trimmings between certain scenes of a multi-set show. Although the stage manager may check a few important small properties, it is up to the property crew to be responsible for the majority of the work. Specific assignments are always completed by the same persons; during the run of a show, these duties should become almost second nature.

The offstage placement of the furniture for a multi-set show frequently presents many difficulties. Furniture for a particular scene must often be stacked together in a group so that it can be carried onstage in a hurry. This offstage placing of properties is to be considered in direct relationship to the stacked scenic units. In order to make the best use of backstage space it is advisable to draw up plans of the entire stage floor, scene by scene, showing the exact placement of all furniture as the pieces relate to the entire production. It is only by such a method that shifting and storing difficulties can be minimized. Obviously, the traffic lanes involved in shifting may determine some of the placement decisions.

The Care of Properties

Regardless of the source of the hand or set properties, they must be cared for at all times when they are on the stage. At best, the repair of properties is expensive and time-consuming, even when breakage occurs at a time other than during performance.

Chairs, sofas, tables, and benches are supplied for the use of the actors during the technical and dress rehearsals and performances and should never be sat on by crew members or used by the actors at any other time. Unless there is specific business to the contrary in the script, furniture should be moved by backstage workers only — and then, by the lifting method rather than by dragging. A sufficient number of people should be assigned to a heavy piece of furniture so that it can be moved safely and easily. Furniture should be covered at night regardless of whether it is left on stage or stored in the backstage areas.

During a quick scene shift, the hurried striking of small hand properties from a table or desk top can become a problem; unless small, fragile items are handled carefully, there is danger of breakage. The best solution in such a case is the use of the *snatch basket*, a small market basket with a handle, supplied with pieces of padded cloth. An object can be placed in the basket and immediately covered so that another hand property can be placed on top of it. Thus, in one trip, a single crew member can collect many small objects quickly and silently.

Every stage should be supplied with a property cabinet large enough to hold all the properties of a show except the furniture. This cabinet must be arranged so that tall objects such as vases, clocks, and candelabra can be placed in drawers without danger. Each night after rehearsal or performance, all such objects should be stored carefully and the cupboard *locked*. Never pile one object on top of another without separating them by means of padding. Most non-professional groups that have not followed this practice can recount unpleasant experiences which involve theft and breakage. As a matter of fact, items of unusual value or size should perhaps be locked away in a special room to insure their safety.

It ought to be possible to anticipate much of the damage that is likely to occur to furniture and the various bric-a-brac. Designers will do well to attend a few rehearsals to see what the actors are going to do as they are in the various areas of the stage. A few conferences with the stage manager should clear up any questions of this sort. For example, if a gun or some other heavy object is to be dropped sharply on a table top, it will be well to protect the table in advance by means of cardboard or a sheet of isinglass.

A scene involving scuffling had better be played in or around substantial, solid furniture. A borrowed or rented wooden-arm chair would hardly be a suitable place for a nervous actress to sit if she were loaded with innumerable decorative bracelets. Since face and body make-up will be bound to rub off somewhat, such a production as *Private Lives* had better not be played using a borrowed or rented sofa. A minimum of wear and tear on properties must be expected; therefore, the crew had better be well supplied with cleaning fluid, scratch remover, and dull furniture polish.

PROJECTS AND EXERCISES

1. According to the normal use that they might have on the stage, classify the following as set, trim, or hand properties: book ends, a table runner, a screen, a desk pad, a wall tapestry, a set of law books, a potted plant, a briar pipe, a chaise longue, a recent issue of *The New Yorker*.

2. List at least three of the distinctive silhouette features of the following types of furniture: lowboy, Lawson club chair, Carver chair, bergère, wing-back chair, Welsh dresser, ladder-back chair, comb-back Windsor chair, butterfly table, kneehole desk, console, breakfront.

3. Select a side chair from your property shop and analyze it according to its structure, labelling the parts. Make an orthographic projection of the chair to one-half-inch scale.

4. Examine a few pages of illustrations in a book of English and American period furniture from the point of view of legs and feet. Attempt to identify all types.

5. Study the carving or inlay work on a chair- or table-apron. Analyze the decorative motifs with special attention to their inspirations and classifications.

6. Make a quick sketch of a panel pattern from some piece of furniture. Lengthen and narrow the panel and then attempt to revise the design so that it will be attractive within its new over-all dimension.

7. Contrast the Greek and Egyptian styles from the point of view of silhouette, colors, ornamentations, and choice of materials. Prepare a list of plays which would require mountings making use of these styles.

8. Examine a few pictures of Greek vases and note the furniture and decorative objects which are indicated. How could these best be represented on the stage?

9. If you were designing a Roman play, what particular motifs and silhouettes would you rely on in order to intensify the suggestion of period?

10. Study pictures of Gothic stained-glass windows in an effort to become acquainted with the typical decorative motifs which are displayed. How many of these would be suitable for use as furniture ornamentation?

11. Prepare a list of plays which might be designed in the Italian Renaissance style. What types of furniture might be used in each?

12. Contrast the Louis XIV and XV furniture as to silhouette, ornamentation, materials, and relationship to room architecture. Make a list of plays for which each style would be suitable.

13. In what ways did the First Empire influence English Regency and Biedermeier furniture? The original production of Noel Coward's *Conversation Piece* was enhanced by Regency mountings. What Somerset Maugham plays might be similarly treated? What would be gained by such treatment?

14. The setting for a Broadway revival of *The Green Bay Tree* displeased a number of the critics, mainly because of the room furnishings. Make some suggestions as to the type of décor that should be emphasized in such a play. By means of illustrations from books, select some of the furniture for Mr. Dulcimer's room.

15. Contrast the Sheraton and Hepplewhite styles as to contour, decorative motifs, variety of pieces, and use of woods. For which of the following plays would such furniture be most suitable: *Disraeli, Abe Lincoln in Illinois, Liliom, The Dover Road, Icebound, The Circle, R.U.R., The Show-Off, The Firebrand?* Give your reasons.

16. Contrast Spanish and Italian Renaissance furniture as to scale, proportion, decoration, and use of wood. List the specific problems you might expect to encounter in building or renting such furniture.

17. In what respects have the oriental styles influenced period and contemporary design? Illustrate by precise references.

18. Study a piece of contemporary furniture that is exhibited in a local store. Apply the accepted principles of contemporary design. Would the furniture combine readily with certain traditional pieces? Could the furniture be copied easily for stage use?

19. Contrast the hardware on French and English eighteenth-century furniture. How does it contribute to the decorative effect? How would you simulate such hardware inexpensively?

20. Investigate the used-furniture stores in your community as to the variety of goods, the rate of turnover, the quality of merchandise, the attitude of the management, and the rental fees.

21. Select a table and study it carefully from the point of view of remodeling. Into what styles might it be developed? What applied ornament might be used? What wood finishes might be considered?

22. What types of window treatment would be most satisfactory for the following plays: *Little Women, Pride and Prejudice, The Winslow Boy, The Sea Gull, Night Must Fall?* What kinds of materials and trimmings would be suitable for the draperies?

23. Obtain samples of fringes and other trimmings from department and drapery stores. Analyze their make-up and be prepared to offer suggestions as to their possible use on the stage.

24. Plan a wall picture arrangement of six frames of assorted sizes to be placed over a chest in a Greenwich Village musician's apartment. Arrange six other pictures in a manner suitable for a college girl's dormitory room.

25. Draw rough floor plans for the following plays indicating especially the placement of lamps, chandeliers, and sconces: *The Late George Apley, Deep are the Roots, Affairs of State, Foolish Notion,* and *Goodbye My Fancy.*

26. Consider the arrangement of bric-a-brac on the desk for the following plays: *Counselor at Law, The Winslow Boy, John Loves Mary, The Damask Cheek,* and *Blithe Spirit.* Be prepared to defend your decisions.

27. What could you use as substitutes, if any, for the following foods and beverages: cold chicken, caviar, filet mignon, lobster, beer, sparkling burgundy, tomato aspic, and cold cuts?

28. Visit the various utility stores of your community in search of artificial flowers of as many varieties as possible. Note the prices. Prepare a list of plays which must make generous use of flowers for decorative purposes. Estimate the cost of flowers for these plays.

29. Read a one-act play in order to prepare a property list. Classify all items under such main headings as furniture, rugs, pictures, vases, food, etc.

30. Consider the remodeling problems concerned with changing a wooden side chair to an upholstered piece. List the materials which would be required for such alterations.

31. Approximately how many property-crew members should be needed
    to handle the properties during performances of the following plays:
    All My Sons, O Mistress Mine, Years Ago, The Corn is Green? Be pre-
    pared to give your reasons.

32. Consider such a play as *State of the Union* from the point of view of
    offstage placement of properties.

33. Which of the following plays will require unusually substantial
    furniture which must take abuse: *The Hasty Heart, Anna Lucasta, Uncle
    Harry, Claudia, Angel Street, The Skin of our Teeth?* Point out the specific
    scenes involved.

9

Stage Lighting

SINCE STAGE LIGHTING is an integral part of the stage picture, it should be given special consideration by the director, the designer, and the lighting technician during the various phases of the designing process and the rehearsal period. If a scene design is to be successfully translated to the stage, the designer needs to know what instruments must supply the light, the intensities of the light sources, and the light colors that are to be represented. Similarly, the director should know in advance the relative intensities of light which he may expect in the various areas so that he may plan his stage movement accordingly. Visibility is the chief responsibility of the lighting technician; but after the visibility requirements are determined and analyzed, the technician is then ready to consider such lighting refinements as will help to unify and define the entire stage picture.

Broadway productions are often lighted by the designer or by someone working in close association with him. The fact that a professional designer or technician sometimes injudiciously under-lights rather than overlights in no way indicates that he does not understand the importance of light on the stage. In the non-professional theatre, the designer also often lights the productions, at the same time working closely with the director — who, like the Broadway director, frequently has a great deal to say regarding the lighting. In neither the professional nor the non-professional theatre should lighting be thought of as a mysterious production device which takes precedence over the other theatrical elements or is beyond the comprehension of the director. Occasional productions, however, may permit the lighting technician to demonstrate spectacular creative work which will be of special visual interest to an audience.

The Lighting Materials

If a designer or a lighting technician is to light a show with any degree of practical or aesthetic satisfaction, he must have knowledge of certain fundamentals of electricity, the mechanics of stage lighting equipment, and the nature of light. Although wiring and electrical installations are usually the concern of specially trained commercial electricians, those who use the current on the stage must understand what is involved in order that safety rules will not be neglected. Since stage lighting equipment is an expensive investment, it must be used efficiently with a minimum of wear and tear. An understanding of the nature of electricity as related to light will prove of invaluable assistance in assuring such efficient usage.

ELECTRICITY

Although electricity provides light, sound, heat, and motive power for daily living, its use on the stage is chiefly concerned with light. An electrical current is made up of a flow of electrical energy along a wire or other conductor. The cheapest and most common electrical conductor in commercial use is copper wire. Non-conductors of electricity are commonly called *insulators*; some of these insulating materials are rubber, porcelain, and fiber. This flow of electricity within a wire (forced through the wire by "pressure" maintained by a generator in a central power plant) is often likened to the movement of water within a pipe (forced through the pipe by "pressure" maintained by a pump). Like water, electricity flows only from a higher to a lower level of energy; and this difference in level of energy (or "potential") is responsible for the *electromotive force* (E.M.F.) — i.e., the pressure — which causes electricity to flow. Electromotive force is measured in terms of a unit called the *volt*.

Electrical energy in actual movement through a conducting circuit is known as *current*, and its rate of flow through the conductor is measured in terms of a unit called the *ampere*. Unlike water, electricity flows only through a complete *circuit* — i.e. a path like a closed loop, through which the current can move. In a circuit, the electricity flows along one wire from its source of supply (e.g., the feed wires from the power company) to its point of "consumption," and then along another wire back to the source of supply. *Direct current* (D.C.), which as its name suggests flows in one direction only, is no longer available in most communities; and *alternating current* (A.C.), which reverses its direction at regular intervals, is much more common in theatre installations. However, these A.C. reversals occur with such rapidity (120 times per second, in the case of a frequency of 60 cycles) that the eye does not perceive any change as the current alternates in direction through a lamp filament. It is important for the beginning student to note that most equipment designed for use with alternating current can not be used with direct current.

To return to the analogy with the water system: just as a greater pressure is required to force a certain amount of water through a small pipe than through a larger one over a given length of time, so a higher pressure (i.e., voltage) is required to force a certain amount of electricity through a small wire than through a larger one in a given length of time. In electrical terms, the smaller wire offers more *resistance* to the flow of electricity than the larger wire. This resistance, which is always in direct relation to the size, length, and composition of the wire used, is measured in *ohms*. A wire or other conductor has a resistance of one ohm if a current of one ampere flows through it under a pressure of one volt. If the lighting technician knows the voltage and the amperage in an electric circuit, he can compute the resistance in ohms by the use of *Ohm's law*, one form of which can be expressed as follows:

$$R \text{ (resistance in ohms)} = \frac{E \text{ (electromotive force in volts)}}{I \text{ (intensity of current in amperes)}}$$

On the other hand, if the voltage or the amperage is not known, either can be computed from the two other factors involved in the relationship expressed in Ohm's law. That is to say, the formula given above can be rearranged as follows:

$$E = I R \quad \text{or} \quad I = \frac{E}{R}$$

Application. If we wish to know the resistance of a lamp carrying 3.5 amperes at 115 volts, we may compute this as follows:

$$R = \frac{E}{I} \quad \text{or} \quad \frac{115}{3.5} \quad \text{or} \quad 32.8 \text{ ohms resistance.}$$

Similarly, if the amperage is required and the voltage and resistance are known:

$$I = \frac{E}{R} \quad \text{or} \quad \frac{115}{32.8} \quad \text{or} \quad 3.5 \text{ amperes.}$$

Electrical *power* is measured in terms of the *watt*, which is defined as the power of a current of one ampere as it flows under the pressure of one volt. Wattage can be expressed as the product of voltage and amperage:

$$P \text{ (watts)} = E \text{ (volts)} \times I \text{ (amperes)}$$

This formula may be rearranged so as to make it possible to compute amperage (when wattage and voltage are known) and voltage (when wattage and amperage are known):

$$I = \frac{P}{E} \quad \text{or} \quad E = \frac{P}{I}.$$

Application. If we wish to know the current drawn by a 500-watt lamp at 115 volts, the following computations are necessary:

$$I = \frac{P}{E} \quad \text{or} \quad \frac{500}{115} \quad \text{or} \quad 4.3 \text{ amperes.}$$

Stage cable is rated in amperes; and in order to determine the capacity of a given cable in watts, the electrician will find frequent use for the $P = E I$ formula. Capacities of standard theatrical dimmers (see page 329) are rated in watts. As a handy rule of thumb, each unit of 1000 watts (a *kilowatt*) of power at 115 volts involves a matter of about 9 amperes.

Circuits are of two basic kinds: *series* and *parallel*. Since there is only one path for the current to follow in an electrical circuit wired in series, the current has the same intensity in all parts of the series.

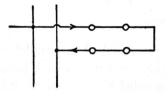

Fig. 110   *The series circuit*

In order to measure the current in a series circuit, the technician must know the voltage and the total resistance. The resistance (R) in such a circuit is the sum of the resistances (r + r, etc.) of the separate units making up the circuit:

$$R = r_1 + r_2 + r_3 \ldots \text{etc.}$$

Application.   If four lamps each have a resistance of five ohms and if the voltage is 115, the current could be obtained by adding the single resistances and applying one of the formulas derived from Ohm's law:

$$I = \frac{E}{R} \quad \text{or} \quad \frac{115}{20} \quad \text{or} \quad 5.7 \text{ amperes.}$$

Since in a series circuit the current must pass through each of the lamps in the circuit, a single dead lamp (or single lamp not making full contact in its receptacle) will black out the entire series; old-fashioned Christmas tree lights, which were so wired, will serve as a simple example. When, however, an electrical circuit is wired in *parallel*, the current passes through each of the two or more branches or paths of the circuit. Since each branch is independent of the other branches, this method of wiring is commonly used for interior lighting in public buildings, and for theatre installations.

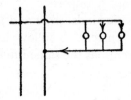

Fig. 111   *The parallel circuit*

If a number of lamps are wired in parallel on branch lines, the voltage will be roughly the same for each lamp. To compute the total resistance of a parallel circuit however, it is necessary to apply the following formula:

$$R = \cfrac{1}{\cfrac{1}{r_1} + \cfrac{1}{r_2} + \cfrac{1}{r_3} \ldots \text{etc.}}.$$

Application. If the three lamps in the above diagram for a parallel circuit have resistances of 25, 50, and 100 ohms respectively, their total resistance may be computed as follows:

$$R = \cfrac{1}{\cfrac{1}{25} + \cfrac{1}{50} + \cfrac{1}{100}} = \cfrac{1}{\cfrac{4}{100} + \cfrac{2}{100} + \cfrac{1}{100}} = \cfrac{1}{\cfrac{7}{100}} = \cfrac{100}{7} =$$

14.28 ohms total resistance

By the application of Ohm's law, the technician can determine the current flowing in a parallel circuit as whole, or in its separate branches.

Obviously, the technician will need such information if he attempts to build (or to remodel for theatre purposes) a *rheostat.* This is a device for effectively varying and controlling the resistance in a given circuit; in its simplest form, it consists of an insulated frame wound with wire of fairly high resistance, and equipped with a sliding contact. As the contact is moved to include more and more of the resistance wire in the circuit concerned, there is a decreasing flow of effective current and an increased dimming of the lamps in the circuit. The rheostat is wired in series with lamps or other electrical equipment, and is rated in amperes (total current carrying capacity) and ohms (total resistance). The resistance required to dim out the lamps in a given circuit completely is usually considered to be three or four times the hot resistance of the lamps.

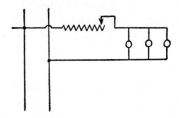

Fig. 112 *Circuit including a rheostat*

Rheostats manufactured expressly for use on the stage — i.e., theatrical *dimmers* — are discussed on pages 329–331.

The diagram of electrical circuits on the pages immediately preceding have all shown only two wires. In the theatre, however, a *three-wire* system is ordinarily used; such a system is made to supplant two circuits of two wires each. The use of three wires provides either 115 or 230 volts, as illustrated below:

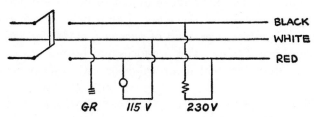

Fig. 113 *The three-wire system*

The center or neutral wire (*never* interrupted by fuses or switches) is common to both circuits. The three-wire system is especially desirable in that it offers a saving of copper wire and a saving of labor in installation.

If a circuit is overloaded, either by adding too much equipment or because of defective insulation, there is always a danger of fire; hence it is necessary that wiring include either *fuses* or *circuit breakers*. A fuse contains a wire or strip of metal which *fuses* or melts when there is an overload, thus opening the circuit. A circuit breaker automatically opens or "trips" as a result of an overload but may be closed after the load is adjusted by turning first to the extreme *off* position and then to *on*; circuit breakers need not be replaced continually. A *short circuit*, an overload involving reduced resistance, is caused by a shortening of the path of a current. The most common type of short circuit is caused by the contact of two poorly insulated wires. Fuses are always placed in series.

STAGE LIGHTING EQUIPMENT

Although the efficiency of stage lighting equipment is constantly being improved, the same instruments are in use today that were developed for the stage early in the century; spotlights, floodlights, borderlights, and footlights are still responsible for the major portion of light on the stage. Some authorities predict radically different instruments within the near future but, until then, we must continue to work with those of traditional form and method of operation. Because of recent improvements in efficiency and convenience of operation, buyers should examine the products of all manufacturers before making purchases of new equipment.

Lamps. The light source for most stage lighting equipment is the incandescent lamp. First of all, these lamps are classified as to the shape and size of the base. Lamp bases are of the *screw, pre-focus,* and *bi-post shapes* and of *miniature, candelabra, intermediate, medium,* and *mogul sizes.* The pre-focus and bi-post bases are constructed so that they will fit into the socket in one position only. Lamps are also classified as to shape of bulb: *Cone* (C), *Straight side* (S), *Pear shape* (straight neck) (PS), *Flame* (F), *Globe* (G), *Household* (A), *Tubular* (T), and *Reflector* (R). Lamp filaments are usually of the *coil* (C) and *coiled-coil* (CC) varieties, and the type of filament determines the burning position of the lamp. Pear-shaped lamps may be burned in any position. Globe-shaped lamps are base-down lamps since they have a concentrated filament and no neck for cooling. Most tubular lamps are base-up lamps. Considerable waste is involved when lamps are burned under their rated voltages.

Spotlights. Many theatre groups have on hand a number of old-fashioned spotlight instruments which they must use in conjunction with their more recent models. The basic construction and part relationships are the same for all spotlights, old or new. The

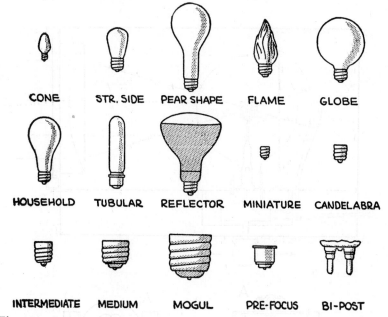

| CONE | STR. SIDE | PEAR SHAPE | FLAME | GLOBE |

| HOUSEHOLD | TUBULAR | REFLECTOR | MINIATURE | CANDELABRA |

| INTERMEDIATE | MEDIUM | MOGUL | PRE-FOCUS | BI-POST |

Fig. 114 *Lamps and lamp bases*

traditional spotlight is a lens instrument which provides *specific illumination* for the acting areas of the stage. An efficient spotlight has a metal hood which is light in weight and not oversized; the instrument ventilates readily, adjusts easily, and is not difficult to mount. The lamp socket, to which are attached the *lead wires* of the spotlight, holds the G-shaped lamp backed by a *spherical reflector* of mirror or polished metal. The socket may be moved forward and backward, according to the focal length of the lens, by means of a *focusing knob* underneath the instrument. There must be easy access to the interior so that lamps may be changed easily. For the most part, instruments of 500 watts or larger are equipped with mogul bases; 100-, 250-, and 400-watt instruments use a medium base. A *plano-convex lens* and a *color-frame slide* complete the instrument proper.

The ideal color frame is made of two pieces of sheet metal with round openings, hinged at one edge and equipped with a clip at the opposite side. Gelatine is placed between the layers of metal and the frame placed in the color-frame slide. If the slide is of the vertical variety, there is no possibility that the color frame might

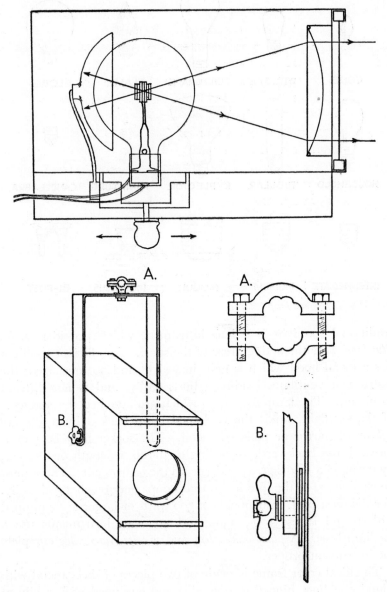

Fig. 115 *The traditional spotlight*

fall out. As for mounting, although a number of methods are used, the *yoke* or *yoke swing joint* and *pipe arm* are the most satisfactory. The use of leather washers and wing nuts makes it possible to adjust the angle accurately.

The plano-convex lens has one plane surface and one convex surface. Lenses are classified according to diameter and focal length; an 8 × 10 lens has a diameter of eight inches and a focal length of ten inches. The *principal focus* of a lens is the point at which all the rays which are parallel to the axis meet or focus. The *focal length* of a lens is the distance between the center of the lens and the principal focus point. (This is true for all practical purposes, although the optical center of the lens does not necessarily coincide with the geometrical center.)

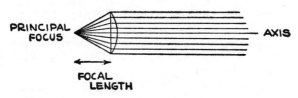

Fig. 116 *Focal length of lenses*

When the rays of light from a spotlight are parallel, the lens is in its proper position as determined by its focal length. The focal length of the lens varies with its shape and thickness. A lens with a short focal length must be near to the light source in order to produce parallel rays of light; a thin lens has a longer focal length than a thick lens. If the light source is moved in front of the principal focus, the lamp filament will appear in the pool of light. The pool of light sharpens and becomes more intense as the source approaches the principal focus.

Many so-called "baby" spotlights which use 250- to 400-watt lamps are fitted with lenses five inches in diameter with focal lengths of eight inches; large 1000-watt instruments are often equipped with 8 × 10 lenses. Tiny spotlights which burn 75- to 100-watt lamps usually have lenses which are from two to three and a half inches in diameter.

Black *hoods* or *funnels* are valuable as a means of helping to con-

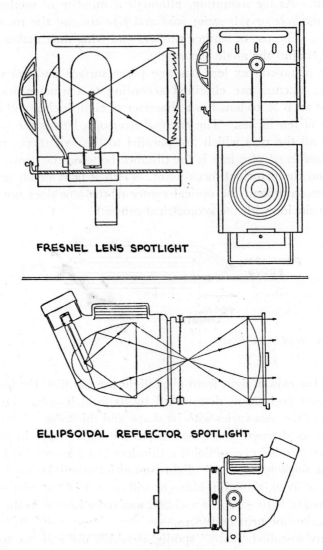

FRESNEL LENS SPOTLIGHT

ELLIPSOIDAL REFLECTOR SPOTLIGHT

Fig. 117 *The most recently developed types of spotlights*

trol the spread of light from an old-fashioned spotlight. Hoods are temporarily placed in the color-frame slide as needed. *Pevear* instruments, popular some years ago as tormentor lighting units, made similar use of black flippers for shaping the beams of light.

The *ellipsoidal reflector* spotlight is one of the most recently developed instruments of specific illumination. This spotlight uses an ellipsoidally shaped Alzak (spun-aluminum) reflector which insures that most of the light is reflected to a secondary point of focus and then through the lens, thus preventing loss of light within the hood. The light source in a spotlight of this type is never moved since the instrument uses a base-up pre-focus lamp. Although the smaller instruments (up to 500 watts) include two plano-convex lenses, the larger units (1000 to 2000 watts) are usually equipped with only one eight-inch lens. No funnel or flipper shutters are required with the ellipsoidal spotlight since special *beam shapers* and *iris shutters* are often built into the unit. Standard equipment includes a color-frame holder and a yoke. Although the instrument is expensive, it is extremely sturdy and two or three times as efficient for long throws as the older type of spotlight.

The *Fresnel* (stepped lens) spotlight, another recently developed instrument, has almost replaced the older type of spotlight for short throws. The Fresnel or stepped lens makes more efficient use of the available light for this type of throw than does the lens it replaces, and it does not require that the light source be quite so close to the lens position (with the attendant danger of cracking glass). As an additional efficiency aid, most Fresnel spotlights are equipped with spherical reflectors. Moreover, a short focal length makes possible a small housing, thus decreasing the size and weight of the spotlight. Most 1000- to 2000-watt instruments use an eight-inch lens; 250- to 500-watt instruments are usually equipped with six-inch lenses. A T-shaped pre-focus, base-down lamp with a monoplane or biplane filament is required for this instrument; if access to the interior is from the front, the color-frame holder is part of the front door. Although the pool of light from the Fresnel lens has a soft, diffused edge which tends to blend and spread, funnels can help to control the light more accurately if necessary. Technicians sometimes place a Fresnel lens in an old-fashioned spotlight. Although the resulting pool of light is characteristically diffused, the

BEAM PROJECTOR FLOODLIGHT

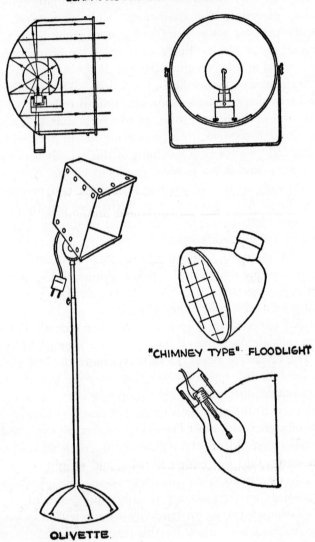

"CHIMNEY TYPE" FLOODLIGHT

OLIVETTE.

Fig. 118 *Floodlights*

instrument itself continues to be over-sized and awkward to manipulate.

Floodlights. Although the old-fashioned *olivette* is still available, equipment of this sort has very limited use in relation to present-day stage lighting. The olivette is a large metal box, the interior of which is coated with white paint; pear-shaped 1000-watt lamps with mogul bases provide the light source. These lighting units are commonly mounted on *telescopic pipe stands.* Regardless of where they may be placed on the stage, they are too cumbersome to handle and are extremely inefficient as to use of light.

A most satisfactory floodlight is the "chimney" type which, by means of yoke and C clamp, can be hung to a pipe batten. This type of floodlight has an ellipsoidal aluminum reflector and offers a wide to medium spread of diffuse light. A pear-shaped 500-watt lamp ordinarily serves as the light source. A similarly shaped model in the 1000-watt size, but containing a parabolic reflector, is available for use on stands. Chimney-type floodlights are ideally suited to lighting the upper portions of the cyclorama. Color-frame holders are, of course, standard equipment on all such instruments.

The *beam projector floodlight*, sometimes called a beam light projector or "sun spot," is a most satisfactory instrument for suggesting the direct rays of sunlight or moonlight. The apparatus consists primarily of a deep parabolic short-focus reflector and a series of *louvers* or spill rings. If a small Fresnel lens is placed within the center spill ring, there will be no center "dead" spot. Projectors are available in wattages of from 500 to 1500 and are equipped with lamp sockets requiring the use of base-down mogul, prefocus, or screw-base lamps. It is necessary that the instruments be provided with color-frame holders and yokes for hanging. The farther away the instrument can be placed the more natural appearing will be the narrow beam of parallel rays. The light from the instrument is not easy to control and the units are somewhat clumsy and awkward to handle.

Footlights and Borderlights. Despite the fact that some authorities discourage the use of *footlights*, such equipment is extremely useful for lighting the act curtain, toning the scenery, and helping to re-

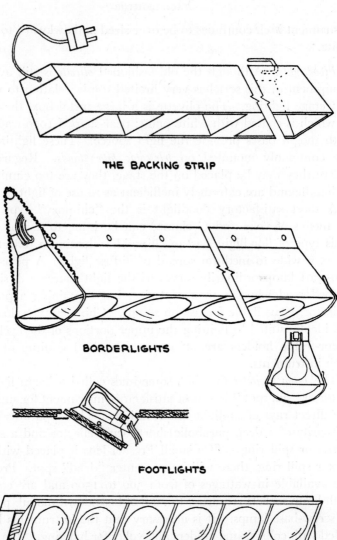

THE BACKING STRIP

BORDERLIGHTS

FOOTLIGHTS

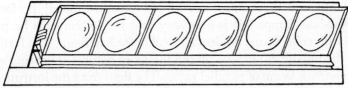

Fig. 119 *Footlights, borderlights, and backing strips*

move unflattering shadows from the actors' faces. The old-fashioned type of footlights makes use of dipped or natural-color lamps in an awkward, high, open trough which extends the full width of the apron. Very often the lamps are placed at such an angle that the entire proscenium wall is conspicuously lighted. The most satisfactory footlights in use today are placed with a built-in trough which protrudes above the floor about three inches. One-hundred-watt lamps with screw-base sockets, individual Alzak reflectors, and red, green, and blue glass roundels serve as the light source. Some authorities suggest that there be provision for the use of gelatine frames in place of glass roundels. The footlights need not extend the full width of the proscenium arch; since the lights are sold by the foot or in five-foot sections, it is a simple matter to divide the entire length into three sections, the center of which is as wide as the two end units. Occasionally the center unit alone will be all that is required for toning purposes. Footlights should be wired in three circuits so that there can be individual color control. Disappearing footlights, considerably more expensive than the above-mentioned units, are usually necessary for a stage which doubles as a recital hall and a theatre.

Old-fashioned *borderlights*, like the out-of-date footlights, consist of a long metal trough with a white interior and dipped lamps of red, blue, and amber. Row after row of these lighting units may have been necessary in drop-and-wing days but, today, two border-lights are usually considered as sufficient. The first borderlight, sometimes called the concert border or the x-ray border, is placed directly upstage of the teaser; the second border is hung far enough upstage to light a drop for an exterior scene. The most efficient borderlights are equipped with individual Alzak parabolic reflectors, glass roundel holders, and medium screw receptacles; and they use 200-watt lamps. (There is also considerable advantage to having the units designed so that gelatine color frames can be used in place of glass roundels.) Borderlight units may be hung on pipe battens with chains or by means of pipe arms with a swing joint or stud mounting at one end and a C clamp at the other. These units need not extend the full width of the proscenium opening since their chief purpose is to tone the setting and to blend the acting area lighting. To permit flexible color control, the units should be wired in three circuits for three colors.

Backing strips. Sheet metal backing striplights are used to provide light for door openings or between a series of ground rows. The units are hung two or three feet horizontally above a door or arch opening, or may be hung vertically the same distance to the side of the opening. Many of these units are supplied with hooks or rings so that the equipment may be hung in a horizontal or vertical position. The instruments are either of the open-trough variety (with four compartments, the interiors of which are painted white) or the compartment type which makes use of gelatine color frames. The light is supplied by 40- to 60-watt natural-colored lamps wired in one circuit.

Cyclorama-Base Lights. Cyclorama-base lighting is best accomplished by means of a number of four-, six-, or seven-foot *horizon* striplight units placed around the curve of the curtain. These units, like borderlights, should have individual Alzak reflectors and provide for the use of color roundels and gelatine color media. One-hundred-fifty-watt lamps, wired in three circuits, are usually sufficient for a medium-sized stage although most equipment will handle 300-watt lamps if necessary. These horizon strips (or "cyc" foots) are sometimes placed within specially built traps or pits so that they may be made to disappear when they are not in use. Free standing movable units should be equipped with stud mounting and placed on frames which are fitted with casters.

Stage Cable and *Stage-Cable Connectors.* Stage cable connects all lighting instruments to the lighting outlets and floor boxes, which in turn, by means of concealed wiring, are connected to the controlboard. Twin-conductor stage cable is much heavier than the cord which is used in ordinary households; each wire is made up of many small wires twisted to make a single conductor. Insulating material covers each group of wires; additional insulating material, preferably rubber, covers the two wires to form a cable. Cables with a large gauge number are smaller than those with a lower number; the larger the wire the greater the current it will carry. For example, gauge #18 will carry 3 amperes; gauge #14, 15 amperes; gauge #12, 20 amperes; gauge #6, 50 amperes. The National Electrical Code forbids the use of stage cable smaller than #14.

The heavy stage-cable connectors used in the professional theatre are unnecessary on the non-professional stage if 15-ampere *pin connectors* are substituted for over-all use. The pin connectors are in two parts: the *load connector*, the male part, with brass prongs, is always attached to the instrument leads from a lighting unit; the *line connector*, the female part, with two brass openings, is always placed on the live end of the cable. These connectors are made

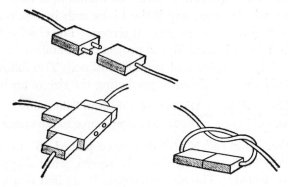

Fig. 120 *Cable connectors*

of fibre and are sturdy, compact, and inexpensive. A special over-hand connection knot can be tied as the cable connectors are united so that the units will not come apart. The multiple (15-ampere) *three-way connector*, a female unit, will prove valuable when it is necessary to group two or three circuits together. Borderlight and footlight units are equipped with three pigtails (short lengths of cable) to which are attached male connectors at one end of the unit and a corresponding set of three with female connectors at the other. Industrial *twist-lock* connectors, preferred by many non-professional groups, are satisfactory on either instruments or cables.

Linnebach Lanterns and *Lens Projectors*. Lighting instruments which project images to a screen may be classified under two main headings — those without lenses and those equipped with lenses. The least expensive of the two types, the non-lens Linnebach lantern, or shadow projector, consists of a large metal box painted black inside, a concentrated light source, and a glass slide. The size of the projection on the screen is determined by the size of the slide and its distance from the light source and the screen. Unless the slide is parallel to the screen there will be distortion in the image; if the slide cannot be parallel to the screen, the shadow design must be planned to allow for this distortion. In order to get a relatively distinct image, the light source should be as far as possible from the slide. If the Linnebach lantern must be placed on the floor in front of the screen, the top of the screen will be lighted with less intensity than the lower part. In addition, a much stronger light source will be necessary if the Linnebach is required to project an image through a translucent screen. The chief value of the Linnebach lantern is its ability to project non-detailed forms which depend mainly on color and general outline. The following formula will aid the technician in predicting the size of an image:

$$\frac{\text{Size of slide}}{\text{Size of image}} = \frac{\text{Distance of slide from light source}}{\text{Distance of light source to the image}}$$

Application. If a 12″ × 18″ slide were placed 18″ in front of a lamp and the lamp were 14′ from the screen, what size projection might be expected? The above formula is applied first to one dimension of the slide and then to the other.

$$\frac{12''}{I} = \frac{18''}{168'' \,(14')} \qquad 18\,I = 2016 \quad I = 112'' \quad \text{or} \quad 9'\,4''$$

$$\frac{18''}{I} = \frac{18''}{168''} \qquad 18\,I = 3024 \quad I = 168'' \quad \text{or} \quad 14'$$

A projection 9′ 4″ by 14′ could be expected.

In order to obtain projections which stress detail instead of form and color, it is necessary to use a lens projector of some sort. A 1000-watt spotlight with a six-inch lens or a 1500-watt ellipsoidal unit with an eight-inch lens will be satisfactory as the projection instrument. However, the spotlight must be provided with an additional condensing lens (plano-convex), a slide holder, and two objective lenses. Slides are always inverted and may be of photographic or painted subject matter; the images may be projected as far as twenty feet without any difficulty. The longer the throw the longer should be the combined focal length of the objective lenses.

By the use of the following formulas it is possible to determine

Fig. 121 *The Linnebach lantern*

the size of the image from a lens projector or to compute the combined focal length of a pair of objective lenses:

$$\frac{\text{p (distance from the slide to the optical center of lenses)}}{\text{P (diameter of slide)}} = \frac{\text{q (distance from instrument to screen)}}{\text{Q (diameter of image)}}$$

$$\frac{1}{p} + \frac{1}{q} = \frac{1}{F} \quad \text{(focal length of lenses)}$$

Application of first formula. What will be the distance from a 4″ slide to the optical center of a pair of objective lenses if the image is 10′ square and the throw is 20′?

$$\frac{p}{4} = \frac{\overset{2}{20} \times \cancel{12}}{\cancel{10} \times \cancel{12}} \qquad p = 8''$$

Application of second formula. What is the combined focal length of the objective lenses where the distance from the slide to the optical center is 8″ and the distance from the lighting unit to the screen is 20′?

$$\frac{1}{8''} + \frac{1}{20 \times 12''} = \frac{1}{F} \qquad F = 7.7 \text{ inches}$$

In order to produce a clean-cut image, it is sometimes necessary

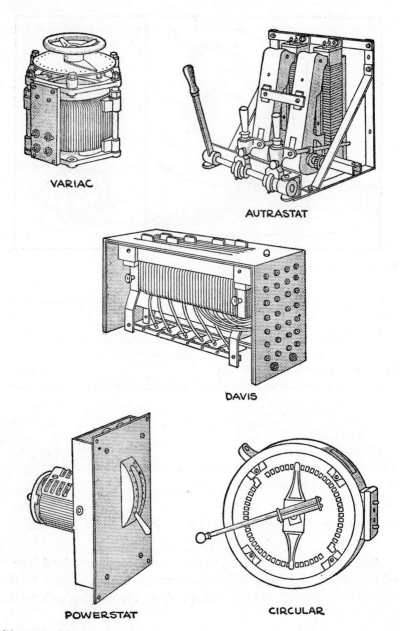

VARIAC

AUTRASTAT

DAVIS

POWERSTAT

CIRCULAR

Fig. 122   *Dimmers*

to know how far apart to place the objective lenses. The following formula will be useful to help compute this figure:

$$\text{F (combined focal length)} = \frac{f_1 \text{ (focal length of first lens)} \times f_2 \text{ (focal length of second lens)}}{f_1 + f_2 - d \text{ (distance apart)}}$$

Application. If the combined focal length of an 8″ and a 12″ lens is 6″, how far apart are the lenses placed?

$$6 = \frac{8 \times 12}{8 + 12 - d} \quad \text{or} \quad 6 = \frac{96}{20 - d}.$$

The distance (d) is in this case 4 inches.

A lens projector for presenting moving effects such as clouds, snow, rain, and flames is called a *sciopticon*. This device consists of a flat drum which holds a large circular slide, painted or photographic, which is moved continuously by means of a clock or a motor. Since the apparatus is expensive and has limited use, it is better to rent the attachments as needed rather than to purchase them outright.

Dimmers. The intensity of light on the stage is controlled by means of dimming devices of one kind or another. Since present-day stage lighting requirements are much more complex than they were in the early part of the century, old-fashioned dimmers are often too inflexible and clumsy to afford satisfaction to a sensitive lighting technician. The change of light intensity must take place subtly and quietly and involve the efforts of only one or two people. However, since so many theatres are equipped with dimmers which are reasonably adequate to the needs of the theatre, the demand for the most newly developed equipment is not great enough that it can be manufactured inexpensively.

Many of the older theatre plants are equipped with *resistor* or *resistance* dimmers. The most popular of these units are of the circular-plate variety and are wired in series with the lighting units; slidewire units are also available. The circular-plate type consists of a bent wire having a high coefficient of resistance, mounted to a steel disc and covered with baked enamel. A hundred or more contact studs are left exposed along the wire and a contact arm controls the amount of wire included in the circuit and hence the voltage at the lighting instrument. When, for example, the contact is moved to the medium-off position, more of the wire is brought into the circuit; more resistance is offered, the voltage drops, and the lamp grows dim. Although the resistor dimmer heats more than other dimmers, it is dependable, simple to maintain, and available in many sizes. However, the units are overlarge, are often stiff in operation, and must be loaded to full capacity in order for them to dim properly. The placement of a *phantom load* or load resistor of the correct wattage (a heater element or extra lighting equipment) in parallel with the dimmer and the instrument to be dimmed will build the dimmer load up to its proper capacity. When professional lighting control equipment must be transported from theatre to theatre, the resistor dimmer is usually the choice since, although it is heavy, it is easily connected and will operate on direct current if necessary.

The most satisfactory resistor dimmers are equipped with handles which, in addition to their connection to the contact arm, are attached to a horizontal steel shaft which crosses in front of an entire row of dimmers. These handles have latches which allow the handles to be affected by the movement of the shaft when desirable; a master handle on the shaft will move all the dimmers that are latched.

The *autotransformer* dimmer consists of a coil of copper wire surrounding an iron core; the dimming is accomplished by means of a sliding contact which is moved around the core. This dimmer reduces voltage by transforming action instead of, as in the case of the resistor dimmer, absorbing heat. Although the *Variac* and *Powerstat* circular types of dimmers, with dial knobs, are compact, efficient as to operation, relatively inexpensive, and have complete variable capacity, the slider type of autotransformer (Powerstat) lends itself more readily to master control and interlocking. Ward Leonard has recently developed the *Radiastat* which is radial in form but uses control handles of the type common to resistor dimmers. Another autotransformer dimmer, made by the Ariel Davis Company, consists of six sliding contacts (2400-watt capacity each) operating on a single coil. Thus, the operator can dim several circuits (up to a total of 6000 watts) by using one coil. Although all autotransformer dimmers are light in weight and portable and will dim all the wattages within their capacities smoothly and evenly, they must be operated on alternating current.

An *electronic* tube-reactor (reactance) dimmer requires the use of remote control and allows very small controlboard units. The dimming apparatus consists of a core with two windings of wire — one coil carrying alternating current and wired in series with the lighting instrument, and the other carrying direct current from a rectifier tube controlled at the board. This dimmer permits successful proportional dimming even when the lamp is as small as one fourth the capacity of the dimmer; and there is always immediate response to the movement of the control levers.

Although, at this writing, only a few theatres are equipped with *Izenour* dimmers and controlboards (Century Lighting), many authorities are of the opinion that this method of dimming, when it becomes less expensive, will eventually replace all other forms. This dimmer, developed by George Izenour at Yale University, makes use of two large electronic tubes and two control tubes for each dimmer — the electronic tube *is* the dimmer. The bulky part of the apparatus (the tube rack) is placed away from the stage, thus permitting a small controlboard. Any size of lamp may be dimmed completely out regardless of the capacity of the dimmer; multi-preset and proportional dimming arrangements are characteristic. Alternating current is required.

Controlboards. Stage-lighting controlboards must be compact and as small as the dimmers will permit. The handles should be aligned vertically and horizontally so that there will be no confusion during operation. Between twenty-four and thirty circuits are generally considered as adequate for the average controlboard. If the board is of the tube-reactor variety, there may be two dimmers for each circuit so that scenes may be set up in advance. Since controlboards are usually set up in two or three banks of dimmers and switches, if a master dimmer and a master switch can be provided for each bank, the operator's work will often be simplified. Where a choice must be made as to the number of dimmers or the use of an interlocking system (manual or electrical), the former is suggested as preferable since an additional hand or two can often take the place of interlocking handles. Dimmer

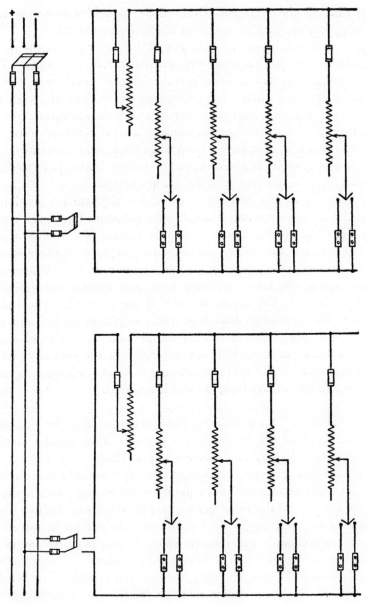

Fig. 123 *Sample layout of circuits for a controlboard*

capacities should probably vary from 500 to 4000 watts with emphasis on the lighter capacities.

All controlboards have certain parts in common regardless of their size and facilities. First on the list is the *master switch*, connected directly to the wires from the main line. The two *main fuses* of the cartridge variety are next in line. Both the master switch and the master fuses should be of from 200- to 300-ampere capacity depending upon the combined dimmer capacity of the board. Special circuit breakers or *circuit fuses* are necessary for each circuit — a 1000-watt dimmer, for example, should be served by a 10-ampere fuse, or a 1500-watt dimmer by a 15-ampere fuse. Circuit fuses are usually placed in a special magazine panel. *Circuit switches* of the single-pole or transfer variety are also required so that a circuit may be broken or transferred from one outlet to another. *Board outlets*, connected to a plugging panel, complete the controlboard.

Regardless of the type of dimmers used or the location of the dimmers, the controlboard or switchboard should be flexible in design. No equipment should be permanently connected to a dimmer; it should be possible to connect any outlet to a dimmer that is not in use. If the various outlets about the backstage area are connected directly to some sort of interconnecting panel, when it is desirable to connect two or three outlets to one dimmer, this can be accomplished readily. Certain interconnecting panelboards resemble a telephone operator's plugging panel while others are designed with no visible cables. (Kliegl's *Rototector* has been designed to facilitate interconnecting.) Old-fashioned controlboards sometimes permit the connection of outlet cables directly to the front of the board; although this method often involves considerable cable-confusion, it at least provides flexibility. Obviously more stage outlets will be needed than dimmers or board outlets (some technicians suggest a 50 per cent ratio); thus a smaller controlboard can serve satisfactorily with less dimming equipment.

Light and Color

About 95 per cent of the energy which goes into an incandescent electric lamp changes into heat; the 5 per cent that is not thus dissipated is changed into light energy, the visible part of radiant energy. As sunlight passes through a prism, it is refracted into the spectrum, which includes colors of various wave lengths. Although light includes infrared and ultraviolet rays, radium rays and radio waves, no colors in the spectrum are visible to the naked eye which have longer wave lengths than red or shorter wave lengths than violet. Light from an incandescent lamp contains more red and yellow than does sunlight, and less blue and purple.

In considering light colors physicists and lighting technicians use different terminology from that which is usually applied to pigment colors by painters. *Brilliance* or *brightness* replaces "value" as applied to reflection, and *saturation* is preferred to "intensity" in relation to amount of chroma. The *light primary colors* — red, green, and blue — can be mixed to provide white light, just as the three pigment primaries theoretically produce gray pigment. However, many physicists consider the *light secondaries* — blue-green, purple (magenta), and yellow — to be a more accurate indication of the true pigment primaries than the common designations of "blue," "red," and "yellow." Black and white are considered to be non-spectrum or achromatic colors.

The light secondaries (and also white light) can be achieved by *additive mixing* of the light primaries — i.e., by lighting a clear surface with two or more light primaries which, as they combine on the lighted area, become a third color. Blue-green is the result of thus mixing blue and green; yellow is the product of red and green; purple, of red and blue. When all three light primaries are thus mixed, white is the result.

Pigment primaries (i.e., light *secondaries*, blue-green, purple, and yellow) are, however, mixed by *subtraction*. That is to say, color in pigment is not apparent to the eye unless light is reflected from it; the particular rays of colored light which are reflected (and not absorbed) determine the hue of the pigment. For example, when blue-green and yellow pigment are mixed (to produce green pigment) and are covered with white light, the blue-green pigment will absorb or subtract the *red* rays of the light and the yellow pigment will absorb the *blue* rays; thus only the *green* rays (the remaining light primary) will be reflected, and the mixed pigment appears green.

White light, directly from the lighting instruments, is rarely used on the stage; hence it is necessary to provide *color media* for the instruments. The type of medium that is used will depend on the purpose and location of these instruments. In any case, just as the use of pigments under stage light involves selective absorption and selective reflection, so the use of color media involves selective absorption and *selective transmission*. That is to say, when any color medium is placed in front of a lighting instrument, the medium subtracts one or more of the light primaries and transmits others. If the medium is green, for example, the blue and red light primaries are absorbed and only the green primary is transmitted. Using any color medium therefore involves a considerable waste of light. However, until better means are developed, the lighting technician is limited to the use of colored glass, colored gelatine, and lamp dip.

Although in recent years a greater variety of colors has become available in permanent, heat-resistant glass, the most generally useful colors are red, medium blue, green, and straw. The use of primary light colors is particularly wasteful since only 3 to 10 per cent of the light can be transmitted through the colored glass. Glass color media are used mainly for borderlight and footlight equipment which provides general light; therefore, the color range of the media need not be so great.

Colored gelatine is always used for spotlight and floodlight equipment which directs the light to specific areas. Gelatine is available in an extremely wide range of colors from frost to the various primary colors and tints and combinations of these colors. Colored gelatine, like colored glass, absorbs a great deal of light; hence it is more efficient to use the tints whenever possible. Gelatine tends to fade and crack under the light and must sometimes be replaced during the run of a show. The following colors are generally most useful:

1. Frost
2. Light Flesh Pink
9. Dubarry Pink
17. Special Lavender (Surprise Pink)
25. Daylite Blue
27. Light Blue
29. Special Steel Blue

54. Light Straw
57. Light Amber
62. Light Scarlet (Bastard Amber)

The primary light colors are best represented by these gelatines:

65. Medium Scarlet
36. Non-Fade Blue
49. Dark Green

The secondary light colors are approximated by the following:

46. Dark Blue-Green
58. Medium Amber
11. Medium Magenta

Since not all dealers use the same names for these gelatine colors, it is well to become familiar with the numerical index as well as the nomenclature.

Lamp dip, a colored lacquer, is not a satisfactory substitute for gelatine or colored glass. Since lamps of more than forty watts may not be dipped, the use of lacquered lamps is definitely limited to small backing striplights. Despite the fact that many colors of lamp dip are available and the expense is moderate, the colors are not all permanent on the lamp. Lamps made from colored glass are more useful, even though the color range is somewhat limited.

Since stage scenery is usually viewed under artificial light, filtered through color media, it is necessary to understand the effect of colored light upon the various pigments. Since, for example, yellow light contains only the green and red light primaries, yellow light thrown on blue pigment will result in a muddied gray or black; to reflect blue light and therefore to appear blue, any blue pigment must be bathed in light rays containing some of the blue light primary. On the other hand, since purple (magenta) light does contain both blue and red light primaries, a blue pigment will show up blue under a purple light. The point is that no pigment color will show up in its intended hue unless its corresponding light primary is falling directly on it from some source on stage.

As a general guide, the following rules-of-thumb may be of value to the technician:

Purple light on *yellow pigment* results in *red*
Yellow light on *blue-green* pigment results in *green*

Blue-green light on *purple pigment* results in *blue*
Blue light on *red, yellow,* or *green pigment* results in *gray* or *black*
Red light on *green, blue-green,* or *blue pigment* results in *gray* or *black*
Green light on *red, purple,* or *blue pigment* results in *gray* or *black*

Colors also change under artificial light because of impurities in both pigment and color media. Because of such impurities, it is therefore wise to test actual paint samples under light before they are used for scenery. Colored fabrics, as well as paint, should be tested under various colors of stage lighting since, despite the apparent hue of a fabric, the designer cannot be certain what dye colors may have been used. Finally, the texture of a material may have some influence on its color effect. If a white light is thrown on a piece of red velour, the color can be seen with especial vividness, because of the sheen of the material; in contrast, a piece of red cotton flannel would not tend to reflect the same vividness of hue.

Speaking more generally, one can say that the amount and the nature of the light reflected from any surface depends directly on the surface-material involved. Rays of light falling on a *diffuse reflector* like rough-textured white paper are broken up in all directions. This principle is applied when direct shadows would be undesirable. Light falling on a mirror or on highly polished metal

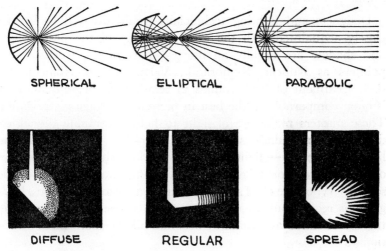

SPHERICAL   ELLIPTICAL   PARABOLIC

DIFFUSE   REGULAR   SPREAD

Fig. 124 *Reflectors (above) and reflections (below)*

obeys the rule of *regular reflection*, in which the angle of incidence is equal to the angle of reflection. (The angle of incidence is the angle between the incident ray and the normal or perpendicular ray.) *Spread reflection* directs light in such a manner that its reflection angle bears a direct relationship to its incidence angle, though the light is spread somewhat. Etched, oxidized, and spun-aluminum reflectors will provide spread reflection.

Lighting Methods

A thorough knowledge of the lighting materials will not in itself guarantee effective stage lighting. Truly creative stage lighting is the result of experience and sensitivity coupled with an intelligent, inquiring point of view. The technician must guard against repetitious effects and strive for inconspicuous originality. Despite the fact that the use of lighting equipment on the stage inevitably assumes certain patterns, the routine use of the same equipment, from show to show, can hardly be a satisfying practice. The lighting problems for each production must be studied with an open mind; any similarity to past productions should be considered as coincidental.

SHADE AND SHADOW

Designers and lighting technicians would do well to become closely acquainted with the great paintings of the past. Shade and shadow are usually an integral part of the work of such painters as Rubens, Rembrandt, Vermeer, and Holbein, and their treatment of backgrounds in relation to the human figure is often comparable to the best in present-day stage picturization. These masters make use of light to help accentuate dimension, depth, shade gradations, and tonal blending. They always use light intelligently — light through a window, shadows from a tree, or light in relation to architectural composition are often represented. When the chief subject matter is a person or persons, backgrounds recede but do not disappear, and the human figure, by the use of shade and shadow, becomes all the more three-dimensional.

The flat stage lighting associated with the theatre prior to the time of David Belasco flooded the actors and the painted backgrounds with equal intensity. Such lighting was primarily for purposes of over-all illumination; all shadows were painted directly on the scenery. Backgrounds therefore tended to glare and often took on more importance than the actors. This flat, general illumination only accentuated the painted quality of the scenery without suggesting atmosphere or mood. Today's more specific stage illumination, when used, for example, with painted ballet scenery, enhances the painting and often provides special motivation for the painted shadows and shading of the scenery. In other words, the backgrounds recede, the performers are visible, and the stage becomes a beautiful picture with well-related parts.

A study of light in nature is as important for the lighting technician and the scene designer as it was for the great painters of the past. Light patterns, plane contrasts, the length and sharpness of shadows, definition, and highlights are all represented in nature at various times of day and in particular seasons and climates. Although color is of considerable assistance in this connection, the source, intensity, and direction of light must be considered first. Since natural-appearing shading, shadows, and highlights are produced on the stage by directional light, a stage setting may appear subtly or sharply different each time the curtain opens.

Directly after World War I, on both European and American stages, there was a tendency to think of light for its own sake, often with little relation to the actors or to the scenery. Sharp shafts of light illuminated small portions of the stage, as in space staging, and actors often appeared stark and severe in pools of light. Although this method was, of course, in direct reaction to the even overlighting of the past, some years passed before this tendency to play with light was checked. Today, when a sharp, single shaft of light is noted on the stage, it is likely to have been suggested by the script rather than to represent a whim of the lighting technician. Although a shaft of light may provide interesting and pictorially pleasing shadows, the sharp contrasts which accompany such lighting are too hard on the eyes to permit satisfying visibility.

The designer must never expect the lighting technician to paint his scenery for him. Light can assist the painter and the designer but cannot shade and mold a flat, painted background. A dark corner must be painted dark; an indistinct wall must be painted by means of a diffused painting technique; heavy architectural shadows must be painted in order to bring out the dimension. The designer who expects light, or the lack of it, to tie together his stage picture may be disappointed. Light from the acting areas is sometimes reflected to wall areas which the designer might prefer to keep in semidarkness. Similarly, inexpert painting cannot always be lighted to its best advantage. Lighting, however, can intensify the scenic ideas which are held by the director and the designer, provided those ideas are already a part of the scenery.

Most realistic plays are lighted in rather conventional manner with little or no unmotivated changes in shade and shadow during the particular scenes. Although spotlights produce short shadows the use of footlights and borderlights helps to make shadows less conspicuous and to cut down on the contrasts between the acting areas. Non-realistic productions, however, make considerable use of light changes during the various scenes. Often these changes enhance the pictorial beauty of a scene or point up an acting area for purposes of dramatic emphasis. Formalistic settings, such as might be used for Greek drama, offer unusual opportunities for light changes which will exaggerate the three dimensions. None the less, regardless of the type of play or setting, the lighting must not be so spirited as to violate the rules of good taste. Furthermore, the actors' faces must always be lighted so that they will never appear as puppets parading before a display of shadow and shade.

LIGHTING THE ACTING AREAS

A minimum of six ellipsoidal reflector spotlights of 1000-watt capacity are usually considered necessary for the *ceiling beam* positions in the theatre auditorium. Three of these lights are placed at each extreme side of the ceiling opening so that crosslighting (double diagonal) may be supplied to each of the three downstage areas (see Fig. 125).

Instruments B2 and B5 will light the center downstage area (2). Area 1 on Stage Left will be lighted by instruments B1 and B4; Area 3, Stage Right, will be lighted by instruments B3 and B6. An eight-inch condensing lens with a focal length of ten inches is

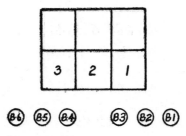

Fig. 125 *Lighting the downstage areas*

suitable for the average throw from this position — roughly twenty feet at a forty-five-degree angle. If ellipsoidal reflector spotlights are not available, the older type of 1000-watt instrument may be used provided it is equipped with a funnel to aid in directing the light. Instruments are either mounted on stands or hung from a horizontal pipe, depending upon the attic space which is free. Individual control from the board must be possible for each instrument.

Complementary tints are usually used for these acting areas. For example, instruments 1, 2, and 3 might be supplied with pink (warm) gelatine and 4, 5, and 6 with (cool) blue. This will give the appearance of greater plasticity and three dimensions to the actor. These colored pools of light should overlap to the extent that there are no "dead" spots; it should be possible for an actor to walk across the stage without getting out of the light at any time.

Five-hundred-watt tormentor spotlights, mounted on a vertical pipe, are sometimes used to assist in the downstage lighting; these instruments must make use of flippers to help shape the beams of light.

The upstage acting areas are most satisfactorily lighted by six spotlights mounted just upstage of the teaser. These spotlights, sometimes called *teaser spotlights*, are usually of the 500-watt capacity and equipped with either six-inch Fresnel or plano-convex lenses. Two instruments are placed on the Right, two in the Center, and two on the Left (see page 342).

Light from instruments T1 and T4 is directed toward Area 4; instruments T2 and T5 light Area 5; and T6 and T3 light Area 6. If Fresnel lenses are used, the light from the instruments will be somewhat diffused; the use of frost gelatine with an oiled center will

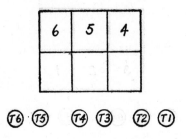

Fig. 126 *Lighting the upstage areas*

give a similar soft edge to the light from a plano-convex lens. Obviously the arrangement of the six acting areas must be varied occasionally because of settings that are different in shape. Extremely large settings and large stages may sometimes be divided into eight acting areas instead of six. Regardless of the shape of the setting, the technician must guard against light spills on the walls of the setting and be on the lookout for "hot" spots (overbright areas) and "dead" spots.

If each of the twelve spotlights is controlled by an individual dimmer and the instruments are carefully focused and directed, it should be possible to offer unlimited three-dimensional composition to the stage picture. The use of complementary tints should provide contrasts which will contribute pictorially; the various intensities should provide accent and shade gradation. If color changes on a given area are required during a performance, it will be necessary to change gelatines between scenes, or to provide a second set of instruments (with other gelatines) to light this area for later scenes. Considerable experimentation is always necessary regarding the levels of area lighting intensity, final decisions usually being made as the rehearsal period progresses; seldom is it possible to predict in advance the exact relationships of light intensity. In order to help emphasize certain locations or objects on the stage, it may be necessary to use extra spotlights, hung in special positions. A door is sometimes spotted in this manner, with a special mat shaping the light beam which is directed toward the door. Since the primary purpose of spotlighting is for visibility, subtle lighting effects must occasionally be discarded if they prevent the actors from being seen.

BLENDING AND TONING

Borderlights and footlights, the chief sources of general illumination on the stage, are necessary for blending and toning purposes. The proper amount of light from borderlights ties the various acting areas together without erasing the original contrasts supplied by the spotlights; footlights are invaluable in helping to provide a color tone for the setting. In present-day theatre, visibility should never be considered as a function of these lighting sources, although the actual wattage used may be as great as or greater than that available in the spotlight instruments. If the walls of a setting receive an excess of light from the blending and toning equipment, undesirable reflection may take place and the actors are likely to be placed in unflattering relief. Too great an intensity or the incorrect selection of color can also ruin the appearance of a carefully painted setting.

Although direct light from the instruments of general illumination is kept from the walls of a box setting, drop-and-wing settings may require borderlights between the foliage borders in order to illuminate the scenery properly. Unless foliage borders are toned with colored light, they are likely to appear black instead of emphasizing the soft green variations which are so characteristic of foliage. Furthermore, an unpleasant shadow will be cast at the top of a drop unless some sort of borderlight hangs between the drop and the painted border. As for elaborately painted drops such as are used in revivals of certain historic plays, if they are to contribute to the production, they must be seen clearly and toned pleasingly.

If a theatre is equipped with spotlights on the front of the balcony, the lighting technician may find the use of footlights unnecessary. However, since balcony spotlights will cause shadows on the back wall of the setting, additional light from the borderlights is often necessary. If footlights or balcony spotlights are used primarily for visibility rather than for toning purposes, it is likely that the results may seem artificial. Musical shows often demand this overlighting and extra toning; large groups of colorfully dressed performers can be toned in much the same manner as expanses of scenery. Shadows cast in a musical show are of relative unimportance since realism is not stressed. Although a considerable variety of color will be afforded if footlights and borderlights are equipped with the three primary light colors, extra wattage must be allowed due to the amount of light that will be absorbed.

Many borderlights are adjustable to the extent that their light can be more or less directed to the acting areas and the lower portions of the setting. This partial control of light simplifies the problem of *reducing* contrasts — the older type of borderlight was more inclined to *remove* contrasts. Although *indirect* footlights, light from which is directed back from a reflective surface, will also reduce contrasts in a subtle manner, such light will also soften facial shadows and shadows which appear under projecting hats and headdresses.

BACKGROUND LIGHTING

Background lighting involves the illumination of door and window backings, ground rows, and cycloramas and sky drops. Even though an audience is aware that backgrounds are lighted, there should seldom be any definite attention called to backgrounds as such by means of the lighting. Side door backings are not usually seen by many people in the audience, but window backings are often quite visible and occasionally painted to represent a definite locale. Detailed painting of this sort should never be overlighted to the extent that the backing seems to take on more importance than the setting. Backings of this type, like backdrops and foliage borders, must be lighted by means of borderlights or backing strips.

The chief problem in connection with cyclorama lighting is that of achieving even distribution of light. To accomplish this, cyclorama-base lights and floodlights are needed. Several base light units are placed as far away from the base of the cyclorama as is possible — three or four feet is usually a sufficient distance. Special built-in lights are sometimes as close as one foot to the cyclorama; such lights need not always be masked by ground rows. The primary light colors may be used, or gelatine of various shades of blue will be satisfactory. (Obviously, no two colors should be controlled by the same dimmer.) However, sunset effects are more easily produced by means of the light primaries. Since the actual sky is lighter at the horizon line, the lighting technician should not be disturbed when his sky appears brighter near the bottom. Although a stage sky must never appear to be excessively bright, there must be enough brightness to counteract unwanted shadows cast by scenery or by actors.

The top portion of the cyclorama should be lighted by a row of floodlights, preferably of the ellipsoidal type. These units are mounted on a pipe batten as far downstage from the sky effect as is possible. Unless there is considerable distance between the floodlight and the sky, every wrinkle and imperfection in sewing and painting will be noticeable. Color-frame holders must be adjusted carefully or peculiar light spills will mar an otherwise even lighting.

The sky effect obtained by the use of the cyclorama is extremely pleasing if it is lighted by the correct equipment. However, the same equipment will light the curved top of a plaster sky dome with much more subtlety. On the other hand, a well-lighted plaster dome may easily take on more importance pictorially than it properly deserves; if it becomes too "interesting" or "beautiful" in its own right, it may of course attract attention that rightfully belongs elsewhere.

Lighting for the book backings to stage doors is best supplied by small four-sectional backing striplights. Since most of these units do not have provision for the use of gelatine, colored lamps are necessary. If the light from the unit is directed away from the opening toward a nearby sheet of white cardboard, a much softer light will be provided and no shadows will be cast. The chief purpose of backing lights is to help give the realistic impression of another room or area. Obviously, backing lights are not necessary with certain forms of minimum scenery which involve only a small area of the stage. Although floodlights are not suitable for door backings, such instruments might very well be used to supply the light for window backings.

Motivating Light

Motivating light, sometimes called natural-source light, attempts to suggest that some such light source as the sun, the moon, an electric fixture, or a flickering flame is responsible for the illumination within an area on the stage. In a realistic play we expect such motivation, although a certain exaggeration is, of course, necessary to add theatrical interest. Light must only *seem* to come from certain sources; supplementary equipment must actually be mainly responsible for the effect. Highlights and shadows are sometimes accentuated by means of motivating-light instruments and, by the use of colored gelatine, the correct light color can be exaggerated in a manner which will suggest the source.

If warm light is directed toward an acting area which is near a window, sunlight is suggested. Since such an area would naturally be lighter than a corner of the room which the sun could not reach, a type of realistic motivated light has been supplied. If two spotlights are directed toward the area, the light on the far side might best use a cool gelatine. The projection of parallel rays from a beam projector through the window will add to the realism although it may or may not appreciably change the amount of light within the area. The direction, the slant, and the color of the rays from the "sun spot" may very easily help to suggest the time of day. By using a variety of lighting instruments, placed in various positions, a number of sunlight or moonlight effects may be obtained for a particular production. Various shades of amber will serve nicely as sunlight colors and light purple-blue or deep steel-blue are useful for moonlight.

All table lamps, electric wall brackets or sconces, and chandeliers must be equipped with lamps of very low wattage; in addition, and regardless of how they are shaded, it will probably be necessary to dim the lamps to prevent glare. In order to make it appear that a light source such as a table lamp is supplying the light for a particular area or areas, special spotlights ("cover spots") must direct light toward the area. The light from these instruments will *seem* to be produced by the lamp, thus suggesting a slightly exaggerated realism. While lamp shades of translucent material will be more noticeable when they are lighted than will opaque shades, the latter type is often more suitable for a stage room. If a light source is against a wall, care must be observed that light from the "cover spot" is sufficiently diffused not to call attention to itself. As a matter of fact, there should never be too much support from any of the "cover spots." Furthermore, if the stage business requires that one of a number of electrical fixtures or table lamps be turned off, half the stage should not be darkened as a result.

A light source such as a chandelier presents additional problems; area spotlights may have to be angled so as to avoid casting shadows of the chandelier on the back wall of the setting. However, chandeliers do not present the same "cover spot" problems as do table lamps and wall brackets. Since a chandelier is hung quite far downstage, it is likely that the light from a pair of the beam spots will "cover" it sufficiently. If more than one chandelier is used, further adjustment may have to be made; a large chandelier might even have a small spotlight mounted within it. A chandelier can add a distinct decorative note to a setting and its use is usually well worth all the trouble it entails.

The representation of an open flame on the stage is at best artificial and rather unconvincing. However, when such an effect is demanded by the script, the audience will usually accept the more or less conventional results. The use of a real flame on the stage presents an element of danger and, since the light flickers and cannot be controlled, it might easily attract an excess of attention. Although the use of old-fashioned chimney lamps, candles, and torches can add considerable atmosphere to the stage picture, they should be used only when absolutely necessary. A flashlight lamp and battery can supply the light for a lamp or a candle flame if a twist of amber colored gelatine encloses the lamp bulb; this method will also be useful for torches although the results are never very satisfying. A fireplace grate with burning coals can be suggested by means of a wire box containing a lamp and covered with bits of amber glass. Convincing fireplace logs are made of wire and papier-mâché and a lamp is placed within to suggest burning embers. Elaborate moving flame effects, complete with fan, bits of silk, and a moving color wheel attract undue attention and are therefore not usually desirable for realistic productions. The "cover spot" is just as necessary for use with a flame motivating light as it is for an electric fixture although the gelatine color should perhaps be warmer.

Lighting Plots and Cue Sheets

Before setting up and angling the stage lighting equipment, it is necessary to make some sort of lighting plot which will show the locations of the instruments and the areas that these instruments must light. At this time, gelatine colors must also be considered in

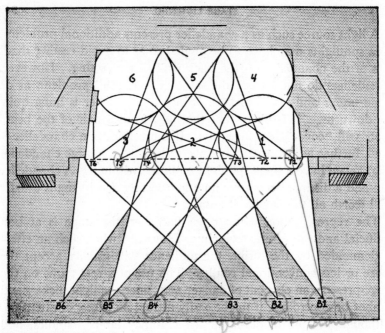

Fig. 127 *The lighting plot*

relation to light sources, time of day, season, and mood of the play. The question of dimmer readings, however, cannot be determined exactly until it is possible to view the entire production as it is set up on the stage. As the lighting technician becomes experienced at such plotting and has frequent opportunity to observe the results of his assumptions, he will come to learn pretty much what to expect from certain equipment. The arbitrary instrument locations noted on the previous pages will, therefore, serve as a workable starting point from which to consider the over-all lighting problems.

The setting for *Blithe Spirit* (p. 21) is an example of a realistic box setting which would require rather conventional night and day interior lighting. Since the play is a comedy, the use of warm green walls, panel moldings applied in gold, gold damask for the sofa and draperies, and red leather for the chairs and hassock will keep the room mellow and cheerful. If the green walls are sprayed or flecked with a dark green and a grayed yellow, the walls should take on a pleasant quality when toned with various combinations of light amber (#57) and light blue (#27), depending upon the time

348

of day or night. If the borderlight is equipped with the light primaries, these lights can be dimmed so that the red and green are similar in intensity and the blue dimmed considerably — thus producing a warm yellow for the day scenes. The blue can be brought up more strongly for the night scenes in order to cool the general effect a bit.

Since the play is bright and merry, it seems only natural that the acting areas should be lighted warmly and with considerable intensity. Light scarlet (#62) should be pleasing for the warm side, theoretically supplying the light from the window or the piano lamp, with Dubarry pink (#9) serving as a sort of cool complement from the opposite instruments. This contrast between the two colors will accentuate all dimension and be especially flattering to the actors. Beam Spot #1 (p. 348), for example, should be equipped with light scarlet and Beam Spot #4 with Dubarry pink in order to light Area #1. Similarly, Beam Spot #2 with light scarlet and Beam Spot #5 with Dubarry pink would light Area #2. The same principle should be applied to the upstage areas in order to suggest more warmth from the window side of the setting. Since a lamp is also on Stage Left, the question of intensity is of chief concern as it relates to the particular day and night scenes.

Motivating light from the Stage Left window can be supplied by a beam projector floodlight which is fitted with light amber for the day scenes and medium blue special (#32) for the night scenes. Although in the *Blithe Spirit* production which is under consideration it will not be possible to have window light from more than one angle, it is sometimes desirable to use two sun spots, each from a different angle and fitted with different gelatines to suggest different times of day or night. In this connection it might be well to point out that while everyone knows that moonlight is not necessarily a colorful blue, audiences are quite willing to accept such on the stage because of its attractiveness.

If sufficient light does not fall on the various pieces of furniture, it may be necessary to direct an extra spotlight to the chair or sofa. The intensity of the extra spotlight, however, must not kill the plasticity obtained by cross-lighting. Light in the hallway can be handled by placing one or two small striplights over the door. A combination of amber with green or blue lamps might be used, depending upon which combines most pleasingly with the paint. Undoubtedly it will be necessary to direct one or two small spotlights in the hallway just upstage of the double doors so that as actors pass through the hall they can readily be seen. It will also probably be necessary to focus a spotlight directly toward the double doors, matting the gelatine frame carefully so that the beam conforms to the shape of the door; an approximation of the toning color would be suitable for this purpose. Two small spotlights, temporarily hung from the teaser batten, can serve as cover spots for the table and piano lamps and thus give extra emphasis to these areas. A glow of red or deep amber, produced by a small spotlight within the fireplace, would be especially effective for the scenes played in semidarkness.

Blithe Spirit is perhaps an easier production to light than many plays with interior settings. Its light cues are sharp and distinct and its chief lighting requirements are either excellent visibility or almost absolute darkness. Certain other productions, however, require unusual mood and atmosphere and will be a challenge to the lighting technician as he attempts to provide both visibility and atmosphere. Such plays as *Angel Street*, *A Streetcar Named Desire*, and *The Glass Menagerie* require exceptional skill with the use of light. Beginning lighting technicians might do better to obtain their experience by working on plays like *Born Yesterday*, *Affairs of State*, or *Years Ago*. It is better not to attempt effects which, because of inexperience, are bound to come across haphazardly.

As for the exterior setting, aside from the difficulties of cyclorama lighting, there is much greater opportunity for experimentation since no ceiling is in the way. Leaf patterns may be projected, shafts of light may pierce the foliage borders, and the fourth wall may be ignored to provide light sources which a box setting cannot offer. Provided they do not attract too much attention, subtle light changes may take place during the action of a scene. Exterior floor plans, like those for the interior, may be divided into acting areas which should be lighted after consideration is given to motivation. Obviously, exterior lighting requires the use of a great many instruments. Many groups are not well enough supplied with equipment to attempt elaborate exterior settings.

Since controlboards differ so much as to size and set-up, it would be difficult to plan an electrician's cue sheet which would be usable for every type of board. It is therefore up to the lighting technician to study his board, his interplugging panel, and the locations of the various outlets throughout the backstage area in an effort to plan a series of printed forms which will be useful for his specific theatre. Even though the lighting plot shows which instruments are used, where they are directed, and what dimmers control them, such a plot does not supply sufficient information to run a show accurately.

Rows of dimmers are usually considered in banks, and arbitrary designations such as colors or letters from the alphabet are assigned to the banks. If the board makes use of transfer switches, these must be taken into account as well as the regular circuit switches. Most technicians find it helpful to prepare a cue-sheet form which includes a chart of the controlboard at the top of the page with a space at the bottom for the various cues and the dimming and switching operations involved. If such a sheet is filled out in detail for each scene of the play (more than one sheet for each scene may sometimes be necessary), there will be little opportunity for error. The chart should have spaces to indicate the dimmer readings, the stage areas that the instruments cover, and the colors of the gelatines for each circuit on the bank.

It is in connection with the interconnecting plugging panel that errors are most likely to occur. When such a panel is used it is often necessary to connect dimmers to different stage outlets in the course of the minute or two allowed between scenes. Crew members are sometimes in such a hurry that they make mistakes which, of course, can hardly be corrected easily once the curtain has gone up. Thus flexibility breeds complications. For example, during one scene a dimmer could control part of the first borderlight; during the second scene it might be connected to a beam projector floodlight; during a third scene it might be responsible for the cover spot for a table lamp. It would seem, then, that an interconnecting panel chart should provide spaces to indicate both the dimmers involved and the location of the instrument which is connected to the dimmer at the moment. An electrician who knows what his switches and dimmers control is of more help in an emergency than one who works blindly.

PROJECTS AND EXERCISES

1. If the following lamps are to be dimmed on one circuit:
   3 of 250 watts at 115 volts,
   2 of 1000 watts at 115 volts,
   what would be the proper resistance for the dimmer?

2. If a stage setting requires four three-bulb wall brackets (40 watts — 115 volts), what would bet he total wattage and total current required if the lamps were connected in parallel?

3. A 75-watt (115-volt) lamp is to be used in a hearth. If it were to be dimmed with a 500-watt dimmer, what would be the required "phantom load"?

4. Why is it undesirable to use a single color to light both the setting and the costumes of a play? What method do you suggest?

5. Experiment with the various commonly used colored gelatines as to their effect on certain colored fabrics. Do any of the results surprise you? Attempt to explain any unusual results which you note.

6. List the advantages and disadvantages of three-color foot and border lighting. What system is used in your theatre? Try to find out why.

7. What color would be produced by a mixture of separate yellow and blue beams of light on a white surface? Why?

8. Make a simple chart which will illustrate the important differences between the old-fashioned spotlight, the ellipsoidal reflector spotlight, and the Fresnel lens spotlight. Investigate the prices of the various instruments.

9. Examine the lighting instruments on your stage from the point of view of mounting equipment. Analyze the advantages and disadvantages of each method.

10. Contrast the olivette and the ellipsoidal type of floodlight. How may each be used most satisfactorily? How do these instruments differ in construction from the beam projector floodlight or "sun spot"?

11. How many rows of borderlights are hung in your theatre? What determined the choice of this number of units? How frequently are they used?

12. If a Linnebach lantern is to be used which has a 10″ × 16″ slide, what size projection can be expected if the slide is 12′ from the screen?

13. Make a list of plays for which lighting effects from a sciopticon would be suitable. Be prepared to give reasons for your opinions.

14. Prepare a chart which will show at a glance the advantages and disadvantages of the various types of dimmers. What type of dimmer is used on your stage? What determined the selection of this equipment?

15. Make a simple drawing of the front of your controlboard. Study the switch and dimmer arrangements from the point of view of clarity and ease in operation. What suggestions would you make as to simplification?

16. Examine the paintings of some of the old masters. Note the use of shade and shadow as related to light sources.

17. Select a realistic play which requires the use of a single box setting. Make a drawing of the floor plan for this play. Divide the stage into the areas which must be lighted. List all the equipment which would be required to light the play.

18. What colored gelatine would be the most useful for lighting the acting areas for the following plays: *Antigone, John Loves Mary, The Patriots, The Rivals, Angel Street?* Why?

19. Contrast beam spotlights with balcony-front spotlights. In what cases might the latter be used with satisfaction?

20. Examine illustrations of various stage settings as shown in books and magazines. Attempt to discover examples of light motivation. Does the light *seem* to come from these sources?

21. Plan light-cue forms for your controlboard. If your theatre is equipped with an interconnecting panelboard, devise a cue sheet for this board also. Examine the light-cue forms used by several other theatres. What do all the good forms have in common?

10

Sound Effects and Special Visual Effects

RADIO WRITERS and directors are constantly advised to use sound effects sparingly. If such advice is suitable for those who work in a medium which deals primarily with sound, surely those who work with a medium such as the theatre, where sight and sound are both important, should find the suggestion all the more applicable. Film patrons, however, have come to expect every available *creak* and *groan* and *slam* and *bang* and are sometimes disappointed when noisy, literal sound effects do not accompany the stage play. Since the visual element and the spoken word of the theatre are its chief concern, the stage director often prefers to allow the imagination of an audience to supply many of the sound effects.

Recorded Sound

In recent years the use of recorded sound has become increasingly popular for both radio and theatre drama. Obviously, recorded sound in radio and film drama is in no way objectionable since

354

neither type of performance is usually *alive* before an audience. On the other hand, recorded sound in the theatre becomes a "canned" accessory to an otherwise "alive" dramatization. Since recorded sounds are available in anything from an auto accident to zooming airplanes, it is the line of least resistance to turn to such sound effects despite the fact that a little ingenuity might provide more satisfying manual substitutes.

The best type of sound-effects records have been made from life "on location." The sound is first recorded on tape and then transferred to vinyl-plastic discs. Recordings of this type have a minimum of surface noise. The sound technician must take pains to select only those recorded sounds which are accurate and authentic, clear and undistorted. Better to use no sound at all than to rely on vague, scratchy, wavering recordings. Purchases should be made with an eye to future use; the development of a sound library involves considerable investment.

If a recorded sound effect provides distant sounds such as train or boat whistles, animal noises, or the singing of birds, the volume might better be so low that the results will not seem "canned." If there must be sound of great volume and reverberation like that made by a pneumatic hammer or the blast of an explosion, recorded sound may be a necessity. Sometimes recorded background sounds can be livened; a crowd noise recording will take on dimension if a few people *ad lib* backstage as the crowd recording is being played. In such a case it is possible that all the sound will seem to come from a "live" crowd.

Since the *loudspeaker*, the *electronic amplifier*, the *mixing console*, and the *turntables* are the backbone of the stage sound apparatus, it is false economy to purchase inexpensive equipment which will break down continually. It is not necessary to buy elaborate, expensive cabinets to hold the equipment — serviceable frameworks can be constructed in the shop. In order to provide flexibility, at least two turntables and three pick-up arms should be provided so that there can be a blending of sound effects when necessary. While a high fidelity loudspeaker and amplifier with a frequency response of from 100 to 6000 cycles are desirable, less sensitive equipment will be adequate for the average production provided tone control is included. (Some specialists insist that a frequency variation of from 30 to 12,000 cycles is absolutely necessary.) A fifty-watt amplifier will be satisfactory for most stage use; nothing less than twenty-five watts should be considered.

Although most of the commercial sound-effects records are of the 78 R.P.M. variety, there are many advantages to the use of variable speed turntables. It should be possible, by turning a knob, to change the revolutions per minute from 15 to 85. Many of the new $33\frac{1}{3}$ R.P.M. records could then be used as background music for various stage scenes, providing music for almost as long as necessary. Also, "dubbings" of recordings are more satisfactory if the $33\frac{1}{3}$ speed is used. Varying the speed will, in some cases, provide a slightly different type of sound. A slowed-up airplane motor will, for example, resemble a dirigible motor — or an automobile motor recording can be given a "chug-chug" quality when it is played more slowly. When the volume is increased for wind and wave recordings, the sound will change from a comparatively calm representation of the elements to the suggestion of a tempest.

Certain sounds are almost always necessarily represented by means of recordings regardless of volume or speed. Hurdy-gurdies, carousels, bagpipes, carillon chimes, cathedral bells, fanfares, and automatic pianos require the use of recordings when they occur as offstage sounds. The real article had better be provided for effects such as a music box, a Klaxon horn, drum sounds, door buzzers and bells, dinner bells, cymbal crashes, and gongs. Unfortunately, manufacturers sometimes place a number of unrelated sounds on a single side of some of their sound records. This occasionally causes confusion in playing and blending and makes logical cataloging rather difficult.

Unless the sound-table operator is especially skilled at fading the sounds in and out, recorded sounds will never be even remotely convincing. Unpleasant "pops" and "wows" and abrupt "blasts" can be expected to disconcert an audience. As the sound technician operates his more or less simplified controls, he follows cues similar to those of the electrician at the controlboard. Sensitivity and understanding are required of the operator even though the director of the production is responsible for the selection of sounds, their arrangement throughout the various scenes, and the decisions as to intensity and pitch.

The loudspeaker should not be permanently placed in one location; it is often advisable to change its backstage location in order to help suggest that sound is coming from a particular direction. Obviously, if the loudspeaker is placed in the auditorium, serving as a part of the public-address system, the sound effects will stand little chance of being realistic. Although the flats of a box setting will serve to muffle the sound considerably, a relatively open exterior setting will not diminish the sound to any great extent. Introductory music, before the curtain opens, will always prove to be a problem since the act curtain *and* the scenery will deaden the musical effects. The use of two loudspeakers, therefore, is sometimes indicated — one in the auditorium and one in the backstage area.

Since it is occasionally necessary to amplify sounds or voices from a microphone which is placed backstage, the sound apparatus must provide such facilities — complete with all the necessary controls at the mixing console. An occasional play may even require the use of a microphone onstage with the placement of the loudspeaker in the auditorium proper. The use of an offstage microphone would be especially suitable for such an atmospheric sound as the ticking of a clock, or to amplify the sounds from an electric vibrator or a utility-store toy siren. The microphone should probably be of the unidirectional (sensitive on one side only) variety so that extraneous noises will not be picked up.

Some sound technicians advocate the use of magnetic tape recordings in place of the usual discs, claiming that tape recordings are so subtle that an audience is not specifically aware when they are in use. All the sound effects for a production can be recorded on tapes in the order in which they occur and, since most tapes will play as long as half an hour, considerable background music may be included if necessary. If plastic-backed tapes are used, it will be possible to play and replay the tapes throughout the rehearsal and performance periods.

Every sound technician is aware of the opportunities for error which are presented as he fades, cross-blends, and changes speed and volume. If these operations are recorded correctly on a tape, the sound problems are simplified and the operator merely has *on* and *off* cues to follow. When special *live* sounds are recorded on tape for a production, this had better be accomplished in a studio so that various echoes and reverberations will not interfere with the sound definition. Combinations of recordings and live sounds are also quite successful on tape; a crowd recording combined with one or two special voices calling out phrases pertinent to the scene should make a useful sound effect. Since a good tape recording and play-back apparatus involves the expenditure of several hundred dollars, many groups must be content with the traditional turntable and disc arrangements for sound.

Sound technicians usually find it advisable to follow a *Recorded Sound Cue Form* of some sort which will show at a glance the records used, the equipment level readings, and the specific line or business cues. Although the particular apparatus which is in use will determine the necessary equipment level blanks on the sheet, all recorded sound cue forms should probably indicate the number of the record and the side and cut that are to be used. As for precise cues, both *in* and *out* data should be listed, together with approximate timing information.

Manual Sound Effects

Unlike recorded sound effects, manually produced sounds (see pages 360 and 361) are not usually subject to the whims of this machine age. When the sound apparatus develops contact trouble or tube difficulties, a property-crew member with blank cartridges and pistols is much more dependable than the finest of recorded sounds. Thus, a manual sound effect offers the added inducement of dependability in addition to its representation of authentic sound. Furthermore, a manual sound effect is so easy to time that there is seldom any question as to its correlation with the rehearsed reactions on the stage proper. The definition of manual sound can be sharp and conclusive; the sound thus seems to relate itself to the part of the play which it assists. Some effects, of course, must be produced at considerable distance from the stage setting if they are to sound realistic.

Many manual sound effects require the use of specially built, bulky, space-consuming apparatus. Such devices must be accurately and precisely built if they are to operate satisfactorily;

they should be considered as permanent equipment and stored carefully when not in use. Although the sound technician provides these sound effects and knows how to use them effectively, it is up to the director to indicate his desires as to the intensity and the direction of the sound which the devices produce. Considerable rehearsing is usually necessary if the sound device is to provide well-defined, convincing effects.

As in the case of recorded sounds, offstage manually produced effects should probably be used sparingly if they are to help the play. Sound effects may sometimes "open a scene" and then fade out so gradually that the audience will be unaware of the changes. No kind of sound effect should serve as an unnecessary "crutch." However, it is possible that a well written or well acted play may have one badly written or poorly played scene which needs the extra bolstering which atmospheric music and sound might provide; in such a situation, the "crutch" might be necessary in order to help de-emphasize the weaknesses. Unless a sound must provide a motivation for reaction by the actors, its use is often open to question. Extraneous traffic noises, surf sounds, and farmyard effects, for example, may even distract unless they are carefully controlled and used with discrimination.

A *Manual Sound Cue Form* is usually necessary if the crew members are to supply the sounds with consistent accuracy. Although the form need not be so detailed as the recorded sound cue form, it must usually include such items as the cue number, the apparatus to be used, the intensity of the sound, and the exact *in* and *out* cues. Since the main purpose of the form is to guarantee accurately timed and responsive sound effects, needless "busy" work should not be required. A simple cue sheet will be much easier to follow than a complicated and detailed form. Since directors frequently wish to make sound effect changes during the late rehearsal and early performance period, it is possible that a cue sheet, at the final performance, may bear only a slight resemblance to the original.

The following list of manual sounds includes almost every type of device which has been found useful at one time or another. The sound technician will frequently find it advisable to combine the sounds from a number of devices or to vary the procedures and

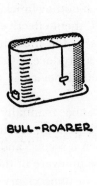

BULL-ROARER

SOLDIERS MARCHING

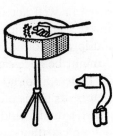

AIRPLANE

BOMB

CHIMES

HORSE'S HOOVES

Fig. 128 *Manual sounds*

LOCOMOTIVE

OLD-FASHIONED AUTO

SHOTS STARTER'S PISTOL

WIND

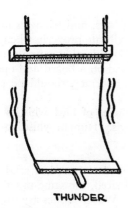

THUNDER

SURF

Fig. 129 *Manual sounds*

methods listed below. Although expensive electrically driven wind, rain, and thunder machines are on the market, the home-made varieties are satisfactory in most cases; ingenuity will perhaps lead to the discovery of interesting new effects. In all cases, the results are more important than the means.

Animals. Saxophones and oboes are useful to suggest cow and frog sounds. The human voice is also effective. The roaring of a bull or lion is well imitated by means of a large can or bucket and a string which has been treated with resin. When there is tension on the string or cord, and it is rubbed with a glove containing resin, the sound will be amplified by the can.

Automobile. A large metal can serves as the basic unit for automobile sounds. When a stick with attached pieces of leather or a wire duster is rotated against the inside walls, a motor sound is indicated. As variations, an egg beater, a Mixmaster, or an electric vibrator might be used. A starting and stopping sound is sometimes accomplished by placing the tip of an electric egg beater against a bass drum and turning the apparatus on and off on cue.

Airplane. The automobile devices will provide this sound if speed and intensity are increased. The snare drum is also sometimes useful. If an electric-bell unit, without the bell, is placed against a bass drum, an airplane motor will be suggested.

Bomb Explosion. When a shotgun (using blank shells) is fired into a large metal can or barrel, the explosive sound will carry a considerable distance. To change the quality of the sound, the can may be wrapped with a blanket or rug.

Bells. Bells, brake drums, chimes, wrecking bars, and triangles must be hung in a free position so that they will vibrate properly when struck with a hammer or a wooden mallet. Considerable experimentation is desirable. An actual doorbell, mounted on a board and operated by batteries or electric current and transformer, should be part of the permanent sound equipment.

Birds. Utility and novelty stores have supplies of bird whistles representing the calls of a wide variety of birds. Human whistling is also suitable if it is expertly done.

Chimes. See Bells.

Crash. When a box of broken glass is dropped or jarred, a crash effect will result. When a metallic crash is desired, the same practice can be followed using a box of scrap metal. Wood crashes are suggested by the breaking of orange crates or lengths of thin wood.

Crunching Sound. A large box filled with flake glue and covered with cloth will provide excellent crunching sounds when the contents are walked on.

Door Slam. An actual offstage door is required if a door slam is to be convincing; a small door such as is used in a radio studio should prove satisfactory. The "bang" produced by slamming a short length of 1″ by 3″ to the floor is a poor substitute for this effect.

Gong. See **Bells.**

Hail. See **Rain.**

Horns. It is best to use the specific horns that are called for in the script. The horns may be sounded manually or electrically. A storage battery can supply the current for an automobile horn.

Horse's Hooves. The standard method is to strike coconut shells against a padded or hard area. A considerable variety of rhythmic sound patterns is possible.

Locomotive. A satisfactory locomotive sound is created by the rubbing together of sandpaper blocks. A much stronger locomotive effect is produced by striking sheet metal with a wire duster. A snare drum might also be used for this purpose.

Machine Gun. If the tips of a couple of limber wood slats are held against the fast turning slats of a wind machine, the staccato effect of a machine gun will be indicated. Firecrackers are also sometimes used for this effect; they are, of course, not completely reliable.

Marching Soldiers. Loose dowel sticks, wired within a wooden frame, will supply this effect if the frame is raised and lowered so that the sticks strike a table or the floor with regularity.

Motorboat. The motor which supplies the power for the spray gun is a possibility for this effect. Experimentation with the various automobile and airplane effects might also be in order.

Rain. A large, round, tin pan filled with dried peas, beans, or rice will suggest the sound of rain if the contents are in continual circular motion. If a visual rain apparatus is in use, its accompanying sounds will be most effective.

Shooting Gallery. A number of repeating toy cap-guns can suggest shooting-gallery shots if some sort of sound pattern is worked out in advance.

Shots. Pistol or gun shots are required if the sound must have intensity. Blank shells are always used.

Siren. Sirens operated by hand or by electricity are required for these sounds. Storage batteries or dry cells may supply the power.

Splash. The sudden pouring of varying amounts of water from one pail to another will suggest a splashing sound without the dampening effects of a real splash.

Squeak. A large, resin-coated, pointed peg will cause a squeaky sound when it is deliberately moved about within a wooden hole of similar diameter.

Steam. The release of air or a harmless gas from a tank will indicate a most satisfactory abrupt or continuous escaping-steam sound.

Surf. A large, rectangular tray, with a floor of heavyweight screening and containing dried peas or beans, is the best basis for this sound.

The contents of the tray should roll from one end of the tray to the other at regular intervals.

Thunder.   A thunder sheet consists of a 3' by 6' sheet of 26-gauge sheet metal which is sandwich-battened at the narrow ends.   If the sheet metal is hung in a free space and shaken in crescendo and diminuendo fashion, a reasonably satisfactory thunder effect results.   Thunder sheets are sometimes beaten with a bass drumstick or a padded hammer.   The thunder drum, a much more complicated and expensive thunder apparatus, produces an especially realistic sound.   The unit consists of a heavy frame covered on one side with specially treated and stretched leather.

Wind.   A wind machine is a rotating drum consisting of wooden slats which rub against a taut strip of canvas.   Considerable variation in sound is possible.

Whistle.   All types of whistles are available in the stores; there are usually no substitutes for these particular sounds.   Large wooden whistles are particularly effective.

Waves.   *See* Surf.

Special Visual Effects

Many special visual effects used on the stage are relatively simple to handle but none the less impressive to an audience; the elaborateness of the apparatus does not always bear a direct relationship to the final results.   Since audiences enjoy tricky visual effects, directors and technicians should never lose opportunities to include them even though extra labor and rehearsal time may be involved. Although special lighting apparatus is often employed for the direct projection of moving waves, falling snow and rain, and moving clouds, manual on-the-spot visual effects are also used with considerable success.

When realistic rain effects are required on the stage, there is no satisfactory substitute for actual water.   Productions such as *Rain* can make good use of an apparatus which will supply both the visual and sound effects.   A long pipe with two rows of holes can be placed above and behind each outdoor opening to the setting. Water, forced through this pipe by means of a hose, will fall in a steady stream to a trough beneath the opening; it may then be collected in buckets or by some more ingenious method.   The play of light on the downpour helps to give emphasis to the falling water.   The contraption is much like a long lawn sprinkler except

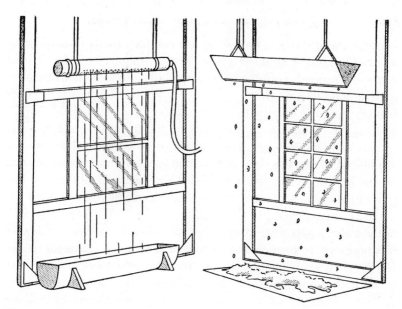

Fig. 130 *Rain-effect apparatus (left) and snow-effect apparatus (right)*

that the holes in the pipe are more limited. Now and then a play will require that water dash against actual glass window panes. When this is necessary, the backs of the window flat and window frame must be waterproofed and the pipe tilted so that the water is directed toward the glass. Directors need never fear that a good play, well acted, will be overpowered by such mechanics, especially if the effect is an inherent part of the play.

Snow is more difficult to represent than rain since the flakes must fall rather gently without the use of force. The usual procedure is to suspend a trough-shaped cradle upstage of a door or window and to rock it back and forth gently. The cradle must be built so that it has a narrow slot through which soap or mica flakes will fall whenever the cradle is moved; bits of irregularly shaped paper are so not satisfactory since they tend to clog the slot. Technicians will do well to place a removable floor covering underneath the cradle so that the snow may be cleared from the floor quickly and easily.

Smoke effects are sometimes obtained by the use of an elaborate apparatus which forces ammonia vapor through hydrochloric acid. The use of such a device involves considerable expense and is not without danger; therefore, less complex methods are preferable. One of the simplest smoke devices requires only a heating element wrapped around a cone-shaped tile form which is equipped with a screw base; these cones are used in inexpensive electric heaters and are available at hardware stores. Sockets can be mounted in tin cans or on fibre boards, and the units are then ready to produce smoke. Small quantities of powdered sal ammoniac are placed within the cone and as soon as the element becomes hot, an inoffensive smoke will rise. The Katherine Hepburn production of *As You Like It* used this method successfully for an open fire down center. Several of these units may be used on various parts of the stage, and a little experience will indicate how far in advance it is necessary to turn on the current or how much chemical to use. If a property-crew member can be masked so that he can have easy access to the cone, smoke can be provided more or less continuously. A heavy, hanging white smoke can also be produced by soaking cotton batting with tritanium tetrachloride; as the chemical comes in contact with the air, the smoke is formed.

A sudden burst of light followed by a cloud of smoke is best obtained by the use of a *flash pot*. This homemade device, often in the form of a fibre box, makes provision for fastening the metal strip from the inside of a cartridge fuse to either end of a wire which is to carry current. A small amount of magnesium ($\frac{1}{2}$ teaspoon) is placed on the metal strip so that, when the current goes through the wire, the metal strip melts and ignites the powder. A simpler version of the flash pot merely involves the removal of the mica from a screw-type fuse and the addition of a small amount of chemical. Care must be observed that nothing inflammable is placed near the flash pot. The device is especially useful for disappearing acts; the audience is so startled by the flash that characters may run quickly from the stage unobserved.

An ascending and descending stage elevator is more easily represented if some portion of the door or doors is equipped to suggest translucent glass. A permanent light can be placed behind the door, and a shutter, next to the door, raised and lowered on cue. A more realistic effect can be obtained by using a box-like frame to represent the top of the elevator. The frame should be closed at the top and equipped with a dome light. As the frame is raised

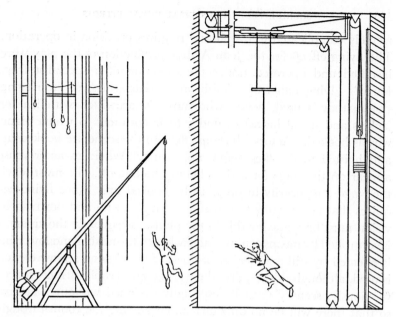

Fig. 131 *Flying apparatus*

and lowered by means of a top center line, guided by wires at the four corners, light will show through the doors and the door cracks. An effect of this sort is practicable for a one-set production but, where scene shifts are involved, it will probably be better to use the shutter method. The hospital corridor scene from *I Remember Mama* is enhanced by the use of a practical elevator as is the loft-apartment in *The Closing Door*.

By means of a specially placed ring in the fly loft, and the use of black, braided, nylon fishing line, objects can be raised and lowered, seemingly of their own accord. For example, if the witches' caldron in *Macbeth* were placed on a hollow base large enough to hold a crew member, the first apparition could be raised, accompanied by a puff of smoke, and then lowered into the caldron, after which the crew member could attach the second apparition, etc. A production of a play like *Blithe Spirit* might make good use of this ring and fish-line system, especially for some of the tricks at the end of the play. As simple as this device is, it never fails to mystify an audience.

The *flying apparatus* necessary for such a play as *Peter Pan* is extremely complicated to install and requires precision in operation. The flying effects for the Jean Arthur production of the play were installed and operated under the direction of a specialist from Kirby's Flying Ballet of English fame. Regardless of the rigging system that is used, actors who must fly are fitted with leather jackets and metal harnesses under their costumes to which piano wire is hooked. Actors who must fly into the scene are hooked up and hoisted to the flies before appearing. When an actor must appear on the stage for a time before "taking off," he must leave the stage temporarily in order to be hooked up. Since flying requires that actors cross the stage as well as go up and down, provision must be made for this in the plans. Frequently the crossing is controlled by means of a special track, and the raising and lowering is effected by still another set of lines. Sometimes a seesaw device is used, although this requires the use of considerable offstage space. Obviously, scenery must be especially designed without a ceiling so that there will be no difficulty about leaving the room through the air.

PROJECTS AND EXERCISES

1. Examine the catalog of some firm which sells recorded sound-effects. Note the variety of areas covered. Check the effects which would be especially suitable for stage use.

2. Which of the following plays would be aided by the use of recorded background music: *Goodbye, My Fancy, Death of a Salesman, Dream Girl, The Madwoman of Chaillot, Life with Mother, The Glass Menagerie,* and *Julius Caesar?* Be prepared to give your reasons.

3. What type of sound system is used on your stage? What are its specific limitations?

4. Attend a motion picture in order to note the various off-the-set sound effects that are used. How many effects were absolutely necessary? How many were merely helpful? How many were unnecessary?

5. Devise a *Recorded Sound Cue Sheet* for use with your specific sound equipment. Make the cue sheet as simple and clean-cut as possible.

6. Make a list of manual sound effects which might be somewhat un-

dependable. Why? Which manual sound effects would require the most skill in operation?

7. Read the first act of *Command Decision* from the point of view of noting the sound effects required. What do these contribute to the scene? Could any of the effects be omitted? Which effects would necessarily be recorded? Which must be manual effects? Do you see any objections to combining both recorded and manual sound effects within one scene?

8. Investigate the various types of whistles and horns which are available in one of the local utility stores. For what plays might they be useful? Does it seem likely that the items would be durable enough to last throughout the rehearsal and performance period?

9. What would you use to obtain the following sound effects manually: a Paris taxi horn, cricket calls, an ambulance siren, a dentist's drill, Indian yells, subway turnstiles, a door buzzer, billiard-table sounds, and a farmhouse water pump.

10. Prepare manual and recorded cue sheets for the first act of *Command Decision*. Which cue sheet is the more complicated? Which type of sound will require the more expert timing?

11. What are the special visual effects required in the following plays: *The Green Pastures, Blithe Spirit, Mr. Roberts, Ah Wilderness, On Borrowed Time, Storm Operation*? How can these effects best be accomplished?

APPENDIX

**THE SCENE DESIGNER'S AND TECHNICIAN'S
VOCABULARY · A GLOSSARY OF TERMS**

BIBLIOGRAPHY OF SUGGESTED READINGS

SOURCES OF SUPPLY

INDEX

THE SCENE DESIGNER'S AND TECHNICIAN'S

VOCABULARY · A GLOSSARY OF TERMS

---

acanthus leaf A Greek and Roman decorative motif based on a luxuriant flowering leaf. Used in most succeeding periods as well — sometimes naturalistically and occasionally stylistically. Found on the Corinthian capital. Illustration on p. 229.

acoustics The behavior of sound in an auditorium as determined by architectural features of the room. Ceiling and walls act as distributing surfaces and must be designed to insure that the sound will neither lose its intensity nor become distorted. Since angles of reflection of sound waves are always the same as angles of incidence, charts can be drawn showing the sound distribution in a room. Poor acoustic conditions are often caused by excessive reverberation and not enough absorption of sound. (Time of reverberation in a small auditorium should not exceed one second.) Echoes and dead spots can be located in a model by means of special physical apparatus; these tests are accurate enough to insure equal distribution of sound in a completed room. Older theatres with much ornamental plaster (Empire Theatre, New York City) have better acoustics than many of the contemporary free-of-ornamentation type. The use of porous surfaces of fibrous materials may help overcome some types of acoustical difficulties. *See Acoustics and Architecture.* Paul Sabine. McGraw-Hill, 1932.

acroterium *See* **antefix**

act curtain A curtain which separates the audience from the stage. Placed directly upstage of the fire curtain. On large stages with a fly loft, the curtain is preferably of the drop variety (*act drop*), but smaller stages without a fly loft must use the draw type of act curtain. Illustration on p. 8.

acting area The area of the stage visible to the audience and used by the actors after the curtain rises.

Adam Brothers, Robert and James Late-18th-century English architects and designers whose work includes the years 1762–94. The Pompeii and Herculaneum excavations were responsible for the classic formality stressed by the Brothers Adam. Noted for the unified designs of their architecture, furniture, china, silver, floor coverings, and textiles. Illustrations on p. 260.

additive color mixture *See* **color mixture**

alternating current Electrical current which changes its direction at regular intervals. A current with a frequency of 60 cycles reverses its direction 60 times in one direction and 60 times in another — in one second. Although most communities have this type of current, it is always necessary to investigate, since direct current is sometimes provided and since not all equipment will function by means of either type of current.

alum A chemical, useful in solution, for painting over old scene paint which has deteriorated and may rub off.

aluminum reflector (*polished*) A reflector (spherical, ellipsoidal, or parabolic in shape), placed behind the lamp in a lighting instrument. The efficiency of the instrument is therefore improved as more light rays will go through the aperture or lens.

alzak reflector A spun-aluminum reflector considered by some authorities as superior to polished aluminum for use in spotlights.

amber A color medium which is similar in color to sunshine.

amorini Winged cherubs. Either the entire figure is used or the head alone. Illustration on p. 229.

ampere A unit of measure in electricity applying to the rate at which electricity flows through the wires. *See* **ohm** and **volt**

amplifier (*electronic*) That part of a sound system which, operating between the turntables and the loudspeaker, magnifies the strength of the electrical impulses carried by the system.

analine dye A strong alkaline dye, useful for painting curtains and toning scenery, and for over-all dye jobs. Putnam and Diamond dyes are a good substitute for analine scenic dyes. Available in a wide variety of colors.

analogous colors Colors next to each other on the color wheel. *See* p. 108.

antefix A Greek leaf ornament used on the roof corners of temples. A common motif in the late 18th and early 19th centuries where the classic influence was felt. Illustration on p. 234.

anthemion A conventionalized radiating cluster. Egyptian in origin. Illustration on p. 229.

antimacassar A Victorian doily placed on chair backs and arms as a protection to the upholstery.

antique Furniture or bric-a-brac which is at least one hundred years old and can therefore be brought through customs, duty free. Most Victorian furniture and bric-a-brac is not antique. Usually it is not safe to use actual antiques on the stage; reproductions, especially those with non-glossy finish, are better.

Antwerp Blue *See* **blue**

Appia, Adolphe (1862–1928)   A Swiss scene designer.   Appia and Gordon Craig were largely responsible for the change from two-dimensional to three-dimensional scenery in the early twenties. Many theatre students think of Appia merely in terms of stage lighting and the third dimension which is emphasized by lighting.   Actually, Appian theories included several different phases, culminating with his experiences at Hellerau, where audience and actor were almost indistinguishable.   His early designs were for Wagnerian opera, but his later work became formal — the stiff, flat surfaces of the scenery contrasting sharply with the actors.   He was the author of the following: *La Mise-en-scène du drame Wagnerien* (1891), *Die Musik und die Inscenierung* (1899), *L'Oeuvre d'Art Vivant* (1922).

appliqué   A three-dimensional paint treatment applied to scenery. Makes use of sand, sawdust, asbestos, and other rough materials.

apron (*furniture*)   A connecting support for the front legs of a piece of furniture.   Found just beneath the top of the seat.   Illustration on p. 226.

apron (*stage*)   The stage area in front of the act curtain up to the edge of the orchestra pit.   *See* diagram on p. 3.

arabesque   A framed design of floral or geometrical forms.   Illustration on p. 229.

arbor (*counterweight system*)   *See* **carriage**

arc spot   *See* **carbon arc**

arch flat   A flat with a large to-the-floor door opening.   Illustration on p. 72.

architrave   The lower portion of the entablature.   *See* **column** on p. 94.

arena staging   A method of staging which permits a close actor-audience relationship and allows the audience to view a production from three or four sides.   There is usually no scenery or proscenium arch as such, and all shifts of properties are accomplished in darkness or between the acts in full view of the audience.   While the show is on, lights are focussed on the arena; during intermissions, the seating sections are lighted but not the playing area.   Performances can be given in ball rooms, halls, and lounges, or in theatres specially built for the purpose (e.g., Penthouse Theatre, University of Washington).

arm pad   The upholstered pad on chair arms.   Common in Louis XV and XVI periods.   *See* pp. 226, 243, and 245.

arm stump   Support for the arm of the chair.   Illustration on p. 226.

arras   A tapestry originally woven in Arras, France.   Used to drape walls and beds in Medieval times.   Also used for the curtain in some Elizabethan stages.

Art Moderne   The term applied to French contemporary design of the twenties.   Considerable unnecessary ornamentation and overuse of heavily textured materials.   Illustration on p. 272.

Art Nouveau French contemporary design of the early 1900's. Much use of realistic vegetation as motifs. Illustration on p. 272.

asbestos curtain A curtain which, in case of fire on the stage, can be lowered to protect the audience.

atlantes Male figures used as supporting columns for furniture and architecture. Illustration on p. 229.

Aubusson Tapestries and carpets of extra fine quality woven originally in the village of Aubusson, France. Scenic and figure designs were common. These tapestries can readily be simulated for stage use by means of dye and burlap.

Ayers, Lemuel (1915–   ) An American designer and producer (*The Pirate, Angel Street, Oklahoma, St. Louis Woman, Kiss Me Kate, Out of This World*). Known for his free and meaningful style and acute sensitivity to color.

baby spot A small lighting instrument with a four-and-a-half- or five-inch lens, and using a 250- or 400-watt lamp. Used for specific illumination.

backdrop (*back cloth*) An unframed unit with sandwich battens at top and bottom. Can be used for both interiors and exteriors.

backflap Loose-pin or tight-pin hinges. May be purchased at regular hardware stores. The use of tight-pin hinges is preferred when the crack is to be covered by a dutchman. Loose-pin backflaps are for temporarily fastened units. Illustrations on p. 54.

backing A two- or three-fold masking piece placed behind doors or windows to cut off the view of the backstage area.

backing strips Lighting units used for general illumination from behind doors, windows, and ground rows. Lights are arranged in sections up to six feet in length. Illustration on p. 322.

back painting Necessary to prevent offstage lighting from showing through scenery when onstage areas are dimly lighted. A standard practice in professional scene painting studios.

backsaw A stiff-back saw used in a mitre box. Very small teeth. *See* p. 49.

backstage The stage area which the audience does not view during performance.

Bakst, Leon (1866–1924) A Russian designer known for the rich, oriental-styled scenery and costumes he designed for the Diaghileff Russian Ballet (*Scheherazade, Daphnis and Chloe*, etc.). He continually stressed the necessary unities of the stage picture.

ball foot A round, ball-shaped, turned foot used on chests. Same as *bun foot*. *See* p. 227.

ball fringe A trimming for draperies which consists of ball shapes made of cotton, wood, silk, crystal, etc. *See* p. 286.

balsa wood An extremely soft and lightweight wood. Ideal for easy carving and commonly used in the construction of model airplanes.

Suitable for the building of furniture and bric-a-brac for model stage settings.

baluster-back chair A chair back with spindles similar to the balustrade of a stair rail. Common in late-17th-century English and American furniture. Illustration on p. 219.

balusters A series of columns supporting the stair rail of the balustrade. Turned or plain, depending on style. *See* p. 82.

balustrade A unit consisting of a row of balusters (or spindles) and a stair rail. *See* p. 82.

bamboo A wood used in Far Eastern furniture. Also used in the Occident somewhat in the 90's and early 20th century. Chippendale bamboo turning is similar in shape to actual bamboo.

banister *See* **baluster**

banquette A long, built-in wall bench frequently found in night clubs and restaurants where space is at a premium. The backs and seats are often upholstered in the fluted or tufted manner.

baroque An exaggerated 17th-century architecture and design trend. Huge ornamental curves and oversized moldings, masculine in feeling, were its chief characteristics. Dorothy Draper has been responsible for popularizing and theatricalizing the plaster baroque curve.

barrel chair A chair shaped like a barrel cut in two. Usually upholstered with a fluted back. A non-period commercial style. *See* p. 218.

base (*column*) The lower part of the column which rests on the pedestal. Illustration on p. 94.

baseboard (*mopboard*) The trim which finishes the lower part of the wall. Molding usually trims the top of the baseboard, occasionally making it as much as one foot in height.

base-down lamp *See* **incandescent lamp**

bas relief A sculpture term which applies to ornament which projects slightly from the background.

batten: *Wood* A long strip of lumber such as is used at the top and bottom of a drop or for framing flats. *Pipe* A length of pipe to which a set of lines of the rigging system is hooked or tied.

batten clamp A type of stage hardware which clamps onto a pipe batten. The lower portion opens to clamp to the wooden batten of the drop. Made of cast iron. Illustration on p. 150.

Bay, Howard (1912–   ) An American designer. Former president of United Scenic Artists. Noted for the sharp, incisive comment expressed in his designs (*Carmen Jones, The Little Foxes, Up in Central Park, As the Girls Go,* and *Come Back, Little Sheba*).

bay window A typical feature of early-16th-century English rooms. A series of windows forming an alcove which is sometimes large enough to become almost another room. Common in turn-of-the-century houses as well.

bead (*beading*) Small half-round molding. Illustration on p. 52.

beam lighting Lighting from spotlights placed in front of a beam above and in front of the proscenium. Used for lighting downstage areas.

beam projector floodlight (*sun spot*) A lighting unit which permits the throw of intense rays of light to simulate sunshine. Contains a color filter holder, parabolic reflector, and blinder or Fresnel lens. Some units are equipped with louvers. Illustration on p. 320.

beam spot A spotlight used in beam lighting.

Belasco, David (1859–1931) An American producer and director. Associated with naturalism in the early-20th-century American theatre (*The Easiest Way, The Girl of the Golden West, The Return of Peter Grimm*).

belaying pin A metal or wooden pin used on the pinrail and the tie-off rail. *See* p. 12.

Bérard, Christian (1902–1949) A French painter and designer. His sketchy designs for the ballet and for numerous Cocteau plays illustrate unusual flair and taste. The Bérard scenery for *The Madwoman of Chaillot* and the Jouvet production of *L'Ecole des Femmes* was most favorably received on Broadway.

bergère A French armchair with closed upholstered sides. Common in Louis XV and XVI periods. *See* p. 243.

Berman, Eugene (1899–   ) A Russian virtuoso painter and designer. One of the founders of the imaginative Neo-Romantic school in Paris in the twenties although his present designs might better be called Neo-Baroque. His atmospheric designs often involve unusual use of three dimensions in paint. Berman designs have included *Romeo and Juliet* and *Giselle* for the Ballet Theatre and *Rigoletto* for the Metropolitan Opera.

Bernstein, Aline (1880–   ) An American designer. Scenery for *Reunion in Vienna, Grand Hotel, The Late Christopher Bean, The Children's Hour.* Costumes for *The Little Foxes, Harriet, Regina.*

Bibiena (Galli) family A 17th- and 18th-century Italian family of architects and scene designers and painters. Noted for their use of intricate perspective, baroque styles, and splendid proportions.

Biedermeier German Empire style. Named after Papa Biedermeier, a German comic character. Fruit woods were used extensively. Much more provincial than French Empire. Illustration on p. 269.

birdseye reflector spotlight bulb A lamp intended originally for show-window lighting, satisfactory for the stage when more expensive equipment is not possible. Built-in features are a plano-convex lens and a reflector. Available in 150- and 300-watt sizes with a medium screw base. Some sort of spring-clamp louver is advisable. If a swivel socket is used, the lamp will be adjustable to most angles.

bit A tool used with the bit brace to bore holes in wood. The bits have size ranges of $\frac{1}{16}''$. A bit which would bore a $\frac{1}{4}''$ hole is stamped #4 — i.e., $\frac{4}{16}''$. Illustration on p. 49.

black: *Ivory Drop* A fairly satisfactory dry pigment. Dissolves reasonably well. *Swedish Black* Comparable to Ivory Drop. *Hercules Black* Extremely black and easily soluble.

blackamoors Decorative Negro figures used frequently in Victorian times. Large and small figures, dressed with turban and loin cloth, and used separately or as a part of furniture.

black walnut An American wood of dark gray-brown color and simple grain. Much of the less valuable Victorian furniture is made of this wood.

blending A method of texturing which involves the blending together of several colors over a damp ground coat.

block foot A square blocklike foot on the end of a chair or table leg. Common in Chippendale furniture. Illustration on p. 226.

block-front chest A late-18th-century American furniture form. The front is in three panels; the center is concave and the ends convex. Illustration on p. 222.

blue: *Ultramarine* As a dry pigment, the closest to primary blue. Relatively inexpensive. *Antwerp* A wet pigment.

bobbinet A delicate, net-like material which is woven with oval-shaped openings $\frac{1}{8}''$ or $\frac{1}{4}''$ in size. Comes 30' wide so that no seams are required.

bolection molding A projecting molding framing a fireplace or panel. Has an outward roll with an ogee shape. Illustration on p. 52.

bombé A swelling and bulging surface noted in the Louis XV period. Particularly common in chests and commodes.

book Two flats hinged together, or the process of hinging two flats together. The crack and hinges are usually covered with a dutchman before the unit is painted.

book ceiling A stage ceiling consisting of two hinged rectangular frames hanging parallel to the curtain line. Three sets of lines are required to hold it over a setting. Only the middle set of lines is required when the ceiling is flown out of the way. Illustration on p. 98.

boomerang A two- or three-step rolling platform used for painting scenery at different levels. Illustration on p. 116.

"Borax" Badly designed commercial furniture with meaningless, pretentious detail, often faintly reminiscent of period pieces. Usually features poor scale, awkward proportion, and bad construction. Frequently available in *suites* or sets.

border A horizontal masking piece, either framed or unframed, for the space above a set. Necessary when stage draperies are used, but most unsatisfactory as trimming for a box setting.

borderlights Overhead lighting units containing reflectors but no lenses. Used for toning and blending. Several rows of these units may be necessary for exterior settings. *See* p. 322.

Boston rocker An American 19th-century painted rocking chair. Features a wide top rail as well as a chair seat which curves upward at the back. Illustration on p. 219.

Boulle work (*buhlwork*)   The ornamental inlay of brass into wood or tortoise shell. Popular during the reign of Louis XIV. Takes its name from André Charles Boulle of Versailles fame. Sometimes spelled *boule* or *buhl. See* p. 242.

bowline   A knot useful for tying rope directly to a batten. Allows a secure and tight attachment. *See* p. 150.

box plaiting   The gathering of material in small folds, pressed flat and sewed in that position. Useful for valances and for the skirts on upholstered pieces. *See* p. 283.

box setting   A setting with three (sometimes two) walls, the "fourth wall" being the proscenium arch. Necessary for most realistic plays demanding interiors. Illustration on p. 21.

brace cleat   A small, flat unit of stage hardware to which the upper end of a stage brace can be attached. Screwed to the stiles at regular intervals and on either side of doors. Illustration on p. 54.

brace jack   A triangular frame used in place of the stage brace to hold up scenery. Usually hinged to the scenic unit. *See* p. 142.

bracket   A small decorative shelf to hold a vase or clock. (Sconces 'which have been wired for electricity are sometimes called brackets.) Also used between leg and seat of a chair or table as ornament.

braided cotton rope *See* **sash cord**

breakaway scenery   Scenery constructed to allow scene shifts in full view of the audience. Especially effective when both interiors and exteriors must be shown.

breakfront   A bookcase in which the center of three sections projects further forward than the other two. Eighteenth-century English. Illustration on p. 223.

breasting   The process of pulling a unit backward by means of an upstage line attached to it and controlled by means of special pulleys.

Brewster chair   A many-spindled wooden Pilgrim chair. Might be called provincial Jacobean. A wooden seat and sturdy, turned posts are characteristic. *See* p. 219.

bridle   A type of rigging which allows the flying of a wide drop by means of two lines instead of three, or of three lines where four are needed but not available. Illustration on p. 150.

brightness (*brilliance*)   The lightness (tint) or darkness (shade) of a color. Painters usually use the term *value.*

brocade   A substantial fabric which resembles embroidery. The threads of its conventional or floral patterns are carried across the back when not needed on the front to develop the design.

brocatelle   A fabric which resembles an embossed damask. Has a satin-woven pattern against a twill background.

buffet *See* **sideboard**

bun foot *See* **ball foot**

burl   A veneer cut from a growth on the trunk of a tree. Burled walnut is often found on Queen Anne table tops and cabinets.

burlap A loose-weave hemp material such as is used for gunny sacks. Useful for covering tree trunks and rocks. Can also be painted to resemble tapestry.

Burnt Italian Sienna An inexpensive dry pigment, reddish in color. Somewhat difficult to keep in solution.

Burnt Turkey Umber A dry-earth pigment which is more brown in color than it is red.

butt joint The joint usually most suitable for scenery construction. Illustration on p. 62.

butterfly hinge A Colonial hinge used on cupboards and doors. Butterfly in shape and usually made of hammered metal. Both large and small sizes.

butterfly table A small early-18th-century drop-leaf table. The leaves are supported by brackets in the shape of butterfly wings. Illustration on p. 222.

Byzantine Late-fifth-century Near Eastern design based on the Roman. Noted for overdecoration (carving, gold and glass inlay, etc.) and stiff, sharp decorative motifs.

cable (*stage*) Insulated rubber-covered copper wires used for connecting spotlight and floodlight instruments to electrical outlets.

cable connector A fibre block used at either end of a stage cable. Male plugs, or pin connectors, have copper contact prongs. *See* p. 325.

cabriole leg A double-curved furniture leg. The top and foot swing out. First noted in 17th-century Flemish furniture. Illustration on p. 227.

calcimine A powdered paint containing a small amount of pigment and powdered glue, and much whiting. Not usually suitable for stage use unless considerably more pigment and glue are added. Also spelled *kalsomine*.

candelabra lamp base *See* **incandescent lamp**

canvas duck Heavy cotton material suitable for drops, ground cloths, and flats. Available in three-foot, six-foot, and ten-foot widths.

capital The top of a column. Common Greek capitals are Doric, Ionic, and Corinthian. The capital names the architectural order. Illustration on p. 94.

carbon arc A lighting instrument useful for long throws. Provides powerful clear light by means of an electric arc between two carbons. Instruments are self-adjusting as the carbon wears away.

Carlton table A table with drawers and compartments placed on top of it. Frequently used by Sheraton and certain early-19th-century designers. Illustration on p. 222.

Carolean *See* **Charles II**

carpenter's level A tool which permits the testing of the accuracy of perpendicular or horizontal building. Sometimes called a *spirit level*. *See* p. 48.

carpet hoist A method which allows a heavy unit to be removed from its lines when set on the stage. An extra line keeps the sandbag or counterweight at the grid when the scenic unit rests on the floor. The lines are then unhooked and taken out of sight. *See* p. 148.

carriage (*step unit*) Two or more parallel notched planks which support the steps. Sometimes called *stringer*. Illustration on p. 82.

carriage (*counterweight system*) A carriage holds the slip counterweights and is guided up and down by means of either T bars or steel cables. An operating rope is fastened to the top of the carriage and extends through the head block around to the floor block and then to the bottom of the carriage. Sometimes called an *arbor*. Illustration on p. 12.

carriage bolt A bolt which varies in diameter from $\frac{1}{4}''$ to $\frac{3}{8}''$ and in length from $4''$ to $10''$. The use of wing nuts is advisable. *See* p. 54.

cartouche A decorative motif which represents an oval with the edges rolled. Can be either painted or in relief. Originally from the Italian Renaissance.

cartridge fuse *See* **fuse**

Carver chair A turned, Early American rush-seated chair with rather high arms. Originally constructed of ash or walnut. Named after Governor Carver. Illustration on p. 219.

caryatid A female figure supporting a table, chair, or cabinet. Originally a Greek ornament but often used in 17th-, 18th-, and 19th-century furniture. Illustration on p. 229.

casein glue A powdered waterproof cold-water glue made from milk. Very satisfactory for fastening canvas to frames.

casein paint A paste paint with a casein glue binder. Comes in tints and strong colors. Extremely easy to mix and covers very evenly. *Texolite* is a common brand.

casement window A window, usually hinged on the side so that it will swing out. Some casement windows swing in.

casing *See* **trim**

cassone An Italian Renaissance chest or box with a hinged lid and carved sides. Small boxes were often used for jewels while large chests served for clothing storage. Illustration on p. 239.

cavetto A concave molding with a curve similar to a quarter circle. Frequently used in cornices. Illustration on p. 52.

ceiling plate A metal plate with an attached ring, useful in fastening together the parts of a roll ceiling and in hanging that unit from lines. Illustration on p. 54.

center of vision The intersection of the *central visual ray* with the *horizon line* on the *picture plane*. In one-point perspective this is obviously the vanishing point for all lines parallel to the line of vision since it is on both the *eye-level line* and the *C.V.R. See* p. 192.

central visual ray A line, perpendicular to the *horizon line* and at eye-level height. This will indicate the distance from the eye to the picture plane.

chain hanger An adjustable chain used to hang borderlights to a pipe batten and to regulate the angle at which they hang.

chair rail A room molding at chair-top height. Sometimes called the *dado cap*.

chaise longue A long chair or upholstered day bed. Typically 18th-century French. Occasionally in two pieces. *See p. 243.*

Chaney, Stewart An American designer (*The Old Maid*, *The Late George Apley*, *Blithe Spirit*, *The Voice of the Turtle*, *The Moon is Blue*). Also successful as designer for the following classics: *Hamlet* (Gielgud), *Twelfth Night* (Hayes-Evans), *The Winter's Tale*. Noted for elegance of design and use of high styles.

Charles H *See* **Restoration**

Cheney, Sheldon (1886–   ) An American author. One of the first editors of *Theatre Arts Quarterly*. Author of *The Art Theatre* (1925), *Stage Decoration* (1928), and *The Theatre* (1929).

cherry (*wood*) A light-brown wood used in old American furniture. Much Biedermeier furniture made with this wood.

chimney piece A decorative, period wall unit (including mantel) placed over the fireplace opening. The term *fireplace* is often misused in this connection.

chinoiserie Chinese motifs and subject matter used by Western designers particularly during the late 18th century.

chintz A fine printed or plain cotton material, often glazed. Suitable for draperies and slip covers.

Chippendale, Thomas (1718–1779) An English furniture designer. Except for the use of mahogany, his early work was similar to the Queen Anne styles. Straight legs are shown in his Gothic and Chinese adaptations. Chinese latticework backs, ribbon backs, and ladder backs were common in his later designs. Illustrations on p. 254.

chroma A color term used by the Munsell system and certain physicists. Sometimes called *intensity*. Refers to the strength of the color or its distance from the gray of the center of the color wheel.

chromium reflector A lighting-unit reflector similar in efficiency to those made of aluminum. An etched surface is usually more satisfactory than a polished surface.

circular saw *See* **table saw**

clamp (*tool*) A tool whose two movable ends are forced closer together by means of screws. Either the C clamp or the furniture clamp will hold wood in place while glue dries.

claw and ball foot A furniture foot carved as a bird's foot clutching a ball. Common in Queen Anne and early Chippendale. Illustration on p. 227.

clew A flat, triangular-shaped piece of wrought iron used to join one rope to a number of other ropes in order that all the ropes may become a single unit. *See p. 148.*

clinching plate A piece of cast iron about $\frac{1}{4}''$ thick. Clout nails will clinch as they go through the wood and strike this iron. Sometimes this plate is built into the template.

clout nail A blue nail with a flat, rather soft point. When $\frac{1}{4}''$ three-ply is used, a $1\frac{1}{4}''$ clout nail is advisable. *See* p. 54.

clove hitch A kind of knot. Useful for tying rope directly to a wood batten or to tie a wood batten to a pipe batten. *See* p. 150.

cloven foot An 18th-century furniture foot in the form of an animal's cleft foot. *See* p. 227.

club chair A comfortable, tailored, over-all upholstered chair. Non-period. Illustration on p. 218.

cock's head hinge An early English hinge cut in the shape of a cock's head. Brass or iron. *See* p. 276.

cold chisel A tool with a sharp edge at the end of a blade, used in cutting metal. The chisel is pounded onto the metal that is to be cut.

Colonial An indefinite term often applied to American furniture and architecture before 1800. A better classification for the same years would be: Early American 1608–1720, Georgian 1720–1780.

color frame Metal or wooden frames of various sizes to hold gelatine before lighting instruments.

color medium (*filter*) Colored gelatine or glass. Placed in front of a lighting instrument. Produces color by selective transmission.

color mixture: *Additive* The mixing of two or more light colors on a surface. If a spotlight with a green color medium and one with a red medium are focused on a white screen, the result will be yellow. *Subtractive* The selective transmission process. If a white light is directed through a red medium, blue and green will be absorbed and only red light will be transmitted.

color wheel The colors of the spectrum arranged in a wheel with the complements opposite one another. *See* p. 108.

column An architectural support made up of a capital, a tapered shaft, and usually a base. *See* p. 94.

comb-back chair An American 18th-century Windsor chair with extra spindles at the top of the back shaped like a comb. Illustration on p. 219.

commode A low chest with legs, usually placed against the wall. Particularly common in the 18th-century French periods. Illustrations on pp. 223 and 243.

compass saw A cutting tool used for removing center portions of a design without disturbing the outer sections. *See* p. 49.

complementary colors: *Pigment* Red, yellow, and blue. The pigment primaries are the light secondaries. The red is actually nearer to magenta and the blue nearer to blue-green. *Light* Green, red, and blue.

console A wall table sometimes supported at the wall or by its front leg or legs. Illustration on p. 223.

constructivism Non-realistic arrangements of steps, platforms, scaffoldings, etc. Used by the Russians after World War I in an effort to stress the anti-decorative and mechanical. Scarcity of materials was also responsible for the development of this style. *See* p. 181.

contemporary The best non-period styles of a particular era. A more accurate word than *modern* which is likely to be confused with *reproductions* as compared to *antiques*.

contour curtain The main curtain at Radio City Music Hall offers the best example of this device. Makes it possible to shape and change the size of the proscenium opening. Illustration on p. 8.

controlboard The distribution point for the electric current used on the stage. The parts of the controlboard include the master switch, the circuit fuses and switches, the dimmers, and the board outlets. Controlboards for professional productions are of the portable variety since Broadway controlboards do not provide sufficient outlets and dimmers.

Copean stage The *Théâtre du Vieux Colombier* in Paris had a formal stage specially designed by Jacques Copeau and Louis Jouvet. During the early 20th century this theatre accommodated many different types of productions with very little in the way of scenic backgrounds.

coping saw A cutting tool which is satisfactory for use on small, irregularly shaped designs which must be cut from three-ply. *See* p. 49.

Corinthian *See* **column**

corner block Small triangular-shaped piece of $\frac{1}{4}''$ or $\frac{3}{8}''$ three-ply. The most common dimensions are 9″ by 9″. Holds the corners of the flat together. *See* p. 64.

corner brace A mitred length of 1″ × 2″ placed in the upper and lower right- or left-hand corners of the flat. Usually between three and four feet in length. Illustration on p. 64.

corner iron (flat) An L-shaped piece of strap metal. *See* p. 54.

cornice The projecting topmost portion of the room architecture. A necessity in 18th- and 19th-century period rooms.

cornice board A wooden valance which serves as the top support and decoration for window draperies.

cornucopia An overflowing horn of plenty. Fruits and flowers are the main decorative motifs. *See* p. 229.

countersink A tool used with a brace to bore extra wood from a hole so that screws or bolts can be placed flush with the surface. A countersink is available for metal work as well. The process of countersinking applies also to the removal of wood or metal so that applied hardware such as hinges will be flush with the surface.

counterweight system. A permanent installation whereby arbors or carriages are guided by wires from the stage level or fly gallery to a loading platform. Three or more lines run through the head block and are fastened to the top of the carriage. A purchase line runs from the bottom of the arbor to a tension block (or floor block) at the floor and back around through the head block to the top of the arbor. From a loading gallery, counterweights are added as necessary to balance the load on the end of the ropes. A locking rail controls the purchase line. Illustration on p. 12.

Craig, Gordon (1872–   ) An English designer. A great visionary and one of the first to stress the unification and simplification of scenery. Is often criticized for the extreme variety and impracticality of his ideas. Actually very few of his scenic designs were ever presented on the stage since his chief interest was in a new type of theatre.

credenza A low, Italian Renaissance cabinet used like a sideboard. Contains doors and drawers and is usually placed against the wall. Illustration on p. 239.

cretonne A cotton fabric of heavier material than chintz and usually with much less detailed designs.

crewelwork A type of fabric design in which the pattern is in wools of various colors embroidered on unbleached material. A winding stem with large flowers is a typical design. Although commonly used during Jacobean times, present-day commercial East Indian rugs are often decorated in this manner.

crosscut saw A tool used to saw across the grain. Ten to twelve teeth to the inch.

cubism A form of stylization emphasizing apparently meaningless, blocklike arrangements of color, line, and mass.

Cut Awl A portable electric saw for cutting elaborate scroll designs. *See* p. 43.

cut-down scenery A form of minimum scenery which is complete as to floor plan but not normal in height. Flats are often placed horizontally rather than vertically. *See* p. 31.

cut drop A drop in which designs are cut out and netting glued to the rear to hold the openings in proper shape for hanging or rolling. *See* p. 101.

cyclorama A C-shaped sky representation, hung without folds and requiring at least two sets of lines for the hanging. Pale blue or white are the ideal colors, and the material should show no seams or wrinkles. Must be high enough and wide enough to suggest a great expanse of sky. Illustration on p. 102.

cyclorama trough A built-in series of floor lights at the base of the sky dome or cyclorama. Formerly fitted with the light primary colors, but present-day practice is to use special gelatines. *See* p. 102.

cyma recta An ogee molding. Its double curve starts and ends horizontally. *See* p. 52.

cyma reversa A molding which is the reverse of *cyma recta*. Starts and ends vertically. *See* p. 52.

dado A section of the wall below the chair rail and above the mopboard. Decorated differently from the upper wall, usually by means of panels, marble, or contrasting color.

Dali, Salvador (1904–   ) A contemporary Spanish surrealist painter, noted for his expert draughtsmanship, use of color, and weird, Freudian subject matter. Designed the backgrounds for the ballet sequences of the film *Spellbound*. Also has done some designing for the Monte Carlo Ballet Russe.

damask A fabric with a flat taffeta weave pattern. Takes its name from Damascus where such patterned silk was first woven in the 12th century. Suitable for both draperies and upholstering. Occasionally used to cover entire walls.

Dante chair A heavy X-shaped Italian Renaissance chair with curved legs and arms as continuous pieces. Cloth or leather back and seat. Illustration on p. 239.

davenport A furniture term often used incorrectly in place of *sofa*. A davenport is more accurately described as an unpleasant, awkwardly stuffed, and poorly designed sofa. Illustration on p. 218.

decalcomania A type of decoration, popular in the early 19th century, which involved the transfer of printed designs to wood or metal.

dentils A series of toothlike projections. Originally used on Greek and Roman entablatures, and later in Georgian design.

diamond point Geometrically shaped designs, often carved or inlaid in the panels of 17th-century French and English furniture.

diaper Diagonal repeat patterns used in wallpaper, fabrics, and furniture carving or inlay. *See* p. 229.

dimmer An electrical apparatus which permits the intensity of stage lighting to be changed during performance. *Resistor* The popular circular-plate type consists of a bent wire mounted on a steel disc covered with baked enamel. The dimmer is connected in series with the lighting instrument; and the dimmer capacity and the wattage of the instrument should be the same. *Electronic tube-reactor* Consists of a core of two windings of wire — one carrying alternating current in series with the lighting instrument and the other carrying direct current from a tube controlled by a resistance pilot. *Autotransformer* Includes a coil of copper wire surrounding an iron core. The dimming is accomplished by a sliding contact which is moved around the core, thus reducing the voltage by transforming action. *Izenour* Makes use of two large electronic tubes and two control tubes for each dimmer — the electronic tube is the dimmer. *See* p. 328.

direct current An electrical current which flows in one direction. Alternating current is more commonly available today although some sections of large cities are provided with direct current.

Directoire A French transitional decorative period extending from 1789 to 1804. Military motifs (spears, drums, stars, trumpets) helped to distinguish this period from the Louis XVI and First Empire periods. Illustrations on p. 247.

dolphin A sea-animal shape used for furniture legs, hinges, and carved and painted decoration. A common Empire and English Regency motif. *See* p. 229.

door casing A carpenter's term for the trim and thickness of the door. Includes all of the door unit except the shutter.

door facing A carpenter's term for the door trim.

door flat A special flat with a door opening. Door units are either built or set into this opening. Usually 3′ by 7′. *See* p. 68.

doorjamb A carpenter's term for the door thickness.

door shutter The opening and closing part of the door unit. Should be as light in weight as possible. *See* p. 84.

doorstop Strips of wood (1″ × 1″) on the door thickness which stop the shutter within the thickness and in proper relationship to the door latch.

door thickness The part of the door frame which corresponds to the wall thickness and is perpendicular to the trim. Sometimes called the *jamb*. *See* p. 84.

door threshold A strip of wood at the floor connecting the side thickness pieces. Usually bevelled. Thresholds of strap metal are sometimes used. Illustrations on p. 84.

door trim A border at the top and sides of the door frame, parallel to the wall. May be either plain or decorated with moldings, etc. Sometimes painted instead of built. *See* p. 84.

Doric The oldest Greek architectural order. Plainer than the Ionic or Corinthian orders. The column has a very simple capital and no base. *See* p. 94.

dormer window A perpendicular window in a sloping roof. Common in attics.

double-hung window A window divided into two up-and-down sliding sections. For stage purposes only the lower section must slide. *See* p. 88.

down center A stage area which means the center of the stage near the footlights. An actor might be directed to go in that direction from another location.

drag *See* **dry brushing**

drapery hanger and socket A device for hanging drapery poles quickly to a wall. The hook is attached to the pole and the socket is flat against the wall so that it does not interfere with the storage of flats. *See* p. 284.

draw curtain A type of stage curtain which opens by parting in the middle. A two-sectional track and carriers are part of the necessary equipment, together with a continuous length of rope. *See* p. 8.

dresser-sideboard A tall cabinet, open at the top and containing drawers in the lower section. Fully developed during the 18th century in England and France. Illustration on p. 223.

drills Boring tools used with the hand drill or power drill. It is necessary to have both metal and wood drills on hand. *See* p. 49.

drop An unframed canvas unit with double wooden battens at top and bottom. May be painted a solid color to represent the sky or painted with representational or stylized picturizations.

Drop Black *See* **black**

drop curtain A type of stage curtain which can be raised and lowered, thus shutting off and revealing the scenes in clean-cut fashion. The unit is usually counterweighted.

drop holder A type of stage hardware which clamps onto the wooden batten of the drop. If this hardware is not available, the drop can be tied directly to the pipe batten or to the lines. *See* p. 150.

drop-leaf table (*flap table*) *See* **gate-leg table**

drum table A table with a round drum-shaped top and pedestal base. There are usually drawers all the way around the apron. Common in England during the last half of the 18th century. Illustration on p. 222.

dry brushing A method of texturing which involves the dragging of a semidry stiff-bristled brush over a surface to simulate graining or rough plaster. *See* p. 128.

duck A good quality canvas useful for stage scenery. Available in seventy-two-inch widths. Has an interesting texture and offers a minimum of shrinkage.

dumbwaiter A three- or four-tiered table with revolving shelves of decreasing height. The *Lazy Susan*, used on a dining table, is a type of dumbwaiter. *See* p. 222.

Duncan Phyfe A New York designer whose work was based on Directoire and Sheraton types. Prominent during the first half of the 19th century. Known for his lyre-back chairs and pedestal tables. Illustrations on p. 269.

dutchman A strip of cloth used to cover cracks where two flats are joined together. Must cover the hinges as well. If the dutchman is soaked in water first, it is easier to apply. New material is easier to manage than strips of painted material.

Dutch Pink (*English*) A tan dry-pigment color, more intense than Raw Sienna.

duveteen A soft, sturdy material suitable for stage draperies and upholstering. Has a flat nap on one side.

dye *See* **analine dye**

earth colors Inexpensive colors, the most common of which are Raw Sienna, Raw Umber, Burnt Sienna, Burnt Umber, and Yellow Ochre. More glue is necessary as a binder for these colors than is required for purer, stronger colors.

ecru A pale, tan color similar to that of unbleached muslin. Glass curtains, draw curtains, and overdrapery linings are often of this color.

effect machine *See* **sciopticon**

egg and dart A carved or painted continuous ornament using alternating egg and dart designs. Of Greek origin. Illustration on p. 229.

elevation A form of drawing which shows no perspective. The object or a wall is seen as if it were immediately in front of the eye. The front elevation of a chair would show the back, the apron, and the front and back legs, but not the seat.

elevator stage A mechanical device for lowering or raising the stage. The Radio City stages can be raised in sections or as units. Extremely complicated hydraulic engineering problems are involved.

Elizabethan An English period named after Queen Elizabeth. Last half of the 16th century. Oak was the prominent wood, and furnishings were heavy, massive, and uncomfortable. Italian motifs were crudely imitated. Illustrations on p. 250.

ellipsoidal reflector spotlight A very efficient lighting instrument which contains an ellipsoidal reflector. The lenses are not adjustable, but framing shutters cut down on the area of illumination. The *Lekolite,* manufactured by the Century Lighting Company, is available in several different sizes. Illustration on p. 318.

Empire (*First*) A French period beginning with the coronation of Napoleon in 1804. The period began to wane after Waterloo in 1814 and was definitely over by 1830. David, the painter, and Percier and Fontaine, architects, were the artistic leaders of the period. Wine red, emerald green, bright yellow, and rich purple were common colors. Greek and Egyptian decorative motifs were popular. Illustrations on p. 248.

Empire (*Second*) A mid-nineteenth-century French period associated with the reigns of Napoleon III and the Empress Eugenie. Noted for eccentricities and immoderate use of capricious forms. Tassels, fringes, and gilt often contributed to the trimming of furniture which was basically overdesigned. Often considered as a sort of French version of the Victorian period.

entablature The upper portion of the architectural order. Includes the cornice, frieze, and architrave. Supported by the column. *See* p. 94.

entasis An architectural term referring to the amount that the upper two thirds of the column tapers toward the top. According to the architectural orders, the diameter at the top of the shaft should be five sixths of that of the base. *See* p. 94.

étagère A type of French tiered cabinet built especially to display objets d'art. Found in the Louis XVI and both the Empire periods. Used in England and America as the *whatnot.*

eye-level line A perspective term which means the same as the horizon line. The eye-level line and the ground line are on the picture plane.

exotic woods Woods used in Art Moderne, Art Nouveau, and some contemporary styles. Common for inlay and veneer work. Eucalyptus, harewood, palisander, pearwood, primavera, snakewood, tulipwood, zebrawood.

expansive bit A tool which can be adjusted to bore holes from $1\frac{1}{4}''$ to $2\frac{1}{2}''$ in diameter. *See* p. 49.

expressionism A style of scene design (the term is borrowed from painting) usually involving distortion, and attempting to interpret the mental quirks of the characters in the play. Involves color and light as well as style. *See* p. 172.

false proscenium A frame which is used to cut down the size of the regular proscenium opening and often, by means of its design, to help unify the production. Used frequently in musicals in combination with a show curtain. Sometimes several such frames are useful in one production in order to simplify masking problems.

fan light Originally an over-door or over-window design with radiating muntins, *q.v.* Used as furniture and wall panel decoration in painted and inlaid form in late-18th-century England.

fasces A decorative motif in the form of a bundle of rods and a projecting axe. Originally Roman in design. Particularly popular during the First Empire.

fascia A facing molding of broad, flat general shape. Similar in purpose to the fillet. *See* p. 52.

fauteuil A French open-arm upholstered chair with arm pads. 18th and 19th centuries. *See* p. 243.

Federal A classical American period from about 1780 to 1830. The American versions of the Adam, Hepplewhite, Sheraton, Regency, Directoire, and Empire periods appeared during these years. Duncan Phyfe and Samuel McIntire were the leading designers. Mahogany, fruitwood, and rosewood were used and there was considerable veneering. Lion's paws, lion's heads, lyres, swags, pineapples, and cornucopiae were the chief decorative motifs.

fender A low ornamental metal rail which rests on the hearth and encloses the fireplace opening.

festoon A painted, carved, or inlaid decoration consisting of scalloped drapery, chains of flowers, or rope loops. Popular during the late 18th century. *See* p. 245.

fiddle back A chair back typical of Queen Anne and early Chippendale chairs. So called because of its violin shape. *See* p. 253.

fillet A small band molding which separates larger moldings. Serves the same purpose as the fascia. *See* p. 52.

filter *See* **color medium**

finial A decorative ornament which completes a pediment or post. Metal finials hold lamp-shade frames to the central unit.

finishing nail A thin nail with a slight head. Especially useful for moldings. *See* p. 54.

fir A Western wood which is not suitable for scenery construction because it is heavy, resinous, and splintery. Available in long, wide pieces.

fire back A decorative piece of cast iron placed in the back of the fireplace, the purpose of which is to help reflect the heat. Decorative motifs include human figures, flowers, trees, coats of arms, etc.

fire curtain *See* **asbestos curtain**

fireplace flat A scenic frame with a small opening at floor level in front of which a three-dimensional chimney piece or mantel can be placed.

flameproofing The process of preparing scenic units to withstand fire. A solution of four pounds of sal ammoniac and four pounds of borax to three gallons of water should be sprayed onto the frame and the canvas. Canvas may be purchased which has already been flameproofed.

flap table *See* **gate-leg table**

flat A framed scenic unit in screen form, covered with canvas. Usually not higher than sixteen feet nor wider than 5'9". *See* p. 64.

flecking *See* **spattering**

Flemish scroll A double scroll (C scroll and reversed C scroll) design used on chair and table legs. Particularly common in late-17th-century English pieces.

fleur de lis A decorative motif in the form of a conventionalized iris. Originally a heraldry design.

flies The space below the gridiron and above the acting area, not within sight of the audience. Flown units hang in the flies.

flipper A narrow flat hinged to a wider flat. Often used on the front of ceilings to mask the front edge. Also used on the offstage edges of returns and the onstage edges of tormentors.

flipper jack A brace jack which is loose-pin-hinged to the unit which it is to support. A foot iron holds the jack to the floor.

floating The process of letting a flat (not a door or window flat) fall to the floor. Many theatres do not approve of the method since considerable dust is stirred up when the flat falls. However, the fall is silent and no harm is done to the unit. *See* p. 147.

floodlight A lighting instrument used for general illumination. Often includes a parabolic or ellipsoidal reflector, provision for color frames, and a mogul receptacle. There is no lens. Illustration on p. 320.

floor box (*pocket*) A metal box, the cover of which is hinged and level with the floor, containing electrical outlets for the stage.

floor cloth *See* **ground cloth**

floor plan A diagram, preferably to scale, showing the shape of the stage setting. The view is from above, looking down. Usually the floor plan is approved before work on the perspective is begun. The proscenium opening and the tormentors and returns should be shown in detail. *See* p. 186.

floor plate A metal plate, countersunk in the floor. When stage screws are not permitted, the lower end of the stage brace can be thumb-screwed to the floor plate.

flour paste A powdered wheat paste used by paperhangers and scenery workers. When water and dissolved ground gelatine or white flake glue are added, a paste is formed which is suitable for use when covering flats.

fluorescent paint A type of paint which seems to glow in the dark when ultraviolet light is directed toward it. Especially useful for bizarre costumes in musical shows.

fluting Concave grooves in the shaft of a column. Also frequently found on furniture legs in the Louis XVI and Adam periods.

fly A verb indicating the backstage vernacular for raising scenery into the flies by means of lines.

fly floor The floor of the fly gallery. The men who handle the flown units stand on the fly floor.

fly gallery A backstage area containing the fly floor, the pinrail, and the tie-off rail. Ideally, this region should be sixteen feet above the floor level, provided, of course, there is a high fly loft.

fly loft The place directly below the gridiron in which scenery hangs.

flyman One who works from the fly gallery and whose job is to raise and lower scenery by means of lines which terminate at the pinrail.

focal length An optical term relating to the distance between the center of the lens and the principal focus point. A lens has both a diameter and a focal length, and the distance of the instrument from the stage determines the sizes to be selected. *See* p. 317.

foliage border A long, horizontal masking piece fastened to a wooden batten or tied to a pipe batten. Used in combination with wood wings to complete the stage exterior. Illustration on p. 101.

foliage brush A stubby, chiseled, stiff-bristled brush suitable for painting leaves. The results will be suggestive rather than realistic. *See* p. 118.

follow spot A lighting unit, usually placed in the projection booth or the front of the balcony, which can be moved so as to keep a performer in a constant pool of light. Carbon arc instruments are usually most satisfactory for long throws.

foot Backstage language for holding one end of a flat to the floor while the other end is raised until the flat is perpendicular. One worker puts his foot at the edge of the flat so that it will not slip as another worker *walks* it up. *See* p. 147.

foot iron A type of stage hardware used to fasten scenery to the floor.

One edge is screwed to the unit and the other receives the stage screw. There are hinged and solid types; the former will not foul when units are flown. Illustrations on p. 54.

footlights Striplights placed at stage level or in a trough below stage level in front of the act curtain. Available in five-foot sections with glass roundels. Used for general illumination. *See* p. 322.

forestage *See* **apron**

formalism A type of scenic background which remains aloof from the play. Usually noninterpretive and only slightly decorative. While Greek and Elizabethan theatres were formalistic, similar backgrounds today do not usually recede so much as they did in historic times. Illustration on p. 176.

Fortuny, Mariano (1838–1874) An Italian who experimented with indirect colored lighting. Spotlights were shone onto offstage pieces of colored silk and diffuse light was reflected from the silk to the stage.

fragmentary scenery A form of scenery referring to small incomplete sketchy sections. Especially effective in non-realistic productions where many locations are necessary and scene shifting must be accomplished in seconds. *See* p. 34.

French heading (*pinch plaiting*) A method of sewing folds into material. Cloth is gathered into groups of three small folds about six inches apart and sewed together four inches from the top.

French Provincial Furniture and architecture developed in the provinces. Reminiscent of the Louis styles but always less ornamental. Oak and fruit woods were used extensively. Sometimes called Provençal, after the province in southeastern France.

French Orange A dry-pigment color, brilliant orange in hue.

French Ultramarine Blue *See* **blue**

French windows Floor-length hinged windows. The frames are divided into small oblong panes which are a shade higher than they are wide.

French Yellow Ochre *See* **yellow**

Fresnel lens *See* **lens**

fretwork Carved, interlaced, geometrical, ornamental work often found on the aprons of chairs and tables. Used frequently by Chippendale for his Gothic and Chinese styles.

frieze A flat, decorated surface between the cornice and the architrave of the entablature. *See* p. 94.

fringe A type of trimming useful for upholstery and drapery work. Main classifications include cut, uncut, ball, tassel, and molded forms. Elaborate fringes often made up of a number of forms combined together. Available in cotton, silk, wool, rayon, etc.

frizé A type of upholstery material with a pile of uncut loops.

Fuchs, Georg (1868–1932) The German author of *The Revolution of the Theatre*. Founder of the Munich Artists' Theatre. Stressed the shallow *relief* stage, a sort of bas-relief method of staging, with light particularly important in developing the stage picture.

fuse A device to prevent damage due to overloads of electricity and short circuits. The size of the fuse limits the amount of wattage that may be used. The metal within a *cartridge* (clamp) fuse may be replaced, but a *plug* (screw) fuse must be discarded when it has blown. The latter has an isinglass face which shows when the fuse has blown.

futurism A form of expressionistic stylization which is completely non-emotional. While this style is sometimes decorative, it is often confusing to an audience.

gadroon A carved or pressed ornament in the shape of short ruffle-like flutings. Chippendale used this decoration as an edging for table tops. Also found on the top of Elizabethan melon bulb legs and on Sheffield silver.

gallery A metal or wood railing placed partially or completely around the top edge of a piece of furniture. Often a strip of ornamental punched brass.

galloon (*galon*) A flat gimplike braid used as drapery or upholstery trimming.

gargoyle A Gothic architectural figure of weird, animal design. The gargoyles of Notre Dame Cathedral in Paris are famous.

gate-leg table A table with hinged flaps. When its swinging legs (or gates) are open, the table is larger. Common in England and America during the 17th century. *See* p. 222.

gauze (*scrim*) *See* **bobbinet**

Geddes, Norman Bel (1893–   ) An American designer. His grandiose and expansive designs for Dante's *Divine Comedy* are characteristic of his philosophy of the theatre. The *Futurama* of the New York World's Fair is an example of his industrial design theories. For Max Reinhardt he designed *The Eternal Road* and *The Miracle*. He is also noted for his famous *Dead End* waterfront exterior.

gelatine A color medium made up of thin sheets of gelatine. Commonly used numbers are #1 Frost, #2 Light Flesh Pink, #17 Special Lavender, #62 Light Scarlet, etc.

Georgian An architectural and furniture term loosely applied to English designs of the last half of the 18th century. Includes late Chippendale, Sheraton, Hepplewhite, and Adam. American Georgian designs are somewhat less detailed.

gimp (*guimpe*) A narrow flat braid or tape used to add a finish or trim to upholstery work. Also occasionally used as drapery trim.

girandole (*girondole*) A type of wall bracket or sconce with a mirror back. Developed in France and England during the last half of the 18th century.

glass curtain A thin curtain hung next to the window glass. Usually hung straight although sometimes looped up with tiebacks.

glazing   A method of toning scenery which involves the painting or spraying of size water or diluted shellac.   Gives a slight gloss to the paint job and blends the texturing colors.

glue   An adhesive which serves as the binder for scene paint.   *Furniture glue*   A cold liquid glue obtainable in cans.   Also available in bar form.   Not waterproof.   *White flake glue*   Made from bones, hides, etc.   Not very flexible.   *Gelatine glue*   Stronger than white flake glue. A flexible gelatine product.   Available in flake or ground form. *Casein glue*   A powdered, skimmed milk product.   Waterproof.

gooseneck   A design form frequently found as the pediment of highboys. Sometimes called *swan neck*.   Double-curved in shape.

Gothic   An architectural period at the end of the Middle Ages, roughly related to the 12th through the 15th centuries.   Much use of the Gothic pointed arch and perpendicular lines.   The common wood is oak.   *See* p. 238.

grand drapery   An elaborate upper proscenium arch trimming, usually made of material similar to that of the act curtain and trimmed with fringes, tassels, braids, etc.   Seldom found in theatres which are contemporary in design.

grass mat   Woven, raffia, pile matting placed on the floor to represent grass.   The bright green color must be toned down if a realistic effect is desired.   Also useful for hedges.

Greek key   A band decoration in the form of a continuous square, hook-shaped form.   Sometimes called *Greek fret*.   *See* p. 229.

green: *Light Chrome Green*   The lightest available green dry pigment. *Medium Chrome Green*   The most useful inexpensive green dry pigment.   *Dark Chrome Green*   The darkest of the inexpensive greens. *Emerald Green*   A wet-pigment color, vivid in hue; sometimes called Kelly Green.   *Malachite Green*   A dark-green wet pigment.

gridiron   The frame work directly below the ceiling of the stage house to which sheaves are attached.   *See* p. 2.

griffin   A grotesque decorative motif originating in the Renaissance and continuing as late as the First Empire.   Half lion and half eagle. Often used as furniture legs.   *See* p. 229.

grille work   A wire or pressed metal lattice work used on furniture doors. Fabrics often serve as background for the grill.   Used on many late-18th- and early-19th-century French and English pieces.

grip   A backstage name applying to a stagehand.

grommets   Small metal rings which are placed at the top of stage draperies to hold the tie lines.   The rings are clamped together by means of the grommet *set* and *die*.   Illustration on p. 100.

gros point   A coarse French embroidery in cross-stitch style.   Stitches made of either silk or wool.   There are about 140 stitches to the square inch.

ground cloth   A large canvas used to cover the entire acting area.

Snapped, lashed, or tacked to the floor. Useful to help deaden sound and to cut the glare of the wood floor.

ground coat The last coat of paint which is applied before the texturing is begun.

ground line A drawing term referring to a line directly below the eye-level line. The line where the picture plane meets the ground plane.

ground plan *See* **floor plan**

ground plane A drawing term referring to the floor on which stand the one who draws and the object drawn. Perpendicular to the picture plane.

ground row A long, low horizontal masking piece. Useful to hide the lower batten of the sky drop. It is not necessary to use a ground row to mask the lower batten of a backdrop. *See* p. 76.

guard rail A railing placed in front of the lines at the side of the stage when the pinrail is at stage level or less than sixteen feet from the floor. The lines are thus always available even though scenery is stored on that side of the stage.

guilloche A running band ornament of overlapping curves. Illustration on p. 229.

hack saw A tool used for cutting metal. Similar in shape to a butcher's bone-cutting saw. Blades are inexpensive and are replaced rather than sharpened. Illustration on p. 49.

half leg drop *See* **leg drop**

hall tree A stand for hanging wraps. Either wooden or metal and occasionally more like a frame than a stand.

halved joint A carpenter's joint, useful when it is necessary for two battens to cross, meet cornerwise, or be placed end to end and at the same time retain the same thickness. Illustration on p. 62.

hammer A driving tool. The *claw* hammer has curved prongs and the *rip* hammer, straight prongs. The latter is more generally used. The magnetized *tack* hammer is useful to workers as they cover flats. Illustrations on p. 48.

hand properties (*action properties*) Articles used in stage business by the actors. Although occasionally a large decorative furnishing may be so classed, usually the hand property is limited to such items as books, food, luggage, tobacco, etc.

hanger iron A type of stage hardware bolted to units which are to be flown. Those fastened to the bottom of extra heavy frames have a hook, while those used at the top are merely a flat strip of cast iron and a ring. Illustration on p. 144.

harness hook *See* **snap hook**

hassock An upholstered footstool usually with no visible wood.

hauling rope A rope serving as a lifting aid for heavy flats. Attached near one end of the lower rail.

head block A type of hardware used for counterweight and rope-system rigging installations. Must contain three or four sheaves, depending upon the number of ropes in the system. Placed at the edge of the gridiron directly above the pinrail. Illustration on p. 12.

header A small horizontal flat, placed between two tall perpendicular flats to form an arch. Especially useful when the assembled unit is too large for easy transportation. May be attached by hinges or, from the rear, by mending plates.

Hepplewhite, George An English designer identified with the late Georgian period, 1770–1810. Furniture noted for veneer, slender lines, and delicacy of contour. Oval, interlaced-heart, and shield chair backs were characteristic and the Prince-of-Wales motif was used frequently. *See* p. 257.

Herculaneum *See* **Pompeii**

Hercules Black *See* **black**

herringbone A design form involving alternating slanting lines. A common fabric weave but also used in inlay work.

highboy A chest of drawers supported by a lowboy with long legs. This piece of furniture was developed in the William and Mary and Queen Anne periods. *See* p. 252.

Hitchcock chair An American painted chair similar in line to some Sheraton styles. Decorated with designs of flowers, foliage, or fruit. Illustration on p. 219.

hoop-back chair A chair whose top rail and upright pieces form a continuous curve. Certain Windsor chairs illustrate this line.

horizon line A drawing term referring to the eye-level line on the picture plane. Usually the height of the person's eye as he stands on the ground plane.

hue The color itself. Red, blue, yellow, etc. As the colors on the wheel approach those next to them, they take on the hues of those colors; i.e., as red approaches orange it takes on an orange hue.

illustration board A type of cardboard useful for making models and for matting renderings. Available in thin and double-thick grades.

impressionism A painting term which is frequently applied to a type of scene design; a non-realistic representation of what the designer feels or sees. Mielziner's scenery for *A Streetcar Named Desire* has impressionistic qualities as does his setting for *The Glass Menagerie*. Pure impressionism is seldom found in the theatre. *See* p. 170.

incandescent lamp A lamp whose light comes from filament incandescence. A-type lamps are gas filled and the B-type, vacuum. This prevents the lamp filament from oxidizing. The lamp must be burned at the proper voltage printed on the glass. An A lamp is inside frosted, a G lamp is globular in shape, a T lamp is tubular, and a P.S. lamp is pear shaped. Lamp bases (the part that fits into the receptacle) are classified as follows, from small to large: miniature, candelabra, intermediate, medium, and mogul. They are also classified according to shape — screw, pre-focus, or bi-post. *See* p. 315.

India print A painted or printed cotton material with patterns based on Persian or Indian designs. The tree of life is a popular motif on such prints. Illustration on p. 229.

inlay A type of furniture decoration involving the removal of small areas of wood and the replacing with woods of contrasting grain. Can be simulated by paint for stage use.

intensity (*color*) A color characteristic determined by the amount of its complement that a color has mixed with it. Also concerned with its nearness to the center of the color cone.

intensity (*light*) The effective power of a light source, as measured in candles.

interior design The correct designation for the complete designing of a room, from architecture to furnishings. The term "interior decorator" is often applied to one who actually paints or wallpapers the room after the interior design work has been completed.

intermediate lamp base *See* **incandescent lamp**

Ionic An architectural order, the columns of which are characterized by a base, and a capital with two volutes. *See* p. 94.

iris shutter A spotlight mask made like the iris shutter of a camera. Possible to have pin-point or full-area lighting. Especially useful for ellipsoidal reflector spotlights where the lens is not adjustable.

isometric projection A type of drawing which allows the measuring of its principal lines. Diagonals may not be measured, however. The up-and-down lines are either slanted or perpendicular. Drawings of model dwellings are often shown in this manner, with the roof removed. Stage settings drawn with slanting lines will permit the showing of the rear of some of the flats. *See* p. 204.

Italian Blue *See* **blue**

Italian Raw Sienna An inexpensive dry pigment of the earth variety.

Italian Renaissance An Italian period of intense creativity inspired by the styles of antiquity. Usually divided as follows: 1. Quattrocento — 1400–1500. Representative of both Gothic and classical designs. 2. Cinquecento — 1500–1550. The high period. Exclusive use of classical forms. 3. Baroque and Rococo — 1550–1750.

Ivory Drop Black *See* **black**

jack *See* **flipper jack**

jackknife stages A scene-shifting device involving two wagons which pivot from opposite sides of the proscenium. Jackknife stages are ideally suited for multi-set shows, since while one wagon is in view the scene can be changed on the other. These stages are also often used in combination with regular wagons.

Jacobean An English decorative period concerned with the early 17th century, during the reign of James I. Furniture was more comfortable than in preceding periods and there was considerable decorative strap-work carving. Twisted-rope and spiral carving replaced the bulbous Elizabethan supports. Illustrations on p. 250.

Jenkins, George (1910–   )   An American designer formerly engaged in industrial design and architecture. Assistant to Jo Mielziner for four and a half years.   One of the first to use small fragmentary settings in front of large atmospheric backdrops.   Productions have included *Mexican Hayride, Dark of the Moon, I Remember Mama, Strange Fruit,* and *Lost in the Stars.*

Jessner, Leopold (1878–1945)   A post-World-War-I German director. His work of this period is best remembered for his *Steps* or *Jessnertreppen.*   These steps offered many opportunities for playing levels and were often vivid in color.   According to Jessner, the various levels allowed the actors a chance for full orchestration instead of merely a single melody.   Just before World War II he went to Hollywood.

jigger   *See* **tumbler**

jig saw   A power tool for use in cutting intricate designs on three-ply. The blade is fastened above and below the saw table and the motor drives it up and down like a sewing machine.   Since blades are inexpensive, they are replaced rather than sharpened.   *See* p. 43.

jog   A narrow flat, two feet or less in width.   Often hinged to wider flats.

Johnson, Albert (1910–   )   An American designer whose work for musical revues in the thirties was noted for its robust comment. Broad, theatrical use of color and interesting changes of scale from scene to scene for purposes of creating tempo.   *The Band Wagon, Jumbo, Face the Music, Three's a Crowd, As Thousands Cheer.*

Jones, Inigo (1573–1652)   A Restoration architect and designer.   Designed settings for court masque productions.   After studying Italian Renaissance designs, he introduced the representational perspective setting to England.   As a scene shifting device, he used sliding wing flats and grooves.   Responsible for the use of the Palladian style of architecture in England.

Jones, Robert Edmond (1887–   )   Often called the Dean of American scene designers.   Noted for his sensitive use of color and complete understanding of all the elements of stage picturization.   His background for *The Man Who Married a Dumb Wife* (1915) is generally considered to be the first authentic example of American scene design. Author of *Continental Stagecraft* (with Kenneth Macgowan), *Dramatic Imagination,* and *Drawings for the Theatre.*   Has designed such plays as *The Green Pastures, Philadelphia Story, Lute Song, The Iceman Cometh, The Enchanted.*

kalsomine   *See* **calcimine**

keeper hook   An S-shaped piece of stage hardware.   Two or three are used to keep a stiffening batten in position at the rear, top of an ,opened book.   *See* p. 144.

keyhole plate   A piece of decorative hardware, brass or cast metal, which surrounds the keyhole of the door lock.   Many present-day stock plates are useful on the stage but specially designed plates are usually necessary for period rooms. Sometimes called *escutcheon*.

keystone A piece of three-ply used to hold the ends of the toggle rail to the stiles; six inches long with the grain running lengthwise. The widest end is three and a half inches and the other end is two and a half inches.

kick plait An inverted box plaiting placed at the corners of chairs and sofas that are skirted. Suitable for either upholstered pieces or slip covers.

kidney table An 18th-century English and French writing or dressing table, oval in shape and with a concave front. The kidney shape is also sometimes found in bench form. *See* p. 222.

klismos An ancient Greek chair with a back rail which is curved in concave form. Legs are usually plain and curve to sweep out. The Roman versions of this chair were of inspiration to the First Empire and the English Regency designs. *See* p. 234.

kneehole desk A desk with an open space under it for the knees, and drawers on either side. Used extensively during the last half of the 18th century in England and America. *See* p. 222.

knife box A wooden case for holding flat silver and carving knives. Originally square in shape but in the late 18th century, urn-shaped boxes were often placed on pedestals. *See* p. 260.

knob turning A type of 17th-century leg or stretcher carving which consists of a series of knobs.

knots: *Bowline* A method of tying rope when the object is to be lifted straight up. Forms a loop which will not slip. Unties quickly. *Clove hitch* Useful when the object is to be pulled at a diagonal. When completed, the direction of the rope on either side of the batten is the same. Unties easily. *See* p. 150.

knotty pine A type of wood first used for wall panels in the early 17th century. Usually left in its natural yellowish color. Particularly popular in early Georgian times.

kuppel-horizont *See* **plaster dome**

ladder-back chair A 17th-century English and American tall chair with a back consisting of a number of horizontal rails. Some Chippendale pieces have similar slats on chairs with backs of normal height. *See* p. 219.

lamp dip A colored lacquer in which lamps may be dipped to give them color. May be used in place of gelatine and glass for footlights and borderlights. Not a satisfactory practice.

lamps *See* **incandescent lamp**

lash line A braided cotton rope (sash cord) used for fastening two flats temporarily together. The line is cut so that it is a few inches shorter than the flat. *See* p. 64.

lash-line cleat A type of stage hardware around which the lash line is hooked as two flats are lashed together. The number of cleats which are placed on a flat depends on the condition of the flat and its height. *See* pp. 54 and 64.

lash-line eye A type of stage hardware used for attaching the lash line to the top of the flat. The rope is put through the eye and knotted. Substitutions often include a hole in the corner block or the use of a large screw eye. *See* pp. 54 and 64.

lash-line hook A type of special stage hardware, hooklike in shape, which is used instead of a lash-line cleat when the lash line might otherwise pull off. Also frequently substituted for the tie-off cleat. *See* p. 54.

lath nails *See* **shingle nails**

lead block *See* **head block**

leatherette An artificial leather made of nitrocellulose or some similar synthetic. Sometimes the material is stamped to indicate certain types of leather graining. Very suitable for stage upholstering.

leg drop A type of drop from which a portion of the center is cut, leaving two legs which hang to the floor. Especially suitable for exteriors requiring tree trunks and foliage-border effects. Also useful for representing painted palace interiors, etc. A *half leg drop* is designed for only one side of the stage.

lens A specially shaped piece of glass used to change the direction of rays of light. Used on the stage in spotlights and projectors. The following lenses are most frequently used: *Plano-Convex* A condensing lens with one flat and one convex surface. Used in the simplest types of spotlights. *Fresnel (step lens)* Contains concentric rings like an automobile headlight. Allows an increased focal length without using an unusually thick lens. Spreads light more than a plano-convex lens. *Objective* A double convex lens used for projecting designs from an effect machine.

level *See* **carpenter's level**

lid A scenery unit which serves as the floor of a parallel. Often covered with Ozite and canvas. *See* p. 78.

life mask A paper and glue mask which is made after a plaster of Paris casting has been prepared. The face of the subject is coated with grease before the application of the plaster, and breathing is possible through straws which are placed in the nostrils.

lift jack A triangular-shaped lever device, equipped with a caster and an adjustable arm. When the jack is attached to a heavy object, the arm can be forced down, thus raising the unit so that it will ride on the caster. Usually used in pairs. Illustration on p. 157.

linen A crisp material made from flax. Hand-blocked linen is especially suitable with 17th-century English decorations. The Egyptians were the first to use the material.

linen fold A Gothic, Elizabethan, and Jacobean decorative motif which is similar to folds of linen. Usually found as carved panel decoration. *See* p. 229.

lines Manila (hemp) ropes arranged in groups of three or four to complete the rigging system and permit the raising and lowering of heavy objects. *Long line* The stage line which extends the farthest distance from the pinrail. In a four-line system, this line is often called #4; if three lines are used, it may be called #3. *Short line* The rope which is nearest to the pinrail. Sometimes called line #1.

lining brush A small brush ($\frac{1}{4}''$ to $2''$) for painting detail and lines. Either long- or short-bristled. *See* p. 118.

Linnebach projector A non-lens projector suitable for throwing images which do not include detail. Since the instrument cannot be placed directly in front of the screen, the design must allow for distortion as it is painted on a glass slide. *See* p. 327.

loading door The door through which scenery is brought onto the stage from the truck. Must accommodate wide units if necessary. *See* p. 2.

loading platform A backstage location referring to the level at which counterweights are placed in the carriages. The term also sometimes applies to the raised area directly outside the loading door of the stage. Such a platform must be exactly the height of the floor of an average-sized truck. *See* p. 2.

locking rail The part of the counterweight system which includes the rope locks. Usually about two feet from the floor. *See* p. 12.

loft blocks Single, framed sheaves, one for each line, through which the lines of the rigging system are run. Available in both *underhang* and *above-the-gridiron* styles. *See* p. 2.

loose-pin backflap A type of regular hardware which is very useful for temporary fastening. Two units can be hinged together and, when the pin or wire is removed, the units will separate. *See* p. 54.

Louis XIV (1643–1715) The French king who was responsible for the construction of Versailles. Décor of this period is considered as the first of the native French styles. The architecture was of more importance than the furniture, and painted panels and elaborate ornamental carving were characteristic. Cabinets were noted for elaborate Boulle work, ormolu work, and marble tops. Although straight lines dominated the main lines of the furniture, the baroque curve was the most frequently employed decorative motif. Illustrations on p. 242.

Louis XV (1723–1774) The French king whose name identifies a decorative period noted for rococo (shell) motifs and the use of free curves. Some Chinese designs were popular, but artificial and sentimental pastoral subject matter was more favored. Fabrics included satin, brocade, taffeta, and toile de Jouy. The chaise longue and the bergère were introduced at this time, both with the cabriole leg. Illustrations on p. 243.

Louis XVI (1774–1789) French ruler during a period influenced strongly by the Pompeii and Herculaneum discoveries. The architecture was symmetrical and involved considerable use of rectangular panels decorated with panels, garlands, bouquets, and cupids. Furniture was straight in line and legs were tapered and often fluted, topped by a square block with a rosette design. Popular fabrics were moiré, brocade, damask, and toile. Illustrations on p. 245.

louver A series of metal circular strips or concentric rings which prevent the spill of light from an instrument and tend to straighten the rays of light which come from it.

love seat A two-section sofa or a double chair. Much used in French and English 18th-century periods.

lowboy An English and American table with drawers. Useful as a dressing table or a wall piece. Popular since the 17th century. Illustration on p. 252.

lyre The lyre motif had its origins in the Renaissance but was particularly popular in English and French 18th-century pieces. Associated today with the Duncan Phyfe style. *See* p. 269.

Magenta Lake An intense purple color, useful for painting accents. Contains a noticeable amount of blue.

mahogany A reddish-colored hardwood used consistently for 18th- and 19th-century English and French furniture. Known for its subtle, rather straight, grain. Mahogany varnish stains can suggest this wood for stage use.

Malachite Green *See* **green**

Manila rope A hemp rope (preferably braided instead of twisted) used for stage lines. A diameter of at least $\frac{3}{4}''$ is usually desirable. This rope is sold either by the pound or the hundred feet.

mantel The shelf or top to the chimney piece. Some fireplace openings have a mantel as the only over-decoration.

maple A light-colored hardwood in straight or bird's-eye (curly) grain. The straight grain is ideal for wall paneling.

maroon: *Dark Maroon* A wet pigment, useful for palette painting. *Light Maroon* An expensive, wet pigment, suitable for painting color accents and important detail. Both *Dark* and *Light* are blue-red in hue.

marquetry An inlay pattern, flush with the surface, obtained by the use of unusual varicolored woods. Sometimes metals and ivory, etc., are used in addition.

marquisette A gauzelike glass curtain material of cotton, silk, or rayon. In the weaving, the threads are twisted and knotted to form the characteristic openwork.

masking piece A unit of scenery which prevents the audience from seeing into the backstage areas. Door and window backings are the most common movable masking pieces. Teasers, tormentors, and foliage borders are also considered as masking units.

measuring points A perspective term referring to points to the right and left of the Center of Vision — on the eye-level line. Unless these points are about forty feet (to scale) from the center, the perspective will seem distorted. *See* p. 192.

medium lamp base *See* **incandescent lamp**

mending plate (*mending batten*) A strip of steel used to repair broken wooden battens or to extend a wooden batten. May be obtained as large as 3″ × 18″ and in many smaller sizes. Two pieces are often necessary. *See* p. 54.

melon bulb leg An Elizabethan and Jacobean leg, bulbous in shape. The upper portion of the bulb is often carved in gadroon design; the lower portion makes use of the acanthus leaf. Featured on cabinets and large tables. *See* p. 250.

Mielziner, Jo (1901–) An American scene designer noted for his monochromatic use of color. His first Broadway job was *The Guardsman* in 1924. Since then his work has included *Street Scene* (both the play and the opera), *The Barretts of Wimpole Street*, *I Married an Angel*, and *Annie Get Your Gun*. His use of scrim in the impressionistic-realistic settings for *The Glass Menagerie* and *A Streetcar Named Desire* has had considerable influence upon present-day scene design.

miniature lamp base *See* **incandescent lamp**

minimum scenery A type of stage scenery which either does not enclose the entire playing area or is not normal in height. Cut-down, selective, fragmentary, and profile scenery are considered as minimum.

Mission A heavy, square decorative style developed by Spanish and Mexican Indians and missionaries. Early-20th-century American adaptations used fumed oak, crude mortise and tenon joints, leather upholstery, and copper hinges and straps. Not developed further after about 1915.

mitre box A tool used for cutting lumber at various angles. Substantial, metal mitre boxes can be adjusted for various angles but homemade wooden boxes are limited as to use and somewhat inaccurate as to results. The backsaw is best used with either. *See* p. 49.

model A three-dimensional representation, built or drawn to scale, and complete with proscenium opening and backings. Constructed of illustration board, bristol board, or sheets of balsa wood and fastened together with airplane glue or Scotch tape. Furniture is sometimes included but usually too much work is involved in the making of it. *See* p. 198.

modern A design term often used in place of *contemporary*. The latter term is more definite since modern can mean *manufactured recently* as contrasted with *antique*.

modernistic A design term occasionally used in place of *modern* or *contemporary*. Designers sometimes use this term to denote the bad and overly ornamental contemporary design of the twenties. *See* **Art Moderne** on p. 272.

mogul lamp base *See* **incandescent lamp**

mohair A durable wool cloth made from goat's hair. Woven in plain and pile fabrics, sometimes in combination with cotton or rayon.

moiré A silk or cotton material known for its water-marked finish. The marks, pressed in by rollers, are especially lasting when the material is synthetic.

molded fringe An expensive trimming made up of wooden ball or pendant turnings bound with silk. Sometimes combined with tassels. *See* p. 285.

monk's cloth A cotton fabric with groups of thread woven to produce a coarse-weave, neutral-colored cloth. Sometimes used for stage draperies but does not take light very well.

mopboard *See* **baseboard**

Morris chair An easy chair probably invented by William Morris in the late 19th century. Made up of an angular, wooden frame with an adjustable back and two loose cushions. Adopted to some extent by the Mission designers.

mortise and tenon joint A carpenter's joint which consists of a slot (the mortise) in the wood through which the tenon fits. Particularly useful for furniture. *See* p. 62.

moss fringe A cut or uncut fringe which is full and thick enough so that it does not lie flat. Sometimes has a fuzzy quality. *See* p. 285.

mullion An architecture and furniture term referring to vertical bars which divide the panes of a tracery door or window. Mullions in Gothic cathedrals are of stone and the pattern produced by the stone is called tracery. Similar patterns of lead are found on furniture doors of glass.

Munsell color system A scientifically accurate system for duplicating color characteristics at any time or in any place. Developed by Albert Henry Munsell in 1905 and now approved by the American Standards Association. This system uses a color sphere and a more complicated color book (p. 108) which is broken down into numbered parts. Munsell prefers *chroma* to *intensity* and discourages the use of *tint* and *shade* in place of *value*.

muntin An architectural term referring to vertical sections of a door or window which divide glass or wood into panels.

muslin A plain-woven bleached or unbleached white cotton fabric often used for drapery linings and plain curtains. Heavy-grade muslin may be used to cover flats.

naturalism A type of design and method of theatrical production which was common in the early-20th-century theatre. Characterized by excessive detail, most of which was unnecessary so far as any inherent needs of the play were concerned. David Belasco's productions were noted for their extreme naturalism. *See* p. 165.

newel post An architectural term referring to the supports for the balustrade. The stair rail is fastened directly to the newel post. *See* p. 82.

nosing A small molding or half rounding such as is used to trim the edge of the stair tread. Also used on shelves and on furniture.

oak An open-grained hardwood of unusual durability and strength. Used almost exclusively in Elizabethan times. Its present-day use is limited to contemporary styles where it is often bleached.

objective lens *See* **lens**

Oenslager, Donald (1902–   ) An American scene designer who has been largely responsible for the present interest in the use of paint on the stage. Particularly interested in new ways of presenting classic plays. Author of *Scenery Then and Now*. His Broadway designs have included *You Can't Take It with You*, *Of Mice and Men*, *Pygmalion*, *Three to Make Ready*, and *Born Yesterday*. On the faculty of the Yale Drama School.

offstage A backstage term referring to the area out of sight of the audience. Can also be used as a stage direction for the movement of actors.

ogee A molding with an S-shaped silhouette. Somewhat similar to the double curve of the cyma reversa. Two such S curves, meeting to form a point, produce an ogee arch.

Ohm's law An electrical principle which states that the electromotive force (E — volts) is equal to the product of the current (I — amperes) and the resistance (R — ohms). $E = IR$ $I = \dfrac{E}{R}$ $R = \dfrac{E}{I}$

olivette An old-fashioned box-shaped flood light either mounted on a stand or hung from a pipe batten. Illustration on p. 320.

onstage A backstage term referring to the area in which the actors play. Also used as a stage direction for the movement of actors.

O.P. side (*opposite prompt*) A backstage term which refers to the side of the stage opposite to the side from which the show is run.

orchestra A theatre architecture term which refers to the main floor of the auditorium. The *orchestra pit* separates the stage from the orchestra. In English theatres the orchestra is called the *pit*. The term originated in the Greek theatre where the orchestra was the circular dancing place containing the altar. *See* p. 3.

ormolu A decorative applied bronze ornament used to embellish 17th- and 18th-century French furniture. Also found on English Regency pieces. *See* p. 248.

orthographic projection A drawing method which shows the exact shape of an object, its length, width, and thickness. Three drawings are shown: the top (plan), the front (the object), and the side (elevation). Illustration on p. 204.

ottoman A stool or bench without arms or back. Originally used in

Turkey and introduced into England during the 18th century.

ovolo A quarter-round molding, often decorated with the egg and dart design. *See* p. 52.

Ozite An inexpensive hemp rug padding suitable for use on platforms and steps. Wafflelike in appearance.

pad foot The flat end of a cabriole leg, padlike in shape. Characteristic of the Queen Anne period. Illustration on p. 227.

paint frame A wooden wall frame which holds flats or drops in place as they are painted. Some frames are held by wires and may be lowered into a well beneath the floor level or raised to ceiling height for the convenience of the painters. *See* p. 116.

Palladio, Andrea (1508–1580) An Italian Renaissance architect whose designs greatly influenced Inigo Jones and, later on, the Georgian periods. Although Palladio was a native of Vicenza, his work in Imperial Rome led to the development of the characteristic Palladian arch — an arch with two columns flanked by two lintels and supported by pilasters. Designed the permanent stage setting of the Teatro Olympico with its three-dimensional false perspective backstage. *See* p. 74.

panelboard A steel cabinet containing switches and fuses. Not useful as a substitute for a controlboard.

paper cambric An inexpensive, highly sized, thin cotton material. Since it has little body, its use is to be discouraged for costumes and curtains.

papier-mâché A molded and shaped paper decoration which has first been dipped into a solution of melted glue, wheat paste, and whiting. Useful for three-dimensional designs, artificial food, bark effects, etc. *See* p. 298.

parabolic reflector A type of reflector used in striplights and some floodlights. Concave in shape. Reflects rays of light in straight lines. *See* p. 337.

parallel A collapsible framework consisting of rectangular hinged frames topped by a lid. The stiles of the frames serve also as the legs of the parallel. *See* p. 78.

parallel circuit An electrical circuit in which the wires are connected so that the current branches in a number of directions. Unlike the series circuit, each lamp on the parallel circuit will light independently of the others in the circuit. *See* p. 312.

parquetry Geometric inlaid arrangements of woods on the floor. Particularly popular during the 18th century.

patera An oval or round ornament — carved, painted, or inlaid — classic in origin, sometimes used in Louis XVI, Hepplewhite, Sheraton, and Adam periods.

pear-shaped lamp *See* **incandescent lamp**

pearwood A light-colored close-grained hardwood used for provincial 18th- and 19th-century European furniture. Useful for inlay work.

pediment A triangular architectural top over a door. Originally the roof line of the end of a Greek temple. Often used to top 18th-century English secretaries. Broken, scroll, swan neck, triangular, segmental, and double-hooded pediments are variations. *See* pp. 222 and 253.

Pembroke table A small drop-leaf table, the leaves supported by brackets. Late-18th-century English. Takes its name from the Earl of Pembroke. Illustration on p. 222.

Pennsylvania Dutch An 18th-century decorative style developed in Eastern Pennsylvania by German, Swiss, Swedish, and Dutch peasants. Considerable use of the fruit woods. Clean-cut painted decorations instead of carving. Developed such pieces as kneading tables, spice boxes, bride's chests, etc.

perspective A method of drawing which allows the representation on paper of objects as they actually appear. *One point* (parallel) perspective, since it easily permits the drawing of three walls, is most useful for scenic renderings. While *two point* perspective is also necessary for these renderings, such perspective is frequently concerned with only two walls. Picture planes, vanishing points, and ground lines are considered in setting up either type of perspective. *See* p. 192.

petitpoint A wool or silk cross-stitch embroidery done on fine net. About four hundred stitches to the square inch.

Pevear tormentor hood A box-shaped spotlight with metal flippers that can be moved so as to help shape the beam of light.

phantom load The use of a heater element or lamp in parallel circuit with a lighting instrument. Necessary where the dimmer has a larger capacity than the lighting instrument.

picture-frame hook and socket Special stage hardware used to hang pictures, shelves, etc. to a flat. The hook is attached to the picture and the socket to the flat. Illustration on p. 291.

picture plane A drawing term which can be likened to a perpendicular transparent sheet of glass between the observer and the object to be drawn. If the observer could draw the object on the glass, the result would be in perspective.

piecrust table A small table with a scalloped, molded edge. Originated during the Queen Anne period and fully developed by Chippendale. *See* p. 222.

pilaster An architectural term referring to a half-round or rectangular column placed flat against a perpendicular surface. Capital, base, and shaft are all usually represented.

pin hinge *See* **loose-pin backflap** or **tight-pin backflap**

pinch plait *See* **French heading**

pinrail A rail at which the lines from the gridiron are tied off. Belaying pins are standard equipment. The pinrail and the fly floor make up the fly gallery. A tie-off rail is sometimes placed directly below the pinrail. *See* p. 2.

pipe batten A length of pipe, measuring at least one inch on the inside diameter, to which is attached a set of lines. Scenery and lighting equipment should be attached directly to the pipe.

pipe clamp A metal device used to fasten the yoke of a lighting instrument to the pipe batten. Illustration on p. 316.

piping A covered cord trimming used at the seam edges of slip covers, upholstery, and some draperies.

pit *See* **orchestra**

plano-convex lens *See* **lens**

plaster dome (*kuppel-horizont*) A stage dome used for sky effects. Developed in the early-20th-century German theatre and introduced into American theatres in the twenties. Gives the effect of great depth to the exterior setting, but ties up a great deal of valuable backstage space.

plaster of Paris A gypsum powder which, when mixed with water, makes a paste which quickly becomes hard. Useful for forming casts.

plate rail A narrow, continuous shelf around a room, about five feet from the floor. Common in late-19th- and early-20th-century houses of nondescript periods.

plinth block An architectural term referring to the base of some door trims. The block and the baseboard are the same height.

plug (*lighting*) *See* **cable connector**

plug (*scenery*) A unit of scenery which fits behind or in front of openings in a setting, thus changing the appearance of the setting.

plug fuse *See* **fuse**

plywood A three-ply (or more) veneer board of fir or similar soft wood. The thicknesses most suitable for use on the stage are $\frac{1}{4}''$ or $\frac{3}{8}''$. Sometimes called *profile board*.

Pompeii and Herculaneum Ancient Italian cities, the excavations of which, during the middle 18th century, created a great interest in classic styles. The influences were most strongly represented in England by the designs of the Brothers Adam and in France during the Louis XVI period.

pongee A thin, cream-colored silk of translucent nature, originally found in India and China. Often used for draw curtains to take the place of window shades.

poudreuse A small powder table developed during the Louis XVI period. One section of the table top was usually hinged so that it could swing up to reveal a mirror.

pounce bag and pounce wheel A small thin-cloth bag filled with lampblack. The bag is tapped against the holes in a pattern which are made by the notched ridge of the pounce wheel. Illustration on p. 118.

power drill (*portable*) A small power tool suitable for use with wood bits, metal drills, and screwdriver bits. A motor of at least $\frac{1}{8}$ horsepower is necessary. Illustration on p. 49

presentational theatre One of the two general forms of theatre — concerned with life *in* the theatre as opposed to a *representation* of life *outside* the theatre. According to Alexander Bakshy, presentational theatre such as is found in music halls is not a forced art and offers great freedom of appreciation to the spectator. Greek and Elizabethan stages were presentational in function and the speeches, asides, and soliloquies were fully justified in such theatre.

prie-dieu A chair with a high back and a very low seat. The seat is cushioned for kneeling at prayer and the back has a shelf for the prayer book.

primary colors: *Pigment* Red, blue, and yellow are accepted by most color theorists. *Light* Blue, red, and green. Sometimes called *additive primaries.*

prime coat The first coat of paint after the size coat. Serves to prepare the surface for the ground coat. A ground coat can sometimes substitute for the prime coat.

Prince-of-Wales plumes A decorative motif consisting of the three ostrich feathers which are the emblem of the Prince of Wales. Common on Hepplewhite chair backs. *See* p. 257.

profile A form of minimum scenery consisting of a silhouette frame specially shaped to suggest a particular location or style. *See* p. 35.

profile board *See* **plywood**

projection booth An enclosed room at the rear of the auditorium (usually the balcony) containing motion picture projectors, effect machines, and carbon arc spotlights.

prompt side The side of the stage from which the show is run. Includes the controlboard and the curtain pull.

proscenium arch The opening in the wall which separates the stage from the seating area.

puddle A method of texturing scenery which involves the running together of various colors. May be used in place of the ground coat if a suitable prime coat has been applied.

purchase line *See* **counterweight system**

Purple Lake An extremely dark purple wet-pigment color.

quarter round A molding the cross section of which is in the shape of a quarter-circle. *See* p. 52. *Also see* **ovolo.**

quatrefoil A Gothic architectural form indicating four lobes with intersecting curves. Like a conventionalized four-leaf clover. *See* p. 229.

Queen Anne period A decorative style named after an English queen of the early 18th century. The cabriole leg, the fiddle-splat chair back, the pad foot, and carved shell motifs were characteristic. The tilt-top table and the settee were developed during this period. Illustrations on p. 253.

rails The horizontal members of a scenic frame. The top and bottom rails are the width of the flat but the toggle rail is two widths of lumber less than the other rails.

rake The amount that the side walls of a stage setting slant toward the center of the stage. As much as a two-foot rake may be desirable for sight line purposes.

ramp An inclined platform to be used instead of steps. May be either a specially built framework or merely a lid hooked onto the edge of a parallel or platform.

rasp A heavy, coarse file useful for shaping wood. Often used instead of a plane or a draw knife. *See* p. 49.

Raw Turkey Umber An inexpensive dark-brown dry pigment.

realistic setting A style of setting which, while containing naturalistic elements, is highly selective in intent. All elements of the realistic settings are necessary both for the play and for the stage picture. Illustrations on pp. 21 and 168.

Récamier sofa A type of Directoire or Empire sofa named after the French society leader, Madame Récamier. One end is considerably higher than the other. Often represented in chaise longue models as well. *See* p. 248.

redwood A soft, reddish-colored wood, available in long lengths. Useful for special properties and for the battens on wide drops.

reeding Two or more small convex molding strips set in parallel lines. The opposite of fluting.

refectory table A long, narrow table which first appeared in dining halls during the Middle Ages. *See* p. 239.

reflectors *See* **aluminum, Alzak, chromium, ellipsoidal,** and **parabolic.**

Régence period A transitional French period between the reigns of Louis XIV and Louis XV. It introduced the typical curved lines of the Louis XV period.

Regency (*English*) An early-19th-century decorative period definitely influenced by Egyptian and Classic styles. Has much in common with the First Empire and Biedermeier styles. Considerable use of black and gold. *See* p. 261.

remote control A type of electrical control in which the current passes through dimmers which are placed in a remote place away from the switchboard. Remote control has also been developed for the changing of color screens and for changing the direction of a beam of light.

rep A corded material woven with heavy thread. This reversible material is useful on the stage for draperies and upholstering.

representational theatre One of the two general forms of theatre — concerned with life *outside* the theatre and removed from the audience. Most realistic plays are of this classification; thus, our peep-show theatre is ideally suited to such representation.

reproductions (*furniture*) Accurate and detailed copies of period pieces. Sometimes made of old wood and passed off as antiques. Present-day commercial reproductions are often somewhat inaccurate.

resistor dimmer *See* **dimmer**

Restoration A decorative period coinciding with the reign of Charles II, 1660–85. The following names are often substituted: Carolean, Late Jacobean, and Late Stuart. Introduction of the Flemish scroll. Illustration on p. 252.

return A two-fold flat to which the box setting may be lashed, thus leaving space for lighting equipment between the setting and the tormentor.

revolving stage A special type of stage floor which may be revolved around a central pivot. While the Radio City Music Hall revolving stage is permanent, most professional usage is limited to separate portable units.

rheostat *See* **dimmer**

ribband-back chair A chair back, developed by Chippendale, in which the splats are carved to represent various ribbon arrangements. *See* p. 254.

rigging The entire system of ropes, loft blocks, head blocks, manila ropes, pipe battens, and belaying pins.

ripsaw A saw used for cutting with the grain. Five or six teeth to the inch. *See* p. 49.

riser The part of the stairs which is perpendicular to the tread and is responsible for the various levels. Six inches is a good standard measurement. Illustration on p. 82.

rococo (*rocaille*) An 18th-century manner of decoration which was in revolt from the chaste classical forms. Extravagant free curves, rocks, shells, leaves, and flowers were characteristic. Noted in Louis XV, Chippendale, and Hepplewhite designs.

roll ceiling A type of stage ceiling made by fastening a large piece of canvas to long battens. Temporary stretchers hold the battens apart when the ceiling is to be used; the unit is rolled up like a drop when it must be stored. Illustration on p. 98.

roll curtain A type of act curtain or fire curtain which is rigged so that it rolls up around a hollow cylindrical framework which hangs at the bottom. Useful where there is no fly loft. Commonly used in late-19th-century theatres. *See* p. 8.

rolling (*paint*) A method of texturing scenery which involves the rolling of canvas or sponge over the units. The cloth or sponge is dipped into the paint and wrung out before the rolling is applied. *See* p. 128.

Romanesque A crude and massive decorative style extending approximately from 500 to 1100. Transitional between late Roman and Gothic. *See* p. 238.

rope lock The part of the counterweight system which makes it possible to lock the purchase line while the flown unit is in a desirable position. *See* p. 12.

rose window A round, Gothic, colored glass window with tracery radiating from the center. May be simulated for stage use by means of combinations of translucent and opaque paints.

roundel (*color*) A concave glass color medium useful for borderlights and footlights. Available in the light primary colors.

running A method of moving scenery without the use of any mechanical contrivance. The units are pulled along the floor by hand.

saddle iron *See* **sill iron**

sandbag A strong canvas bag filled with sand. Used for counterweighting lines, or can be attached to the lines of the gridiron when they are not in use and there are no pipe battens. *See* p. 12.

sash cord A cotton rope with a braided covering. One-quarter-inch diameter is the most useful size for use as lash line.

sash curtain *See* **glass curtain**

sateen (*satine*) A mercerized cotton material, shiny on one side and dull on the other; somewhat silklike in appearance. Useful for lining draperies. Not heavy enough for regular stage draperies.

satin A silk material with one very shiny and one dull surface. Useful for draperies and upholstery.

satinwood A blonde wood with a satin finish and interesting grain. Used for inlay work in England and America during the last half of the 18th century.

saturation A light-color term applying to the measurement of the amount of the hue. Saturation is concerned with the relationship of a color to a gray of similar brilliance. Gray is unsaturated, for example, while pure blue is completely saturated.

Savonarola chair An Italian Renaissance X-shaped chair of interlacing curved slats which form the seat, the legs, and the arms. *See* p. 239.

scale rule An architect's scale rule is specially marked for changing feet to inches. (The engineer's scale rule uses the metric system.) Most scale rules offer $\frac{1}{8}''$, $\frac{1}{4}''$, $\frac{3}{8}''$, $\frac{1}{2}''$, $\frac{3}{4}''$, $1\frac{1}{2}''$, and $3''$ scales, each of which is divided into twelve parts or inches. The scale rule should never be used to draw lines.

scarf joint A carpenter's joint made by cutting away two flat pieces to correspond to each other and fastening them together. The cut is made at an angle. *See* p. 62.

scene dock A storage rack for scenery in the shop or on the stage. Must handle flats as high as sixteen feet.

sciopticon A projector with condensing and objective lenses. Contains a motor or clock mechanism so that effects of moving rain, snow, clouds, etc. can be obtained.

sconce A bracket arrangement of candles hung on the wall. Particularly common during the 18th-century French and English periods. *See* p. 248.

scotia A hollow, concave molding usually found at the base of a column. *See* p. 52.

scrim (*shark's tooth*) An open-weave fabric of coarse twisted thread with square and oblong openings. Thin paint or dye can be applied and the material will remain translucent. Available in 30′ widths.

scroll saw *See* **coping saw**

scumbling *See* **blending**

secondary light colors Blue-green, yellow, and magenta. These colors are produced on the stage by the additive method of color mixture. The light secondaries correspond to the pigment primaries.

secretary A drop-front desk with bookcase above and drawers below. Popular in 18th-century English and American periods. Illustration on p. 222.

selective reflection A method of reflection concerned with light on a colored surface. When magenta (blue-red) light is directed to a yellow surface, blue is absorbed and red will be reflected.

selective scenery A type of minimum scenery which usually includes one or two complete wall sections of normal height. The balance of the setting is often suggested by means of furniture and properties. Especially useful for multi-set realistic plays. *See* p. 32.

selvage The finished edge of a fabric which prevents raveling. Must be trimmed off materials which are used for covering scenic frames.

series circuit An electrical circuit in which the current follows a single path through each of several elements. The current supplied to each element is the same; the voltage of the circuit is equal to the sum of the voltages across the several elements. *See* p. 311.

set properties All stage properties which rest upon the stage floor. Rugs, tables, chairs, etc.

Sèvres porcelain A type of china developed during the reign of Louis XV. Bases and urns were decorated with extremely detailed miniature figure designs. Considerable use of gold leaf.

sgabello A small Italian Renaissance chair with three legs or a trestle support. Originally used as a dining chair. Illustration on p. 239.

Shakers A 19th-century American religious sect which was responsible for the development of a simple type of furniture based on the Windsor designs. Sound construction and excellent scale and proportion. Use of farm woods.

sheave A grooved pulley wheel such as is found in head blocks, loft blocks, and floor blocks.

Sheraton, Thomas (1750–1806) An English designer and cabinetmaker. His work shows Hepplewhite and Adam influences although he favored rectangular chair backs. Especially noted for his use of tricky locking devices. The author of *The Cabinet-Maker and Upholsterer's Drawing Book*, which was more of a catalog than a book of his own designs. *See* p. 258.

shingle nail A small thin nail with a flat head. Resin-coated shingle nails, one inch long, are useful for fastening $\frac{3}{8}''$ corner blocks to frames. *See* p. 54.

ship lap An inexpensive unfinished lumber which can sometimes substitute for tongue and groove for lids or flooring. The lumber has a lip on one edge and these lips can be reversed so that they overlap.

shirring A series of close, parallel, irregular folds in a material which, by the use of a heading, are gathered within a given space. Useful for glass curtains. *See* p. 283.

short circuit The crossing of two wires of opposite polarity will produce a short circuit. The use of fuses cuts the circuit and thus prevents damage when this occurs.

show curtain A specially designed curtain, immediately upstage of the act curtain, which attempts to present the theme and spirit of the production. Especially effective when used in combination with a false proscenium for a musical show.

sideboard A long narrow piece of wall furniture originally developed from two pedestals and a serving table (*see* p. 260). Drawers for silver and shelves for china are always included.

side chair A small chair without arms. The usual dining room chair might be so classified.

sight lines The various lines of vision from the spectators seated in normal and extreme positions of the theatre. Sight lines include upper as well as side views. Since it is usually impossible for all patrons to see three walls of the setting, the scenery is designed so that any two walls will seem complete to the audience.

sill iron (*saddle iron*) A narrow strip of strap metal ($\frac{3}{16}''$ thick and $\frac{3}{4}''$ wide) placed along the bottom of a door flat and attached by means of $1\frac{1}{2}''$ screws. Keeps the legs of the flat from wobbling.

Simonson, Lee (1888–   ) An American scene designer especially known for his early work with the Theatre Guild, of which he was one of the founders. His designs have included *The Failures*, *The Adding Machine*, *Marco Millions*, *Idiot's Delight*, and some recent work for the Metropolitan Opera. He is the author of the following books: *The Stage Is Set*, *Part of a Lifetime*, and *The Art of Scenic Design*.

size water A mixture of melted glue and water (one cup to the gallon). Preferred by some for mixing paint instead of adding glue and water separately to the pigment.

skeleton setting A special scenic framework with various openings, designed to simplify scene changes and to unify the stage picture. Openings can be plugged and unplugged to effect scene changes. *See* p. 29.

skirt (*chair or table*) *See* **apron**

sky dome *See* **plaster dome**

sky drop A backdrop painted a pale blue or white to represent the sky. May be used for exteriors and for interiors when windows are on the center wall.

slip seat A separate chair seat consisting of a frame which can be removed for upholstering.

Smith, Oliver (1918–   ) An American designer known almost exclusively for his work in the ballet and the musical show (*On the Town, Brigadoon, Billion Dollar Baby, Miss Liberty, Bless You All*).

snap hook (*harness hook*) A galvanized steel hook which, by means of a spring, provides a method for the temporary attachment of a line to a ring. *See* p. 150.

snap line A strong, fuzzy cord which is rubbed with chalk, placed at points distant from one another, pulled taut, and snapped. The chalk is discharged to mark a straight line. The *bow snap line*, which includes a bow and a cord, is a variation of this system which can be used by one person to snap short lines. *See* p. 118.

snatch line A short length of cotton rope used to connect a scenic unit to a pipe batten. Especially useful for the book ceiling.

Solferino Lake A wet-pigment dye color of purple-red hue.

space staging A method of staging which involves the focusing of spotlights on the actors to the extent that little or no scenery is seen. Black stage draperies are the usual background.

spattering A method of texturing scenery which involves the shaking of small drops of paint by means of jerky or snapping brush movements. Several different colors may be used on one unit. Dots should not exceed $\frac{1}{8}''$ in diameter. *See* p. 128.

spectrum The bands of colored light which are refracted as the result of passing white light through a glass prism.

spherical mirror reflector A spherically shaped silvered glass reflector mounted directly in back of many spotlight lamps. Not so efficient as metal reflectors.

spindle *See* **baluster**

spinet A musical instrument smaller than a harpsichord. The design of present-day so-called spinet desks is based on early-19th-century rectangular spinets.

spiral turning A type of carving, twisted in shape, used frequently on chairs and table legs during the 17th century. Similar to a rope twist with a descending groove. Illustration on p. 227.

spirit level *See* **carpenter's level**

splat The central perpendicular member of a chair back, plain or carved. The shape of the splat often helps to identify the period. Fiddle back — Queen Anne. Ribband back — Chippendale. Shield back — Hepplewhite.

sponging *See* **stippling**

spool turning A repeated small bulbous turning similar to rows of spools. Particularly popular in America during the 19th century after the invention of the lathe.

spot block and line A specially installed line and pulley from the gridiron over a certain area of the stage. Useful for flying units which cannot make use of the regular stage lines.

squirrel cage   A cagelike framework which supports the top of a pedestal table. Queen Anne. Chippendale. *See* piecrust table, p. 222.

stage brace   An adjustable bracing device for holding up scenery. The hook on one end attaches to the scenery and the stage screw is placed through the eye at the floor end. *See* p. 142.

stage cable   A fabric- or rubber-covered twin-conductor cable with a male connector at one end and a female connector at the other. The most useful sizes are #14 (15 amperes) and #12 (20 amperes).

stagehand   A member of the crew who sets up the scenery, shifts it during the run of the show, and strikes it at the end of the run. Duties are sometimes divided between flymen and grips. In multi-set shows, stagehands will often need rehearsals to increase their efficiency. Stagehands are responsible for keeping the units in good repair.

stage house   The entire backstage area from the floor to the ceiling. Includes the gridiron, fly gallery, etc.

stage screw (*peg*)   A type of special stage hardware used for fastening scenery to the floor with the help of either foot-irons or stage braces. *See* p. 142.

stair rail   An architectural term referring to a railing which is held up by balusters and usually completed with newel posts at either end. *See* p. 82.

station point   A perspective term referring to the position of the eye of the observer. The S.P., by means of the C.V.R. (central visual ray), determines the C.V. (center of vision) and thus the height of the H.L. (horizon line).

steel corner brace (*angle iron*)   A narrow, flat piece of metal bent at a forty-five-degree angle. Suitable for the inside bracing of frames. Illustration on p. 54.

stencil   A cut-out framed design suitable for use in painting repeat patterns on scenery. Guide lines are first snapped on the scenery and the stencil is then placed within the chalk lines. A special stencil brush should be used. *See* p. 118.

step lens   *See* **lens**

stereopticon   A lens projector of the magic lantern type. Suitable for projecting detailed images on a screen.

stiffening batten   A length of 1″ by 3″ or 1″ by 4″ attached to the rear of a book, a three-fold, or separate flats. Battens may be attached by screws or bolts or held in place by S hooks.

stiles   The perpendicular members of a scenic unit. The stile is the height of the flat minus the width of the top and bottom rails. *See* p. 64.

stipple   A type of paint texturing which is applied by means of a sponge or the tip of a brush. The painter must take care that the brush or sponge is not loaded with paint, or obvious patterns may result. *See* p. 128.

stop cleat A type of special stage hardware useful when two flats must be lashed to form a corner of a room. Placed on the flat which is perpendicular to the footlights. Small mending plates may serve as substitutes. *See* p. 54.

stove bolt A type of regular hardware which varies in diameter from $\frac{3}{16}''$ to $\frac{1}{4}''$ and in length from $2''$ to $3''$. Has continuous threading.

stovepipe wire A thin black wire useful where extreme strength and durability are not required.

strap hinge A triangular-shaped hinge used for hanging doors and for holding door frames within door flats. *See* p. 54.

strap iron Lengths of iron which can be used for sill or saddle irons. The $\frac{3}{16}''$ by $\frac{3}{4}''$ size is most useful.

strapwork A carved interlacing strap design used in panels. Often found on wooden chair backs and aprons during Elizabethan and Jacobean periods. Also found on Chinese Chippendale pieces.

stretchers (*furniture*) The rungs which connect the legs of chairs or tables. The various types include: box (continuous all the way around), H-shape, X-shape, Y-shape, and serpentine.

stretchers (*scenery*) The temporary members of a roll ceiling to which the ceiling plates are attached. Also, the lengths of wood which connect the discs of a column or tree.

strike Backstage terminology meaning to remove a unit from the stage. At the end of a run all the scenery and properties are struck.

stringer *See* **carriage**

stripper *See* **dutchman**

studs Decorative upholsterer's tacks, often with pressed designs in brass.

stylization A style of design which, by means of exaggeration, emphasizes a conventionalized design in an individualistic manner. Combines readily with other non-realistic styles. Especially suited to musicals, revivals, and some plays for children. *See* p. 174.

subtractive color mixture A method of producing colored light by selective absorption and transmission. If white light falls on a red gelatine, red light is transmitted and blue and green are absorbed. Similar reasoning applies to the use of the other primaries and to the secondaries.

"suite" A commercial furniture term referring to sets of furniture (sofa and club chairs, bedroom sets, etc.) which are often objectionable because there is no opportunity for variety as they are used within a room. "Borax" furniture is often available in "suites" or "suits."

sun spot *See* **beam projector floodlight**

surrealism A form of expressionism which gives special emphasis to the subconscious and to Freudian theories. Surrealistic designs often present such things as drooping watches, arms with outgrowing trees, and human heads which reveal weird contents. Interesting surrealist ballet designs by Dali have been exhibited recently.

swag　A decoration — carved, painted, or inlaid — representing a suspended festoon of drapery, leaves, ribbons, etc. Used in all periods where classical motifs were prominent.

swastika　A design motif consisting of four equal L-shaped arms at right angles to one another. A popular Greek design although its origin was much earlier. Adopted as an important emblem in Hitler's Germany.

Swedish Black　*See* **black**

Swedish Modern　A contemporary style noteworthy for its simple undecorated lines. Decorative in appearance due to pleasing curves, tapered supports, and the use of light woods.

sweeps　Flat, curved pieces of lumber useful for defining the shape of semicircular columns or the openings of arches. Sweeps are usually cut from 1″ by 12″.

switch　An electrical device to open and close a circuit. The most suitable types for stage use are the *bulldog* (reverse bar), *knife*, and *rotor movement* switches. A *transfer* switch will allow a circuit to be transferred from one outlet to another. The *master* switch controls the current through the main fuses. A *flipper* switch automatically breaks contact after dimming has been completed.

switchboard　*See* **controlboard**

symbolism　The representation of ideas and objects by means of simplified scenic elements.

tab curtain (*tableau*)　A type of stage curtain which is rigged so that each side can be gathered and draped up. Includes special rings sewed to the curtain as well as draw lines. Draw curtains may be rigged for both draw and tab pulling. Tab curtains are better suited to musicals and opera than to plays. *See* p. 8.

table saw　A power tool with a saw blade shaped like a disc. Used for crosscut work, ripping, and angle sawing. It is false economy to buy a cheap table saw. *See* p. 43.

taffeta　A silk or rayon material of plain weave. The material is sometimes chemically weighted to give it extra body. Useful for draperies.

tambour　A sliding furniture panel made of strips of wood glued to cloth. Used by Sheraton for desks and secretaries. Present-day roll top desks are similar to the tambour.

tapestry　A heavy fabric of wool or silk with a pictorial design woven into the material. Useful for wall hangings or upholstery.

teaser　A horizontal masking frame or drapery placed upstage of the act curtain to trim the top of the setting. Black velour is especially suitable for this purpose. *See* p. 2.

teaser spotlights　Spotlights clamped to a pipe batten which hangs between the teaser and the first borderlights. Used to give specific illumination to the upstage areas. A minimum of six instruments is required for the average sized stage — two for each of the three areas.

technical director The staff member of a non-professional theatre who is responsible for supervising the building of the scenery, setting it up, and shifting it during production. A technical director may also be responsible for designing and painting the scenery, the construction of the properties, the lighting, and the sound. In such a case his title might be more accurately described as *designer-technician*. Many large groups employ a technician, a designer, and a lighting technician.

template An open-frame table with raised edges on two sides. Used for building flats of regulation sizes. A much more satisfactory method than building on the floor and much more accurate. *See* p. 40.

tension block A block containing a pulley which is held in place by springs. Can be used beneath the units of a counterweight system. Small tension blocks are useful for draw curtains.

terra-cotta A brownish-red, clay-colored pottery. The Della Robbias (16th-century Italian Renaissance) were noted for the use of ornate glazed terra-cotta plaques and figures.

tertiary color A type of color which is formed by the combination of a primary with a secondary. The hues are extremely difficult to name accurately.

Texolite A paste paint with a casein glue base. Available in white, black, tints, and deep colors. Diluted with water before using.

theatricalism A scenic style which, by means of paint, offers theatre in its pure sense with little attempt at realism. Frequently combined with stylization and often in the form of drops and wings.

three-fold Three flats hinged together which, when opened, will provide a wide wall space. A tumbler is necessary between two of the flats in order for them to fold when not in use. *See* p. 68.

three-ply *See* **plywood**

tieback A small belt, rope- or flat-shaped, which is used to hold draperies or curtains back to the window trim. Usually placed at one third the distance from the top or bottom of the hanging.

tie-off cleat A type of special stage hardware which is used in pairs to tie off the lash line after two adjoining flats are in place on the stage. Lash-line hooks are sometimes substituted.

tie-off knot A type of knot used to tie around the lash-line cleats. The rope is never tied in a knot but is looped behind the length just above the cleats so that it can be loosened quickly. *See* p. 150.

tight-pin backflap A type of regular hardware which has a pin which is not removable. Useful when two units must be hinged permanently. *See* p. 54.

tilt jack *See* **tip jack**

tilt-top table A table with the top hinged to the pedestal so that it may stand against the wall and conserve floor space. Popular during the Queen Anne and Chippendale periods.

tint   A color term referring to a light value of a hue.

tip jack   A rolling jack which is equipped with two casters. Since the bottom rail is perpendicular to neither long member, after the tip jack is attached to the scenery, the unit can be tipped back onto the casters and rolled about on the stage. *See* p. 157.

toggle rail   The center rail of a flat of average height. The toggle rail is the width of the top rail minus the width of the lumber used for the stiles. Tall flats may require two toggle rails. *See* p. 64.

toile de Jouy   A cotton material with rather realistic repeat patterns of groups of people, landscapes, architecture, etc. Originally painted (18th century) but usually printed nowadays.

tôle work   A type of decorative painting on tin especially suitable for such small items as trays, candlesticks, wastebaskets, desk equipment, etc. Developed in France during the 18th century.

tongue and groove   A method of joining which is accomplished by means of specially milled or cut lumber. The planks contain a tongue on one edge and a groove on the other. *See* p. 62.

top rail   The top member of a flat. Extends the full width of the scenic unit. *See* p. 64.

torchère   A tall stand for holding candles or candelabra. First developed in the Italian Renaissance. Important during the 18th century in France and England.

tormentor spotlights   Spotlights mounted in a high position at the side of the proscenium directly upstage of the tormentor. Although a tower is sometimes used, a perpendicular length of pipe is usually satisfactory.

tormentors   Permanent perpendicular masking pieces directly upstage of the act curtain. Usually covered with black velour and used in combination with the teaser. *See* pp. 2 and 3.

torus   A convex molding almost half a circle in profile. *See* p. 52.

T plate   A steel plate of T shape, sometimes used in place of the keystone. Available in sizes up to seven inches. *See* p. 54.

tracery   A type of metal latticework used on windows and bookcase doors. The shapes are delicate in nature and glass panes fill the spaces. Originally Gothic, but used with success by 18th-century English designers.

translucent drop   A backdrop, parts of which have been painted with glue size or dye so as to be translucent. Since light will not shine through areas that are covered with scene paint, interesting lighted effects are possible and unusual dimension can be suggested.

traps   Sections of the stage floor which are removable. Sometimes an entire stage floor is trapped, thus permitting unusual sunken stage effects. *See* p. 2.

traveler   *See* **draw curtain**

tread   The part of the step unit upon which the actors stand. A good standard measurement is twelve inches. *See* p. 82.

tree of life A decorative motif, Assyrian in origin, consisting of inter-lacing tree branches and leaves combined with birds and animals. Often represented in crewelwork. Illustration on p. 229.

trefoil A Gothic decorative motif representing three arcs within a circle. Like the three-leaf clover.

triangle An architect's drawing instrument. Perpendicular lines are drawn as the triangle rests against the T square. Large, plastic forty-five-degree and thirty-sixty-degree triangles are the most useful.

trim The process of hanging a scenic unit so that it will be level with the floor. Since rope is affected by the weather, trimming may be a daily chore.

trim clamp A small cast iron metal box held together by three bolts and equipped with a ring to which sandbags and counterweight carriages may be hung. The Manila ropes of a set of lines go through this box and can be tightened after they are trimmed. Not a very satisfactory piece of equipment since all lines must be loosened in order to adjust one line. *See* p. 12.

trimming chain A link chain which is used to hang lighting units from a pipe batten or to assist with the hanging of a regular counterweight arbor.

trim properties Stage properties which are on the walls of a setting or which rest on the furniture. Pictures, draperies, sconces, bracket shelves, ashtrays, vases, lamps, etc.

trip A backstage process by which a drop can be flown out of sight in a theatre that has a low gridiron. The set of lines directly in front of the drop trips it, folds it up out of sight.

trompe l'œil A type of artistic trickery which attempts to fool the eye. In two dimensions the painter creates the illusion of a third by break-ing the picture plane in the direction of the spectator. May also push space backwards. Used by the Bibienas and other baroque designers.

trumpet leg A furniture term referring to a conical leg with the end flared in the shape of a trumpet turned upwards. Restoration and later. *See* p. 227.

T-(Tubular) shaped lamp *See* **incandescent lamp**

T square An architect's device used for drawing horizontal lines and, with the square, for perpendicular lines. The T square alone is never used for perpendicular lines and should always be used on the same side of the drawing board.

Tudor An English architectural and decorative period which included the first half of the 16th century. While Gothic forms dominated, there was a definite Italian Renaissance influence. Heavy oak furni-ture was characteristic.

Tudor rose A Tudor decorative motif consisting of a circular conven-tionalized rose. Frequently carved in the oak pieces of the period or displayed in the decorative window designs.

tufting An upholstery term applying to the process of tying down upholstery at regular intervals and decorating the indentation with a button.

tumbler A length of 1″ by 3″ or 1″ by 4″ hinged between two flats in a three-fold so that the units will fold up. *See* p. 68.

Turkey Red Lake An intense red wet pigment of lighter value than Vermillion.

turnbuckle An adjustable rigging device often equipped with hook and eye. Useful for tightening the wires at the top of a counterweight arbor.

turnbutton A type of regular hardware consisting of a small bar (about two inches long) which can be turned to hold one object to another. Often used in houses as screen-door fasteners. *See* p. 54.

two-fold *See* **book**

two step A three-dimensional step unit consisting of two steps, usually with supports so that the unit will stand alone.

Ultramarine Blue *See* **blue**

underhang block A rigging pulley which hangs under the gridiron instead of resting on it. Useful when space is at a minimum.

unit setting A form of scenery made up of units which are given interchangeable positions on the stage. Columns, steps, ramps, arches, and plugs are the most commonly used scenic units for this form of scenery. *See* p. 28.

United Scenic Artists Local 829 A theatrical union to which all Broadway designers and their assistants must belong. Admission is by examination and a fee.

upstage A stage location referring to the areas away from the curtain line near the upper boundaries of the setting.

Urban, Joseph (1872–1933) An Austrian designer who started his American career at the Boston Opera in 1911. Began his work for the Ziegfeld Follies in 1915 and also did some work for the Metropolitan Opera. Although his designs show some Art Nouveau influences, he was expert at the use of broad masses of color and his pointillage experiments are well known. His color theories were prominently represented at Chicago's Century of Progress exhibition.

valance The horizontal trimming over the top of overdraperies. May be freehanging plaiting or a wooden or metal frame covered or uncovered. *See* p. 283.

value A color pigment term referring to the light or dark (tint or shade) quality which is usually obtained by adding black or white to the color.

vanishing point A perspective term sometimes called *center of vision*. A point on the horizon line or eye-level line at which parallel lines converge. Perpendicular lines or lines which are parallel to the picture plane do not have a vanishing point. *See* p. 196.

velour A fabric term applying to any material which has a pile similar to that of velvet. Suitable for stage draperies. Rather heavy in weight and quite durable.

velvet A fabric which has a pile on one side and a plain back like a rug. Silk, mohair, or rayon are the usual materials. Plain or patterned velvets are suitable for either draperies or upholstering. *Velveteen* is a cotton velvet.

veneer A thin layer of wood which is glued to a thicker piece of wood for decorative purposes. Entire pieces of furniture may be covered with veneer which has been cut to show unusual graining.

vermilion (*American*) A brownish-red dry-pigment color. A poor substitute for Turkey Red.

Victorian period (1830–1901) A decorative period much of which was in poor taste. Furniture was inspired by Greek, Gothic, Turkish, and Louis XV styles with little consistency as to application. Proportions were awkward and ornamentation was often meaningless. Low chair seats were characteristic. *See* p. 263.

vise A table tool used to hold an object tightly so that it can be worked on.

volt An electrical term referring to the electromotive force of the current.

volute A Greek scroll-shape such as is found on the Ionic capital. *See* p. 94.

wagon A scene-shifting device consisting of a low platform equipped with casters. Small wagons can be used alone or fastened together to provide wagons large enough to hold an entire setting. *See* p. 152.

wainscot chair A 16th- and 17th-century English chair with a carved panelled back. Wooden seats and turned legs.

"walk it up" A method of raising a large scenic unit which involves three or more people. One person stands at one end with his foot against the lower rail. The other two start at the top and begin lifting, hand over hand, until the unit is standing upright. *See* p. 147.

wallboard A quarter-inch paper board sometimes substituted for plywood for bent thickness pieces. Inexpensive but not durable.

walnut A light-brown hardwood especially favored in England after the Restoration and until about 1730. Used widely in France after the Renaissance was in full flower. The grain makes an interesting veneer because of its burls and curls.

watt An electrical term relating to power. Watts equal volts multiplied by amperes. All lighting units are rated according to wattage.

webbing A hemp band interlaced to form the base for a spring chair seat. Also useful as a finish for the top of stage draperies. *See* p. 100.

Wedgwood A type of English pottery first made during the 18th century. Many of the designs were by the Brothers Adam. Blue backgrounds and classic white relief motifs were popular.

Welsh dresser *See* **dresser-sideboard**

whatnot *See* **étagère**

wheat ear A decorative motif — carved, painted, inlaid, or in relief — consisting of several ears of wheat. Used often by Hepplewhite.

wheat paste *See* **flour paste**

wheel-back chair A type of Windsor chair back, round or oval in shape, which contains bars which radiate from the center.

white flake glue *See* **glue**

white pine The most satisfactory wood for use on the stage. Light in weight, non-splintery, and free from resin.

whiting A chalky, powdered substance useful as an aid in mixing tints. Since it tends to settle in the bucket after it is mixed, painters should stir the paint frequently as they work.

William and Mary period A late-17th-century English decorative period of Dutch origin. Trumpet and bell turned legs were typical and walnut the popular wood. Serpentine stretchers were also characteristic. *See* p. 252.

wind machine A sound effects contrivance consisting of a wooden slatted drum which is turned to rub against a strip of canvas. Tempo and tension affect the sound. *See* p. 361.

window flat A scenic frame which includes an opening for a window. The top of the window is usually the toggle rail. *See* p. 68.

window frame The *sash* corresponds to the shutter of the door. (*See* **double-hung** and **casement windows.**) The *sill* is the ledge upon which the frame rests, similar to the floor sill of the door. Some window shutters contain *muntins* which divide the window into panels.

Windsor chair An early-18th-century chair originally built by wheelrights. Common back shapes are comb, fan, and hoop. Splayed legs and rush or carved scoop seats are characteristic. *See* p. 219.

wing A hinged unit of scenery placed at the side of the acting area for masking and decorative purposes and painted to represent walls or trees. The offstage side areas are called the *wings*.

wing-back chair An upholstered chair with side pieces attached to the back. Introduced during the Restoration. *See* p. 253.

wing nut A type of regular stage hardware used in place of square nuts when scenic units must be taken apart frequently. Sometimes called *butterfly* nuts or *thumb* nuts.

wood chisel A tool with a sharp cutting edge; used wherever countersinking is required. *See* p. 49.

wood wing A booked wing painted and shaped to represent tree trunks.

work lights Backstage lights used for scene shifting and rehearsals. Controlled by a switch rather than by a dimmer.

working drawings The building plans from which the scenery is built. One-half-inch scale is usually adequate although occasional bits may have to be drawn full scale. All drawings should be neatly spaced on the page and, so far as possible, should be in the order in which they will be placed on the stage. Hidden parts should be shown by dotted lines. Cross-sectional views may be necessary. *See* p. 201.

working side The side of the stage from which the show is run. The curtain pull and switchboard are usually on this side and the stage manager works from this position.

wrecking bar An iron bar with a curve at one end. Useful for nail pulling and for separating boards which have been fastened together.

yellow: *Light Chrome* A dry pigment, lemon yellow in hue. *Medium Chrome* A dry pigment with a deep gold hue. Similar to primary yellow. *Yellow Lake* A wet pigment deeper and more intense than Yellow Ochre.

yellow pine A heavy splintery wood which contains considerable pitch. Difficult to saw. Sometimes called Ponderosa pine.

yoke A U-shaped device attached to the lighting unit. Supports the instrument from both sides. The yoke must be equipped with a pipe clamp to hold it to the pipe batten. *See* p. 316.

Yorkshire chair A provincial Jacobean chair with a carved, curved slat-back and turned legs and stretchers.

BIBLIOGRAPHY OF SUGGESTED READINGS

Scenery and Lighting

Barber, Philip, *The Scene Technician's Handbook*. Whitlock's Inc., New Haven, 1928.

Bentham, Frederick, *Stage Lighting*. Sir Isaac Pitman and Sons, Ltd., London, 1950.

Burris-Meyer, Harold and Edward C. Cole, *Scenery for the Theatre*. Little, Brown & Co., Boston, 1938.

Cornberg, Sol and Emanuel Gebauer, *A Stage Crew Handbook*. Harper and Bros., New York, 1941.

Fuchs, Theodore, *Stage Lighting*. Little, Brown & Co., Boston, 1929.

Hake, Herbert, *Here's How*. Row Peterson and Co., Evanston, Ill., 1942.

McCandless, Stanley, *A Method of Lighting the Stage*. Theatre Arts, Inc., New York, 1932.

Nelms, Henning, *A Primer of Stagecraft*. Dramatists Play Service, New York, 1931.

Nelms, Henning, *Lighting the Amateur Stage*. Theatre Arts, Inc., New York, 1931.

Selden, Samuel and Hunton D. Sellman, *Stage Scenery and Lighting*. Appleton-Century-Crofts, Inc., New York, 1936.

Scene Design and Rendering

Bishop, A. Thornton, *Composition and Rendering*. John Wiley and Sons, Inc., New York, 1933.

Cheney, Sheldon, *Stage Decoration*. John Day Co., Inc., New York, 1928.

Friederich, Willard J. and John H. Fraser, *Scenery Design for the Amateur Stage*. The Macmillan Co., New York, 1950.

Fuerst, Walter René and Samuel Hume, *Twentieth Century Stage Decoration*. Alfred A. Knopf, Inc., New York, 1929.

Jones, Robert Edmond, *Drawings for the Theatre*. Theatre Arts, Inc., New York, 1925.

Komisarjevsky, Theodore and Lee Simonson, *Settings and Costumes of the Modern Theatre*. Studio Publications, Inc., London and New York, 1933.

Macgowan, Kenneth and Robert Edmond Jones, *Continental Stagecraft*. Harcourt, Brace and Co., New York, 1922.

Melvill, Harald, *Designing and Painting Scenery for the Theatre*. Art Trade Press, London, 1948.

Norling, Ernest, *Perspective Made Easy*. The Macmillan Co., New York, 1939.

Sheringham, George and James Laver, *Design in the Theatre*. Studio Publications, Inc., London and New York, 1927.

Simonson, Lee, *Part of a Lifetime*. Duell, Sloan and Pearce, Inc., New York, 1943.

Simonson, Lee, *The Art of Scenic Design*. Harper and Bros., New York, 1950.

Furniture and Architecture

Aronson, Joseph, *The Encyclopedia of Furniture*. Crown Publishers, New York, 1938.

Cescinsky, Herbert and George Leland Hunter, *English and American Furniture*. Garden City Publishing Co., New York, 1929.

Draper, Dorothy, *Decorating is Fun*. Doubleday, Doran and Co., New York, 1939.

Gerard, Sanford E., *How Good is Your Taste*. Doubleday, Doran and Co., New York, 1946.

Gilman, Roger, *Great Styles of Interior Architecture*. Harper and Bros., New York, 1924.

Gottshall, Franklin, *How to Design Period Furniture*. Bruce Publishing Co., New York, 1937.

Kimball, Fiske and George H. Edgell, *A History of Architecture*. Harper and Bros., New York, 1918.

Parsons, Frank Alva, *Interior Decoration*. Doubleday, Doran and Co., New York, 1915.

Whiton, Sherrill, *Elements of Interior Decoration*. J. B. Lippincott, Philadelphia, 1937.

Wolf, Martin, *Dictionary of the Arts*. Philosophical Library, Inc., New York, 1951.

Historical Theatre

Blum, Daniel, *A Pictorial History of the American Theatre*. Greenberg, Publisher, New York, 1950.

Cheney, Sheldon, *The Theatre*. Longmans, Green and Co., New York, 1929.

Gorelik, Mordecai, *New Theatres for Old*. Samuel French, New York, 1941.

Hughes, Glenn, *The Story of the Theatre*. Samuel French, New York, 1928.

Kernodle, George Riley, *From Art to Theatre*. University of Chicago Press, Chicago, 1944.

Nicoll, Allardyce, *The Development of the Theatre*. Harcourt, Brace and Co., New York, 1927.

Censlager, Donald, *Scenery Then and Now.* W. W. Norton and Co., New York, 1936.

Simonson, Lee, *The Stage is Set.* Harcourt, Brace and Co., New York, 1932.

Smith, Cecil, *The Musical Comedy in America.* Theatre Arts, Inc., New York, 1950.

Theatre Buildings

Bell, Stanley, Norman Marshall and Richard Southern, *Essentials of Stage Planning.* Frederick Miller, Ltd., London, 1949.

Burris-Meyer, Harold and Edward C. Cole. *Theatres and Auditoriums.* Reinhold, New York, 1949.

Pichel, Irving, *Modern Theatres.* Harcourt, Brace and Co., New York, 1925.

Periodicals

Architectural Forum

Architectural Record

Arts and Architecture

Better Homes and Gardens

Dramatics

House and Garden

Interior Design

Interiors

National Geographic Magazine

Players Magazine

Theatre Arts

SOURCES OF SUPPLY

Scenic Studios

Great Western Stage Equipment Co., 1324 Grand Ave., Kansas City, Mo.
Knoxville Scenic Studios, P.O. Box 1029, Knoxville, Tenn.
Novelty Scenic Studios, Inc., 32 West 60th St., N.Y.C.
Charles Teichner Studios, 230 South Wells, Chicago
Tiffin Scenic Studios, Tiffin, Ohio

Stage Hardware and Curtain-Controlling Equipment

J. H. Channon, 1455 W. Hubbard, Chicago
J. R. Clancy, Inc., Syracuse, N.Y.
Clark and Barlow, 123 West Lake St., Chicago
Vallen, Inc., Akron, Ohio

Paints

Aljo Manufacturing Co., 153 West 21st St., N.Y.C.
Gothic Color Co., Inc., 90 Ninth Ave., N.Y.C.
A. Leiser, 48 Horatio St., N.Y.C.
George E. Watson, 417 South Wabash, Chicago

Fabrics

The Astrup Co. (The Gibson Dept.), 39 Walker St., N.Y.C.
Cornell Displays, 53 West 35th St., N.Y.C.
Dazian's Inc., 142 West 44th St., N.Y.C.; 400 Boylston St., Boston;
  203 North Wabash, Chicago; 731 South Hope St., Los Angeles
Maharam Fabric Corp., 170 West 48th St., N.Y.C.; 115 South Wabash,
  Chicago

Lighting Equipment

Ariel Davis Supply Co., 373 West South Temple, Salt Lake City
Brigham Gelatine Co., 17 Weston St., Randolph, Vt
Century Lighting Co., 521 West 43rd St., N.Y.C.; 626 N. Robertson Blvd.,
  Los Angeles
General Radio Co., 275 Massachusetts Ave., Cambridge, Mass.

Kliegl Bros., 321 West 50th St., N.Y.C.
Midwest Stage Lighting Co., 55 West Wacker Drive, Chicago
Superior Electric Co., Bristol, Conn.
Ward-Leonard Electric Co., Mt. Vernon, N.Y.

Recorded Sound

Carl Fisher, 165 West 57th St., N.Y.C.
Standard Radio Transcription Services, Inc., 360 North Michigan Ave.,
    Chicago
Thomas J. Valentino, 150 West 46th St., N.Y.C.

General Theatre Supplies

Stagecraft Supply Co., 536 West 29th St., N.Y.C.
Theatre Production Service, 1430 Broadway, N.Y.C.

INDEX